SONGS OF AUSTRALIA
A Poetic Trilogy

N.B.J.Clayton

Publication data:

SONGS OF AUSTRALIA - A Poetic Trilogy 1st ed.
ISBN: 978-0-6489863-6-2

DRA012000   Drama/Australian & Oceanian
FIC014000   Fiction/Historical/General
POE010000   Poetry/Australian & Oceanian

Warning!

Kulinma! Ngulakujaku-kula!
This book might contain names of people who have since departed this world.

BOOK ONE

AFGHAN - Song of the Desert

SETTING THE SCENE

A little town of Australia's past,
Adheres to new name for the people vast,
What was once called Hergott Springs,
Is now Marree where desert wind sings.

The year is 1883 to be sure,
On this day, 20th Dec no more,
What was a groomed settlement small,
Is now a town and standing tall.

Its growth more rapid than any previous year,
It started as a camp for workers most dear,
An overland telegraph line of sturdiness to build,
Across the great expanse, the responsibility of this guild.

Ethnic population growing, flowing water beneath barge,
Fewer white than blacks, seemingly true and at large,
A nickname employed to accompany its growth,
Christened Little Asia by many, though many do loathe.

Here they arrive, having come to roost,
Afghans and their camels to population boost,
To call this home more than sixty families firmly stand,
This place for Afghans amidst Australian sand.

An Afghan works for near pittance, a smear,
A quarter that the salary of the white man so near,
So no stranger should it be, great advantage took,
Their service taken for granted, at first glance, at first look.

The white mans' bullocks are no match at all,
No match for the camels which seem never to stall,
A single humped dromedary of great worth,
Here for the haul they bring Afghan great mirth.

An Afghan is not just from Afghanistan,
A darkish and very ethnic man;
An Australia is from white background,
Convict, immigrant, or from around.

These Afghans come to work as any other,
To soil and desert sands, there are none tougher,
From Kashmir, Punjab, Persia, most sturdy,
Great men from Egypt and even from Turkey.

Easy it is to grow business here,
Where camels cost little to rear,
For they are to become part of the bush, of the desert around,
Ships of the desert, of sand, and every mound.

Cost effective and sturdy, heavenly great,
They do their work, pull their own weight,
More than a bullock team, for which Afghan hate,
Amongst farmers and homesteaders, are favoured first rate.

Little to no water and no shodding needed,
Little maintenance required and easily tended,
Bullock teams need the more expensive hay,
And less hardy they are that most farmers say nay.

Horse teams too appear to fare little better,
Appearing as though shackled, strangled by fetter,
Taking from white purse most expense,
To employ them goes against good common sense.

New lease to life was government reaction,
To get the railroad built in good fashion,
From Marree to north as fast as they may,
No room for idleness, no room to stray.

Marree was now the centre of attention,
Attracting much work and camels the mention,
Farmers from all over need to get goods to port,
Needing to rent reliable service and good sport.

Supplies are needed by them, their ration,
And someone to get goods from farm to station,
No better way than to bargain, service as cheap as one agrees,
To get the move on the nation, be busy as bees.

Settlements, homesteads and farmers, they stack,
Of Birdsville, Strzelecki and Oodnadatta track,
And less trodden trails to outposts and more,
All around this vast area, transport from farmer, to store.

Alice springs and Broken Hill,
Coolgardie and Innamincka still,
For hundreds of miles around the trend,
Trend for transportation, there is no end.

Area prone to floods and drought,
Sandstorms an upheaval sound out,
Colonists desire good time, this you must maintain,
Get their merchandise to consumers on time by train.

And in Marree a police station, much smaller than any other,
With three men of uniform tending their flock, don't smother,
A general store and post office can be easily seen,
And a few others as well, though little more between,

For all the more it is a place like depository,
A place to deliver goods and collect amidst story,
A place to conduct business, to converse, and never be late,
Rely on the railroad and tell old stories to mate.

The cemetery is as racist as the rest of town,
Split into three quarters to all is renown,
Aboriginal, Afghan and white,
Even here in growth there is great spite.

Derived from an old aboriginal word, Marree was born,
Bore from 'many possums', a story, possums a thorn,
The possums now replaced by camels of varied colour,
They too are everywhere you care to look amidst splendour.

Now in the year 1884, more than 1500 camels here,
Single hump variety, a mosque, date palms near,
A place of worship amidst this date palm lair,
System of flowing water for ablution before prayer.

Small comforts in the bush, desert plains wide,
Flies and ants galore here do thrive and abide,
Forty or fifty degrees does harbour respect,
Hell on earth though people do not neglect.

Hot during the day is unspeakable truth,
And cold by night you chatter until sore tooth,
A desert as many other in seamless drought,
A place to scorn, a horrid place to live, no doubt.

But they come all the same,
Be it many men or a few dame,
Do their work and try to live,
Such is life, and for some life do give.

And so Christmas of 1883 has well and truly concluded,
No Christmas cheer about, population deluded,
But telegraph poles are growing, trees uprooted,
From August 1870 to July 1872 has been noted.

And to Stretch across bare land and flooded plains,
From Port Augusta to Darwin, build a rail for trains,
A time of legendary engineering and great skill,
Cultures do not mix, though only a few wish to kill.

So don't forget the date of this song,
This is 1884, do not get it wrong,
Other dates may appear to be of mention,
But 1884 is most important, no need to question.

THE ARRIVAL

Nak Kadir is 42, a little long in the teeth,
Gums well parted to reveal stains beneath,
Well stained beyond his year,
But nowhere near as some do appear.

But he wore no smile, at this minute, today,
For a scar across mouth and lips, pessimistic and grey,
Lips held back by restraint from forming such in his despair,
Tissue forever damaged beyond repair.

But affect his speech it did not, no, that was absurd,
For this was a man much accustomed to word,
A friendly man with damaged background,
He has come here for a penny to be earnt, not found.

Standing years before at the gateway of Marree,
He had come to stay, regardless of what may be,
To find his fortune through hard work not wrong,
To call Australia his new home amongst the growing throng.

Steeped in desire to earn extended families respect,
Family residing in Afghanistan, he has no regret,
He does all he can to merit good word, no liar,
And keep at bay a majority of sinful ways and desire.

He is awaiting his new worker to call,
A man named Abdul Hassan, apparently handsome and tall,
A 23 year old, no devil, a picture formed in mind,
Whom had a wife and two young, who had been left behind.

Nak surveyed the iron line, from station and down,
Seemingly touched by the best commodity in town,
Turban upon his head, dirty at best,
And a robe of nation cast, for working, not rest.

He had been patient all day for the train,
Its arrival delayed, for no good reason, but a pain and a stain,
No message of lateness was received upon wire so grey,
Telegraph line drooping silently before cooling of day.

Muslim men were quite exotic to the eye,
Though hatred for the most you cannot deny,
From Marree, far north and south abide,
Hard to find one without camel at his side.

Immigration was thick in the 1860s and more,
With their camels to accompany men and their store,
A mix of man and beast, an oiled machine to beat,
Well suited to Australia and the desert heat.

Only 18 men had arrived in 1838, 22 years before,
Growth of importation staggering, seemingly passed by law,
Importation of camels to grow, some saying exponentially,
Quite a phenomenon to see, really quite expectantly.

They were a required asset to this new country,
A new home to take to breast: ethnically contrary,
European men despising camels with grimace,
No love they held for the single humped menace.

But Afghan men loved these beasts, never to neglect,
Treated them fair and gained much, much respect,
Together they were a team, to work hard all day: so it would seem,
Afghans love their camels, eyes never lie, they gleam.

It's a loathing feeling that all white men hold,
Spitting in the wake of all they have, be told,
Not jealous at all, just racist and unfair,
Racist and rude, stubbornly confirmed by fatal stare.

Even after so long at work, working hard as all men should,
Afghan men were without doubt, clearly misunderstood,
White men gave no proof, no time to clarify,
Why they hated them to the core, from ground to sky.

Birdsville was once known as Diamantina Crossing,
Many small homesteads here, and slightly engrossing,
Lake Harry Homestead is one of many, upon desert land,
Mulka Homestead, another to mention, neither that grand.

Birdsville, to town of Marree, was like good brother,
Pastoral properties around, so vast as to smother,
Each the centre of its own action amidst barren landscape shout,
Like core of gold and wealth with veins stretching out and about.

Afghans were here to earn money and send it home,
White man to carve fortune, pastoral lands, forming a tome,
Each endeavour in their own way, to gain their need,
Both striving hard to achieve their ultimate greed.

It was then that Nak heard something warming and familiar,
In the distance a train approaching, sound of bliss to his ear,
Abdul Hassan would be here soon, to aid with camels: a tool,
At Nak's heal, to stand and to work, as was desired and the rule.

Nak then briefly thought of his dear friend,
Shir Adji an accomplice to unwritten contract's end,
His partner to gift hard work, he wished to uphold his name,
He was 33yrs old and ugly as sin, so ugly to eye it was a shame.

A few coins giggled in Nak's pocket, hence not spent, refrained,
Reminding him of Shir and the job most recently obtained,
A homesteader, come farmer, needed Abdul and his camel string,
To deliver goods, commencing tomorrow, vast supplies to bring.

From Marree to just south of Birdsville they would have to tend,
A good long trip to near Pandie Pandie, to test Abdul to no end,
Two jobs here knitted into one,
Much money to be had if working finger to the bone,

Birdsville was fitted with three stores and chemist, parts, a lith,
Butchers shop, two hotels, and one lonely blacksmith,
Though blacksmith, no need the cameleers required of him,
For camels need not be shodded, and no hoof requiring trim.

This homestead near Pandie Pandie also required wool delivered,
Taken from their homestead to Marree, a town tethered,
To be deposited by train, to Port Augusta please,
Then to Adelaide and shops with much glee to appease.

Large responsibility for all through the year, and more to explore,
Three men tasked with many jobs, vastly different, galore,
Their camels worth their weight in gold at time of portage,
Men and their pets working as one, of conviction no shortage.

Rely Nak does on Abdul being a good man true, maturity grown,
As Shir was reliable with his eyes reflecting their tint of brown,
Shir, a good man, was to be married this very night,
To Aboriginal lady, she would treat him right.

Each three needed the other,
Reliance on each as though their mother,
Commanding over many camels does require few men,
But each must be worthy, each one worth ten.

Importance of work could never be underestimated,
Any job could ruin them if not planned, or purposely machinated,
They need to compete, far and wide, against other cameleers,
The name Faiz Mahomet, for one, comes to many ears.

Faiz is a learned man of strength,
A forwarding agent of many years length,
A general carrier of goods in great number,
He is profitable, always alert, never at slumber.

Faiz was a *jemadar*, had been for many a year,
More than four hundred employed and working full gear,
Mainly at Karachi Wharves he displayed his strength, did flourish,
Well respected by all and to all below he seemingly did nourish.

Nak pondered the life to fall Abdul,
Not yet arrived but work ready and available,
He in the Ghantown of small town spoke,
Where homes were built so cheaply as to make a joke.

The road parallel was extremely busy and of great credit,
Its hardened surface portraying wide use and to all a benefit,
Countless hooves having trodden this way in the past,
Many more millions to follow in future, forever to last.

Another camel string and Afghans was passing by,
Considering it Faiz Mohamed's would not be a lie,
One cameleer to every ten camels did steer,
Nak himself desired eight to control and to treat as though peer.

Yes, there was much work in handling a camel,
Work in rearing them too, prior to extensive travel,
Not to mention the young they bore unto the world scene,
Born into the lap of work, it waiting; dirty, never clean.

He brushed once more the flies from his face,
The air stifling and stinking and hot, no display of grace,
His skin hardened by the unrelenting heat,
The rays of the sun seemingly cooking him as though meat.

A BRIEF TOUR

The breaking of the train was methodical screeching,
The sound of which was far reaching,
Engine and moving parts screaming out loud,
Puffs of steam appear, a stream of billowing cloud.

Faces in windows peering out now,
Hard faces all to greet with enthusiasm low,
Creases and cuts in flesh adorn,
Many hours hard labour, stoutly worn,

The engine now fully stationary, much commotion both in and out,
Doors opening and men with baggage pouring out,
And then from last carriage a tall man does appear,
Afghan in semblance drawing Nak's most studying leer.

The man is handsome and with turban, it does adorn,
Pantaloon trousers truly well worn,
Trousers dark in colour but turban not,
High boots too, fine shirt, not rot.

Abdul wore a smile, happy and wide,
Nak's a grimace from past, from battle's tide,
Abdul's story a near reflection of his employer,
And Nak's a semblance of war, the destroyer.

For no real peace can be gained from conflict,
Only bad memories and scars, of joy they do restrict,
Taking sanity away for all so that they do suffer,
In silent pain and pain from much more, from other.

"Are you Abdul Hassan?" Nak does ask,
"Yes, I am he, and ready for task."
"I'm Nak Kadir, I'm sure you are aware,"
His facial grimace demands temporary stare.

"Do you have much with you?" does Nak enquire,
"I have nothing with me, no materialistic desire,
No spare clothes, no blanket for sleep,
No socks for change, or clip for money to keep."

"As poor as the poor, but keen to work hard,
No song for me to whistle, not even a bard,
My soul and good nature is all I have here
It is what I hold most, I hold it most dear."

So says Nak with a stare,
"You have nothing to bear,
Nothing at all but free of burden,
Ready to work hard in this furnace, this horrid garden."

They both shake hands and acknowledge a bond,
They are one and the same, as fish in a pond,
They both appear happy, happy and free,
Two birds of a feather and soon to be three.

"Come with me," says Nak at last,
"Come meet Shir Adji before we set to task,
He's a friend of years past,
Someone to trust to the very last."

Abdul waves a fly from upon his face,
Waving off fly in what is Aussie salute with grace,
For waving flies away from nose, face and cheek, from head,
Becoming second nature: mated: like a needle to thread.

Nak said: "The flies here will drive you crazy,
Just keep waving off, don't get lazy,
Annoying they may be,
But you get used to them, you'll see."

"It's like the work we get with colonist, plenty to be had,
Though good at job you must prove, having patience is not bad,
Once farmer is convinced and consolidated,
Your service will hence be well faired, well rated."

"More work than you can handle will fall your way,
But tough it out, remain focussed, and never stray,
Prove yourself strong and reliable to all confronted,
Be true to your word and ethics, never be routed."

Abdul said: "The office in which I applied,
Advised good work be had, he has not lied,
I care not how hard I need to work,
So long as it keeps my future from unfortunate murk."

Nak is pleased: "You must learn a new way, new rope,
Gain what you can, be reinforced by all hope,
Do not take advantage of any easy road, avoid the easy route,
Keep your head high, and grow from experience, you'll sprout."

"Stay with me, you will have nothing to regret,
I treat men well, and for one to stray I do not let,
Men like Faiz Mahomet, if you excuse me please,
Some of his workers grow lazy in attitude and tease."

"We will depart tomorrow for our first appointment,
A homesteader turning farmer near Birdsville, our agreement,
Sometimes we travel by night, when it's cool,
Especially during Ramadan, we try to follow each rule."

Nak asked further: "So from Kandahar you are?
"Yes," replied Abdul, with half guilty stare, memory afar,
"Well, I am from Kabul, and Shir from Karachi,
You shall be our good friend, and we, good companions for thee.

And Nak pondered more on the past,
To hear all the truth to the very last,
"Did you leave Afghanistan before the war,
Before the British moved in, before all the gore?"

"After," replied Nak, unsteady in breath,
"I fought against the British, to do so till death,
For two years I bore body against them,
And not long after I came to Australia seeking my gem."

Abdul then said: "Receive your gem you may or may not,
But regardless of future you are giving it your best shot,
You once fought the British in your past,
But now you basically serve them in your days so vast."

Nak stopped temporarily upon his feet,
"I serve no one, and for this I shall not be discreet,
I serve my ambition, and you my new employee,
I am as devoted to work as was against Britain, you'll see."

"I shall not be a servant to the British,
But must convey I need work to fill my dish,
Nak then added: "We are both prisoners here as you know,
Getting our lives on track for money and into purse we stow."

Abdul enjoyed good honesty, people being up front,
Nak said: "I was a tribesman back home, maintaining my wont,
But never felt like a pheasant, whether treated as such or not,
For in heart I was forever of own mind, and all good was begot"

"But now I am here, treated as I desire,
I command over my future, I am no liar,
But hard work it will surely be, I do attest,
But always I will do, for you, my very best."

And Nak continued more with solemn song,
"Forever looking over my shoulder, as though wrong,
Seeing if eyes recognise me for all I have done,
But in the end I think I have won."

"I have divided myself from previous incursion,"
Continued Nak as though it were his mission,
"There is no truly escaping their cause or true wit,
Though I shall also never truly join it."

"This country need me more than I need it,
But remain here I shall as I feel I do fit,
For without my service they would shrivel and die,
We use them more than we actually rely."

Abdul then felt to remind Nak once more,
A letter he sent to Port Augusta, an office of lore,
"I served in General Robert's Camel Corps, travelled far,
I was in the march of 1880 from Kabul to Kandahar."

"I know," replied Nak, for he had arranged this day,
Asked friend in Port Augusta to gain worker before they stray,
Abdul had arrived with shipment in 1884
Along with 259 camels in hull, the ship's store.

Nak continued: "It is true to be wise,
Never hide truth behind any disguise,
I served against the British and you served with them,
Neither of us have blossomed from this, their poisonous stem".

"My friend, Jehangir, does well I must agree,
Did his search as though he were me,
Plucked you by choice from a wroughting crowd,
Making a choice of which he can be proud."

"And I trust in his good judgement,
Of his idealisms and character assessment,
Seeing first hand the character you carry,
Understanding you as though his wife did marry."

"Yes," said Abdul, looking Nak in the eye,
"He plucked me right out of there, as plump bird from pie,
He showed me the way to fruitful life and employment,
Into your very hands, and, seemingly, for my enjoyment."

Nak reflects on the past: "Jehangir is a good man to know,"
And changes tone: "I understand him more as I grow,
But our escape was no different than what was yours,
We do all we can to stay alive, pick and choose our own chores."

"We all served those we needed to serve,
But now serve ourselves with great nerve,
I sometimes regret my actions in Afghanistan,
But I had to defend against the invasion of British man."

"But speak of it no more, I wish to advise,
War is a strange bedfellow for the wise,
And wiser we grow with work to be found,
Working our feet into the very ground."

"We are all Durannis, though different than Mahomet,
For he threatens our job prospects as each is met,
Faiz is far better than Abdul Wade,
A common and despicable Ghilzai made."

And Nak trailed off, his thoughts were poison rort,
For the Durranis were not really his sort,
Durranis formerly known as Abdulis,
Nak was just trying to provide similarities.

Abdulis and Abdul, similar in some way,
Strange comparison, not dressed in black, but grey,
But he put nought in it and thought of it no more,
Gave it no further thought, his mind made up for sure.

Abdul asked: "What of Shir and the war?"
And reply: "He will not share conversation, say no more,
He will refrain from asking about your dealings,
As you'll refrain from seeking from him good meanings."

"But we have a new destiny now,
One we share as though of the same brow,
But also different we each are beneath Earth's moon,
You married, me single, and Shir to marry soon."

"Tonight in actual fact,
An Aboriginal with much tact,
Shir has paid his bride price,
And she appears to be very nice."

Nak continued: "You too will grow lonely here,
Nothing to do between jobs, here and there,
You are invited to the wedding of course,
A wedding that Afghan community has decided to endorse."

"But first we must get you sturdy and steady,
A blanket and basic equipment to get you ready,
It can grow cold here during the dark hours of night,
A good blanket will put your weary bones to right."

INTRODUCTION THE SHIR

A great service could be found here in Marree,
And no one could do anything but agree,
For merchandise could be secured for delivery,
And paid for later when wages came flowing like gravy.

It was the culture of the current time,
No prejudice here, no difference between orange and lime,
For the colour of money was the same from each,
From white or from Afghan, money spoke and did not preach.

This place and service was the delivery shed, big business here,
Supplies galore and a service to all, a slogan to adhere,
Bags and sacks of flour, rice, and sugar, an array of stables,
Oatmeal, baking powder, and tea, stacked to roof, no tables.

Items painstakingly ticked off a big list,
A great enterprise that would not desist,
And so here we find Shir as he gathered his sacks and bags,
His shopping list filled as he stood there in near rags.

Shir and Abdul shook hands, each under stare,
Abdul being handsome and Shir as ugly as rear end on mare,
But smile he did for he was happy to no end,
To be wed this night and for loneliness to mend.

Abdul knew nought what to say,
For war talk was banned and he did not wish his mind to stray,
"My time as a cameleer has been varied to vast degree,
But here in Australia I'm sure more to learn there be."

Shir said: "Desert here and desert there,
Ghostly cold by night and peaked at day by sun's glare,
But the colonists are as stupid as stupid can be,
They cannot compete with us, you will surely see."

"We might live in the same town,
But we are the ones steeped in renown,
We command over all transport requirements and need,
Transporting to farmers, supplying all but mead."

"We don't tough alcohol or bacon,
But anything other we are ready to be beckon,
Good reputation with all we have, rigid as a stave,
We are the people's blessing, their mysterious nave."

"We separate ourselves from all those that are late,
And deliver on time, our service is first rate,
We can achieve competitive service cheaper,
And these deals make bartering all the sweeter."

"Once this load is delivered on time as we agree,
We shall transport their wool back to Marree,
But for the minute we must hurry all the more,
For a wedding we attend, for me a great ceremony in store."

Nak saw opportunity, good advantage to take,
"Is she a good cook, good meals can she make?"
Shir replied: "She can cook and furthermore still,
A woman of great passion and able to give thrill."

The others laughed at this, happy to hear a joke,
But spiteful looks were cast their way from other bloke,
For let us not forget - of the populace - the racism here,
Always unfortunate and forever in gear.

Nigel B.J.Clayton

Shir then said: "Please, come and help me now,
Still work to be done but I am ready to bow,
For the day is drawing to a close,
And I need a wash for I grow on the nose."

Nak to both: "Come and we shall finish up here,
Go to our calling, good company most dear,
Many new friends for Abdul to meet and to talk,
Finish up here and with me come walk."

WEDDING ARRANGED

Custom in Afghanistan it was for bride price to be paid,
And for this a man's daughter would be laid,
Upon ceremonial pedestal to be wed,
To then be taken most surely by husband to bed.

Time between words of promise and mattress,
Was for the friends and family, alleviate stress,
Each giving their blessings, strong words of steeple,
As newly wedded couple gave cheer to the gathered people.

It was an unfamiliar custom in Australia, this bride price,
Something alluded as though avoiding lice,
But Aborigine had picked up on the custom fast,
For need of money and comfort to last.

A father standing proud with daughter in hand,
To give her up with smile on face as he does stand,
Seeing daughter's hand taken by an Afghan,
Made no difference to the father, of his house, the man.

Where the Afghan was rich with money to spare,
He may be able to capture more than one wife in snare,
Seen more than once this monstrosity,
Men taking advantage of this opportunity.

Normal it was for a man to be over sixty,
Taking a wife as young as fourteen, seeing her as sexy,
No crime is it here and so few seemed to care,
But some in society do manage to give a rude stare.

An old man with a dirty mind on child,
Running fingers up one so innocent and mild,
Feeling the inside of her leg for joy,
As though his money for bride price was spent on a toy.

18

Though never a complaint is heard upon the wind,
For the suffering do so in the raging of their mind,
But Shir was a good man here,
And to one wife he would adhere.

To behold a wife, slightly plump with a little fat,
Saw reflection of eagerness from Afghan with eyes like rat,
Eyes ready to eat, wishing to devour the fish,
Some call this fetish, others prerequisite to be met and to dish.

Further still can we secure more from this time, this decade,
From this century, within the mix of culture and facade,
For Europeans would have little to nothing to do with either,
But Afghan and Aborigine slowly gave to securing good tether.

Times were changing where they saw eye to eye,
Good friends, Aborigine and Afghan, they could seldom deny,
And of the colonists and all they believed in,
They seemingly portrayed little more than to be of great sin.

There was another obstacle in the way, all agree,
Women forbidden to pray in the mosque at Marree,
Men were granted more spiritual comfort which they did expect,
Whilst women were treated to lesser degree, with lesser respect.

Inside the mosque where Shir was to be wed, to verses say,
There was the *mirab* so placed, which faced a certain way,
To Mecca the Koran must be laid in good tradition,
Wrapped and well rested upon place of distinction.

The Koran was treated as a National flag,
Not just any old piece of worn-torn rag,
For no other book was to be placed upon it,
It must have a good station for it was writ.

Shir's wedding would be taken with no less ceremony,
Special custom as though no limit to money,
Shir's wife called Arika, to join him tonight,
To set straight their loneliness, to make things alright.

THE CEREMONY

In Aboriginal her name meant waterlily, you see,
A name fitting a beautiful wife to be,
Shir was hopeful that his wife was happy and content,
Cared for her, where other men would deny, not allowing consent.

In separate rooms to start out the night,
A *mullah* from Marree to view with delight,
Ensuring all custom was met with alright,
To ensure all ceremony were seamless and tight.

Shir was dressed in *shalwar* trousers, the custom,
Wide at the top and narrow at the bottom,
Largely dissimilar to pantaloons in appearance,
There was a vast amount of difference.

And a turban of white sat upon his head,
Ivory white and of greatest respect,
Arika with dress of white and a veil, musing compassion,
Nothing outlandish but befitting this special occasion.

Arika was comforted in the knowledge of wedlock,
That Shir was a good man who loved her, never to mock,
No unconditional love could she willingly yet give,
But with her new husband she could forever live.

Commit herself to him she would do at will,
Offering goodness to both in their future to fulfil,
Receive great joy from company offered,
Security for life she did hope to be smothered.

To embrace Shir's religion as her very own,
Accustom self to it with maturity grown,
Religion and Afghan were one and the same,
To be married to an Afghan was a religion to claim.

Arika spoke in broken English as best she could,
Shir did the same as expected he should,
For neither knew the others language,
It was a smallish burden, not of real heavy baggage.

And so wed they were amidst all who saw,
Many friends to witness, ceremony of custom and law,
And after good words spoken a feast so huge,
Now married couple, no denying the truth, a new type of refuge.

Showered in blessings from young and old,
Dalak of Marree, being happy, from smile be told,
No circumcision her today, he wore another mask,
The *dalak* of Marree performing many a varied task.

The *dalak* was called Zareen,
A man seemingly wealthy and clean,
Bestowing a bow and a gift,
Giving money, good fortune, opposite of rift.

Zareen was a lowly man, circumciser of boys,
Also the haircutter most sure, though never annoys,
Only two others exist whom are more lowly then he,
The sieve maker, and a dancer who danced with glee.

"My best wishes to you and new wife,
May your future together prove to be a good life."
"Thank you, Zareen," said Shir smiling and steady,
Despite, in his mind, looking for bed with wife, he was ready.

The assembly was large and hungry, keen for supper,
Many tables of food prepared to stifle much hunger,
Women in veils to which they all adorn well,
Men in their turbans; both sexes, their enthusiasm does swell.

Nak stood before all and gave a short speech,
"I congratulate this new couple, tied together, never to breach,
Please now take to these tables of food, all ready for thee,
Eat all that you can and be content, be as happy as can be."

The throng moved about with great patience,
Never shoving with haste, employing a methodical science,
Conversation thick and most friendly, and to friends rely,
A most hospitable congregation, not a single person could deny.

Shir reflected, most dreamily, on life there ahead,
Upon his wife and the young life she had lead,
Living off the land of the desert, digging out roots like mole,
Amongst forages, creeks, and sparsely strewn water hole.

Amongst rivers and streams, amid the heat,
Where the scorching sun does unkindly beat,
A sun-scorched land which does dry and crack,
And then rainy season and deluge across desert and track.

Shir was so happy, so happy at last,
A beautiful wife, one who mused of character vast,
She was sixteen and he was mighty pleased,
Less than half his age, an ambition of his at last appeased.

Shir was ugly on the outside though handsome on the in,
So lucky he never forced her, he was always without sin,
This was wrought from her personal perspective,
He had also proved to be very protective.

One thought remained, a splinter, a sentence within a tome,
It was time to leave the feast room and to go home,
Time to be man and wife,
Time to begin their new life.

21

Nak stood before the two, Abdul to his rear,
Both giving free smile and happy they did appear,
"I wish you both the very best, hopefully, even, a little rest,
Tomorrow's work we attend, to work hard and remain the best."

"Sorry I say, arika, new friend... Ah... new wife,
Four weeks gone, we go, but not... no strife,
I shall look to Shir for you... whilst go away,
Make sure he will not to go... to go astray."

Shir said: "I have some letters for you, for the homestead,
I have to give them to you, but I got distracted instead."
Nak replied: "Do not reflect on it right now,
When we load the camels you can give them a show."

And so Shir and Arika say their good night,
Off they go into the future so bright,
For business is thriving, although very hard,
It is work to last long and never retard.

And in broken English, Arika does speak,
"All nearly go home, we go to, I think."
And Shir asked: *"Are you scared for the night?"*
"No," she says, with sincere foresight.

THE PROSTITUTE

The wedding ceremony is over, good couple new,
Time for Nak to abscond and quench his own desire as it grew,
A secret he keeps to self forever and more,
Only short walk away he does make via misleading tour.

Not too far a prostitute does live,
Of Japanese ethnicity she does give,
Love to those that wish to pay,
For good company as they do lay.

Nak was single and of good moral, good brother,
Though he still had needs as any other,
He deserved love, as per anyone else, without fail,
To feel the warmth of flesh, of a beautiful female.

He was lured more by his loins and his frustration,
A need growing within for great satisfaction,
Wanting to extinguish the desire within,
To accomplish his desire in the midst of his inward grin.

She lived in the Ghantown not that too far away,
Never tempted to find trappings in city, she was here to stay,
For some considered her soul wretched, sinful and worse,
And others a great commodity to be paid for by purse.

Her real name was unknown by the community as it stood,
But Saki to those single men of the neighbourhood,
Leading a reasonably pleasant life away from the town centre,
She was seldom seen away from her shelter.

You could not say she was welcomed by the community, her host,
But she provided a service to the men that needed it the most,
And so to men she became accepted for her services here,
Some finding her irresistible, sneaking behind back of all peer.

She had been married once to a wealthy man,
One of Chinese background, and his name was Chan,
He was old and vicious to say the least,
Who had passions for his cook also, he was a snarly beast.

He died not long after being wed to her fast,
He always had her commit to his desires, to the last,
Rough and ready with heavy hand,
With heavy punch to face he always did land.

After his death she had nothing at all,
Caste away like rubbish upon the streets, feeling small,
Nothing left for her and no money to be had,
She was penniless, homeless, cast out, but not mad.

She reinvented herself to be what she is today,
Self-managed and important to those that pay,
Leaving Adelaide behind she found her way here,
To Marree where she carved a new life for her to steer.

She was a prostitute, destined to please,
Nak was a man who had his desires to appease,
His future ambition a secret untold,
To wed Saki and live a life quite bold.

Though she knew nought of Nak's secret untold,
Knew not of his ambition to be so bold,
But she knew and felt his love more than as though kin,
And loving a man like Nak was far short of being a sin.

Nak knew the truth of it all as it stood,
Afghan and Asian was frowned upon by neighbourhood,
Marriage between these two could never be true; never knew,
And so Nak would always feel alone as in older age he grew.

She felt no prejudice for Nak or his religion,
Nak felt no disgust in Saki and her ambition,
He needed love and paid for it here,
She needed funds to secure future year.

He fell upon the shack by a dry creek bed,
Up river, so to speak, so water clean and good health lead,
But little water flowed at this moment in time,
For the heat of the months dried all and left grime.

A few date palms did grow nearby,
A little fruit picked now and then, lullaby,
A clothes line hanging between house and crooked post,
Looking worse for wear but not quite the ghost.

Nak passed the clothesline and pulled worn shirt from hanging,
A flag of familiarity meaning that Saki was ready for straddling,
This was her work and those words not meant as disrespect,
For she was a good woman, and to mans' needs never neglect.

He knocked twice upon the door to be certain,
Saw then a shadow moving across window curtain,
Saki opened the door with a smile upon face,
Nak could not reciprocate due to affliction, which is no disgrace.

The outline of her breasts issued great pleasure,
Nak had already, without more, received good measure,
His ill-feelings and pressure was already much less,
Already advantage to spirit and anxiety, and stress.

Her hips and slight plumpness were like heavenly gift,
Enough it was to mend the inner torment and rift,
Nak felt his love for her all the more,
Even without the love making which was yet in store.

Looking each other in the eye,
Saki could never, with Nak, deny,
Taking his hand she lead him straight to bed,
To satisfy his hunger, for him to be fed.

As they stepped Nak spoke a few words as best he could,
"Good night," he said, his broken English understood,
"Yes," replied Saki as they walked past single lantern,
Past basin, past small cupboard and then did turn.

Facing each other at the foot of the bed,
Nak felt as though he had just been wed,
Saki felt the desire in Nak for sure,
Comfort was present in Nak, no need to lure.

"I go work, long time, long way,"
Saki simply smiled, Nak happy and gay,
Nak's grimace and smile ugly to eye,
But she knew that in her Nak did rely.

Nak said: *"I stay long time here,"*
And pulled money from his purse, one held dear,
She pushed it away in order to first fulfil her job,
A duty, a repose, a pleasure to aid, never the snob.

To the night she did tenderly tend,
Kissing softly Nak's grimace, his face, to mend,
Nak's feelings abated, lost in splendour this night,
Here he would stay under morning's first light.

THE FIRST DREAM OF CONSEQUENCE

This was Char Asiab, 6th October, 1879,
Abdul stood upon the firing line,
Ready to do duty for British here,
Fighting for all he could gain for family this year.

Three British field guns fire from a single ridge,
Firing upon an Afghan position, distance easy to bridge,
British Highlanders, Gurkhas and the 5th Punjab Infantry,
Do what they can to command over this country.

The British lines advance slowly at first,
From the enemy side of fence the scene could not be worse,
The desert explodes in places upon the field, no place to hide,
The noise of battle carrying both far and wide.

Little damage currently seems the effect,
Upon Afghan position whose stronghold mused to be neglect,
And so the gap closes and slows, a faltering tide,
But distance is eventually gained against the defending side.

Both Afghan and British forces litter the ground,
Many dead and wounded around to be found,
Screams from the dying filling the air,
No time to relax or to give a care.

Volley after volley permeates the atmosphere,
The advance continuing now more rapidly does appear,
Battle noise deafening as deafening can be,
Smoke from cannons and weapons as far as the eye can see.

Abdul then woke with a great start and gasping for air,
It has been a long time since bad dream, it just wasn't fair,
But something had jolted his memory from the day before,
Someone he'd recognised, for sure, to be sure.

PREPARATIONS

The morning broke with the usual ceremonial flare,
Muslim singing, their song, their music blare,
Mystic verses of praise and worship do layer,
Accompanying all as they prepared for prayer.

Afterwards Shir had farewelled his wife of one night,
Abdul departed shed after wrapping turban tight,
Nak arrived last and happy as could be,
No one aware as to where he did flee.

"Good morning to you, Abdul," greeted Shir,
Abdul replies: "A good morning it is, that is for sure,"
"How was your stay in shed, upon bed of hay?"
"The family Bauz were good, comfort I had during my stay."

"And here is Nak, on time again I see,"
"And good morning back," replied Nak, "and to thee,"
To Abdul he had spoken, and Abdul was pleased,
"Thank you Nak, I am refreshed and ready to appease."

Shir said: "All is usually well amongst Afghan swell,
This day is busy and we do all we can to assure we gel,
Each has his place in Ghantown and Marree,
One day you'll see, and will have to agree."

"I already agree," replied Abdul, "of this place,
Friends already I have found, all with profound grace,
This will be a good place to call home, I am sure,
To this friendship, comradery, good cheer, I have bitten a lure."

They had walked over to coral near empty trough,
Their camels waiting, tails waving flies off,
Hardly sun on horizon and already growing hot,
This place in the desert, for the weary it is not.

Nak said to Shir: "You look refreshed after last night,"
"That's because I had a woman to hold me dear and tight,
But where did you go last night, off into the dark?"
"Uh, to see an old friend, and... well... up at first spark."

"And so good company we have all had," Abdul replied to both,
"Each of us rewarded experience to help us in our growth,
For I had good company, shared with the family Bauz,
Greeted this morning with large breakfast on which to gaze."

Shir then started: "We must commence with the deed,
Get these camels from shackle to feed,
Have them packed with goods and ready to move,
For we have a long journey ahead, though little to prove."

Shir then handed a letter to Nak as promised, unread,
"From yesterday, two letters for the homestead."
The last letters to be delivered by hand,
For a small mail service had gripped the land.

Jack Hester was his name,
Delivering mail was his game,
Service to grow in conjunction with demand,
A faster delivery than expected across bleakness, across sand.

"I was handed them by the Postmaster late yesterday,
And promised to deliver them without delay."
Nak said: "If they were Muslim, to receive these,
The Postmaster would be slow to appease."

But the Afghans would deliver them regardless of this,
Their manner different than white folk, this you could not miss,
They had nothing to lose by delaying the mail,
Only good reputation and well earned respect upon trail.

Abdul advied with good cheer: "Maybe another order,
Possibly demand for more wool, a job grafted to shoulder,
Bigger rewards and future job, better terms for wage,
A new beginning for you Nak, upon the camel string stage."

There was always room for growth around here,
Good business to receive if to schedule adhere,
Do well to the residents and farmers all,
Gathering more customers meant you would never fall.

Though to work they must get,
If current schedule was to be met,
For loading of stores to camel's back,
Would take time to ready, just a little time to stack.

Abdul was permitted entry to Australia, rather slender,
A three year lease only, a little short and rather tender,
Though administrational records would sometimes disappear,
And longer stay would many appreciated with good cheer.

If Afghan was married, family still overseas, at home,
It was hard to be satisfied with just desert to roam,
Homesickness was part of everyday life,
Especially if at home you had children and wife.

Some would bring family to Australia, sure,
But very few were granted, lacking tackle or lure,
For Australia needed camels and handlers too,
Not children and women with nothing to do.

Many men before Abdul had abandoned their post,
Taken Australia as new home, accept them as host,
Leaving family to perish in Afghanistan and more,
Feeling one selfish ambition, regardless of lore.

No; Abdul was different, his family came first,
He would aid his family, even if worse came to worst,
And the sharpness of knife then hit his heart hard,
In his mind he was totally devoted to wife, to children, his bard.

If denied his family admittance here,
Home he would go, back to family dear,
Whether alive after three years and feeling well,
Or dead as a dormouse and in coffin did smell.

Whether wrapped in good clothing or rags,
Dressed real proper or like pauper who nags,
Regardless of circumstance he would return,
To be with his family, family he could never spurn.

Whatever the cost, no matter how dear,
He would serve his time, in Marree, right here,
Even working his fingers to the bone,
He would once more be with family upon throne.

The camel string would soon be ready,
Nose pegs in place and camels steady,
Stores loaded upon the backs of them all,
Ready to depart and see the miles behind them fall.

All were anxious to be on their way,
Camels too needed lifting from demeanour grey,
To trek the land north across scorching land,
Hoping to be free of sandstorm, for sandstorm was banned.

No time here for a delay to hit hard,
So prayer this morning they did for guard,
For safe journey they had all wished,
Hoping for all disaster to be missed.

To homestead they must reach,
Drop off their stores in good manner to teach,
Reload with homestead wool and deliver to station,
Get homestead goods to market, distributed to nation.

The camels were tied in order of advance,
Lead camel to front and kitchen to rear, all to prance,
From Marree to near homestead they would attend,
Just south of Birdsville, a hazardous journey, no friend.

With them one camel, pregnant was she in guise,
To leave behind would be unfair, unwise,
The others would miss her, in heads bells toll,
Camels had great character, like people, with great soul.

More like pets than mountainous features,
Near impossible it was to neglect these creatures,
Each and every camel had its place in the string,
Always they travelled in order, so cheerful as almost to sing.

Each of the three men had eight camels to call his own,
Stick in hand to tame and to direct until familiarity grown,
Each and everyone had a name and characteristic,
Never abuse; never employ against them anger or rude mimic.

Varying colours and sizes and towering tall, a great lump,
Hair growing longest at the shoulder and at the hump,
Dull grey or yellowish brown and yoke,
Main coat colour grey, black, cream, and others just spoke.

White was rare and very seldom was seen,
These animals were family and comrades keen,
An Afghan could never work with a horse,
To do so would fill them with sorrow and remorse.

Two Aboriginal boys worked hard and with good grace,
Paid well they were sure never to oneself, disgrace,
They continued to place saddles and supplies where needed,
Much activity undertaken now, as was pleaded.

The boys worked from three lines of stacked merchandise,
With much eagerness they prepared the trip to hell, not paradise,
The Aborigine boys continued to smile as to work they went,
Working systematically they were worth every penny of rent.

Abdul did ask: "To the camels' names, what do you call?"
"That one is Amaroo, and that one Girra, names we have for all,"
Two of the camels, not yet with nose pegs in place,
Did change positions within the string, they seemed to race.

These animals knew their place well,
Understood formalities and in them pride does swell,
They had their own minds which worked like well-oiled gear,
"It's only the lazy ones that need a whisper in ear."

"Never hit hard with your stick or readily provoke,
They take to their jobs superbly, that is no joke,
Very seldom you need to hit them hard,
Most will bend to your will and you will be their guard."

Nak looked at the eight under his command,
Gave an order and all stood as was demand,
Abdul then tried and only two stood,
The other six were as though made of wood.

"They are testing you, Abdul, that's all,
Show them who's boss, shoulders back, stand tall,
Bark out your order and make them react,
They will adapt quickly to your voice and your tact."

And so formalities of the early morning proceeds,
Familiarity for animals and men, fulfilling their needs,
Three men and two Aboriginal boys under occasional gaze,
Toiling away under the growing heat and the blaze.

The front-most camel of each eight camel string,
Had a riding saddle attached for rider to sit as though king,
A saddle of two forks, one in front and one behind,
Leather-covered seat, with stirrups, secure mind.

The camels worked hard for the men as though seemingly agreed,
In return they must attend the camels everyday need,
Constantly checking for sores on camels back,
Checking lashings, and straps, every tack.

Pack saddled may require relining with jute,
Strong fibre from wool bales to remedy, camel discomfort mute,
Unmuzzled camels may require muzzling at times during ride,
Temperamental dispositions seeing one bite another's hide.

They were a team like no other,
Men and camels: camel the worker and men the mother,
Saddles refilled with straw through small slits,
Which overtime turned to chaff, hence replacing with straw bits.

Saddle sores could become infested,
Where infection would be nested,
Fly-blown lesions that caused death,
A worrying sight able to stall one's breath.

Feet too needed to be constantly checked and scrutinized,
To be free of abrasions and cracks, washed and sterilized,
Cameleers loved their camels to the very last,
Like family they were, as though of family cast.

The loads sitting upon a camel's back,
Seemingly stable and resting upon solid rack,
Although sometimes sway from side to side during the move,
Always taken from them at night, delicately removed.

Thongs and cordage were tied secure,
Allowing for quick adjustment and removal to cure,
For unstable loads upon camel was annoying at best,
Quick to hurt and rub, and forced upon string unnecessary rest.

Nose peg of hardwood was connected to each camel,
No need for a bit in mouth like horse to travel,
String attached from peg to other camel's rear,
An easier way to maintain discipline and to steer.

The connection sagged in the middle with ample room spare,
No pain evident unless camel tried to bolt from his snare,
No heat-conducting metal employed for use as these,
For cameleers were fond of their camels, each to appease.

Camels worked hard for their owners, sturdy stock,
The cameleers protected and served these beasts of rock,
Each relied on the other for good life,
Any other form of existence would cause strife.

As packs of merchandise was stowed,
The cameleers fondled their friends, eyes glowed,
Quiet word from cameleers lip,
Deep throaty grown reply or responsive nip.

Playful they are, capable of dry eye or tear,
Own persona each has and matured each year,
If only they could talk it would be a great friendship,
Their disposition one could never dissect or strip.

Everything to love and nothing to hate,
Always on time and never late,
Happy to trudge the extra mile per day,
Before napping at night under stars without hay.

Another easily seen here was the kitchen camel,
Always last in line, in the order of travel,
Water and food, pots and pans clanging about,
Utensils, cups and bowls, all that men could not go without.

Abdul looked into the eye and then upper lip of one,
The camel reminding him of a story long gone,
It was a story of how they did silently move,
And had come about the lip which bear a small groove.

How Muhammad had kissed the lip of a camel,
And since that day hare lips did they have, wherever they travel,
It was a gift from Muhammed to all descendent,
All creatures of this type did display, loudly and most strident.

In little under forty minutes all told,
They were ready to move, content and bold,
The sun had risen above the horizon, moon now tired,
Time to get moving, only one other thing required.

Nak had a rifle, help in crook of arm, you see,
For Al Halal meat was forever available in Marree,
But once out on the sand and running low on food,
For good meat all three may be in the mood.

In the Ghantown where they live,
It is easy to take and to give,
But it is the *mullah* that resides here,
And to him a responsibility for which to adhere.

Adhere to religious law,
Never to flaw,
Always to abide,
Never to wash out with tide.

The guidelines were explained in the Koran,
Everyone knew it, every single man,
Meat was gained by using a sharp knife,
Killing animals whilst still full of life.

Dragging sharp edge over jugular vein,
Blood to come oozing from the artery main,
Then allowed to bleed and die in their sight,
As butcher did accomplish what he believed right.

Long strips of salted meat that Nak had available,
May run out during journey leaving none for table,
This would mean slaughtering a kangaroo or other,
Preparing meat so that hunger they could smother.

Whilst facing Mecca, regardless of how far,
Nak would recite, 'Bismillah Wallahu Akbar',
Sacrifice to Allah is what this does entail,
Whilst animal dies and whines and sometimes thrashing his tail.

But die it must not before conclusion of prayer he did reach,
Animal to suffer as the *mullah* does make his grand speech,
Applying this verse to his one and only God,
He then proceeds as though given the nod.

If the animal dies before prayer is complete,
Leave the animal to rot there at his feet,
So thinking of this he checked his weapon once more,
Prior to placing it away upon saddle, in bag to store.

No sooner than done and they were to farewell their stay,
Camels stood up and they were upon their way,
A long journey ahead but they would return back home,
The Ghantown falling behind them and much desert to come.

OF THE CAMEL

The noble dromedary that Nak had in his string,
Were descendants of India, descendants of king,
Trustworthy and sometimes witty, hard workers and fast,
No lazy bone amongst them, hard workers to the very last.

The camel could go two to three weeks without water,
Glory be, a grand total of abstinence and no slaughter,
Able to drink twenty gallons of fluid at a single sitting,
Able to go so long without drink for a camel is fitting.

The heat of the Australian sun,
For the most part was simple and fun,
Forty degrees in the shade of the coolest tree,
They were simply content and happy with glee.

So much better than a horse or an ox,
Higher than both, tall and witty as fox,
Spinifex never concerned a camel in any way,
So high up they did clear, no damage to stay.

The assortment of goods carried in sacks,
Upon backs and side saddles with glistening tacks,
Nothing was harmed by spinifex at all,
Because, yes, that's right, they were so very tall.

Tell-tale signs of camels having passed by,
Hair upon spinifex does not lie,
Legs three foot long they move through scrub and turf,
Their skin as black and hard as rock on earth,

Their skin becomes as hard as iron rails,
A horse being torn to shreds, it all pales,
For significance is in the breeding,
So why bring horses into a place not needing.

Spinifex, a plant to aid in erosion,
A notorious plant having spread like explosion,
And small birds and animals use the plant wise,
Aboriginals have their uses and weapons to devise.

Saltbush country edged with mulga, as like the shore of sea,
Undulating sandhills as far as the eye can see,
Rabbit burrows infesting the ground,
Easy to see as you look all round.

Plenty of meat here as can be relied,
Dingo, emu, kangaroo, all can be abide,
A single shot from a rifle and it is ready to treat,
A meal to dress, a meal to eat.

But wound the animal Nak would have to try,
Otherwise allowed to rot, and meat for them it would deny,
Religion is religion and in it they trust,
Without it they would simply turn to rust.

And mulga was a good meal for a camel and more,
And against all belief no water in hump does he store,
A camel will absorb the fat from within, a supplementary dish,
The hump falling short and to slowly diminish.

The animal could extract moisture well,
Taking much from mulga and paracelis to aid in dry spell,
Their pads were soft, best for moving over sand,
Quite often the string would avoid heavily trodden land.

Soles hard to take the heat,
Seemingly cushioned and very neat,
Made for hard work, hard labour,
This beast was a legend of all land and Nullarbor.

Uncanny sense of direction and good memory in store,
Knowing where they are going if been there before,
Three miles an hour for up to ten hours a day,
Though stand still in one spot too long and they say nay.

Seeing some sign out of the ordinary would grasp attention,
They would look and stare in that general direction,
Memory with them all of the time to stay,
For next time coming past they look for that sign in the same way.

They were quite remarkable,
They were very, very able,
They were polite and worked as hard as the heart,
They were good friends, never to part.

THE FIRST DAY

They had been moving along at good pace for some hours,
When Nak looked to his camel, Chocolate, who towers,
High above Nak the camel does peer and stare,
Ahead of him something... moving upon track, amidst glare.

Ah, Chocolate, Nak's favourite beast of all owned,
Each camel in his 8-camel string did seem to atone,
For they were all yellowish brown with dark mane,
Everyone and each of semblance they did maintain.

So Nak followed the camels gaze,
And sees a figure upon the shimmering maze,
Seemingly seated in shade not far up ahead,
Looked similarly Aboriginal, his stature easily read.

They came upon him soon enough, quite close,
Passing him by, seeing infliction quite gross,
A victim of his mother's cruelty, no joke,
His lips burnt away from face, with hot embers she did poke.

Nak and Shir had seen him before,
Upon this land on occasion he does explore,
Holding his hands out for a morsel of meat,
But little does the string have to allow him to eat.

A sorrowful sack of bone,
Little real flesh, no body tone,
A shell of emptiness and very weary,
His eyes peering up but looking rather bleary.

His name was forgotten, he was a wanderer of sorts,
Forever on walkabout, or so go the reports,
From a distance he appears happy with smile on face,
But closer, you'll see, bare teeth a disgrace.

No lips to close over mouth forever more,
Mother's torture, bad treatment they deplore,
A punishment inflicted when he was a very young boy,
When he played with his foul dinner as though a toy.

An alcoholic mother of bad spirit and soul,
No sense of pity or remorse, but upon him a toll,
Picking up hot stick from burning ember,
Strike hard until burnt this family member.

But that is the way it is here in the bush,
No one to rush out with aid, just remain hush,
A sadness to see this was pure evil itself,
Something unable to be put from mind, put to shelf.

And then further on another is seen,
Half-caste for sure and extremely unclean,
Neglected and thrown like rubbish about,
No home, no one to say 'come', no one to shout out.

Pasted over the land like freckles on face,
These people discarded as though a disgrace,
No one wants them hanging around anywhere near,
They are called pests of society and all do sneer.

This one here would sell herself short,
Give her body to some white man for good sport,
To be paid a pittance for something to eat,
No family around, no one to greet.

Abdul was the last string, was last in line,
To see soon enough, cold shiver creeping up spine,
He had come here to make money, for family and security,
To send home all he could, yes indeed, a surety.

He had served the great British Empire,
And Australia was part of that which he did aspire,
But the more he did see of this land,
The more he grew ashamed of all he'd played of his hand.

So they continued on their way,
Much time available later to have one's say,
As they moved along, pot and pans continued clanging,
Metallic melody teasing the hungry, and the utensils hanging.

FODDER

The day was commencing to draw to a close,
And time for prayer, time to grasp, to attain repose,
The camels required feeding and so did all men three,
Nourishment provides much strength and the body does agree.

Beautiful reds and oranges spanning the land,
Many colours and hues enough to make a man stand,
Stop walking about and look all you can: feel cheer, feel healthy,
This view is for free and a sight most worthy.

The way and effort in securing good grazing land here,
Was for the cameleers to be wary of land up front and rear,
Always looking for good place to set up camp,
Forcing the camels to not wander off and upon country tramp.

A fine shallow, an old creek bed, sits as though fallow,
Bush and trees and grass yellow,
Everything here needed for a hungry camel to snack,
Just wait for the packs to be removed from each back.

Camels are position, each string of eight aside,
Packs to be removed from their position astride,
Forelegs folded down towards the ground,
Followed by rear legs onto hindquarters as mound.

Thongs and cordage, tacks unfastened too,
Allowing packs easy removal, there was much to do,
Working remarkably fast and Abdul under watchful eye,
He was found to be working tirelessly, no one could deny.

The two front legs were tied by rope shackle,
Nothing the camel with teeth could tackle,
Short hobbles applied to all in their presence,
And let the camels loose to feed, not restricted by fence.

Nose pegs untied to allow free reign for all,
The kitchen unpacked but never let fall,
Much activity to conduct and much to achieve,
Before night was too cold and the flies did all leave.

Each camel knew its place in the line,
Could smell his pack as though rats to lime,
The camels would know where to straddle,
In readiness in morning for replacement of saddle.

Not too far out will they stray,
Most will remain near their masters whom near fire stay,
Hindered by shackle, this restraint good and proper,
To go more than a mile away they would not bother.

When night fell it fell erratically fast,
The heat from the day escaping as though from vacuum blast,
A fire built eagerly for something to eat,
But religious commitment comes before sustenance and meat.

Another moon was expected tonight,
It would provide some very decent light,
But until then all three should work fast,
Get everything sorted before the light was at its last.

THE FIRST CAMP

The camp was relatively easy to appease their need,
The night possibly colder than any other, would not impede,
A campfire for cooking was second important to all,
Second to prayer, from which they would never stall.

They had already placed there sleeping covers and sheet,
Folded up into tight rolls and ready to meet,
And with nearly everything completed,
The Koran was revealed to which all eyes greeted.

Nak was *jemadar* and responsibility was his to be graced,
So with this in hand and prayer mat placed,
He prepared to read the most appropriate,
For their needs and thoughts, for their new associate.

Ablutions should to be conducted in the usual manner,
It was very important and it really did matter,
Five pillars there are here,
Five times per day to recite amidst silent cheer.

But this was the dilemma for cameleers,
They could not do the same as all of their peers,
They could not waste water amidst the desert shades of red,
And so sand they employed in its stead.

Small piles of sand sat beside them each,
A semblance of water but ritual they could preach,
They would perform their duties as good men should,
Just not in the proper way in which it was understood.

Five pillars were also altered,
They could not pray as so ordered,
Salat-al-Fajr, Salat-al-Zuhr, Salat-al-Ast they were,
Salat-al-Maghrib and Salat-al-Isha great emotions stir.

Sunrise, noon, afternoon, sunset and night could not be,
So drop the afternoon and night it was decree,
Longer they would spend during times of other,
To make up for lost prayer and hope for forgiveness from brother.

And one further degree,
In which we sometimes see,
For Nak on occasions sees Salat-al-Zuhr given leave,
The sun was too hot at that hour, which sees each man grieve.

RESPECTFUL NIGHT

The light from the fire lifted the cheer of the men, of all of them,
Faces appeared happy and from this goodness did stem,
They sat cross-legged with mug of tea,
Not a cloud in the sky, they felt as though toil free.

The cold of the night would fall, as cattle herded from croft,
No cloud cover to cover them from aloft,
No cloud cover to keep the heat in by night,
Good need there was to wrap up tight.

The brightness of stars high above,
Was something to easily provide your love,
The Milky Way seen clearly as it spanned the night sky,
So picturesque and clear, enough to make a grown man cry.

Stars winking as though breathing in and out,
No denying that God was mighty, there was no doubt,
It was sheer beauty on a scale worthy to view,
Something bold and grand, all contemplation just grew.

It cast memories to fall upon the mind,
Recalling old friends, some simple, some kind,
Memory of times upon this great earth,
In other countries, in particular the one of your birth.

And of vulnerability did come to thought,
Of the vastness about and no other company to be sought,
So peaceful and quiet, as quite could be,
Where wind was still and solitude alone did spree.

Where they had stopped there was nothing at all,
Not even the telegraph wire above them so tall,
They had moved away from the beaten track, and,
The camels found it easier to move on soft sand.

Away and aside from the telegraph wire,
Gave each man and camel a clearer desire,
No reminder to see how far travelled,
No mark in mind to be chiselled.

Instead they employed landmarks to appease their need,
Vast sweeping plains and hills gift knowledge as though to feed,
Creek lines and familiar large trees give sign,
These signposts in which their minds did design.

Clever thinking during long journeys to last,
Across dry land which seemed so bare and vast,
Better to trek without telegraph line overhead,
Solitude delivered and inwards bred.

Shir added the finishing touches to their meal,
Nak took Abdul for short walk to conviction appeal,
For his need was for Abdul to do as they did,
Regardless of trust in him which had already been bid.

To check on the camels one last time before, to sleep, fall,
Familiarise Abdul with the characteristics of all,
Camel's and their company the lifeblood of all they did inhibit,
All preferred camel than man for company though did not admit it,

So the sun had drawn to a close upon most temporary home,
The seemingly short day from time sun did come,
Very busy it was indeed and all would agree to tell,
But time for a short story before eyelids declared farewell.

Nak began his story after briefly setting the scene about,
Of Aborigine people, small tribe of these parts no doubt,
The fire flickering a melody to reflect his tone,
Devastation as it come to nest, seemingly placed upon throne.

Viciousness and Aborigine were of the same word,
Nothing to part them, they were of the same herd,
It is evil to speak of these things since passed, not paltry,
But Abdul needed to know the truth of this sunburnt country.

A husband did look down upon the face to spurn,
A creature of the opposite sex, ready to burn,
A creature of the incorrect sex, one to neglect,
For the tribe needed a man, take this one as a mark of disrespect.

The disgust upon the man's face was painted clear for all,
Never hid his emotion did he, but allow it to fall,
He felt no connection with this person, this baby so thin,
This child his own flesh that he did not see as kin.

He picked her up by the feet and swung her real fast,
Bashing her head against rock as was his task,
The brain splattering everywhere you care to look,
The mother sobbing frantically as terror, to soul, had shook.

The sorrow within her was like a tidal wave true,
How this had come about she had little clue,
But some men are strange in a land of hard living,
For them it is hard for love to be giving.

No final hug or warning had the mother received,
No time for her to prepare, nothing left on which to grieve,
Her life had just been ended in the flash of an eye,
Her child's life taken from her, good life to deny.

The husband scolded the wife and kicked her hard,
Kicked the mother as though piece of filth from shoe to discard,
Not a shred of empathy lingering about,
No feeling in him of guilt to give shout.

He took the body and disappeared from sight,
Taking limp body, being denied proper cremation right,
He then built a small fire to burn the body away,
Not wanting the flesh and bones on earth to stay.

But the fire would not start and kept going out,
No matter what he did it just wouldn't flare out,
And in short manner of time the smell of blood on the air,
Did bring dingoes galore out of their lair.

And so throw the body down the man did do,
The dingoes rushing in and ripping apart, devouring raw stew,
Some taking a piece of the body away,
For it to remain a part of the land to this very day.

How did the cameleer know this was true,
How could he be sure that in it the truth grew,
For word of mouth it terribly sound and does solidly stand,
Spoken well from one to another across forsaken land.

No writing instruments or other way to communicate,
No messenger at door or solid oak gate,
No history books to fall upon for lesson to learn,
All is verbal and truth spoken in good turn.

Abdul wasn't sure of the point of the story,
Found it to be a little too gory,
But it reminded him of what he had seen earlier today,
And understood viciousness to be part of the Aboriginal way.

Aboriginal people, though sacred they are, so Abdul learnt,
Mused to have a harsh life in this land so burnt,
Their laws and way of life so different than any other,
Afghan or white man, the Aborigine was satanic, tougher.

Nigel B.J. Clayton

Nak had meant it as no rebuff for Shir,
Whose own wife at home seemed to be heavenly pure,
But reflect on the story just spoke he did, not scoff,
Something to contemplate and would be hard to be rid of.

And so the slumber of night is now to take place,
Nothing further of the day to embrace,
Shir to dream of wife, and Nak of Mungerannie Gap,
Abdul of his time on the British line with rifle held by strap.

THE SECOND DREAM OF CONSEQUENCE

A shockingly loud bang filled the air, red flashes of light off glare,
Abdul then saw a soldier hurled backwards, unaware,
His legs torn from torso, feet from limb,
Abdul's possible future, it made him feel grim.

But push on he did towards the enemy now,
Ready to take life and he knew just how,
And he saw a man's head appear up ahead,
The smile upon the face of the enemy easily read.

A soldier behind fortification with grin on face,
A beautiful smile for which to embrace,
The enemy enacting kills upon the field,
The battle around, open, little to no shield.

The man was taking shots at British as they did appear,
No thought to retire, no contemplation to fall to rear,
An enemy of strong conviction and resolution,
He was intent to stay and fight, his only solution.

'Praise Allah,' Abdul heard upon the breeze, it did astound,
Unbelievable to think in the battle noise around,
The smiling man again aiming over rifle sight,
To take another life from the British fight.

Abdul realised them that the gun fire had slowed,
The British behind him had momentarily been stowed,
This was not good for being on the front line,
No fire support, life harder to preserve: "Please preserve mine."

He then fired automatically at another target ahead,
Unsure really but in mind a target was read,
A puff of smoke filling before his eyes and to temporarily blind,
He shot up in bed, to a new day not yet ripe, his second to grind.

THE GATHERING

When morning broke it was met by three men waking,
Blankets stowed and readied for final packing,
The most important of tasks was met, the grandest priority,
Ablutions and prayer having secured their notoriety.

As Shir took to preparing breakfast the others went to task,
Seeking out camel and herding them, no need to ask,
There was also the checking of stores, essential mapping,
Checking of saddles and all manner of strapping.

Few birds there are to greet the morning activity,
Where flies commence the annoyance in life of brevity,
Though sounds can be heard they are seldom allocated,
All part of the chorus, of the song of the desert so associated.

This was the hour of birth given to light of day,
A gift to the morning from all creatures that lay,
Hidden from view but all appearing to be gay,
Always to be heard and part of the play.

Other sounds could be heard upon the light wind and afore,
A storm in far, far distance, a hundred miles away or more,
And regardless of this grand music to ear,
It was silent and calm, atmosphere enough to bring on a tear.

The camels are relatively easy to find,
As with mouths busy, their food they grind,
Bells on necks giving their general locations away,
Affixed the night before, prevents them going too far astray.

Within a half mile of campsite,
It was quick and easy to put string back to right,
Chocolate found by Shir and used as a lure,
Many camels following his lead, their leader most sure.

They had eaten the night before,
Good sleep and then eat some more,
Ready for a hard day's travel ahead,
Their heads held high, contented moods easily read.

Abdul confided in Shir so as not to impede Nak,
But he was feeling the isolation, wishing for home, to be back,
"I feel the weight of it upon my shoulders,
My desire for my family, forever embers within me, it smoulders."

"I feel the weight of it here every day,
The feelings are detrimental to my stay,
I don't wish to burden Nak with my quandary,
My family comes first, not secondary."

"I must be here to earn for family's sake,
But being away is like being hit with toothed rake,
I cannot win for whatever I decide,
I feel I am casting my family aside."

Says Shir: "It is true, to be sure,
The love of family, sincere and pure,
But look to the bright side if you may,
Only three years here and then forever with family stay."

"Do not think too much on it, heed not the misery you take,
Just think on the work ahead and the money you'll make,
Your wife and children will flourish ever more for your sacrifice,
For all you do here your life will be all the better and very nice."

"I suffered too," continued Shir,
Feeling as though stuck, forever a pessimistic mure,
"And Nak too has his facial affliction,
But he has forced for himself a solid conviction."

"It is all the same to us now, no essential cure,
We simply do what we must in order to secure,
Our futures grace and temperance,
To have a grand future, a deliverance."

"You will get used to the condition and the loneliness,
Never give your future a second guess,
What lays ahead of you is paved in gold,
For you and family to grow, graceful and bold."

"When in Marre you will find community and friends,
To stand by you no matter what your trends,
We are like brother and sister forever,
Caring for one and then for the other."

"But you won't be spending much time in Marree,
We are going to work, all three of us as did agree,
Time will go fast, fast as can be,
Three years will be the blink of an eye, you'll see."

Abdul said: "You are right and it is agreed,
I need to stop negative feeling, which to mind I feed,
But what else to think on, when on the road?
Nothing all day but mile after mile of desert abode."

"That is hard to answer,
Harder still to master,
For each day will be different,
Depending on many, varied predicament."

"Some days are like a year spent,
Others less than a few seconds lent,
Depends on if something does occur,
Or how well trained your mind is to administer cure."

Abdul said in contemplation,
"I suppose it is a simple negation,
Refuse this place and length of each day,
Take them in stride and consider what future lay.

Shir replied: "And that is your answer true,
Another perspective, something new,
Regardless of this you will find a way,
And in three years time you'll consider it a short stay."

THE MISSIONARY

Loading a string of camels was done so in reverse,
Harder than unloading and considered by some a curse,
It was a challenge on occasion for it was strenuous indeed,
For camels could not rest fully loaded regardless of mans' need.

Shir reached for his water canteen,
To quench his thirst he was keen,
His last drink for quite some time,
Water discipline self taught, pristine, prime.

Bells and hobbles to remove,
Nose pegs placed above lip with groove,
Ready to stand the team as one,
Single command ushered in tone.

Standing on hind legs first and straighten them now,
Front legs opened at knees, forequarters raised, camels from bow,
Push forward onto one front leg and then the next,
Up and ready for the day to come, perfect action as written in text.

The camp now clear of their stay that night,
Time for the journey, time to take flight,
Eight to ten hours more, no real delight,
But the song of the desert will appease, devoid of fright.

They stepped off one foot in front of the other,
Much distance ahead, their tracks, grains of sand does cover,
Taking seconds, minutes and hours by stride,
Abdul does all he can to allow feelings to strategy abide.

There are places enroute, for camel, that allow for easier going,
It is all in the knowledge of area, all in the knowing,
Avoid the easy, accept the extreme, fewer horse teams on the track,
And to all degree, avoid the bullocks of the outback.

Not long on the road north and Nak saw something ahead,
Immediately familiar it was and even in the heat easily read,
Chocolate looked up and voiced his opinion, too,
For what they saw was something they both knew.

The silhouette of a man beside covered wagon,
The blemishing waves of heat, mirage, try and imagine,
But no mistaking this, it was easy to decipher, and on guess rely,
No question about it, no need to deny.

Chocolate though was a little confused, not ignorant,
For the last time he saw this was somewhere different,
Though familiarity of image was there to test,
His memory as for humans was always his commodity best.

Nak gave warning to those that followed behind,
"Missionary ahead," a man of sacred mind,
Abdul looked up from the rear, his eyes did strain,
Saw the shimmering picture, pixels, coloured grain.

As the gap between the two diminished,
It was easier to see what could never be missed,
A man of God though of different belief,
The three Muslims only hoped for passing to be brief.

Brother Johann Ernst Jakob [Jacob] was the man's name,
Known far and wide, temperament tame,
A bullock team under control of whip, his sway,
Tails moving to flay flies from buttocks away.

He was walking beside the team,
His body not muscular, rather lean,
Having a short stretch of both leg,
As he went along his way, aiding all, and those that beg.

The Brother of Christian [Lutheran] religion,
On the road every day of the year preaching to legion,
Walking his team or travelling upon wagon seat,
Only stopping on occasion for something to eat.

To and from Port Augusta he did travel,
Supplying the mission at Killalpaninna, a desert naval,
The mission provided a service of religion, to all those around,
To provide good service to men and women of religion found.

For Johann the needless journeys across desert plains and bays,
Were coming to the end of their steaming hot days,
For the train and Marree meant there was far less work to be done,
More time for him to preach, so really he had won.

Killalpaninna Mission, first decided in January, 1867,
Missionaries having first arrived as though gift from heaven,
Having settled out from Langmeil, never to stall,
Three and a half months after, arrive upon desert, all.

Killalpaninna was not too far ahead,
Possibly 25 miles out from of Cooper Creek bed,
Out-stations Kopperamanna and Etadunna Station,
Incorporated into what was Bethesda Mission.

Johann appeared to recognise Nak,
Gave nod of the head as he lightly whipped bullocks' back,
"May God be with you, brothers, let him build an altar within,
Release you of the savagery of your belief, being forever in sin."

Nak understood little of what was said,
Not purely for English spoken, but slight German accent bred,
And so, *"Allah be with you,"* was returned first rate,
Spoken with sincerity and not with hate.

The calling of Allah struck Johann hard,
But reflected not, his mellow smile his guard,
Whether two friends or enemies it mattered not,
They treated each other with respect, right there on the spot.

COOPERS CREEK

Cooper Creek could be allusion,
Cooper Creek could carry confusion,
Spin off from Cooper could be Cooper or rot,
Was creek to their front Cooper or not.

So vast the names and system about,
Cooper Creek so known where trees give sprout,
What other creek could it be,
Not for anyone to guess or disagree.

Cooper Creek was around these parts, yes,
But was this to their front right now, just guess,
Call it Cooper for Afghan was not sure,
But which other could it be, a grand animal lure.

Many years of summer sees the creek dry,
And at others it is running though slow, as though shy,
From Queensland to north, a possible flood,
Flowing down through NSW to south, like veins of blood.

Regardless of the situation found,
To this beauty they were all bound,
Endowed by 3.5 miles of expansive floodplain,
Though hard to decipher from ground, confusion one does gain.

Water was here and creek full of life,
Shadows flickering and flirting, relaxing, little strife,
Fishes and birds, and amphibian life here,
Lucky you'll be if large fish with eyes above water does peer.

The camels would have smelt the water long before,
Though little they would need due to what earlier they store,
Walking leisurely they tenderly approach,
Afghans at their side and ready to coach.

Picturesque as the scene was there would be no respite,
Nak didn't want the camels to lose all for which they did fight,
The camels would grow lazy if given a drink at every stop,
Lazy camels opposed to tough and cream of the crop.

Many Europeans fed water to camels every three days,
Nothing but deterrent and honestly wicked in their ways,
Offering easy way out and never the tough,
Made lazy camels, harsher times rendered rough.

Allowing a camel to water every ten days is finely tuned,
This may procure a total of 20 days when desperate, well pruned,
Water discipline it is and needed to be taught,
A well worn and trained camel was better than distraught.

Call it water fatigue or stress,
Call it what you need, call it a mess,
Treat kindly but harsh,
From desert to marsh.

No matter the climate or predicament,
Good training is rudiment,
Without such training,
Dead camels come raining.

Sixteen to twenty gallons in a single sitting,
If a camel drinks less than it is spoilt by constant filling,
Longer stretches in between is the need,
Water for camels is far different than feed.

Camels are ships of the desert forever more,
Afghans good handlers able to administer as any choir,
Knowledge of surroundings go hand in hand,
Such knowledge sought from Aborigines that walk the land.

Every precaution, all of the time,
Moulding good camel, condition most prime,
Never sway from good training true,
Never underestimate a camels' ability to do.

Nak said: "We don't stop, keep them on the move,
The camels will drink if opportunity does prove
Take a quick mouthful with cup of hand,
Feed yourself, though, by rule to camel we stand."

Abdul said: "A good place to stop and pray."
Replies Nak: "We cannot change our routine today,
Think of the camels and their training we must,
Do not allow them to drink or in future they rust."

"Allah knows we are loyal to him, always to follow and do,
To his beliefs we adhere, we are consecrated and true,
Water is weak and these camels are strong,
To gift them water opportunities is very, very wrong."

The creek depth before them was rather unknown,
So for first time at journey their bodies were upon saddle thrown,
Now straddling the camels the cameleers did ride,
So high above ground, so high astride.

With supplies piled high and far from ground,
Portage goods never exposed to water found,
960 pounds of maximum weight, and more if desired,
Always maintained and convictions never retired.

These were camels and part of a string,
Not caravan or wagons pullers with supplies to bring,
Wagons unless built high were not that great,
They too were subject to gifting supplies in wet state.

Abdul cupped his hand and help it extremely low,
Gifting water to mouth, feeling refreshed, a pleasant glow,
The moisture running the length of his throat,
Like water cascading into dry castle moat.

It was tasty and refreshing,
Naturally good and a blessing,
It was like being in heaven above,
Less the seventy-two virgins to love.

Within minutes the string was across,
"Check their nose peg," yelled Nak, their boss,
"Sometimes they are broken,"
Task already done, even as spoken.

Not much to it, not much at all,
No need to slow, no need to stall,
No need to rest, no need for prayer,
No need to refresh camels amidst water's glare.

NATTERANNIE SANDHILLS

These first four days of travel was a peak, a best,
No flogging dead horse, no putting camels to test,
Simply pushing alone at great pace,
Across land for ten plus hours a day they did trace.

Ahead were the Naterannie Sandhills,
Gorgeous ridges of hue likes grills,
In some places like snakes upon the lands,
Ridges of assorted colour bands.

A wedge-tailed Eagle then caught Abdul's eye,
Magnificent species flying so high,
Wings of fortitude help out upon brightness of sky,
Silently glide, black, long, mysterious, he could not deny.

Diamond-shaped tail,
Talons sharper than any nail,
Chestnut coloured nape,
Unmistakable in shape.

Some parts of the country were appealing but bleary,
Filled with beauty but also quite eery,
So peaceful and quiet, serine,
Bitter and vicious, obscene.

No clear cut way to put it,
A land of own desire and wit,
Characteristics battling against one another,
Life-giving to some but life-taking from other.

Gorges and hills with peak,
Steep hills of high volume they speak,
Low lands flat as can be,
Many contrasts around to see.

But for some it was too much,
Seeing it all the time now failed to touch,
No inner warmth felt by Nak,
And Shir was also quick to turn his back.

Only Abdul saw the raw beauty of land and sky,
Of the country around and all he could spy,
Many weeks and months had the others suffered,
They were not impressed by what was offered.

Nak and Shir must have minds of steel,
What did they think of during stretch from meal to meal,
Long stints of nothing to do but walk,
No opportunity except at night to talk.

Day after day was always the same,
Seemingly nothing to do but play the game,
Working and toiling hour after hour,
What did the mind receive regarding stimulating shower?

Australia seemed better than Afghanistan, but only just,
Fortune would be a long time coming though in it he trust,
He contemplated Jehangir in Port Augusta aiding another,
Even so many miles apart he gave to Nak as though mother.

Abdul had a stomach full of food,
Friends who always appeared in good mood,
A working day that kept him busy at toil,
No time to spend allowing laziness to soil and spoil.

Much unemployment there was in reality here,
Long lines in queue and much scrutiny from unkindly leer,
And in Afghanistan it was even worse, especially with wife,
Being poorly and grovelling upon soil to sustain life.

A man made his life at best he could,
Took the best offer as he should,
Always there was fruit upon the tree,
Ready to pick, branches to move and you'll see.

Carve your own future,
No time to wait for a caring nurture,
Appease yourself and your own need,
No one else will aid you with such greater speed.

But continue on regardless of mind's lay,
Past Mulka to Mungerannie for another day,
Mungerannie is Aborigine for 'big ugly face',
A name that holds very little grace.

MUNGERANNIE

Do not pass into view of the town,
It is as many with white trash acting the clown,
Cursing and blasting their hatred of race,
A short cut would also offer better pace.

It is not just the Afghans that the population hate,
Though they take jobs from many by offering cheaper rate,
But the camels which they believe hideous in every way,
Wishing only that in Afghanistan the camel would stay.

But how hard was it for the idea to sink in,
To replace their frowns with a deep grin,
For white trash here to take heed and discard ideas vintage,
To rear the camel themselves, properly and to great advantage.

To be looked upon disgustingly by the wives of the men,
A cold stare that could kill before the count of ten,
An ungodly glare to Afghan and more,
And of every Aborigine they do deplore.

It was here that Abdul was gifted a lesson,
They were at a junction of deserts, the Simpson,
Tirari, Sturt and Stony, amidst dry air,
And mention of the Strzelecki Desert just to be fair.

Sheer solitude and quiet no matter where you look,
Except that song of the desert which penetrated every nook,
Many variety of bird life crying for water holes and spring,
Calling to young and mates, reverberating calls sing.

Many, many species can be counted about,
So many varieties of birdlife each gifting a shout,
The next generation of life just waiting,
Or hatched already and looking for the season of mating.

But for the most the desert plains around,
Were just that, flat and barren ground,
Emptiness seemingly coming alive,
And upon it, hidden from view, life does thrive.

Vast areas of undulating plains,
Fine-tuned and tiny, miniscule grains,
Large batches of small stone getting underfoot,
Camels feet becoming a point of great moot.

No, life was not easy for the cameleer,
Not for the camel held so dear,
But they shared good company and love,
They fit together like hand and glove.

THE DINGO

Close to camp for the night they did approach,
When Nak saw up front one of the many desert roach,
As the sun commenced its journey, to slowly disappear,
The night air incessantly cooled through progressive gear.

There was a dingo up ahead, a sure sign of trouble,
No matter mind of genius or even mind of rubble,
A dingo at dusk, waiting, looking, standing,
Was a recipe for disaster in the making.

And Nak felt he knew why the dingo was here,
Why the dingo was adamant to remain near,
The reason will be divulged to you soon,
With or without the comfort of light from sun or from moon.

"We have a dingo up front and we'll be camping shortly,"
"Will you shoot it?" asked Abdul rather curtly,
Nak replied: "Not just yet but on him maintain,
Good visual in order to counter his desire to gain."

"No need to upset the camel,
Too close to end of days travel,
Nose pegs to be removed,
Maybe after safety has been proved."

Shir asks: "What did you say?"
"I say keep your eyes open in case he decides to stay,
This damn dog called dingo looking for camel to play,
But deny him great sport I shall this day."

Shir says: "I know why,
Why he is here, why he is not shy,
My camel Slate is ready to give birth,
And I am prepared to receive great, ecstatic mirth."

"Slate has been grumbling a little now,
This past few minutes, that I do know,
Not long now I am sure of that,
Used to the signs I am, but now is no time to chat."

And not much further along,
They are ready for camp and for song,
"We camp here for the night,
Keep good visual, right and tight."

The procedure for setting camp was the same as before,
Though Shir made time to see Slate and to assure,
Unloaded her first and getting ready for birth,
Ready for young one to fall and to grow great girth.

Nak could see that the dingo had retreated a short distance,
But he did not retreat very far, ready for deliverance,
So Nak had to stroll over to Chocolate,
Get ready his rifle, he was not obstinate.

Prefer to let live the dingo,
Wishing him to be free and let go,
But camels came first before this creature,
Whose desire was for blood, it was in his nature.

He untied and prepared rifle for firing,
Feeling it a choir, this killing quite tiring,
The string of camels had all been seated,
He set the sights of weapon as was needed.

But waste the meat of dingo he would not,
Try all he could to wound and not allow to rot,
To kill according to law, for the good of all,
To not waste a bullet, or meat, forced to feel abysmal.

Bringing the rifle into his shoulder,
Looking out to front, through brush and past boulder,
Honestly too far even for Nak to shoot,
A missed target meant nothing to loot.

Nak did not wish to kill for the sake of killing,
Did not find it at all thrilling,
Didn't wish the dingo to crawl away and die in great pain,
But calf was under way, unto world of desert plain.

The other two men stood by their camel,
Abdul pleased their familiarity had grown during travel,
Slate rather slow to react to orders given,
Men busy unloading packs, skilful and driven.

No real telling how long before delivery,
But seemingly soon, be rid of the drudgery,
For even camels suffered the pains of labour, did stress,
Walking Slate may aid in the matter, avoid a stressful mess.

Nak aimed the rifle as best he was able,
The dingo standing front on, on all fours, stable,
But Nak missed his target completely,
Hardly jarring the dingo, it moving rather discreetly.

The animal then stopped and turned to stare,
A loud noise only, what did he care,
He'd barely moved, even to side, when shot was fired,
As the bullet whipped through the air, to vacuum retired.

Shir laughed and stirred a few camels, their glanced lent,
His laugh more disturbing than bullet just spent,
"Good shot, Nak," was what he did say,
"Concentrate next time you should, maybe another day."

"Lay upon target of flesh and bone,
Not stir him slightly as though throwing a stone."
Nak replied: "If you bend over, Shir, I shall not miss,"
And turned again to the dingo, "Watch this."

He reloaded and squeezed more gently this time, good site picture,
Breathed in and out, good comfort, good posture,
Fired his shot and the dingo he did hit,
Now sprawled on the ground, and Nak did spit.

A carcass wasted, no good to them now,
To the dark of the forever night the dingo did bow,
Now raw pickings for the creatures that do seek,
An easy meal to be had, slim pickings for the meek.

THE BIRTHING

Not long after fireplace set,
Slate gave birth, new calf was met,
Of similar colour to mother,
Nothing out of ordinary than other.

The calf sought out the udder, no need to mention,
Good size and good son to mother interaction,
Good nourishment, great gift, an attraction,
Young calf with good sucking action.

Good looking calf," said Nak, "he looks great,
You need to get a bag ready, prepare ride for Slate,
She can also carry the kitchen, with blessing,
A lighter load with rations diminishing."

"Take up the rear and follow from behind,
Not distract the others of duty and mind,
I shall go seek some more fodder to stow,
Abdul with me, please, to task, do follow."

Abdul pondered the request of company to keep,
Wondered on Nak's need to speak,
Nak was awaiting to divulge news in good turn,
Something to listen to, something to learn.

Abdul complied to the request, the bid, the need,
He could see it ahead, conversation a budding seed,
Leaving Shir with camel in newfound fame,
To return later to circle and talk around near fire and flame.

And of the calf we must briefly accost,
For they are heathen to look after but a blessing, no cost,
Much good rearing before working track can they take,
For their place on earth as movers, for living to make.

And currently to spare the anguish of walk ahead,
Calf would be bundled and bound instead,
Wrapped in bag and onto mother's back,
Along with cargo, added to stack.

During the trudge across desert plains and mound,
Slate would look over shoulder, joy bestowed and found,
Young calf blinking adorably at mum,
All content, all love, clear to see, an insurmountable sum.

Slate would be content to continue the move,
A part of the string, moving great trove,
Her body churning to make milk for her young,
Seven pints of milk from bladder to mouth and over tongue.

Until back in Marree would the unnamed calf be carried,
Until three years old, too young to be married,
To string with heavy load, not for long or short haul,
Much hard work in future but currently none at all.

After weaning it would be able to accompany its mother,
But no loaded store to kill and to smother,
A separate string attached to the caravan,
A nose peg worn as any other, it was not ban.

But this was not necessity, not entirely required,
Only if Slate needed would calf join as though wired,
It was capable of keeping up with the string, all would agree,
But preference would be for calf to remain in Marree.

From three years the calf would meet with work,
No time to be lazy, no time to shirk,
At eight years it would be mature,
Entirely and appropriately of good stature.

Nak and Abdul took a few steps more,
Before stopping in front of pantry, a store,
Spinifex available, easy picking,
Tussock grass easily cut like whittling.

Much Mulga around,
Grey foliage abound,
Seeds and pod,
A meal for which to nod.

Weeping mulga bush with silvery leaves, a good feed,
Saltbush from salty soil, good fodder suiting their need,
Covered in a white powder, blue-grey leaves do tease,
Sturts Desert Pea a favourite to see and appease.

Camels happy to eat whole bush and root,
Pulling from ground and shaking free the soil to loot,
Seeds dormant during dry times, little moisture,
Hairy grey-green stems, easy to eat, no torture.

It was all free, as free as can be,
As far as any man can see,
Filling hungry camels with much glee,
Cameleers could do nought but agree.

A camel would grab a branch in its jaw,
Not in teeth, pull down, stripping to gnaw,
Regurgitate, chew and chew,
Grinding all down until mellow like stew.

"You've been working hard," of Abdul, Nak did praise,
"How do you find it here, where camels for free do graze?
How do you like this Birdsville Track?
Few towns, few settlements, few homesteads, few shack."

"Much like the rest of the country I have seen,
Already growing dull but I am still eager and keen,
The scenery is beautiful and night skies are a gift,
Something to look forward to, to one's spirit it does lift."

"Ah, yes," agreed Nak, "Not much change about,
No gauntlet. No maze, no strict route to lay out,
But like you say it fills you up with something special,
Gives you purpose, feels gratifyingly simple; not social."

"For the nights do similar for me, it does lure,
Lifts my precious soul to heaven, no restriction, no mure,
Splendid feelings of solitude and private thought,
To contemplate the meaning of life, an understanding sought."

"But you still have much to see and experience,
Possibly rainy season to bring a little flood and grievance,
Flooded plain in some areas, for miles and miles around,
Nowhere dry, not a piece of dry ground to be found."

Abdul askes: "You have experienced this all?"
"All, around four years that have to me come to fall."
"And yet you have not made your fortune to date."
Nak looks Abdul in the eye, "One day: one day, it is not too late."

Nak educated: "It favours a man to keep many friends."
"Friends like Jehangir who mitigates, to new arrivals he tends?"
"Yes," said Nak, "friends to aid you always, in many ways,
We aid each other, many times over the years, across many days."

A compliment Abdul then did make,
"You have made much from nothing: much risk you did take."
Nak rpelied: "We have suffered risk and much, much more,
A reminder to me and Shir, a reminder of gore."

Abdul pressed on: "You do not speak of war?"
"No, no, I do not, but something more,
Of a man named Muschky, a good friend to adore,
I recall his death as though scribed, as though lore."

"He was shot dead, his head hit by a bullet,
Whilst doing a delivery, running goods as though through gauntlet,
Too close to a town we had travelled,
And we paid for it, most expensively, our empathy levelled."

"Little pity can I feel for most,
I feel more for Muschky even if a ghost,
I am not easily startled or made distrait by nature's mess,
Too much bad fortune, too much anguish, too much stress."

"Listen to me, Abdul, listen well,
Too few to be trusted here, no matter how you gel,
If no Koran they carry,
Then do not tarry."

"It is why we keep clear of the worn track,
Not just to appease the camel, upon softer sand, their knack,
But to remain aloof and away from the racism,
Save us from falling into cataclysm."

They moved over to where Slate was mothering,
Placed the harvest food before her, patient and waiting,
And Shir arrived at their side, no lag,
Having finished making, for calf, his travel bag.

Nak said: "The rifle I carry is not just for dire need,
It is also for self defence against growing, racist creed,
I have never yet needed to use it for much,
And never yet for defence, against maliciousness and such."

"When I look at the rifle I can see Muschky clearly,
Wishing to be a businessman, his heart set dearly,
Wished to work via contract with miners,
Supplying hotels and bars, to appease their diners."

"He wished to blend with the country about,
Not be lazy, to never be the lout,
To help this country in growth the best he could,
Was ambitious and keen, and tell a lie he never would."

"Never a sore word to say about anyone,
A heart made of pure love, not stone,
But last year was the undoing of it all,
His end met due to this racist gall."

"It was upon this very track,
We were near Mulka and checking some tack,
For a load had become a little loose,
And he wished to get camel's discomfort from noose."

"He then dropped dead, shot in the head,
Came out of nowhere, our hearts instantly filled with dread,
Possibly meant to scare, it came, a mighty *thwack*,
But it ricochet off some supplies on a camel's back."

"Maybe murder, maybe a mistake,
But little action could we take,
They rode away extremely fast,
Several people on horseback, we were simply aghast."

Nak asked, after a few seconds more,
"Why tell me this now, when past Mulka's door?
You could have told me of this before,
Instead of holding it within mind, in store."

Nak explained: "I've been fighting my soul since,
My feelings shrivelled, ground, turned into mince,
Killing the dingo reminded me so much,
Of Muschky and his kind heart, seemingly always in touch."

"I know I have proved to be reliable with weapon,
But the evil of killing has been a lesson,
Ever since Char Asiab and war,
My feelings have changed as though, from me, tore."

Nak a little astounded,
Shocked; grounded,
"You were at Char Asiab, just over four years before,
And then came here, hoping to never see more."

Nak continued: "Every day I experience fear, and I tire,
Of what the colonists may call my betrayal to Empire,
You, Abdul, fought for the British and have little to hide,
I tend to look over my back all day during my long ride."

"My ride to acceptance,
My ride from grievance,
My ride to great friendship,
My ride to avoid the punisher's whip."

"You are now a good friend,
And with friendship our inner souls do mend,
You felt strongly about fighting for them,
And I am the opposite, of different branch but same stem."

"But my life is here, now and forever, for the greater,
I shall never return home to be placed within fetter,
I wish to grow old and knowledgeable,
Of able body and mind, in old age be financially stable."

"I cannot be caught and found out,
To be convicted by any means, always silent, never to tout,
These people here will never listen to me,
Understand I am innocent, should be set free."

Nak, with furrowed brow: "What are you trying to say?"
"With my feelings, every day I do prey,
I want you to carry the rifle for me,
Of course, to refuse, you are free."

Nak said: "No, I am sorry your feelings do grapple,
But I cannot take it as though from tree to take apple,
Yes, I fought with the British,
But only in order to fill my family's dish."

"Sure, there were other reasons too,
To be fair there are many to throw in the stew,
But my families needs always came first,
And if I lie, may I die here in the desert, die of thirst."

Nak said: "I hold this not against you, I say,
But I appeal to your greater understanding, and may,
May you see it from my perspective,
For, from me, the outlook is only the negative."

"It would be easier for you to plead innocent,
If before court of law you are made present,
A greater scrutiny of my past,
Could see my days on earth made my last."

"But, I am aghast,
I have offended you to the last,
Just please understand my predicament here,
Of my past and the ashes I carry from last year."

Shir then spoke: "You should know everything,
I shall open to you and hide nothing,
You are the only one can carry the rifle,
With all these words we do not trifle."

"Nak is a wanted man and so am I,
It is nothing that I can really deny,
I am wanted, dead or alive,
For against the British I did strive."

"I should not tell you this but I shall,
It may hit you on head, like mallet to ball in pall-mall,
I am wanted as a spy by the British,
And for killing one, a mission I did wish."

"Only Nak and Muschky knew this before today,
And now you, and I hope that with you only it does stay,
We can both be easily sentenced, and heavily, put to death,
Death and no glory, no sanctification, to ground beneath."

"And I hear that question, set behind your eye,
The one that lingers but does not pry,
And the answer is no, do you, of me, hear?
You do not deserve judge and jury, before them to appear."

"But it is simply your ability to go against conviction,
To be announced innocent is an easy prediction,
If those that killed Muschky appear again,
Steady hand I fear I cannot maintain."

"A seconds delay in pulling the trigger,
Will see our misery grow all the bigger,
They will get away with another killing,
And we shall have to quit, give up this grinding."

"This is all upsetting to speak,
Our feelings are mixed and never seem to peak,
But I say to you now of my regret,
My poor feelings for British spy I killed, after we met."

"For without my prior, murderous killing,
I could easily do for what may be bidding,
Help defend Muschky's good memory,
To give closure to this entire story."

"I would happily take up rifle against these non-believers,
Defend against these devils, not grievers,
For they have not an ounce of pity for any living thing,
They do not care for anything breathing."

Abdul reflected on all that was spoken,
His heart torn, as though broken,
"Your secrets are safe with me, you need to know,
But I won't carry your rifle, on my camel never to stow."

Nak said after reflection, a second's thought:
"That's fair: you've heard the truth, we both have taught,
And I think soon we have to conclude with day,
Finish with prayer and share a meal if we may."

And all three have learnt a fair bit,
Of commitment: characteristic; being woven, being nit,
And before each closed his eyes for the night,
Each considered the company they had, and in it the great delight.

THE THIRD DREAM OF CONSEQUENCE

The Punjab Infantry continued their advance,
Upon defensive position, battle at a glance,
Abdul having prepared his weapon once more,
Looking for a target, for life to take, a notch to score.

Dust flew up here and there,
Nothing but from enemy the evil stare,
And then from destiny of horror within dream,
He is snatched from it by voice, fluid as though from stream.

"Abdul, it is time to wake,"
Said Nak, for early day he wished to make,
"No time for sleep, prepare for the day,
Time to prepare, to be on our way."

Nak and Shir appeared to be happier than normally gifted,
A great weight from shoulder having been lifted,
But they saw reflection and uneasiness there,
Abdul's dreaming, his glancing off to distance in stare.

But all in all the truth had been revealed,
No longer was guilt of any description to be sealed,
And yet Abdul did seem off put by something unclear,
Something in his heart, something he did not hold dear.

Regardless of this predicament,
The homestead was a destiny set in cement,
Many hours and days remained to be cleared,
Many more miles for camels to be seared.

Abduls reflections of mind continued unabated,
Mostly for the worst they had been rated,
His dreams continued each night, ending never near,
And he felt he knew why but it wasn't entirely clear.

Feeling faintness was experienced on occasion,
As though his mind suffered a lesion,
And with the reflections of his mind,
Each day fell faster, the miles piling behind.

Time passed quickly, never regressed,
To the issue of delivery on time always stressed,
The second last night before homestead falling almost into sight,
The sun saying its farewell, praising its goodnight.

The camel string pulled up late as was normal,
Time for good rest before another day could fall,
Wide orange expanse on horizon, nice and tight,
A band of beauty, supposedly a sailors' delight.

Cicadas claimed the night for their own,
Their song joining that of the desert as though sewn,
Many voices of the night coming together as one,
Always together and never alone.

This was nature at its most splendid best,
Always at work and never at rest,
Cicadas song, male calling to mate,
A call to be heard, female attending as though fish to bait.

Their song was majestic, a repeated vibration,
Helping men sleep, after being filled with elation,
Nothing like life by a campfire at night,
To fold away worries and gift that feeling of delight.

To sleep that soundless sleep at night,
To wake in the morning feeling alright,
But the song needs to get gotten used to at first,
Like the suckling of a baby from mother, ecstasy burst.

A calming effect which is hard to explain,
Though from it good feelings we all can gain,
Though Abdul mused once more to be of a different mould,
Something having come over him, something clearly untold.

HOMESTEAD, COME FARMER, NEAR

It was almost time, the time almost done,
The time of delivery and coin to be won,
Before saddling up again for return journey,
Goods from homestead to port, their conviction sturdy.

Little by little the world around was divulged,
Abdul taking it all in, names of places, a hidden map, it bulged,
The more he saw, the more was shared, and onwards drive,
And coming to last night before homestead they did arrive.

It was important for Abdul to know the land,
The whereabouts of settlement, homesteads and,
A police station, in future, its existence along the track,
Compared to a meal, not even a snack.

A police station was to be built near Diamantina to the north,
Just 15 miles shy of Queensland border for what is was worth,
A line marked on the map, not on land,
Hard to know in which state you did actually stand.

Diamantina Police Station most assuredly to arrive,
This year in fact, and little from it could you derive,
It would house three officers of the law,
The pitiful job and lives clinging as though to straw.

The police here would support the wider community,
A town on the grow, a much given opportunity,
Employed to enshrine the rules of society,
Ensure taxes were paid, not to be taken likely, a novelty.

Strict rules here, nothing left to slide,
Selling of unlawful alcohol would not be abide,
To become a sticking mess and sorrowful life,
The officers here married and single, possibly bringing wife.

Nak said: "The police station will require occasional supply,
With them a contract on which to possibly rely."
Shir added: "A reasonable job we can try and secure,
Maybe an opportunity to expand business for sure."

Abdul asked: "What will you do to contract mend?"
Nak replied: "I shall consider a friend of a friend,
I know a man in Marree that may be able to sway,
Voice good word and bring business our way."

"Fulfil Muschky's dream, one day we will,
Secure our futures, jobs similar to this will fit the bill,
Not much rest do we desire between jobs, we are men,
Rest can come later when we are with many strings, and then."

"I just pray that Ahmad Mohammed has something,
A job for us on return to Marree or we have nothing,
He is very gifted in many ways,
Well guided of mind, much conviction, strong stays."

"Who is he?" Abdul does ask,
Says Nak: "A man, for Faiz Mahomet he does work at many task,
And with small coin provided from my pledge,
He gifts us information and a little knowledge."

"He also has a weak spot and spends this on a prostitute,
Soft as melon in her company his mouth does shoot,
Divulges much more information, you would be aghast,
She provides this to us for errands of the past."

Abdul said: "The power of a woman,
Can never be underestimated: no confusion,
No doubt either do I have for their courage,
I believe it with all the sincerity I can manage."

Nak: "And Shir can attest to that, can you not?"
"I can, and do, so we all agree, here on this spot."
"Ha,ah!," voiced Nak, pointing a finger, "I see in your eyes,
You'd forgotten about her, your wife; tell me no lies."

"You care more for that camel, Slate and her calf,
Than any wife white man calls his other half,
Your camel is your real wife,
And will be for life."

Shir: "To think I care more for a camel instead,
Means that of me you clearly have misread,
I am devoted to Slate... I mean Arika ever more,
So... stop teasing me, before, before..."

"Before what?" jokes Nak, "That sound like rot,
Come, we are friends here, are we not?"
Abdul was laughing with Nak trying to smile wide,
Shir seemed to be happy to accompany on this ride.

"It was the delivery of the calf, being on my mind,
I grow tired of the hard, extra work, to you I wish to remind,
Hard work for me alone to carry out,
And never complain do I, never do I give a painful shout."

"Work!" continued Nak, "is not feeding a calf,
There is harder work for you in taking a bath."
"I'll have you know," said Shir quite seriously,
"I had a bath before married: twelve months early."

NEAR THE QUEENSLAND BORDER

All three men woke just prior to the crack of dawn,
No time to reflect on lost sleep, no time to mourn,
Ablutions, prayer, breakfast, and pack and gather,
After which already covered in sweaty lather.

Though this morning was provided a little more time,
For homestead was not far, conversation to mime,
Broken English would need to be employed,
Sometimes hard to gather meaning, slang to avoid.

Meanwhile, amidst their thoughts during packing,
Shir was busy with Slate and calf, calf napping,
Nak busy with the camp and other chores,
Abdul gathering stray camels out-of-doors.

Abdul contemplated, as he walked,
That the rifle he should carry, forever on mind it stalked,
But he did not wish to carry it, not anywhere near,
It was hard to understand why, and he considered it could be fear.

Abdul heard a bell not too far ahead,
Silhouettes of camels easily read,
Eating the spinifex and anything else found,
If they could they'd eat it right to the ground.

On occasion the camels were hard to spot,
Blend into the surrounds more readily than not,
But cameleers were used to searching them out,
Whether by sound of bell or by simply looking about.

Abdul saw then that one of the camels was blowing its bladder,
Excitement building within it, and not to slander,
Looks unappealing, but to another camel,
Ready for mating, quite healthy and natural.

Of the mating ritual, another creature does not mimic,
Cameleers used to camel smells, even the most prolific,
And the sight of soft palate hanging from mouth, seemingly stout,
Repugnant sacks, and foot long foam, hanging thereabout.

The male will then deposit upon bark, and the like, a great stink,
Big slatherings of black patches, of tar-like-ink,
Rubbing against bark and anything else which vision does fall,
Anything to brush against, anything at all.

When Abdul arrived back after his achieved recovery,
He divulged to Nak of his discovery,
Told him it may be Joy, of the blowing bladder,
Not sure of its name but feeling all the gladder.

Nak advised: "Yes, that one is called Joy, your right,
When at the homestead we shall keep him out of sight,
They will not appreciate the smell,
And our relationship needs to further gel."

"I am trying hard for next years contract, too,
Much work for us, much work for us to do,
The man's name is Alfred, seemingly, though unlikely lazy,
His wife's name sounds quite simply crazy."

Abdul responded: "A strange name indeed,
And a new name she is in much need."
"No, Abdul, that is not it, not her name,
I was advised her name is Marge, crazy but tame."

"We must refer to them as Mr and Mrs Stapleton,
I'm told that both are walking sticks, mere skeleton,
Hard times in the bush, they are as thin as thin can be,
Unlike in the city where food does, to all, agree."

"I see you have all the camels gathered,
Good work, Abdul, now time to get them tethered."
Abdul explained without need: "They followed Chocolate,
As though leading to great waters they did come, first rate."

Nak said further: "Maybe they know, maybe they smell,
That tomorrow at homestead they shall water well,
But seeing them gathered so easily gives pleasure,
Maybe we are in time for good fortune and in good measure."

OF FARMER AND WIFE

The homestead came into view, quite picturesque,
Beauty bound, a home, an office without front desk,
A small business to sprout, to serve the couple's need,
Time to grow, time to fill wont, desire, inner greed.

For all men and women alike toiled through life,
Quest for money and avoid anything rife,
Future retirement, old age always on mind,
But to get there most people, through life do grind.

There was a wooden house here,
A storage shed beside it did appear,
Another for the shearing of sheep,
Another in which for wool to keep.

A small windmill drew water from ground,
Ample quality and quantity had been found,
Not far sat a dry creek bed,
With water in wet season to be wed.

Slightly set upon higher ground,
More so than what around them did surround,
It was a place to call home, but not so happily,
Not a place to live forever, for most just temporarily.

Mulga grew in many places upon this 'farm',
Culled back by the eucalyptus, causing no harm,
Large Australian trees found nation-wide,
Eucalyptus the camels could not abide.

Of all the things in the bush to eat,
Eucalyptus, to camels' stomach, would unlikely meet,
It is untrue to say that they do not eat these,
More so that they do not, at all, to their needs appease.

Standing before the door to house rubbing his hands,
Hand in the dirt before he then stands,
Abdul can see the farmer [pastoralist] getting ready for meeting,
To shake hands in this, their formal way of greeting.

A feeling of surprise by what happened next could not be denied,
The shaking of hands was never met, was not to meeting applied,
But a nod of the head was exchanged instead, no grace,
This was the most solemn hello to be found upon this place.

Nak greeted Alfred as the man stood there in trousers, unclean,
Holes in shirt aplenty could be seen,
Worn fabric, stains and blemishes galore,
Poor man in tatters, conclusion drawn from what he wore.

Alfred removed his hat most temporarily away,
Not for good manners but to wipe sweat aside this hot day,
He returned it fast before communication did commence,
Nak wishing to open in order to establish good trade for pence.

"So," said Nak, *"wool ready, where this token?"*
Alfred understood that broken English was to be spoken,
"You see, over there beside the house, you look,
You take and put on camel, after unload, then took."

Nak asked: *"Where unload; what you mean?"*
"Oh, look; I wish to work fast, get done, I am keen...
Over there, in the shed,"
Alfred then indicated with a move of his head.

Nak heard the frustration, the words in his head toiled,
Didn't wish to unload his stores upon ground to be soiled,
Thought he understood, finally, he was to unload upon floor,
The floor of the shed on which to place his stock, his store.

Nak was initially concerned for the rainy season,
He had forecast good care for the goods for this reason,
Was it possible that Alfred would move them again later,
Was it that the shed's ground was safe from water.

"Ah, okay. You lucky," said Nak, *"No vermin this place."*
"No what?" asked Alfred with a curious look upon his face,
"No rat; you no rat here in shed."
"Ah; yes, plenty rat, but we cat, the shed is his bed."

"Rats are right across this damn country, all over they appear.
What do you think; we don't have rats up here?"
Alfred was forgetting himself, felt this might take all night,
Nak tried to confirm: *"Unload on ground, yes; is this right?"*

"No!" replied Alfred in a huff. "off ground, up; away from wet."
"Okay, I work now," said Nak and turned away, his duty to be met.
Nak turned to Shir and Abdul, explained it all,
Of the work to be conducted, no time to stall.

Nigel B.J.Clayton

Good quality of wool, good product to be giving,
If you could master hard work and hard living,
Fight against the the bouts of 'farmers' depression,
And stress a future of grand life, even if an illusion.

Two alternatives and from these a choice to make,
Bullock teams or camel strings, which road to take,
Bullock teams were mastered by white folk,
Camel strings by Afghans, holding the invisible yoke.

Strings were preferred for speed and agility,
What a shame they were immigrants, despite ability,
Delays could not be risked by any degree,
And so camel strings were employed, despite lack of glee.

To Alfred the camel industry had expanded vigorously,
The need and desire for them was spreading contagiously,
And for Nak the longevity of work came at a price,
That you were willing to work hard and always play nice.

Be courteous and cool to customer,
Shrug off all poor sentiment and slander,
Swallow your pride and be humble,
Never, before a customer, be caught to grumble.

The homestead here was isolated,
Far from train station, to market, related,
Unconditional contact was here for the taking,
Stores dropped and picked up, good work in the making.

Nake looked to the camels, all in a line,
Several having fidget slightly, waiting to dine,
But more than this they needed water,
No need to punish them, no need to slaughter.

Chocolate was spied chewing on cud, hidden behind lip split,
Hidden behind thick lips covered in dust and ready to spit,
30lbs of pressure and half gallon of filth upon white man to spill,
A vision Nak saw in momentary dream state, a shrouded ill-will.

The unloading of camels was taken to fast,
Alfred having filled water trough, from tower, to last,
Each camel to water and water in stomach to swell,
To take all he could, lesson of water gluttony, learnt well.

The Afghan men continued to work,
When Shir saw the wife, on lips a light smirk,
Approach a package bound in red cloth, well wrapped,
Like a map, big X on paper, well mapped.

70

She turned to see her only child of three quite safe from camel,
Safely hitched with rope, to home, not underfoot to be trample,
Shir saw Nak speaking with farmer, unaware,
Shir continued to watch with unsavoury flare.

Marge, clearly stupid and plain,
Took the parcel to unwrap for all to see, insane,
Risking all for something, nothing at all,
A hunk of salted pork, soon to be slivers onto frying pan to fall.

This woman, half-witted and hellish,
Openly rude and condemningly selfish,
Pig meat, from pig, having rolled in its faeces and muck,
Physically and spiritually unclean, for Shir the horror struck.

The Koran forbid the eating of pig,
The *mullah* prohibited its transport with any string or rig,
Even transporting tin cans with no label was fury tempting,
Was not permitted, was shunned, was extremely offending.

"Nak; Nak!" shouted Shir, with fluster and need, with great desire,
Terror in his eyes wrought with horror, attention he did acquire,
"What is it!" blurted Nak, suddenly concerned for friend,
For much empathy did he have for familiar, to the very end.

"There, the woman," pointed Shir, eyes scourging upon pig,
Finger pointing, "We've been transporting bacon, a piece so big."
Nak stomped over to Alfred with grimace upon mouth,
Scarred lips twisted in fashion, *"What this?"* empathy gone south.

Alfred saw the importance of the matter,
But reliable transportation he did not wish to shatter,
Putting hands up in denial and trying to defend,
His mind working hard as ever, to fix this issue, to mend.

"Wait!" said Alfred as he stepped back and blurted,
"Sorry; me sorry," and by now all had been alerted,
"You damn man," cursed Nak. *"You very bad."*
"You are crazy, so crazy, you is... very mad."

He was now steeped in perspiring anger,
His only way out was for he to discipline her,
Alfred stepped up over towards his wife,
And delivered a smack to face, his hardest in life.

The sound clapped out for all to hear,
She had been administered, it was plain and clear,
The bacon falling to the dry and cracking ground,
Alfred jumped up and down on the meat, and it did astound.

Nigel B.J. Clayton

The woman burst out sobbing,
To red mark on face so deep did commence rubbing,
Alfred yelled: "I need this sale to go ahead without a hitch,
You stupid, stupid, stupid bitch."

Alfed peered over at the Muslim men three,
Hoping for his transport of goods as was agree,
Said Alfred: "My wife is so ridiculously stupid; I did not know,"
"It is finished now, The meat is ruined and into desert I throw"

But this was not enough for Nak today,
Even seeing the wife upon ground where she lay,
"No," said Nak, sorry for what had been done.
"No more work. You do wool, no us, do it... alone."

"No, wait," pleaded Alfred, forgetful to whom he was speaking,
His broken English was overwhelmingly leaking,
"I didn't know about the bacon, I swear it, from me to thee.
If I'd known I would have stopped it in Marree."

Alfred could see the contract falling from grasp,
Needed to gather his wits, use any ploy to grip, to rasp,
Alfred needed money from trade for future to nurse,
More than Nak needed coin or banknote in purse.

Alfred calmed a little then: "I pay more, little extra for you,
New contract, no string, we do business, much to do,
I pay for five more days on road, can we upon this agree,
And you get paid at post office in Marree."

Alfred had one more piece of leverage to employ,
"You give note to John Arthur O'Brien, then no more annoy,
You give post office and he pay much; you understand?
We together good commerce, you, me, and this land."

Nak was slow to respond but nod his head he did,
Having looked at the others they were waiting to see his bid,
But Nak had nothing he wished to pry from this man,
His only real wish was to deliver goods, as was his plan.

Alfred said: "No more bacon, come sunshine or rain,
Never any more; all finished; never see again."
"Okay," said Nak. *"We do... job, for... relationship and for you.
We water camel, load wool; we go Marree, this thing, we do."*

"Oh, thank you, thank you," said Alfred so happy,
His anxiousness now replaced by contentment real snappy,
"Ask for more money," said Shir in his native tongue,
"Take from him what means the most, for all he has flung."

72

"No," said Nak. "I won't become one of them, never at all,
We do job, is okay," said Nak. *"Bacon no more, in lap to fall."*
"Yes, yes; thank you," said Alfred and with Nak shook his hand,
Not much can be said, really, for Alfred's final stand.

And so with sudden forgetfulness and with great ease,
Camels were lowered upon their knees,
Stores unloaded, watering still to be done, in this yard well fenced,
Loading of wool then pursued before return journey commenced.

THE BILLABONG

It was late of day when reloading had been complete,
Their parting with white folk politely discrete,
The farmer optimistic and pressuring,
The wife, confused and befuddled, meandering.

The cameleers were respectful and courteous,
Though these outwards feelings were tirelessly laborious,
The camels, seemingly nocturnally, oblivious,
Not caring for either, but their nucleus.

Nak did mean to attend a billabong nearby,
One such passed, not far, where shade did lie,
A place to further water the camels, to quench,
To tighten up their resilience as though with wrench.

With bags of wool loaded and ready for market,
A scratch on calendar their date, their target,
Get goods to station on time and save,
The extra day's wage that promissory note gave.

It did appear as all was travelling well,
Though boring their days, their confidence swell,
Work had now been established and confirmed,
Their position and standing with Alfred well termed.

The water hole did not take long to reach,
Very small but solemn, solitude to teach,
Unpack the camels one more time this day,
Before much later heads lowered upon ground to lay.

But rituals and prayer were the usual items of respect,
Their religion never did fade, was never prone to neglect,
And watering of camels did continue for awhile,
Waterlilies and fronds, both visions, opposite to desert most vile.

The camels stood politely upon the edge of small pool,
Unlike oxen that bath in drinking water like fool,
Afghan men also heeding good sanitary rule,
No need to inhibit this sanctuary, its cleanliness, don't maul.

A water fowl was then seen amongst the slightly thicker scrub,
Not wishing to be the centre of attention, the nub,
And air bubbles in a few places within the shade of the few trees,
Did cry out in silence as though trying to tease.

You could not associate the farm of Alfred with billabong near,
A complete change to the homestead which to heart did tear,
A beastly, hurtful husband and pouting wife,
Too short is our time here on earth, too short is life.

The amount of water here was enough for their need,
Enough for them to continue on journey, to complete their deed,
Enough moisture here for the circle of life to drive,
Drive the combine of nature though it did not thrive.

Abdul went to fetch some wood for fire,
When lifting small log something did occur, rather dire,
He was stung savagely upon the little finger of left hand,
A deep red circle of fire around puncture, a band.

An unfortunate occurrence to be struck so swiftly in a flash,
By a scorpion of the bush having been disturbed it did lash,
Lash out with stinger as was its defensive nature,
A sting so brutal despite tiny stature.

Though a scorpion bite is not deadly in Australia,
This being widely accepted as idyllic, as though realia,
It was no fault of the scorpion so black and afraid,
Defending against intruder, upon his territory a raid.

The upturned wood disturbing the peace,
The tranquil solitude, the scorpions niche,
The fear bestowed upon it unfair,
As though looked in the eye by evil stare.

Abdul was so fast to withdraw his hand,
He failed to look for the assailant, the brand,
For to know the species by description may aid, provide,
Provide aid when advising the others, their knowledge a guide.

He cradled his left hand against his chest,
Raced back the short distance to campfire and nest,
His confusion and panic not helping at all,
Thoughts for his family at home, the first to call.

Abdul was strong and young,
His body able to deal with being stung,
It should be nothing for him to deal with grief,
But the pain of the wound made him grit his teeth.

The finger of his hand was already pulsing,
His thoughts now gone from family to pain engrossing,
This engrossing pain that should mean nothing to him,
But it was a fixture upon his mind, his frame, his figure trim.

"Shir! Nak!" yelled Abdul so loud,
Desert kick up behind his heels as though cloud,
Those of the campfire a little astounded,
Abdul yelling and usually quite rounded.

The silhouette of his two and only real friend,
Assured him and provided a temporary mend,
His sanity levelling and now restored to formal,
Though pain was quite evident, not deemed normal.

Nak had dropped his mug of tea and stood real fast,
Shir too, ready to aid to the last,
Bliss of the night stirred irregularly out of place,
Gone was any scene or picture of grace.

"Nak! Look; I've been bitten," Abdul explained,
He controlled his emotions, his sanity now reigned,
"Over there, by the wood, where the ground...
Look at my finger; the pain does pound."

Nak said: "Move closer to the fire, I can see better by the light."
Shir looked as closely as Nak: "It's not a snake bite."
"No?" said Abdul, not a question, wishing to optimistically agree,
"No," concurred Nak. "It's a scorpion sting, see."

Nak confirmed: " Look, one tiny puncture mark,
No single or double fang... of snake this does not loudly bark,
The redness is clear and no venom seeping from puncture,
Asked Abdul: "How do you know? Are you sure of this lecture?"

"I've seen bites before, Abdul," Nak explained,
"Plenty men have died by snake bite gained,
But you will not die, my friend so keen,
Besides, it is too late in the day for a snake to be seen."

Abdul complained: "But it hurts so much,
I cannot even, to wound, softly touch."
Nak said further: "The pain will go away,
Though meanwhile it will, with you stay."

Nak continued: "I know the basic treatment to the letter,
Maybe tomorrow you will feel a lot better,
Though other than that there is not much we can do,
Other than give you rest, and ensuring rest is up to you."

"Wash delicately in cool water as best you might,
Allow exposure to cold air this very night,
That is the best and only strategy I know: come sit by the fire,
You should be fine by tomorrow, early to bed, to retire."

AMPUTATION

They sat around the fire and looked one another in the eye,
Two thankful and confident that Abdul would by no means die,
Abdul had faced death many times in his short life,
In some people religion did aid, in others pain of death was rife.

So what is the meaning, whether true or not, this internal myth,
One may say that God will greet them when cold and stiff,
That long life be had in heaven amidst peace and God's thrall,
Why still cling to life, shrug off death, and cry that inner waterfall.

Each and everyone is not built the same,
Some panic and thrash, some remain tame,
Others lose all sanity, no grasp on situation's gravity,
But others offer cheery smile, to comfort those living in perplexity.

No need to be baffled though by life or by death,
We are each born, we blink, we die with last breath,
Though it is always better to die with grace,
Rather than greet one's last day in disgrace.

The fire of the camp was by now well lit,
Nothing left of the day but to talk and to sit,
But the pain of Abdul's finger was on his mind,
Was attacking his sanity, it began to grind.

Abdul said: "It's getting late, it's almost dark,
The visions I see of my finger are indeed stark."
Asked Nak: "What can we do?
I think we discuss it no more, it is through."

Said Abdul from heart: "I need to amputate it now,"
Nak looked from Abdul to Shir, empathy did not show,
Nak reprimanded then with: "Are you mad?"
But Shir defended Abdul: "No, a gift of mercy should be had."

Abdul pleaded of Nak: "This thing must be done, for me,
With you from bottom of heart I do plea,
My arm has already starting to blossom red,
The poison is flowing, this is easily read."

Nak did lecture: "What is amputation of finger going to achieve,
I see in your eye, I know you do grieve,
But the poison is pain, in your arm, not your finger,
It will dissipate, it will go, it will not linger."

Abdul said: "The finger is my source of pain,
Please take it off, now, I do ask you again."
Nak: "The source of your pain is your arm,
The poison in finger is doing you no harm."

Abdul: "It will take away the source of the pain, I say,
And it is my finger, my decision to make if I may,
Trust me Nak, it will not affect my efforts, nor my work
Missing a little finger will not see me, responsibilities shirk."

Nak said bluntly: "And your arm, the poison...
Amputate that, me, take an arm from person?"
"I hope not, Nak, but if it must be done,
Allow this poison to fester and this blasted country has won."

Shir knew that a lost finger was better than worse,
And so from him his true feelings, not just to nurse,
"He's right," concurred Shir. "He should take off the digit,
Take no chances, secure a future, move fast, not fidget."

Shir continued: "I recall a man from Afghanistan village,
Whose sanity and mind was savagely pillage,
They took off his finger under similar circumstances,
There are in fact few differences."

"Yes," said Abdul. "I too have heard, sanity, no sense of bliss—."
Burst Nak: "Yes, yes, we have 'all heard' of this,
That story is old, and has been told many times over,
Much forgotten in translation, from one mouth to another."

Nak continued: "You cannot believe in fables,
A story that float the breeze, as though it ambles."
Pleaded Abdul with sincerity, "Look at me,
Look into my eyes, what do you see?"

Nak did as was asked and felt the hurt within,
Recalled how he felt, scarred mouth, unable to grin,
A torment of life since Char Asiab which did adhere,
To be with him now and forever, from year to year.

"Okay," said Nak. "I'm the *jemadar*, my responsibility.
But it is a great shame, a great pity."
Said Abdul: "Thank you, Nak, thank you,
I believe it is the best thing to do."

Shears... clippers for the cutting of hair,
Employed for many reasons and in good repair,
Cast in rust stains but oiled well,
Miniature guillotine about to leash hell.

Nak said: "These will do," as he held up the sheers,
And he received voiceless nods of head from peers,
"It'll work as good as a knife... for sure,
I shall use them speedily, avoiding built pressure."

"I'll not use them as I would normally,
I need to apply sharp force, one cut, strategically,
"Abdul," explained Nak. "I'll simply hold the sharp edge,
Hold it over, to hilt of finger, at palm's ledge."

Of reassurance Abdul did give: "It's okay, Nak, of this I am sure,
Of the pain I honestly cannot take much more,
Of this dilemma I actually never considered, never saw,
Of all the things in life, this was never of mind, never in store."

Nak said: "Place your finger here, upon this rock,
Other fingers held back, under palm do lock,
I will place the edge of shears just here,
Before hitting on back of blade, the finger to shear."

"It will hurt Abdul, more than I'll know, so hold steady."
Abdul: "It can't hurt me any more than I hurt already,
I can't take much more of this absurdist pain,
Let the rock fall, a single harsh hit, no tepid drops of rain."

Nak looked to Shir as he placed the blade over receiver,
Places the rock in own hand ready to deliver,
"Look away, Abdul, so you don't flinch,
Don't move a muscle, or we could be in a pinch."

"Are you ready Shir, with the bandage and cloth?
Are you ready, on command, to willingly doth?"
Said Shir: "Yes, ready and steady, right now, I am—."
And then Abdul said, "Me too, I am—" but it was a sham.

For Nak hit hard before Abdul had finished, delivering the gift,
Nak having delivered powerful hit after rock he did lift,
Momentum of rock coming down fast behind Shroud,
Token words to prepare, but given, followed by shriek so loud.

And in this Abdul was fortunate,
For the finger came away, not obstinate,
Did not hang from flesh or strip of skin,
It was clean and quick, Nak did inwardly grin.

And within a split second of the hit being made,
Abdul pulled hand back so fast, to chest it was bade,
But Shir interfered and pulled hand out for wound to patch,
To cover it with white cloth and bandage to match.

Within a few seconds more,
Abdul did open the door,
"The pain is horrible and bad,
But nowhere near what was sending me mad."

Abdul then looked to hand where finger was normally found,
And then he saw it there, upon the ground,
Nak picked it up and threw it away,
Amongst the spinifex, the land a disarray.

Nak said: "That's it, there's nothing left to do,
Now rest, for you until morning, nothing for you,
 If the paralysis in the arm does not go away,
Rest you must gain for at least another day."

Said Abdul: "My arm may..."
May have to come off, I don't wish to sound grey."
Nak replied: "That's not grey, that is black,
But such expertise I do lack."

"If the arm is to be removed it is not for me to do,
Only a doctor can do this... this voodoo,
Heinous it is to do such a thing, even if no choice can be made,
If worse comes to worst we will try and gain aid."

"Our task is now to see you well,
And get camels to station with instructions to sell,
If you die upon journey then that is not for me to decide,
It is unfortunate and by no means a comfortable ride."

"Maybe we will be delayed by a few days or such,
But the delivery will be made, another trophy to touch,
There is always a train ready at Marree to depart,
Let's be optimistic, turn bad fortune to good, become it an art."

Shir asked: "Will Stapleton be settled with that?"
"Possibly not, but it's for a bad man and wife with brat,
Thou even he knows that you can't rule the weather,
As such: no matter what brand of animal does make the leather."

And unfortunate it was that Nak should say this,
For even a healthy heart can a beat miss,
Sunny days and clear nights are not guaranteed,
It is not something in which you can plead.

But Shir had something up his sleeve,
Something he held back, something he could not alone, leave,
"Listen, Abdul, I have something saved for future,
It may help you, digest it, it may nurture."

He pulled from his pocket a container, a small vile,
A glass bottle with dry herbs, or other: a trial,
"I had this thing stored with Slate,
This will aid your well-being, lift it from grate."

"It's an Aboriginal concoction, provided me by Arika,
A gift before leaving her side, I do miss her,
She advises to add a little water, take all if infection sets in,
I give it to you, so lift up that chin."

"Thank you, Shir, I know not what to say,
I am feeling great friendship now instead of feeling grey,
I shall try this medicine, try it right now,"
And so added water and drained it all, and coughed, "Wow."

THE FOURTH DREAM OF CONSEQUENCE

Abdul is ignoring the moaning of the dying as it grew,
And sees an enemy soldier, head appearing into view,
It bobs down and up again several times in a row,
The anxiety in the enemy can be seen to grow.

The enemy suddenly leaps from the small fortification,
Ready for evacuation, giving up on his pride and nation,
Abdul points his rifle at the enemies head,
Fires off a shot as trigger is manipulated and read.

The enemy's head turns at the same instant,
It is Nak, plain as day, a militant,
Abdul's bullet strikes him in the mouth, ending the task,
Nak is shot, the grimace on face, his eternal mask.

THE STORM

The next day revealed much unpleasantness for all,
Particular for Abdul; the gathering of camels seemed to stall,
Normally much easier to gather but today one hour more,
Wider area of ground covered across desert, a longer tour.

It was in the mind of the camel, animals were able,
They knew what was coming, inward feelings unstable,
A storm was coming and would be upsetting to most,
A smell upon the wind, a warning strong with ambition to boast.

Abdul put the kitchen away,
None happy with the delay,
Nak and Shir had also been slow in retrieval,
Nak said: "Something has upset the camels, some evil."

Shir also: "And your arm, Abdul, better than when you woke?"
"I think that vile of medicine, is working, no need to joke,
Just this past hour alone has seen an improvement,
I feel much better, and my arm, much freer movement."

Nak: "It's all in the head,
It is easily read,
I have no faith in concoctions,
Only for Allah and his revelations."

Shir: "We all agree with that doctrine,
But with good faith and medicine...
Joining the two in union,
Racked layers around the core of onion."

"The more good we do the better off we are,
Whether from Koran, vile, onion or jar,
Remedies to improve one's health,
Just charge in and heal, no reason for stealth."

Nak applauded: "Maybe you are right,
Self help and remedies do keep a mind tight,
But so long as Abdul gets better I really am not concerned."
Shir returned: "And I believe in Arika, will not have her spurned."

Nak said: "Well, let us all agree on this one thing,
No matter the remedy or belief it has taken potency from sting,
Abdul is feeling better and together we are strong,
But with the camels there is something wrong."

Abdul smiled and turned, work to be found,
Proud of what he had accomplished with one hand bound,
In more pain than Shir and Abdul could ever realise,
But awkwardly unable to slow down: full of enterprise.

Nak said: "Just get the camels loaded, and ready to move,
Once loaded it will be time for us all to get in the groove."
They all smiled at the sound of this tune,
When Abdul looked up, ghastly image, to temperament prune.

His expression did change and become rather solemn,
Knew now the reason for the camels, their problem,
The others saw his jaw drop and followed his gaze,
There before them was something to amaze.

Out upon the horizon and approaching them fast,
Was something more than mythical, and it was going to last,
From north to south and across the entire expanse of sky,
Something clear as day, something you could not deny.

A darkened mass of billowing red sand, fiercely mean,
A thick curtain so tall it was absurdly obscene,
Within all their courage had taken a dive,
They had but three minutes to react before it did arrive.

Sandstorms are not very frequent,
But bestowed much fear, much fear to be lent,
The storm approaching was the most ominous Nak had ever seen,
Currently silent but growing, so menacing and mean.

Dark cloud and sand pelleting around,
And then came the feeling, the vibrating ground,
Enormous bellowing surge of force of nature,
Seen now as mushrooming balls, an unstoppable structure.

A storm may last a few hours to several days,
Endeavouring to navigate through such was like walking a maze,
You can hardly open your eyes to see,
No knowing from whence you come and where you need to be.

Nak ordered: "Quickly, Shir, get the shelter from the saddle,
Put it up over there next to the mulga tree, away from camel,
Abdul, get the water and some biscuits from saddle of Slate,
We don't have much time; quickly now, before it's too late."

The men rushed to their assigned task,
Their actions the complete opposite of bask,
Shir saw to it that the calf was also untied,
No need to hobble, he would remain at mother's side.

Hobble! They had no time, with this could not be concerned,
The camels may wander off, no telling as events in time turned,
Nak had already unrolled and hastily erected the shelter,
Having performed well amidst the helter-skelter.

The shelter was set sturdily, ground level, low,
To avoid the worst of the storm as it did blow,
Avoid the storms menacing, overpowering thrust,
The billowing hate, its desire to deliver harmful lust.

Enough protection here to avoid sand though not flying debris,
Not enough room to sit and enjoy a mug of tea,
Not enough here to cook and chat away,
Only room to lay and to pray.

"Nak!" jolted Shir for the *jemadar's* attention,
"I did untie the calf from Slate, I thought I should mention."
"Again with you and that damn calf of yours,
Surprised I am you didn't bring it here, indoors."

With camels quickly forgotten and shelter briskly erected,
Quick and vast thought was spent on anything neglected,
And most important of all: "The Koran! We need it," Shir blurted,
Nak and Abdul now alerted.

Nak was the *jemadar*, knew where it was stored,
Strategy quick to form, the storm had to be ignored,
Without further ado he crawled from beneath their protection,
An attempt to now gain what was of mention.

For Nak this was the storm of all motherly storms that exist,
As though a blanket was cast upon the world, a mist,
But this mist was such a dark mass or sand blown red,
That it was hard to see, to blindness this lead.

If one cannot open his eyes to see around,
To see where moving, to view the ground,
If unable to negotiate any given track,
Then this is blindness, sense of sight Nak now did lack.

The sun was also blot out or sight and mind,
There was no solace in the world to find,
This was sheer bleakness on a tremendous scale,
Last straw to camel, to coffin last nail.

Nak relied upon common sense and thought,
Rational thinking and evaluation heavenly sought,
It was day and now it was night, you could not hear anyone shout,
The howling of wind and storm was so loud, all about.

Nigel B.J. Clayton

No sense of direction,
No sight to mention,
No sound for clarity,
This storm a rarity.

Nak felt his way slowly and surely,
Memorising every shrub and stone, the morning still early,
Camels untied and near ready for loading,
Would be lined in a file, easy for finding.

He would move on hands and knees,
Feeling his way with relative ease,
Angle of approach set upon his mind,
Counting camels for Koran to find.

The camels, built for weather, were much better off,
Treating it as though kings and queens, acting the toff,
Closing their nostrils and breathing through slit,
Denying penetration of fine sand, any form of grit.

Hair within nose filtering what may penetrate,
Built in, natural, as good as any filtration or grate,
The camel's eyes were also fifty percent opaque,
Easier for them to negotiate safe track to take.

The severity of storm was obvious from onset,
The absolute worst Nak had ever met,
The stinging grains thrashing against flesh of face,
His mind scrawling map, and for Koran a race.

The noise had become deafening to say the least,
Camels were silent, laying in wait, a most resilient beast,
No sound for Nak to go by or vision to appease,
Death from becoming lost, fear to mind, it did tease.

He then fell upon a camel and felt around,
Remained on knees, camels also upon ground,
They were weathering out the storm,
And the temperature around was still very warm.

For the breeze was coming from the desert's heart,
Where heat was like furnace, from where storm did start,
Dry and humid, hot and dry, the storm so wide, so tall,
A devastating condition, the worst conditions of all.

Stacked against Nak, no favour,
Nothing around to savour,
But familiarity with camel string he did hold,
Knew where to find his Koran, felt inspired and bold.

The pressure upon his eyelids was beginning to build,
He had nothing to aid him, nothing to shield,
The pressure of quitting was present at large degree,
Continue he must, this was about 'team' not 'me'.

Suddenly, and with great relief,
He fell upon the place of Koran, a lifting of grief,
The great book soon secure, pushed inside clothing with finger,
No time now to stay and consider, no time to rest or to linger.

He remained on the ground, kept on crawling,
Making his way back, foot by foot, upon mind scrawling,
He pressed onwards picturing all in his mind,
Hoping way back to easily find.

He screamed at the top of his lungs for Shir and Abdul to hear,
Wondered whether or not they may be quite near,
Ferocity of the wind shredding his words into mince,
Even he, himself, could not hear himself, and he did wince.

Back under shelter Abdul did try to speak,
Now yelling to Shir, hoping his words, to Shir's ear, would leak,
He placed cup of hand over Shir's ear then tried again,
"Will Nak be okay?" expressing concern, he did not refrain.

Shir reached for Abdul's ear and yelled in reply,
"Nothing is wrong, on his ability you can rely,
There is nothing we can do as this storm continues to pound,
For if he is lost then he will never be found."

DILEMMA AND DESPAIR

Upon Nak time was taking its toll, torment to shower,
He'd been in the storm for almost an hour,
The thrashing upon body was too much to take,
Try for some form of shelter he must make.

He fumbled on in the darkness, Koran now held in tight of hand,
Providing him with some feeling of peace, a resilience, a stand,
A stand against adversity, against this devastating storm,
Respite received, wriggling upon the ground like a worm.

Happy and content with Koran in grasp, medicinal, a nurse,
Prepared to accept the worst of the worse,
And then he thought of his friends in the dark that last,
They had no Koran, "Blast this storm; blast, blast, blast."

He remained upon the ground and then grain upon grain,
Grains of the storm pillared around, upon him a great stain,
Commencing to bury him partially, his human nakedness,
To become part of the landscape, undulated in darkness.

Buried alive! Would anyone find him?
Would his burial place be discovered, could death be so grim?
His body to be fodder for ants and for more,
What of Saki of the Ghantown, the one and only he did adore.

How he would miss her, for she was his choice,
He did so cherish her comfort and her soft voice,
No! He wouldn't allow this to happen,
Would not allow this lonesome death to shapen.

Even if he had to remain outside in the storm,
He couldn't freeze to death, it was too warm,
Time without food: his thoughts could, any hunger, smother,
A little lack of water; Meh, so a little he may suffer.

But what if the storm lasted longer?
How long could it last; was he, of storm, the stronger?
He would search out a large rock, procure safe hide,
Or even a camel, lay beside it, avoid the sand, this devilish tide.

Inside the shallow shelter created,
Nak's possible survival was on term to be rated,
Abdul and Shir were both concerned for their friend,
Though this misery of theirs they could not mend.

They had biscuits to eat,
Water for which lips to meet,
Each other to comfort despite lack of sound,
Unable to see well and huddled so close to ground.

An endless cycle of emotions raging within,
Thoughts of home and life to be never dwindling,
A roller coaster of feelings pouring through souls,
Like soup swirling effortlessly, contained in bowls.

The shelter they had erected was certainly not spacious,
Despite this they were extremely gracious,
The slashing of wind and sand against fabric, their tent,
The storm's fierce anger was freely spent.

The two men had moved closer as best they could,
Their backs against the coarse material, wishing it were wood,
A little space, so tiny at best,
Formed between them, their bodies at rest.

So here they lay with biscuits and water,
Nak not here, his absence a torture,
How was Nak coping with the storm outside,
Same as them, wishing it over them, to quickly ride.

It was hoped that he'd curled up beside a camel,
Protection from camel, order restored as though by court's gavel,
All they could do was pray and hope,
Like a dead man pleaded to God before being hung from rope.

So Shir sat in silence as best he could in the dark,
The constant sandstorm, its continuous howl, unrestrained bark,
His thinking of Nak, his best friend that ever stood,
Even in death he'd be there, he would.

A *jemadar* without fault, no fault could he constitute in his mind,
The best man to walk the earth, never another could you find,
Only a man lacking good character could think badly of him,
Despite his scarred mouth, despite always looking grim.

Shir was a free man and lived with a free spirit,
Followed his belief to the ends of the earth, no limit,
But Nak could be followed for longer, of this he was sure,
No one on earth could salt Shir's mind, never lure.

They would all hold tight to their belief, their religion,
Would live to see the end of storm devouring this region,
Each would ride out this storm in his own way,
Even if it lasted a week they would survive its efforts to flay.

THE DARKNESS

Before Shir and Abdul did realise,
The day had fallen, night to polarize,
Darkness from storm and shelter about,
Hard to know time of day, no aid to give shout.

Their biscuits had gone,
Shared, one by one,
Water held precious,
Forever desirous.

Boredom a tedium,
Tiredness a medium,
Wont for a mend,
For storm to end.

Shir needed to pass urine, it was time,
Pressure built, so depart tent so sublime,
He cupped his hand against Abdul's ear,
Making his intention quite clear.

Shir then departed on hands and knees,
As though grovelling, or praying to appease,
Abdul then knocking his finger in a bad way,
The throbbing pain for some time to stay.

The laziness of doing nought,
Was straining upon all thought,
With boredom this lead to tiredness,
Having achieved nothing all day, this was madness.

Shir returned not long after, to storm did beg,
Most of the urine ending on inside of leg,
But dry in short time, no need to be concerned,
Of this entire experience he would grow, would have learned.

Abdul was then startled, the feeling of crushing weight upon him,
A suffocation of ill-will, clutching to life so grim,
The sand upon shelter, upon his body, causing panic,
Difficult to move, difficult to breath, was he manic?

Shir then found Abdul's ear once more,
"What happened, I felt disturbance at your door,"
"I had a bad dream, was in its thrall,
Is Nak back yet? I wish to see him, is all."

And to what reason is he concerned over Nak's health,
What is it that transcends, a sprint over stealth,
Realization that he was to blame,
For causing Nak his facial grimace of shame.

"He will not move far amidst this storm of sand,
He will know what to do, not wander, or try to stand,
He will find shelter in one form or another,
Not allow this pestilence to grab him and smother."

"All we can do is be patient, sit the storm out,
Be optimistic, await for it to make route,
It cannot last for much longer, not more than an hour,
There's not enough sand on earth to continue this shower."

Abdul did shout into ear, cupping well, amidst their mess,
"What time do you think it is, what is your guess?"
"I have no idea," said Shir in reply,
"Even an educated guess I could not rely."

Shir said: "I think we should rest some more,
Ready our energy for what will be in store,
There will be much work after this storm has lifted,
Much devastation left in its path, much being gifted."

The two men then slept unpleasantly, off and on,
The storm ever empowering, an Italian don,
An eternity of sitting and pushing sand off body,
An eternity, soul-shattering, no melody.

Abdul had never before, in his entire life,
Never had so much time to contemplate his wife,
The friends he had treated poorly,
And those he had treated well, surely.

Question his own sanity and reason,
Whether or not to good friend he had risen,
Had been a good husband and father,
Of his home had he been master?

In reality, one was no different than another,
No tonics of life, nor character, could lather,
One may be weak, one may be strong,
There was no real right way in life, but to steer from wrong.

He would, from this day forward,
Treat each and everyone the same, self reward,
Many thoughts to himself revealed,
No way other than for actions to be appealed.

Shir too thought hard on his life,
Of all he had caused, of all the strife,
The way his life had unfolded to lead to this day,
Of mother and father, dead, in Afghanistan did lay.

Had he done the right thing in his fight against the British,
His actions as spy, forever on tenterhooks, skittish,
The long day before Shir now paved his train of thought,
A promise to never kill again, but happiness with Arika sought.

And the contemplations of life continued for them both,
In the end finding happiness within, nothing to loath,
Just promises to self that they hoped they could keep,
But for the moment all they could do was try and sleep.

Nigel B.J. Clayton

AFTERMATH AND HERDING

It was quite some time later, a marathon,
When Abdul awoke, not sure, exactly, how long,
Long enough it seemed for him to get enough sleep,
Before the wind appeared to die down, enough to take a peep.

And so he rolled over their upon the ground,
Corner of shelter lifted, once found,
Exposing a desert world for he to see,
It looked as though the storm was clearing: could it be?

And so for no reason at all of which he could account,
A panic fell over him, nervousness to start, before it did mount,
And then he closed his eyes to what he could see,
Opened them once more, to what was to be.

The tail of the storm was just passing overhead,
The sky bright and open behind it, hot day to dread,
He shook Shir awoke in order to be at the ready,
After they pray, breakfast and gather herd, upon feet unsteady.

For as he stood he almost fell over,
Bloods circulatory and its hidden power,
His feet seemed weak but confidence quick to gather,
Already his skin commencing to lather.

Neither man spoke for a minute or two,
Evaluating around them and searching for clue,
For the whereabouts of Nak and where he hid,
And call his name, Shir repeatedly did.

And from behind some shrub, mulga to adore,
A vision of pleasure fell upon them, they saw,
Nak came wandering in from fairly close by,
Feeling better than he looked he could not deny.

They all gathered and sat at what would have been their fire,
Each looking around and seeing a scene rather dire,
Equipment was strewn all over the desert floor,
And more than half the camels not at their shore.

The storm was well and truly gone, had made its pass,
Their situation quickly calculated, Nak took class,
"We have about three hours before the day does conclude,
We have to consider prayer later, camels prelude."

"We must gather the camels, herd them together,
Ensure the calf is provided Slate and with tether,
Collect the stores from about, place them beside...
Place them beside their camel, for tomorrow we ride."

"Good time we need to make on the morrow,
Good sleep and courage tonight you must borrow,
We need to make up the time lost to date,
We have to make haste, apply good speed, never be late."

Everything, all around, seemed to be covered in sand,
If it had been snow, beautiful to look at, very grand,
But this was the desert, being hot and dusty as hell,
The difference now? Camels far, far off, they could hear their bell.

"We have not a minute to lose,
We all must get the camels, follow sight and nose,
Listen hard, listen well, get the camels via best way you know,
But have yourselves a drink of water before you go."

Shir was the first upon his feet,
Three hours of daylight and night once more to greet,
With abruptness he turned to look for the camels to be netted,
Jolted by the devastation, but it had been expected.

Wool and pack saddles were strung all about,
Two thirds of the camel missing, but they were stout,
Slate and her calf were seen straight away,
The calf, to nature and impulse, did not far, from mother stray.

Sand clung to stores like glue, ridges tall,
Concave buttresses of loose sand ready to fall,
Several camels now let out lofty bellows,
Moans and groans, unabashed fellows.

A few pack saddles had been moved twenty feet or more,
Several bales of wool loose, straps shredded, tore,
But for the most it appeared not to be too bad,
But at first glance you'd think the world gone mad.

Nak considered Alfred and his wife,
They would have experienced the storm in all its rife,
They could not blame Nak if a few pounds of produce were lost,
Unfair to make the cameleers pay for the storm and its cost.

Meanwhile Shir tried with his entire might,
Listen for the bells of the camels and put things right,
And for the remainder of the day it did take,
But for good prayer and meal they did eventually make.

Nak said: "We are missing eight camels more,
But we have managed to gather all of their store,
Tomorrow we shall search here about,
And if worse comes to worst, continue our journey without.

Abdul stood up then and stepped towards Chocolate,
Removed his bell from neck before it grew too late,
Shir asked: "What are you doing, Abdul, with that?"
"Use the sound of this familiar bell, sound them out like rat."

Shir said: "Like rat. What do you mean?"
"It's called a fable, of a man, a town he did clean,
By employing music he drew all the rats from town,
Amongst the colonists the fable is renown."

Nak smiled, he knew: "I understand… yes, the bell,
This is a good plan, you are thinking well."
Nak explained briefly for Shir, unclear,
"Sound the familiar bell, the camels will come here."

Shir thought and spoke: "This is good; Abdul, a genius,
The camels will desire company, loneliness so tedious."
Abdul stepped off: "Even if it takes me all night,
All camels will be here by first light."

Nak said: "Try for two hours, no more,
Then return here, I do implore,
We shall take turns until they are found,
Bring them back here, to camping ground."

Abdul nodded his head in receipt,
Stepped off, his work to meet,
"I'll sleep," said Nak, "and then I shall take turn,
From this bad experience we all can learn."

"Oh, and Abdul," said Shir most clear,
"I shall stay by fire, most dear,
And if camels should return here by own faculty,
I shall ring a bell thrice for you, of the reality."

And so Nak went to sleep, Shir looked up to heaven,
Looking up and contemplating, life seemingly leaven,
Calamity just suffered, but here he was, alive,
Risen from the depths of despair, had not taken a dive.

The stars were out in all their glory,
Each and every one having its own story,
The moon was also, later, to offer its help,
To help light the night as the bell did yelp.

Nak was fast asleep, having suffered the most,
During the storm his soul and body almost the ghost,
He was the most worn out by the ordeal,
But now he was at rest having eaten a good meal.

Abdul could be heard from time to time,
Ringing the bell, as though in rhyme,
Three dings at a try and listening for bellow,
Though they may not holler, being rather mellow.

But by first light the next day,
Nak realised he'd not been woken, all was gay,
Abdul had found the missing camels that night,
Though four hours out he still awoke fresh and bright.

CONTEMPLATIONS

Abdul did exit the tent to find the sun on its approach,
They had all slept in late, to which they did not broach,
Their morning routine commenced as per any other,
Consuming breakfast and mug of tea like lover.

Nak asked Abdul: "How is your arm this morning?"
Abdul moved it around in display, without moaning,
"It's getting much better. No red blotches on skin glowing,
Good circulation, the blood flowing."

"Probably true," said Nak, "but please don't overdo your effort,
Much of the loading of wool can me and Shir meet in comfort."
Said Abdul in response: "But the wool must get back to Marree,
Urgency there is, our reputation is sacred, we all agree."

"We're late as it is," reflected Nak. "like I said,
Contemplating further I think our situation can easily be read,
We've lost very little wool and only a few hours time,
We'll be okay with this, nothing but a little salt from lime."

Breathe sweat and tear,
Do loathers tone fear,
It matters not a little grain,
From work we do not refrain.

Hard work is not tame,
And we are not lame,
So work shall be done,
Our oath will be won.

Abdul did ask: "Will future contract be burnt like toast?"
Nak replied: "I do not wish to always boast,
But we are favoured above the oxen and horse,
Our camels are the best, always staying the course."

"I do not see how we can lose future work,
With so many jobs in shadows do lurk,
We will always come out on top,
We will win the day, we will never flop."

Abdul felt much assured by each spoken word,
Great security as though from shield and sword,
All camels had been found but some under the weather,
Hard to fathom how none had gone hell for leather.

Though not injured and just nourishment they did need,
Some redistribution was conducted, all had agreed,
Though with a working string as good as this,
It was hard to consider what further could go amiss.

They hadn't been on the road more than an hour,
When they came upon a sorrowful sight, just another to empower,
Empower and enforce great empathy within,
A small Aboriginal group on the move, product of the storm's sin.

The Aboriginal way of life seemed to be in turmoil,
The white man, of the land seeming to spoil,
Expanding into the desert regions of this country,
Taking its toll on all that once was poetry.

The way of the road for Aboriginal life,
Changed forever, for many one to strife,
But some Aboriginal people themselves also stood in their way,
Shunning any improvement, little to be gained in life everyday.

Chinese, Italians, Japanese, in this desert, this cataclysm,
Appeared to cater well for themselves amidst racism,
Improvements were coming at an extremely fast rate,
Leaps and bounds, straight from the starting gate.

Abdul had heard, though unsure on the truth,
And for this he was still rather aloof,
Alcohol with Aborigines was like stripping hair from leather,
Was their Achilles heel, their mother, their tether.

How pitiful to say or to think,
What a mess, what a stink,
To be suffocated from the land,
To castrate due to liquor, liquor mostly banned.

Aborigines absorbed with claiming rights, to make a stand,
When their dreaming proved that man did not own the land,
The land owned the people, upon which they existed,
But claiming land rights they still persisted.

Five men, four women, and six children,
Each something to portage, looking lowly as though stricken,
Vessels for carriage of water, or implement for the digging of root,
Bags or bed rolls, other utensils, a spear or two, nothing to shoot.

Several swags came into view,
Nothing special, nothing new,
Rolled within were a few condiments, dried bread, tea in a tin,
Cooked kangaroo, or wallaby, anything to feed the thin.

The camel string continued past them, going the other way,
No need to stop, no need to delay or stay,
The women were quick to ask for food as though they had none,
"No," said Nak as he passed. "No food; is all gone."

The sad faces of the children did hit the most,
Hitting like hammer upon head of post,
Their hands too, held out, deplorable, seemingly brittle,
Scarred from falling into campfires when little.

Shir did as Nak and ignored the pleas,
Their shallow faces, thin arms, boney knees,
But Abdul did different, being last in the line,
Reached his hand into pocket, for something on which to dine.

Giving one some jerked meat,
It was taken in silence, a silent treat,
If the other of the group had seen this, against his wish,
They would have stormed him, with open hand, with empty dish.

Nak gave Abdul a sturdy look,
A look that Abdul saw, Nak's finger then shook,
Nothing further needed to be said,
Of this lesson Abdul immediately read.

Nak had served as cameleer the longer,
Was *jemadar* and was the stronger,
Abdul had been forgetful of this lesson from the week before,
But would not allow this to happen again, it would occur no more.

By late afternoon all misery was now past,
Time for ritual, setting of camp, take advantage of all as it last,
To consider another storm approaching anytime soon,
Was far from mind, not considered, you would need to be a loon.

The episode with the bacon at homestead was recalled,
A lesson learnt here, could have seen negotiations stalled,
The differences between Christian and Muslim were not few,
Were clear to them all, it was so easy to separate the two.

Of Brother Johann Ernst Jakob and his missionary way,
No easy path for him did lay, but never did he stray,
But no sorrow could be felt for him in general,
No more than the Aborigines, their dreaming essential.

The work was hard and sometimes intolerable,
Abdul and the scorpion bite, the pain insurmountable,
Feelings of incompetence, of missed family, nothing tougher,
The responsibility each of the three held for the other.

Abdul had his family in Afghanistan,
Nak loved Saki, a love which was ban,
Shir had Arika , awarding him a grin,
They each held something close within.

They had taken all that nature threw,
But they would pull through, this they all knew,
No sandstorm or bacon could stand in their way,
Not with each of them having their say.

They were obliged to continue as best they could,
To even better the relationship with colonists as it stood,
Combined they had the reputation of good quality and spirit,
A good understanding of life in Marree as was knit.

Of Marree, other towns and settlements were similar,
Much hope they had as a business built upon strong pillar,
Like a well-built damn able to handle insurmountable weight,
Their characters would not breach, never too narrow but straight.

To do or to die was a figurative,
Nak never liked to delve into the negative,
Shir was seemingly, always so confident and sure,
Abdul hard-working, though occasionally easy to lure.

A team is a team for a contribution of differences,
Together as one as assorted meat grinds and minces,
So it was that these three men, each carved from granite,
Gave their camel string great strength, each to each a magnet.

By the time they had reached near Mulka, a confidence bolster,
They were back on schedule, not a day missed, as per roster,
Many extra miles being covered each day,
To make up everything due to the storm, their delay.

FIVE YOUNG MEN

The three cameleers trod ever onward,
Proud of their accomplishments, it's own reward,
Misfortune and disappointment encountered along the way,
Pick themselves up they have done, from the fray.

But something more sinister was now near,
Something to impede, something to make clear,
That cameleers were not wanted here,
From this country all Afghan should steer.

They were being watched, a far-off gaze,
Through the shimmering heat, vacuum of haze,
Five pairs of young eyes looked upon them with hate,
Like fish to a hook they had come for the bait.

They had heard that a camel string was nearby,
A reliable source of talk on which they could rely,
It was spoken of three men and camels galore,
Travelling afoot, camels stacked high with store.

The five young white men barely of age to drink,
Not enough maturity to stoke fire but old enough to think,
Residents of Mulka and all that was close at hand,
This was their country and by it they would stand.

Some of their fathers had lost jobs to these few,
So their fathers had told them, so this is what they knew,
The soil beneath their feet was their honour and religion,
They would not allow these ethnics to take from the region.

This country did lack water during the summer,
It was hot as hell, drive you mad, make you stammer,
But love it they did, for it was all that they had,
Each and every thought they had was not good, was bad.

The five young men tied up their individual horse,
In the low ground of dry creek bed, a cracking course,
The area around was sparse and slightly undulating,
Scorched earth, weather dry, nothing of interest worth relating.

Snake, Horse, Bullock, Fly, Scotty: on society a stain,
Small jokes to fathers, to women folk and mothers a pain,
Christian names amongst them would never be employed,
Scotty was for Scott; easy to pressure, easily annoyed.

Snake: for he was thin and rather lean,
Bullock: he was large and rather mean,
Horse: some say gifted by nature,
Fly: for his tiny stature.

Scotty pulled a can from his saddle bag,
Held it up for his friend Fly to see, to brag,
A label wrapped around a can of bully beef,
Meat in which you could sink your teeth.

An invention of a man from the Booyoolee Station,
Adopted into the Australian psyche and this nation,
Chunks of beef drowned in gravy, pleasant smell to snout,
Now a staple that could not be lived without.

Scotty asked: "What do you say to some bully, Fly?"
Horse scolded: "Shut your mouth! If you can try,"
"Calm down, Horse," said Bullock, rather monotone, not shy,
Pushing from lip of creek, good visual it would not deny.

Continued Bullock: "They're still a ways off yet."
"I'm gonna clobber me one, damn good," said Fly in threat,
"You and what army?" said Snake, palm to cheek, stroking,
Punching Fly in shoulder, smile on face, joking.

Fly looked around, disgruntled by activity, a little perplexed,
Eager to get going, eager for what was to occur next,
To fulfil their act of revenge upon the men as they should,
By heinously striking their camels as they said they would.

"Shut up, Snake," defended Scotty, "leave him alone."
"You don't have to defend me," said Fly, feeling as thou grown,
Puffing out his chest he said: "I might be the youngest,
But I can lick those men, even their toughest."

"You won't need to," said Bullock, the eldest,
"I got me-self something hidden away, within my nest"
He then twisted and turned, drew out a rifle from hiding,
From deep within bed-roll, still upon horse, striding.

"Where the hell you get that?" asked Horse, "It's the best."
"It's me dad's rifle," replied Bullock, "Stolen from his chest."
"You're not gonna use it, are ya?" asked Horse,
"Why the hell wouldn't I?" said Bullock, "Of course, of course."

"What the hell do ya think I bought it for?
It's not for show, or to scare, but to score,
Score victory by killing their camels,
Tired I am, of seeing them on their travels."

"Scare them," protested Fly. "No; shoot the bastards!
They are nothing but stinking blacks, retards,
Those men should be killed, one and all, not just the camel,
No; hey; kill the lot, be judge and jury, heavy handed with gavel."

"No, no, no," interrupted Scotty, "that's the last straw,
We don't need any trouble with the law."
"What law?" said Snake, he too took a rifle from bed-roll,
"What the hell!" stumbled Scotty, the new reveal taking its toll.

Said Snake: "If you don't want in then go home now,
But I'm staying and will not, to these bastards bow."
"They're just men," said Horse. "Scotty's right,
The law'll get us all, so let's just give them a fright."

Said Bullock. "The closest police you will never see,
With this killing, this action, we must agree,
We're not gonna get caught, unless one of you does tell,
Unless in your weak head, consciousness sounds like a bell."

"Don't look at me, Bullock," pleaded Scotty, wishing to quit,
"I do what you think best, but I don't like it, not one bit."
"It's what they deserve," said Fly,
"Catch them, bind them, feed them pig shit from sty."

Said Scotty in appraisal: "Huh... shut up, give it a rest,
You're just power-hungry, but you're not the best."
"Hey; he's with us," said Snake, "aren't ya, Fly?"
"Sure am," answered Fly as he looked at Scotty on the sly.

And then more direct from Fly: "Ah, come on, Scotty, listen.
Them fellahs aren't even Christian."
"He's right, Scotty," said Bullock. "The lines gotta be drawn,
They're not of this country, of which I was born."

"Come on, Scotty," urged Fly, "It's the right course."
Asked Scotty: "What do you think, Horse?"
"I don't know," something inside was saying 'this is wrong'.
"Ah, come on," said Bullock. "We're in this together, five strong."

"I don't think we should," said Horse. "It aint right."
Said Snake: "If you're not with us, you and ya horse, take flight."
Horse looked around, "I'll go," prepared to move with his horse,
With the killing he could not really endorse.

"You'll go not near," insisted Bullock, "away from them you steer,
I don't want them stinking camel herders to know we're here."
"I got ya, Bullock. You don't need to tell me anything, mate,
You should change your mind, Scotty, before it's too late."

"Shut ya mouth, Horse!" said Snake as he spat,
With that said Horse turned away, "You brat."
And then to Scotty, "You know ya don't have to stay."
He stroked his horse's head before heading away.

"You're either in or out," said Bullock. "What's it going to be?"
He was going to stand his conviction, his ground, not flee,
He was tired of the cameleers, had used up all of his patience,
"I'm in," said Scotty after a little silence.

"That's great, Scotty," said Fly with a smile, "fantastic,"
Scotty simply smirked, then frowned, features elastic,
The remaining four then sought some good ground,
A position from which they had good visual all round.

What was about to unfold was the culminating, the pinnacle,
To come would break the camel's back, the cutting of iron shackle,
Bullock had failed to realise the door to Australia had opened,
Lost focus on all, peripheral blunted, not sharpened.

Many more Afghan handlers would storm this country,
A great awakening, the telegraph line but pittance, paltry,
Many advantages could be reaped after sewn,
And even in early years Australia had vastly grown.

But regardless of Bullocks knowledge on any current event,
It was near impossible to change him, no one could prevent,
Prevent what was about to unfold,
For the story which is about to be told.

But there was something else that infuriated this boy,
More than words could express, concealed as though of troy,
A story having been passed onto him,
From father to son, every word, not a single letter to trim.

Bullock told Scotty, as he stood there, the story,
A story of filth where there was found no glory,
This Afghan that they saw before them, this minute, right now,
Purposely bypassing Mulka, was a villain, tooth and nail.

They looked upon this *jemadar*, through branches and spinifex,
Lean of body, not a muscle to flex,
He was surely the one; he looked the same,
According to Bullock he was fair game.

That grin, the way his mouth presented itself,
steadfast in a grimace one would wish put to shelf,
It was said that he and several others, along this track,
Did stop near a water hole, for a wash and a snack.

But that wasn't the crime in itself, oh no, out of the question,
The crime was in ritual of prayer, their required ablution,
It was said that he removed his socks and shoes,
Washed his feet in the drinking water to wash away his woes.

"That's one of me many stories I know," said Bullock of the rot,
"It has to be stopped. I can't take no more, cannot."
Scotty looked at his friend, searching for sense, trying to lure,
"Do ya think he deserves to die?" asked Scotty, absurdly unsure.

"I do; for all he's taken from me father, for all he's done,
For all his grievances against us, for the employment won."
Snake appeared then, "Come on; you ready or what?
Get back here, spread out proper, not just stand there or squat."

The four congregated in the low ground behind some bush,
Prepared themselves as best they could, remaining hush,
Snake and Bullock taking position so as to be closest to the string,
When it passed them by they would commit an audacious sin.

NOW FOUR YOUNG MEN

Four men, as seen through their own eyes strong,
Four boys as seen through those to whom they do wrong,
They had settled into wait and watched the caravan,
Three cameleers drawing ever closer, ready to reveal their plan.

Bullock thought little of a cameleers' life,
Heathen persons, life unforgivingly rife,
He failed to even briefly consider the work that they did,
The time they sacrificed to bring a little luxury as bid.

It was all for nothing as far as he was concerned,
Ideas quickly syphoned, intellect burnt or spurned,
He was to put to waste this unwelcome string from upon his stage,
His eyes fell to the barrel of his rifle, bullet resting, coming of age.

He'd never killed a man before,
But the hatred within him he did not deplore,
Hatred was self-motivating, the strongest urge,
Ready he was to shoot, to kill, to purge.

Snake was of dissimilar view,
Of life and death he still had no clue,
Only thought on how bad these cameleers actually were,
Ready to follow Bullock, ready to attend pot, to stir.

Snake knew of their callous ways,
Denying his father wages, removing stability, his stays,
Removed was his family's ability to put food on table,
Unable to comfortably stack merchandise to roof of stable.

For Snake the killing would come easily enough,
Never considered the consequences, whether easy or rough,
Only wishing the cameleers were on camel's back,
Further for them to fall when shot, upon ground to stack.

Questions rose within Scotty, a heavy burden, not trifle,
He wondered on the blood and guts, on the effects of a rifle,
He'd seen rabbits and dingoes killed sure enough,
Did a Afghan bleed the same as a rabbit, or was flesh tough.

Did a man squirm upon the ground in the same dying fashion,
Did he yelp like a wounded dog, was this his body's reaction?
But last of all he considered what they were about to do,
No rifle he had, and so he Picked up two large rocks in lieu.

Fly had a smile upon his face as he did watch,
The approaching string, camel kills to notch,
When he looked over and towards Bullock, the menacing look,
To his very core, he was shook.

The cameleers had no names to the young men,
But features enough to distinguish their 'humanity' from 'them',
Was it fair, was it honest, was it just,
To decide these men's fate, the young men's hatred, their lust?

Nak was at the front as usual, leading Chocolate ever so close,
To the torment that was about to befall them, about to disclose,
Shir to the centre and Abdul to the rear,
All now closer to trouble, so very near,

Nak was thinking of the love he held for Saki so bold,
He and her seemingly bound, moulded from same mould,
Shir considered his wife, for he missed her dearly,
An Aboriginal woman, different than the rest, immensely.

Shir looked upon his life with wife, they were lovers,
There was simply no way that you could compare her to others,
Those that were seen upon the desert were scroungers,
Despising life in desert to become reliant on pity, loungers.

As for Abdul, he was by far different than the other two men,
Nothing meant more to him then wife and children,
For him there was no other place on earth,
No other soil which smelled so good, devoid of turf.

THE AMBUSH

Nak frowned, confused by the behaviour,
Chocolate becoming unsettled, acting out of flavour,
Upon the highest portion of high ground to their left,
A small lip of extended ground and a cleft.

Nak thought that a snake might suddenly appear,
His eyes scoured the area for something near,
Looking rather intently for any sign of reptilian life,
Least expecting to find the most heinous of strife.

"What is it?" asked Shir, anxiety peeking all the more,
"I'm not sure," replied Nak, eyes taking a tour,
"Chocolate senses something... I don't know... his despair."
Suddenly an unmistakable sound of a rifle shot pierced the air.

"My god!" yelled Abdul as he took to the ground,
Forgetting his finger, security to be found,
He fell with all his weight upon his hand, giving a shout,
Releasing his hold on the camel, tossing his head about.

Nak too, was quick to find comfort in security, comfort binding,
The second shot rang and he had his own rifle pulled from hiding,
"Shir," yelled Nak, seeing then a body laying flat on the ground,
"Shir; are you okay?" a question, no answer, more than profound.

There was no answer and so Abdul chanced a look,
Saw the prostrate form of his friend dead, to his core it shook,
The four Australian boys then broke from cover,
Raced down towards the three cameleers, it soon to be over.

Bullock took a brief look towards Snake with hate,
Snake having fired a little slow for his liking, too late,
But snake had killed, had made up for his poor showing,
And now the first to reach the string, knife pulled, blade glowing.

Snake's eye fell upon Shir's lifeless form as he lashed,
With knife in hand cutting the strings, Afghan lives trashed,
Camels reacted accordingly and nose pegs broke here and there,
Several camels running off still loaded, unable to care.

The kitchen camel simply pulled away,
Not for a second more would he stay,
All along the line camels reared their heads,
Breaking all connection, free of all threads.

Blood was oozing from Shir's back,
Snake callously thought, no blood did he lack,
Lying there flat, dead as an autumn leaf,
No Arika here to care, no Arika here to grief.

Abdul quickly stood as Scotty and Fly swooped past,
Slashing at all manner of string and throng to the last,
Camels buck and pull, race away, no restriction, no trouble,
No hindrance at all, no short hobble.

All of a sudden, the man named Snake,
Pulled himself up, gave himself a shake,
With clarity not to be steeped, and no delusion,
He snappily realized something amidst the confusion.

He had killed a man, dead as a doornail,
Life gone in a snuff, as easy as stepping on snail,
A great wave of guilt,
From all pores it spilt.

A great surge of sorrow leapt from him,
Had cut him short of morality, more than grim,
Why was it so important to have killed this cameleer,
Because he was from Afghanistan? He could have been a peer.

So hard it was to consider enemy and ally,
Where was the truth, was it standing nearby,
This man was living flesh, spoke, ate, and walked,
Now he was condemned to hell, Snake's belief, balked.

Like smoke on the air, no tobacco to inhale,
Putrid air and life, life which now felt stale,
And whilst he stood their considering this life poorly,
His comrades continued to cause all manner of strife most surely.

Fly grabbed hold of a camel, quick as a flash,
It then bit his hand, a nasty gash,
Fly pulled the hand back from the pain and fright,
Before thrusting his knife into camels throat: good night.

Abdul was able to hit hard Fly in the side of the leg,
Whom fell upon the ground, brief cry of pain to beg,
Abdul rallied his strength, pulled himself upon the coward,
Commenced lashing out with closed fists, the strings steward.

Steward for he cared for the kitchen camel,
Cared for the camel during their trek as they travel,
Scotty then came in from behind, unknown,
Began with his own bout of fists, rapidly thrown.

With the pain of his amputated finger recalled and then forgotten,
Abdul now had to contend with a flurry of new pain most rotten,
Blind punches to the kidney, it was thereabout,
The pain, gaping mouth, no air, no audible shout.

Fly was upon his feet in seconds and prepared to run,
Scotty close on his heels, away from danger, this was no fun,
Bullock, meanwhile, having forgotten to reload his rifle,
Now lashed out with butt of weapon against Nak's jaw to stifle.

An audible crack could be heard,
It was as though the world had been stirred,
Nak grasp his own rifle heartedly as he fell,
Bullock took no time, no thought, no spell.

He continued with his merciless killing spree,
Quickly reloading weapon, bringing a camel to its knee,
By this time Nak had gathered his senses, powered from within,
Pulled his rifle up near slightly cracked jaw, his head in a spin.

Nak took a sight picture, time having slowed down,
Slight contortion to mouth, a scowl, and then a frown,
But he couldn't do it, not even now,
Tired of death, from death he took a bow.

But no, this was wrong, bright in head were the lights,
Fly suddenly appeared within his sights,
Nak fired a single shot whereby Fly fell down dead,
Nak was not happy, not sad, no identity on face could be read.

"NO!" yelled Scotty who went to his aid amidst the fray,
Tripped over then by Abdul from where he lay,
His face came down hard upon the ground in a streak,
His nose breaking, now flat against cheek.

Snake suddenly shook the reality of the dead man from mind,
The fourth rifle shot fired shook him awake, reality he did find,
He saw his friend, Fly, fall hard upon the ground and knew,
Right there, Fly was dead, sorrow now exponentially grew.

THE SINGLE RETURNS

Horse heard the first of the rifle shots in the distance,
The attack had commenced, the boys and their deliverance,
He should have done more in preventing this from occurring,
Instead of within, thinking of self, contemplating, purring.

On hearing the second shot, he pulled upon the reigns of his horse,
Steered it away and to a halt from its present course,
He commenced contemplation, his thoughts not easily read,
The third shot then sang out and Horse turned his head.

He commenced riding towards his friends, slow moving,
They having been left to their own vices, their evil doing,
Suddenly overcome with different emotions,
Many scenarios forming in his head, many notions.

The fighting within himself was little more than a question,
Good over bad, bad over good: not yet an answer to equation,
Bullock wanted, by the sounds of things, to hinder, to bend,
To scatter their camels, ruin their truck, to entirely amend.

The death of the cameleers was simply a bonus,
Bullock wished to feed his desire, independent, autonomous,
Horse, not sure why he was returning; Conviction? Mind strong?
A feeling within, as though something had gone wrong.

For at the same time of his thinking the fourth shot had sounded,
Different than the others, more rounded,
For he knew each calibre held a different tone,
And the sound he had heard struck him to the bone.

This fourth shot fired made all the difference,
By its sound he could see it, make out its appearance,
He was now trotting at a reasonably good speed,
Suiting his desire, fitting his need.

He'd now reached the point just half way between,
Where Bullock had chosen, of heathen to clean,
He pulled at his horse and listened well,
Something not far off, he could tell.

"Bullock," said Horse, "is that you?",
Why did he ask that, he had no real clue,
Still, Bullock lifted his head from behind some brush,
No longer so alive, no longer so lush.

He was followed by Snake whom held his head low,
Gone from him too was the usual glow,
Horse dismounted and walked over to where they were crouched,
Saw them both filled with grief, their look, the way they slouched.

Horse knelt down beside the two,
"Where's Fly and Scotty?" he asked, but he knew,
The silence that followed was clear, but clarity askew,
"Were they killed?" asked Horse, and his anxiety grew.

Bullock looked him in the eye, "Scotty was captured."
"And Fly?" asked Horse, wishing to be told, to be lectured,
"He's dead," said Snake flatly, no semblance of grace,
"I saw him, before I got away," now looking Horse in face.

"Where's your rifle?" asked Horse of Snake for more, even a clue,
"He left it behind," said Bullock. "Now they have two—."
Snake hit Bullock in the face, quickly set upon by Horse,
Friend hitting friend he could not truly endorse.

"That's enough; no more!" commanded Horse,
Not wishing to take this road, wishing to change course,
"I'm more worried about Fly and Scotty than quibbling,
Not your puns, blaming, scolding, wild accusations scribbling.

"It's no good," insisted Snake. "Fly is horse meat, dead,
I know, I saw it, to body a shot from Afghan rifle fed,
Now eternally put to bed,
Never to live life, never to wed."

Horse asked: "So what happened to ya rifle?"
"I guess I dropped it, amidst the scuffle."
"Dropped it!" repeated Bullock sarcastically,
"Enough," stabbed Horse. "We gotta think now, logically."

"We can't just leave Scotty there with those... men,
But it's a matter of acting now, not when."
"I don't think I can do any more," said Snake. "I feel sick inside,
This is not what I signed on for, this is not the ride."

"You should have thought about that earlier," said Horse,
"But it's too late now, so stop feeling remorse,
Instead of feeling sad and dejected,
Consider Scotty, who will not be neglected."

"I still got me rifle," said Bullock, straight to the meat of the bone,
"I don't know," said Horse. "They have two, we have one."
"We'll shoot first and ask questions later."
"That isn't funny, Bullock," spat Snake of the matter.

"No one said it was," said Bullock. "We have to go in ready,
We have no choice now but to go in fast but steady."
"You're right," said Horse. "I don't think we have a choice."
"I killed one of them," came Snake, sound from cracking voice.

Snake looked up dismayed and sad,
Feeling the horrors of his deed growing, having been so bad,
Said Bullock: "Don't feel guilty for what you done,
We still have much to do, they're the losers, they haven't won."

"He's right," agreed Horse looking into Snake's eye,
"We have to save Scotty, in the by-and-by,
And your horses, where are they?"
"Lost; our whistle amidst commotion they would not obey."

Concluded Horse: "Then we'll have to retrieve them,
For a horse thief I shall never accept, but always condemn,
Assuming, that is, the horses are with the cameleers,
...I shall rip out their brains, their minds, from between ears."

THE AFGHANS COALESCE

Shir had been laid in a blanket once able,
Placed in the shade of a tree most suitable,
Picturesque as can be beside the dry creek bed,
Flies trying to annoy whilst with heaven his spirit was lead.

Said Nak: "The flies I hate the worse, so rude,
Poor Shir is dead and all they want is to intrude,
"Forever a pest, never at rest, in our eyes and ear,
And now, even after death, they swarm and appear.

Asked Abdul of the *jemadar.* "What do we do? Flee or stay?"
Nak looked over to where the body of Fly did lay,
Felt as though he had let the team down, a heavy disgrace,
Did nothing to prevent the onslaught from taking place.

"Allow the maggots their feast upon his sin, we must agree,"
And then he looked to the other, tied to the base of a tree,
Said Nak then to the other:. *"What name you, boy?*
Why you is kill us, why you try to... destroy?"

Scotty didn't answer at first; he had a broken nose,
Caked in blood, smelly from sweat, bruised from fight, no rose,
Truly bruised and bloody he was with two black eyes,
Looking a match, peas to a pod, for sinner a suitable guise.

Nak stood up and hurried to him; swiftly, boldly,
Before he could lash out with a kick so unkindly,
He screamed out and tried to curl into a ball,
"SCOTTY!" the kick didn't come at all.

Scotty shaking from his ordeal,
"My name is Scotty and very sick I feel."
"You friend coward, run quick, run fast,
Much far away now, such friendship not last."

"You horse now mine, you nothing, you see.
I get pretty good money of horse for me."
"I don't think he cares," pointed out Abdul of the matter,
Seemingly not caring that his friends did scatter.

Now Scotty was more concerned for his life,
In the hands of these heathen, life on edge of knife,
He knew he could walk home from where they were,
Just needed that opportunity, that chance to stir.

Abdul did ask: "What are we to do now?"
"We'll have to tell the police, Scotty's arse we'll tow,
Hand the boy into the authorities, into jail they'll throw,
Tell them the story and then they'll know."

"I don't see any other alternative, there is none to voice,
I don't exactly trust the police but we do not have a choice,
We can't let the boy go because he'll tell lies: one who deceives,
We could end up being convicted of murder, and horse thieves."

"But with the boy in custody, delivered in bonds, sing our song,
Along with the horses to hand over as proof, and proof is strong,
I think we can fairly well sell our story,
Of self-defence and the savagery most gory."

"I think we should also cover the boy's body, in order to protect,
Before the maggots eat too much, but for him I have little respect,
Leaving him to be eaten, his body already spindly,
The police nor his parents will take kindly—."

"I don't care, Abdul," interrupted Nak, "do you hear,
The people can think what they like, both far and near,
I'm sick to death of them all, I am shattered, I am busted,
Even those we offer good service, none of them can be trusted."

Abdul did ask: "When will we leave?"
"Tomorrow morning," said Nak, "but give me time to grieve,
We'll take the few camels we have remaining,
 Along with the horses, with what food we have, for sustaining."

"The horses can be used to carry the dead,
The white man's ride, now a bed,
The prisoner we'll make walk for a while, put him out of shape ,
After he's so tired he'll not want to escape."

"What about the other camels; the lost, the quick?"
"They'll have to stay lost for now, to our plan we stick,
Maybe we can come back for them, even if late,
We still have the bells from Chocolate and Slate."

"What of the wool that remains, that we have here,
Not much to speak of but our promise was clear."
"You're right," said Nak. "I'll consider it tonight."
"The others may return, they still have a rifle in order to fight."

"We have two," said Nak and then thought of the wool,
"They have no transport, to chase on foot they would be a fool,
We have three camels and four horses, with no time to saunter,
We have lost our stores, have little food and little water."

"My Koran is gone along with our prayer mats,
We have nothing left but pesky flies and a few gnats,
But tonight we'll maintain watch, be as silent as a ghost,
We can set up a small watching post."

"We will set up a fire so it can be easily seen,
Set a trap just in case, our turn to be mean,
If they approach the fire then they must be shot,
We can't afford to be caught unaware, simply cannot."

"They have the advantage," said Abdul knowingly,
"But we have a prisoner and two rifles," added Nak surprisingly."
Abdul said: "I'm just concerned for my family, my wife,
I don't really care for my own life."

"My family back at home will never know what happened,
They will be devastated to never hear of me again, saddened."
"Your wife loves you, Abdul. That's the truth, not a lie."
"And what about you, Nak? Are you afraid to die?"

"There is life after death, dear friend of mine,
I will be 42 years old for eternity: so hard to define,
72 virgins for me, ready to tend my every need,
What more could a man ask from heaven? Nothing indeed."

And he thought then of Saki and his love,
His Snow White, his sacred dove,
"It's good for you," said Abdul, endeavouring to make a joke,
"Me 23 and you 42: bestowed upon you a toke."

Said Nak: "But that will not affect your enjoyment of a virgin."
Abdul smiled: "You're right, still it's too many for me to imagine,
I'll give you some of mine, something to remember, a wreath."
"Ha!" yelped Nak. "Any more and I'll die a second death."

A serious look now falls over Abdul, now a little blue,
"Nak... there's something I have to tell you."
"It's about the battle of Char Asiab?"
Abdul was stunned. "Ah, it is; what a guess, a good stab."

"You fought with the British and I against, against them rotten,
It doesn't matter, Abdul. It's okay; it's forgotten."
Abdul was now more serious than before: "No, something more."
"What?" asked Nak. "What else is there in the cup to pour?"

"That scar on your face; your lips, the one that does mar."
Nak gently passes his fingertips over the horrendous scar,
"It was me. I was the one that wounded you, a scar to stay."
Nak looks at Abdul closely and waved the thought away.

"No; you're mistaken," insisted Nak of the comment,
"I was in Char Asiab, my actions consecrated in cement,
I was in conflict with you, Nak. I saw you get hit,
Out from your defensive position... everything does fit."

"I saw the injury upon your face...I saw your face,
Nak... I know it was you, and I feel a tremendous disgrace."
Nak said: "It could have been any man that fired that shot,
It could have been anyone that fired.... Could it not?"

Abdul smiles lightly and holds out his hand, most sincere,
Nak hesitates and then accepts it, in Abdul's eye a little tear,
"I'm sorry, Nak... truly, for your many years of pain,
For all of these years in which I, upon your body, did stain."

They hold hands for a few seconds and then release their hold,
Nak said: "It wasn't you, Abdul. Even if it was how you just told,
I forgive you. For ever and a day, from this time forward."
"You're my friend, Nak; a true friend, life's reward."

A FINAL STAND

Snake quickly lead the way, Bullock in wake of tide,
Horse lead his horse on foot to match their stride,
The advance was suddenly brought to a temporary close,
Snake put up a hand for halt, scratched his nose.

Asked Bullock: "What is it? What do you see up front?"
"Another camel," and looking to Bullock did grin and grunt,
Bullock lifted rifle into shoulder, looked down the sight,
Seeing the animal he then held his rifle tight.

Horse approached from behind and slammed his palm down,
Expression bane with voice tampered, a growl and a frown,
"Don't be foolish; idiot. Don't act foolishly, filled with remorse."
"Damn; that hurt," said Bullock as he looked at Horse.

"Think before you act,
Get hold of the fact,
We are one rifle, they are men, all three,
They have the advantage… agree!"

Bullock said: "I do agree with some,
But we have advantage of surprise, don't be dumb,
But, yes, I agree we should approach in silence,
I just feel like shooting camels, having been given a new license."

"I got a better idea," said Snake and stepped off,
"What are you doing?" asked Horse, "Stop acting the toff."
"Do ya want these camels to fester the land?" Snake did ask,
"Walking around, drinking at ease, eating for free, free to bask?"

Snake approached the camel for his statement they did accept,
The sun slowly disappearing below the horizon as he crept,
He crept ever closer, more slowly as he closed the gap,
Getting closer to camel, bringing camel to lap.

The nerves of the camel had simmered,
Easy it was to approach untethered,
He was not wild but tame,
Had a slight limp and so was lame.

Snake moved his hands to axe handle and took a good grip,
Not wishing to allow good aim to slip,
Once satisfied and close enough he swung hard and low,
The camel's leg broke as too did his bellowing grow.

He quickly finished the job off in the best way he knew,
Hitting hard upon head the skull splitting in two,
Streams of red came out as a flood,
Axe now covered in membranes and blood.

Bullock approached Snake and the dead mass upon the ground,
The killing he too enjoyed, surprised happiness could be found,
"Come on, Snake, that's enough," he too gratified a tonne,
"It's dead now; give it a rest will ya? Let's get on, you've won."

Snake stopped pounding down upon the carcass, did display vain,
"I'm sick of these bloody animals, this desert they stain,
Good for nothing is what they are, enough I have had,
Taking what work is available away from me and my dad."

"It's not just you," said Horse as he drew alongside,
"We all suffer, and these heathens, our rules they don't abide."
"And now it's time they suffered," said Snake,
"We'll wait till it gets fully dark, comb this land with rake."

Snake continued: "Mmmm.... They'll need a fire for that matter,
I'm sure they will; and then their lives we can shatter."
Said Horse: "You're right, and help Scotty, great idea I think.."
Snake said: "Agreed. Let's get out of here; this camel does stink."

TWO AFGHAN MEN

The sky above was a brilliant dark blue: serine, mature,
A peaceful reminder, man a small part of a larger picture,
Abdul didn't know much about the heavens so bright,
But knew enough to find his way around at night.

He was sitting next to a large bush,
Facing the campfire as it burnt so lush,
Brightness evaporating into the cold of night,
The edge between light and dark, a sheer delight.

A few night creatures sounding now and then,
Scurrying along small crevices, folds in land, a small glen,
And coupled with the light from sky so high above,
All fitting together, serenity, peas in pod, fingers in glove.

Abdul was content to sit where he was for half the night,
To await the boys he knew would return to fight,
He had both rifles with him: he was highly strung, did not tire,
A round of ammunition up the spout of each, ready to fire.

Nak rolled over in his sleep,
From Scotty, stretched out near the tree, not a peep,
He'd had a gag placed over mouth in order to prepare,
To ready their trap, to ready their snare.

A bed roll had been placed out beside the fire,
The dead man Shir, lay here, by Nak's desire,
To trick the others into believing him alive,
Net of trap now set, some lives to take a dive.

Abdul cocked his head a little, heard a horse, far or near?
He couldn't be sure but it was audibly clear,
He strained his ears, leaning his head a little to the side,
The silhouette of a single figure coming out from hide.

Abdul looked over towards where Scotty was lying, dead asleep,
Knew immediately that he was overtired, the night now to keep,
And then another two figures appeared out of nowhere,
Light from the fire revealed the front figure in slight glare.

He wasn't carrying a rifle and so one of the others held that,
A little too close for comfort, Abdul dare not move, eyelids bat,
Abdul decided what to do, mentally tired through and through,
Had sworn to treat all the same, but this he could no longer do.

And so this was the reality of his promise to self,
Forced to put all consciousness to shelf,
For he knew there was a rifle amongst the three,
But hard it was, even amidst light of fire, to clearly see.

Abdul lifted his rifle and without a shadow of a doubt,
Squeezed the trigger of the rifle, fire from muzzle to sprout,
The loud firing of rifle enough to wake the devil,
Drawing the playing field now to level.

For the shot was a success and Snake fell down hard, rolled over,
Wounded in the stomach from which he would not recover,
A heavy gasp for air erupted from him as he commenced to die,
To soon go visit hell, and for eternity to fry.

Nak stirred silently awake,
All reality did receive a good shake,
For Bullock two targets to shoot, one with weapon, the threat,
Time for him to avenge, time for body count to be net.

Having not taken good aim as Abdul had endeavoured to do,
Bullock did miss, firing wide, making a blue,
And so Bullock did panic, he did blunder,
Haphazardly firing his rifle and hitting Abdul in the shoulder.

Abdul did not feel the pain just then from the hit,
Adrenaline coursing through body, hole in flesh ready to knit,
Abdul quickly had the second rifle in is hand,
With swift ease and of great steadiness of skill he did demand.

He pulled the trigger this time, anxious, shooting instinctively,
It hitting Bullock square in the head, killing him instantly,
Bullock's body fell like a sack of spuds upon the desert canopy,
Abdul and Nak now held complete monopoly.

Horse raced over to where Bullock did so heavily fall,
His mind clear and decisive, a power to which he was in thrall,
Understood fully the predicament he and his friends had attained,
He picked the rifle up for the fight to be maintained.

Gasps of pain,
No playing lame,
Grunts of shame,
Everyone to blame.

Nak was now upon his feet and raced towards Horse,
Snake on brink of death kicked out with much pain of course,
The sheer effort, all he had, enough to tax him hard,
But of all his commitment he would not give a yard.

The bleeding of Snake was largely internal,
Like a volcano bursting its banks, ever infernal,
Larva now spouting from the top,
Great pressure within not willing to stop.

Snake gasped for air then, drawing on every effort of breath,
But no more breath came, all was left was death,
Snake died, last fragment of thought, his family at home, he alone,
Here he was, seemingly dying like a dog without bone.

Nak fell hard upon the ground having been tripped,
A blade of spinifex forced into his eye, all sanity now nipped,
The shock of the fall and the pain from protrusion,
There was nothing to paint of this, but pain, and no illusion.

Horse had soon found some ammunition and loaded this into slot,
He brought the weapon into his shoulder and took a shot,
At near point-blank range Nak's body mass hit... life spent,
Nak's stirring fell silent.........................

Abdul saw all of this, everything more,
Nak's life spent, now at heaven's door,
And who now was alive, who was dead,
What was left, what can be said.

It was now that the pain in his arm commenced to build,
Gone was the adrenaline, gone was his shield,
He fumbled around for what he had placed beside his knee,
Found the ammunition for rifle and reloaded it with little glee.

He brought the weapon up into his shoulder as best he could,
The weapon, the pain, he then stalled as he felt he would,
Horse threw his rifle to the ground, an audible thudding sound,
He saw Scotty motionless, there bound upon the ground.

Horse's weaknesses was the fact that he'd just shot a man,
Going to hell was never his plan,
Horse was in a flurry, unsure what he should do,
Kneeling beside Scotty, knife in his hand, his life was through.

Abdul couldn't believe the stupidity, this methodical thinking,
How he'd simply raced up to his friend, amongst all this killing,
Maybe these whites were not much different than he,
Maybe they were the same, more to meet the eye, more to see.

Abdul would not have shot at a defenceless cameleer,
As they made their way from town to town amidst sneer,
Endeavouring to earn a little money for bread,
And characteristically out of nowhere, Abdul shot Scotty dead.

He had squeezed the trigger, given hope to Horse,
Shot Scotty, the bound, the end of remorse,
To let Horse live, seemingly the most healthy,
To live and grow of knowledge wealthy.

Horse heard the shot fired, it was dire,
Saw blood erupt from Scotty by the light of the fire,
Horse felt he understood then the meaning of life,
The meaning was death, whether from old age, rifle or knife.

Nak had instinctively reloaded his rifle, senselessly relating,
Despite considering his life at an end, hangman's rope waiting,
Horse felt he was up against better men, death a formality,
Didn't wish to be a statistic, landing back to reality.

"You go," shouted Abdul. *"You go long way, no come back,*
You got horse, you take and go home. No more attack,
Me forget quick. Me not care. You live, me live; we both live,
You know what meaning is; you understand what it is I give?"

"Yes," replied Horse. "I know what you mean: it's the end."
Horse looked down into the closed eyes of his friend,
Of the five he was the only one left living,
"You've killed four of my friends. That's hard giving."

Lectured Abdul: *"Alive is good, dead is bad,*
You go and me go. We both go, both sad."
"Yes," said Horse as he stood, sheathing his knife, there to stay,
"We both go." Horse turned and commenced to move away.

He stumbled to a stop, had something to say,
"Thank you," he said and continued on his way,
"Okay," said Abdul. *"You do thing, one more for me,*
You make horse speak, me know you gone, we no longer see."

"Yes; yes, okay," said Horse, understanding all,
Abdul wished to ensure that upon him again he did not fall,
"But I'll be back tomorrow, for they I cannot neglect,
Just leave them alone and give them a little respect."

"Okay. I leave horses here too,
Me with them is through,
They not clean as camel,
Hard to… make travel."

ABDUL'S DEMISE AND RETURN TO ROOTS

Abdul was on foot now and staggering a little,
He'd patched his wound as best he could, feeling brittle,
He'd left the bodies of the whites behind,
But his friends were with him, on this long grind.

Nak and Shir were strapped to two of their camel,
The third carried a little water, nothing left on which to marvel,
The thought of riding upon the camel hadn't been considered,
Such was the decay of his normality, mentality slivered.

His thinking was askew, thoughts mostly of the past,
His first real job here was also his last,
Nak Kadir was from Kabul, aged 42 and single,
Shir Adji was from Karachi, married to Arika, was subtle.

He would remember them forever and ever, always,
No matter where, the houses, the countries, the opened doorways,
But for now he had to fend for himself and deliver his friends,
Get back to civilization, across sparseness, around unseen bends.

He looked down upon the sand, town far from drawing nigh,
Unable to see his shadow for the sun was high in the sky,
Daydreaming and staggering, he'd had no sleep the night before,
Looking up as he went: was it real or illusion, that which he saw?

And a few more seconds was all he could endure,
The calling of unconsciousness, lack of blood the lure,
When he fell it was silently and fast,
Upon this heated furnace so open and vast,

But then the jolting of the wagon woke Abdul up from the rear,
And the stirrings of a familiar voice echoed in his ear,
Said Johann: "Ah, praise the good Lord that you have risen,
You've been in and out of your daze for a day, now listen."

"How do you feel?
Hungry for food, for a meal?"
Abdul understood enough of what was said,
But still had a lot of blurriness to contend with in his head.

He rubbed at his eyes and it was suddenly clear,
Of the pain in his shoulder, death of friends, and the fear,
Said Johann: "Ah; I fixed that as best I could,
Took some mending, but flesh is not wood."

"Where we go?" asked Abdul for news of his predicament,
"I found you beside the track, unconscious for the moment,
I was heading north but decided to turn back to Maree,
The least I can do for a man, even one like you, hope you agree."

"Where friend?" Abdul's question a flurry, did smother,
"What friend? Ah; you mean the other?
I don't know. You know; I thought it was weird, a bit strange,
That they should leave you alone like that upon this desert range."

"Did one of them shoot you; were they filled with dread?"
"No. You no see friends? They dead...
No, no. Not meaning. Friend is dead; you find;
You see them and camels?" asked Abdul, words hard to bind.

"Are they dead? I don't know," said Johann: to him it did confuse,
"Here, have a drink," Johann handed him water, began to muse,
"No, I didn't see anyone. No camels, no friend,
Just you; and lucky I did, for you were near your end."

Abdul thought on the past, the hellish weather,
Nak and Shir were strapped, bound with leather,
The camels surely taken off, possibly in search of water and food,
The bodies of his friends lost forever, forever to allude.

Said Johann: "We shouldn't be long into Marree,
"You'll have to report this to the police, you and me… we."
Abdul considered what was said,
This was a problem, deep issue, not easily read.

Without the bodies of Nak and Shir… evidence gone,
What was he to tell the police, his story could not be hone,
The circumstances of being shot could not be proven,
The white boy, on other hand, could bake any story in oven.

Maybe it was time to let sleeping ghosts lie,
Say nothing of what had happened, just simply deny,
He should try and return to Afghanistan whilst he had the chance,
No need to make a storm in a teacup, no need to shout and dance.

"No," said Abdul, loud enough to hear,
Said Johann: "No! It's not my place to say, but Maree is near,
But I think justice should be done, nail on head, a heavy stone,
To those that left you there to die in great misery and all alone."

"I forgive, and forget," but Abdul wasn't so sure that he could,
Never forget the ordeal he'd suffered, never would,
"I'll take you to the Ghantown then," Johann did offer,
"Would you like that? It would not be any bother."

Abdul smiled, looked up at Johann, looked him in the face,
"You good friend," said Abdul with much sincere grace,
"You good man this place. Me never forget."
And of all the week's misery he honestly had nothing to regret.

Abdul had not caused the fight with the boys,
He treated all fairly, filled lives with many joys,
Never did throw the first stone,
Had even apologized to Nak, did atone.

Johann simply smiled and turned his eyes again upon the track,
Life in Australia was too hard, to Afghanistan he would go back,
He smiled and thanked God for he had survived by a mere margin,
What would he do in heaven with seventy-two women all virgin?

BOOK TWO

ORCINUS ORCA - Song of the Ocean

FOR GEOGRAPHY:

Google Maps is a fantastic way in which to find your way around [especially in satellite mode] Eden. Place names and general locations mentioned, with regards to Eden and Twofold Bay, are easily scrutinized. Distances are easily depicted, providing essential assistance and advantage, where a printed map within this book could never do nearly the same in scope or dimension, as may be appropriate to this story.

IMPORTANT NOTE:

Some of the evidence and general information concerning Typee and Jackson, during examination, appears misconstrued and does differ vastly: as to whether or not they are one and the same, I do not know, but I have favoured the opinion that they are two individuals.

This is a work of historical-fiction and should not be used as a source on which to base the history of our protagonists, for whaling events over time have been pruned and extended, rightly or wrongly, to bring to light the charismatic behaviour of the interaction between man and killer whale as best as possible; but it is better to apply the 'historical-fiction' tag than be cursed for telling an untruth that I may not have been sure about. In the chapter 'Mother of Mary' I have completely fabricated the events surrounding the interactions of Orcinus: who is it to know whether or not such attempts by killer whales was made, but it was the thing that was likely to occur if the opportunity did arise: consider it far-fetched or romantic, that is up to you, but where there are no survivors then there is no truth or lie. And last but not least, Orcinus orca is of the oceanic dolphin family: a dolphin.

FAST FISH

A harpoon entering the body of a whale did not kill it; it was meant only as a means by which to secure the line and maintain a measure of control over the whale whilst lancing took place and the animal then killed; this might take some time and some number of lances. It was therefore not surprising to see that a rule was employed by which means a crew could announce quite categorically that 'it' owned the right to the whale in which its harpoon was attached; it went something like this: where the harpoon shall remain in the fish so struck, and a line or boat shall be attached thereto and continue in the power of the striker or headsman, such whale shall be deemed a fast fish, and although struck by any secondary or subsequent harpoon shall be the property of the first striker or headsman only.

COMMON BOAT LAYOUT

Twenty-nine feet long and pointed at both ends with a sag in the middle, wider in breadth around where the centre thwart lay, each differing slightly but built objectively the same, depending on the maker. There was planking across the first 4.9 feet of the stern where the loggerhead could be found, a short post where line was checked, it being drenched with buckets of water during hectic times when whales took off with the line attached, the friction of which was quite easily capable of seeing the loggerhead burn. Tubs which contained the line (fed through the loggerhead) were found between the middle and aft thwarts, depending on the headsman, 200 fathoms of line (manila rope) to each. The line was fed through the loggerhead and continued on through a niche in the bow, under an iron bar and then back over it to the harpoon, where it was attached securely. A typical boat would have anywhere from 5-8 oarsman, the number most favoured being that which allowed for an equal number of oarsman to be positioned either side of the boat once the battle against a whale was commenced, a number derived upon by the headsman.

From the bow the following positions were normally filled: harpooner, bow-oarsman, midship-oarsman, tub-oarsman, after-oarsman, headsman (at the stern); each seated upon his own thwart. The headsman was responsible for exchanging places with the harpooner once delivery of weapon had been secured within the beast, the harpooner responsible for securing 'fast fish'. The headsman, once having exchanged places with the harpooner, would then deliver as many lances as was required to fulfil his duty. The harpooner now controlled the sweep (steering oar) with great precision, it being 22-27 feet in length.

THE FAMILY TREE

Parent:
Stranger [F]

Offspring:
Tom [M]
Hooky [M]

Parent:
Typee [M]
Humpy [F]

Offspring:
Walker [M]

Parent:
Cooper [M]
Big Ben [F]

Offspring:
Young Ben [M]
Albert [F]

3rd Gen:
Charlie Adgery [M]

Parent:
Jackson [M]
Sharkey [F]

Offspring:
Brierly [M]
Skinner [M]

Parent:
Jimmy [M]
Big Jack [F]

Offspring:
Kinscher [F]
Little Jack [M]

PROLOGUE 1: GENERAL INFORMATION

Killer whales; the orca; they are black and white,
Dolphin killers, mammals of the ocean, vigorous, full of might,
Warm-blooded creatures at the top of the food chain,
Man of the land the occasional invader and its only stain.

Their upper and dorsal surface is black and dorsal does tower,
Ventral surface and the face, be known, and much lower,
White with a saddle patch upon their back,
Light coloured underbelly of which black it does lack.

All gels and blends with the surface,
As through the ocean they grace,
For being viewed from above they confuse,
To lose in game hide and seek they do refuse.

Orca attack from below, is confusion: the dark patches,
A head on attack like masquerading shadows, misfortune latches,
Attack from high prey confused: underbelly camouflage,
Ignorance is bliss for Orcinus and so says the adage.

Hence their colouring plays important role,
From the churning jaws so hungry they do not dole,
Blazing head, dark upper, light under, secures his hunt,
Salmon easy victim, as for any, conned, fooled, great stunt.

Menacing and mighty jaws,
One of the many ocean laws,
Killers mouth a big deal,
Always able to secure a meal.

A dorsal fin stands 5.9 feet at best,
Like a gigantic sail upon surface, seemingly at rest,
Though female in much smaller in comparison,
Signature of the ocean, steer wide on sight for good reason.

All rekindles the melody of 'ebony and white',
Black patches of death and angel white delight,
They escape all lucidity,
This is their great security.

A distinctive pigmentation,
Is also of the mention,
Behind the dorsal as though written in text,
An identification mark, one member from the next.

Tail flukes have no skeletal support but are more fibrous,
Propulsion from powerful movement of the tail stock enormous,
Eyes are suited to both ocean and air, vital, do astound,
killers lifting head out of the water to spy on ocean and ground.

Sight plays a major role in the killer's day to day life,
Being as good above the waves as it is below, strategy most rife,
Sound an important ability, able to decipher and rate,
Food seemingly placed before them like dinner upon plate.

Of all the mammals of the ocean they travel narrows and girth,
Widely distributed across all waters of the earth,
Well versed with the oceans of the globe: one as good as the rest,
Although mid-ocean activity is considered less, miniscule at best.

Why this? to preserve energy and feast on flesh,
To feeding grounds well tour and inwardly mesh,
To appease its rituals and endeavours, some seemingly unclean,
Tossing seals, eat rump of a porpoise, feast on tongue of baleen.

Traversing along latitudes of both hemisphere,
When and where temperature most suitably appear,
Close to coastlines where fertility is at its highest,
Leisurely creatures of measurable existence, the mightiest.

With its mouth of teeth, purely owned, no prize,
Born of torpedo-shaped body and of immense size,
It can outplay, out manoeuvre, chase down and intercept,
Extremely intelligent, brain 3 times larger than mans', not inept.

With ability to undertake daily choirs, having great resilience,
Feelings of loneliness and despair, able to hold a grievance,
Can decipher incoming sounds, piece together any required action,
Intelligent, communicative, as a species does travel by faction.

They can be classified into three main groups, to each a flavour,
Each depicting their general displays of feeding and behaviour,
A matriarchal society whereby there is a strong bond and law,
And a structured group be it 'resident', 'transient', or 'offshore'.

'Resident'; no dispersal of individuals from the group does flare,
Dispersal does not occur, quite simply, extremely rare,
Very large groups, pods of related killers, of desire and wish,
Dozens upon dozens who feed exclusively on squid and fish.

A mother, her sons and daughters, 3-10 killers at her side,
Contribute to a group of several dozen per pod, of laws abide,
Matrilineal binding linking all within, agile and full of ability,
Several hundred animals evident in its sustained community.

Matrilineal groups within a pod are created with equal charge,
And where the size of any pod becomes stretched and is too large,
Command and structure form break-away groups of the same,
A sub-pod of matrilineal society is created, well cast, not lame.

Vocal strategies within a sub-pod are adherent and extensive,
Strategies to remain throughout their lives and conductive,
Repertoire of dialect given, to some degree, to another sub-pod,
Or drawn from another as though in agreeance and with nod.

Sub-pods are a 'constant' to which members respond,
Remaining steadfast for the life of the matriarch, possibly beyond,
A killer will not usually defect from one sub-pod to another,
Although extensions from a sub-pod can be created from larger.

Pods also shared their complex mannerisms and talent,
Of their social and vocal range as though valiant,
Including their specific and unique language, never to neglect,
Call it accent or basic understanding of a different dialect.

The 'transient' are less social than our former, the 'resident',
Travel in smaller groups of six or less, seemingly more violent,
Feed upon sea lions, seals and porpoises, given any chance,
Similarly cast may be a throng of thugs at a glance.

'Offshore' constitutes a large group, 30-60 the norm,
Preferring open waters to feed on fish, weathering any storm,
Predatory habits are harnessed, respectful to others highly noted,
An array and vast resources of food seemingly not exploited.

Food, we have touched upon, is as variable as the variety,
Feeding upon distinctive forms of prey for the majority,
The world a large plate upon which is found many a staple,
Penguin, seabirds, dugong, turtle, and manatee, as an example.

Humpbacks are also a heavenly source of food,
Orcinus devouring each, of which they are forever in the mood,
Australia is a known pantry of fat and tongue,
Easy to score, most easily won.

Humpbacks enjoy a frolic near Eden as they follow the coast,
Their migration route in range of Twofold Bay for the most,
From Antarctica, to the north, they travel in groups as we know,
Their migratory range and location the Orcinus in brain do stow.

Most of its life, under the waves, out of view, unique and large,
An orca will stalk its prey like the predator it is, never to barge,
To secure food the orca must act, with complete stealth,
Await the order to move in for the kill, nourishment is wealth.

Large amounts of food it does need, without stretch of a lie,
And without substantial it will most surely die,
If food becomes bare bone, it can sustain self for many a week,
On little to no food, as its demise begins to speak and to peak.

Lack of food isn't the only killer,
Of the orca there is another miller,
For man also plays his hand in its demise,
Cruel and efficient whaling programmes for future to criticize.

Baleen whales, as example, are taken from their dinner plate,
Cleansed from the oceans, hence decreasing numbers to date,
Henceforth arrives the inability to feed as required,
A drop in the population of the killer seen as it is retired.

When food becomes scarce the killer will draw from within,
Energy taken from its high-calorie reserves of blubber under skin,
Its huge bulk serving as a means to survive,
Weeks without food can turn into months, now barely alive.

The Orcinus is able to hold back death for so, so many a day,
But age, whether young or old, decides this length of stay,
Age can alter the survival rate of a killer more readily,
One in mid-life stage of growth able to adapt more steadily.

And there is a strategy in its 'food for the picking',
Young seals or sea lions are preferred for the killing,
Adults rarely being attacked and for good reason, not stupidity,
Adults are dangerous, causing great injury, if given opportunity.

The killers can purposely beach themselves upon the land,
Upon pebbled beach to take a seal pup in its teeth so grand,
Pups that consider the shoreline safe and clear of harm's way,
It is called 'stranding', just another means to secure its prey.

Killers have mastered this skill which is called 'stranding',
Females teach their young as though taking class with discipline,
Occasionally juveniles appear to do this in slow motion,
Not so much for play, but to harness the skill to perfection.

Juveniles may strand themselves by fault during this ride,
Adults coming to the rescue, stranding themselves alongside,
Aiding them back into the water most sublime, their biome,
Most sublime is their atmosphere, their biosphere, their home.

Or act as a decoy,
Thrashing in water as though to annoy,
Distracting pups so immature and unaware,
Orcinus acting with speed, with menacing glare.

It will shake its victim mercilessly and seemingly for thrill,
Though often simply and maliciously to disorientate and kill,
Killers will also take their prey to the pod, their clan,
To feed all equally, calves coming first, always part of the plan.

The calves might then play with their meal,
Harnessing techniques on the killing, life to steal,
Its prey, its captive, meeting its demise,
Lessons to learn as in all of life, no surprise.

A seal might hide within small cave or rock crevice beneath,
A method to extract taken into hand causing much grief,
Two killers will take turns in surfacing and taking a breath,
One maintaining its watch upon the crevice to deliver death.

Once the seal runs out of air,
Tries to escape and in comes the pair,
Always there will be one killer, one at least,
To secure the meal, these orca are an intelligent beast.

They can hold their breath for 5 to 15 minutes in a dive,
216 fathoms or more, for great depth they strive,
Evolution has provided them with unique ability,
In the consumption of oxygen, a necessary commodity.

It is able to exchange gasses more readily,
Each breath manipulated with great ability,
With different ways to cater for different dives and situation,
Being shallow or deep, never a single choice, deny negation.

Its rib cage can collapse under insurmountable pressure,
Surplus air collecting beneath the blowhole in good measure,
And is able to store oxygen reserves in nasal passage,
In its bodily fluid and muscle tissue, their appendage.

Also store in red blood cells of body lean,
Their bodies are a mean machine,
Further more endowed,
Its heart beat can be slowed.

Slow the heart for a deep dive with little strain,
Oxygenated blood diverted to heart and the brain,
Able to reabsorb blood nitrogen when comes the flood,
Avoiding the formation of killer bubbles in the blood.

When a calf enters its watery world, surfacing for the first time,
To satisfy its need to survive it gulps in air most sublime,
The mother and the calf's breathing then becomes synchronized,
Will remain so for much of their lives, to rigidly harmonize.

131

Their breathing aligned now a great benefit, she the instructor,
The mother becoming somewhat of a conductor,
And the remainder of the pod will take its breathing from her,
From this a great symphony, as though purposely she did stir.

For the needs of one and for all,
The remainder of the pod in her thrall,
For the maintenance of good health,
Food, food, food, their constant forage for wealth.

Generations of hunting tactics are taught to the young,
First-hand knowhow for abilities and success to them flung,
Crucial skills passed down from one generation to the next,
Skills individual and social, readily fed as though from text.

Calves acquire the ability to hunt on their own by month six,
Vocalizations and echolocation techniques thrown into the mix,
Social protocol and hunting strategies, good maintenance,
They mimic lessons from mothers all with great patience.

They usually place great distance between pods,
Travel in the same direction, echolocation, the clearest of nods,
When they encounter food they will noisily leap and splash,
In the water and upon surface to lash and lash.

This does signify the find, often with vocalized message,
Though use of sonar is questionable: no clear sign of passage,
Due to alerting specific prey of their presence, may remain mum,
In particular dolphins and other mammals, 'never beat that drum'.

They devour creatures great and small,
Fish and whales, it matters not, for all their gall,
They know they are at top of the food chain and all is fair game,
A kill is a kill, to them it is all the same.

PROLOGUE 2: FLESH OF FISH

A message is received from another pod, a neighbour,
A school of fish close by, the hunt more fun than labour,
Three pods move in to take position and further delve,
Force the school to surface, a single orca, of the hammer, a helve.

Together strong, the school compacted smaller and smaller,
Orcinus then vocalize each move, coordinated is each attacker,
Flash their white markings, a thunder, bad weather,
A school which does panic and then set upon by orca together.

The killers slap the water with their flukes performing magic,
Stunning the herring to stupidity, now seemingly static,
The killers taking a mouthful or two of their prey, these fish,
And take turns so that each has an equal share of the dish.

An orca beneath flashes again his white underbelly,
The herring continue in their panic, grouped tight in rally,
Remaining near the surface where they are in need,
No escape, now taken into mouth, flesh on which to feed.

A burst of fluke-bashing is then commanded by the matriarch,
Further stunning the herring, devoured, their death rather stark,
Taken into jaws as quickly as they float unconscious,
Other orcas continue to keep the herring massed, some oblivious.

Easily corralled and now ready to feed upon flesh they are,
Another killer gets its fill and retreats but not far,
Orcinus orca taking turns to feed upon the herring,
Working as a team, coordinated, minds of strong bearing.

Once all have fed and had their fill,
The killers turn and depart, in for a meal, not the thrill,
Leaving the remaining herring to disperse,
Into deeper water for the school to nurse.

Some bodies half eaten or bitten do remain afloat,
Be they full or half devoured, their gases no time to bloat,
For they are picked up by birds of prey from the wave,
Swooping down to take what's left of the pickings from grave.

PROLOGUE 3: FLESH OF WHALE

Some find larger morsels more rewarding,
A blue whale, being 59 feet in length, most appealing,
Soon surrounded by a deployed pod of experience,
Killers swim either side and below, currently no lenience.

Prevent the whale from making a move towards deep water,
They move in closer and at high speed to slaughter,
Allowing their presence to be known, to cause strife,
Maintaining the fear factor to penetrate as though a knife.

Those either side create white water, like snowy hail,
As they continue alongside the luscious blue whale,
Some move to the front, to slow down any attempt of escape,
Others behind prevent it turning, this bulk, this monstrous shape.

They disturb the whale's rhythm of breath,
They snap their mouths open and closed, predicting sweet death,
Gnashing their teeth together, to terrify their catch,
The chase continues for 20 miles, a lengthy battle, a match.

The blue whale feels self remorse, it does quickly tire,
The killers move in one at a time and then momentarily retire,
Take great hunks of flesh from the whale as he swims on,
The attack continues for five hours, the killers no longer strong.

Either too tired themselves or having had their fill of mass and lip,
They discontinue with the chase, allow the blue whale the slip,
A great gaping mass of white blubber displayed, a battle wound,
Where it's dorsal once existed now nothing to be found.

Death is just hours away and the blue whale is now a beacon,
For sharks everywhere, more teeth, to be further stricken,
Sharks that keep clear of the killers, their unsavoury foe,
Unable to survive a fight against Orcinus they are in the know.

Orcinus orca is strong and resilient,
Feeds to fill, not to just kill, and so, honestly, quite lenient,
But practise its skills it does as any other,
All extremely intelligent, all mother, all brother.

THE BIRTH

Orcas are one of the few animal species to have a distinct culture,
Hunting strategies occasionally unique, in many ways a rapture,
Cultural behaviours are learned, not clearly instinctive,
An individual initiates, others copy, seemingly meditative.

In the case of the seal hunting orcas, of Argentina most particular,
Orcas practice beaching and rescuing themselves until familiar,
Pass the skills on to their offspring in preparation,
Snatching seal pups from beaches, clear statement, no negation.

For thousands of years, before man recorded such an event,
Orcinus orca did hunt baleen whales, no remorse, no relent,
Each pod does seem to relish one meal over another,
Nothing here truly sacred, though enough facets to smother.

Of every ocean upon the planet,
Of all the time man cast to ocean his net,
Only once has it been witnessed,
And truly, with great respect, expressed.

Of the collaboration between beast and man,
For the harnessing of baleen, both meeting with plan,
Great prosperity, understanding and knowledge,
To hunt together, a silent and well endowed pledge.

A family which went by the surname Davidson,
From them we peel back a great comparison,
Scrutinize the efforts of both, and we shall try and be blunt,
Where the killer, in accordance with need, did tax the human hunt.

Fresh meat, the flesh of the baleen,
Coated in oil so fresh and clean,
Source of income for man, meat for the killer whale,
Sheer oppression for baleen, for baleen sheer [archaic] bale.

Taking place at well-known Twofold Bay,
A particular pod of killers would return each year for short stay,
A bay near Eden on the Australian East Coast,
Such an extraordinary story unfolds, one in which to give toast.

This unwritten contract between man and whale stalker,
Evil man and the 'labelled unkindly' Orcinus orca,
This story of the killer is not meant to specifically qualify,
But of all understanding it does tend to superimpose and mystify.

It is a main jest of this story to reflect upon their character,
Give to each that owned, great stature,
Grasp here a true understanding and overall picture,
We start in the year 1862 and steer clear of giving lecture.

From a distance the dorsal of the killers can be seen,
To perforate the surface of the ocean, cutting clean,
Cutting effortlessly through the gentle rolling of each wave,
The road ahead soon to be set, ready to pave.

Each of the mammals beneath are fully aware,
Flippers engaged, gliding through the ocean and sun's glare,
For they surface from time to time, now and again,
More often than not at same instance, similarity it does maintain.

The spouting of water seems the effect of the action,
Air ejected from the blowhole an immediate reaction,
It looks like that of a great cloud of mist,
Exploding from within, an action unable to resist.

Escaping air turning into water droplets, a voluminous sneeze,
Which dissipates in the air, carried away on the breeze,
Fresh breeze coming from the south, prepare for another dive,
By sucking in more oxygen, thriving, staying alive.

It is a wonder in itself to see such a mushrooming cloud,
Each erupting from within, power in which to be proud,
A peaceful cloud of beauty, so serene, one cannot ignore,
Unlike the cloud created by man and his inclination to war.

There is calm about it, no fragment of mind but something surreal,
Where one can become lost in a dream, a fantasy to steal,
Forget not this place in the world, an oyster's pearl,
Nothing like sitting back and watching the event unfurl.

But an even bigger event is about to unfold and take place,
Near land, in the tropics, close to Hawaii, waters of grace,
The pristine waters on which they now lay visit,
Worth all the time in the world to make this transit.

A matriarch so young knows no better place to conclude this ride,
Other bays and inlets that she has visited, all brushed aside,
Her name to be Stranger and young at just 14 years,
Sexual maturity reached at 11 years, mature amongst peers.

Surrounded by members of her pod, an appeal to social science,
Other killer whales that had joined her in her adolescence,
Each seeing that she had purpose and great vision,
She knew of things that they did not, an apparition.

Stranger had been accepted as their matriarch without argument,
Setting themselves alongside for all to learn, behold this moment,
Even now, after the short, 16 months that they had been together,
Their dialect had transposed itself as different from any other.

Uniqueness unfolding with their traits as a unit,
Drawn together through conviction, drawn to a magnet,
She had fallen pregnant when with a large pod of 'offshore',
But departed that life, for she saw that the world held more.

And she departed alone,
Her mate holding heart of stone,
Male did remain with the pod he trusted and knew,
Stranger, now matriarch, of great vision she grew.

So now she has her own pod, her family,
Each joining her as though off assembly,
There was Typee, at 23 years, the oldest, stout, and lover,
He had a mate, whose dorsal was completely bent over.

His mate was Humpy, 17 years, many more in store,
Had partnered with Typee several years before,
Typee having left his previous pod due to the death of his mother,
Of breeding age, you could not part them, eyes for one another.

There is also another pair to meet,
Two more, seemingly young, in which to greet,
The male is Cooper, the female named Big Ben in error,
Both 11 years of age and coupled years before, for their pleasure.

Cooper and Big Ben, dependent on one another,
It was their spirit as a couple, desire to be together,
Desire forcing them to separate from pod the previous year,
Inseparable, even during the hunt, always wanting to be near.

So here they were, a small pod of five,
To soon be swollen by one, beginning to thrive,
Stranger to give birth right here and now,
The beginning of an explosion to population, for them to grow.

For Stranger's abilities in the hunt would become legendary,
To all it was clear, clear and adverse to quandary,
Many male and female alike soon to join them,
Stranger the limb of which would grow many stem.

Little communication was shared between the member so near,
As they continued slowly on their way to waters so clear,
Patrolling waters, considered humanly far from shore,
No alert to prey on which to opportunistically impose much gore.

For prey could be almost anywhere,
Could be here, could be there,
With a new mouth to feed coming their way,
They would remain, always, alert for new prey.

Searching constantly would be its own reward,
Whilst they waited the birth of their newest ward,
But stem that communication between each killer,
Which is a natural part of life, of their society a pillar.

Communication takes place during parts of the day or night,
Times that are more appropriate, to infringe a frightful blight,
Dialect modified over the decades, year to year,
Learnt and curved, for members of the pod all is clear.

Regional variations that are perfected,
Customized and never neglected,
Employed methodically without thought,
It is that which they now suppress, as taught.

This pod as for others are social,
With this there is nothing special,
And a small pod is more prone to seek company,
Even if such is human and unable to join in their symphony.

Nigel B.J. Clayton

In this alone we find it hard to believe,
That creatures of the deep can feel, can grieve,
Or that they have a connection,
With the human race, of any description.

They feel the effects of loneliness,
As well as overwhelming degrees of bliss,
They experience fear and embarrassment, I'm sure,
As men do, with their mistakes they do deplore.

But yet this is still far from their minds, present is a prize,
For a birth is taking place before their very eyes,
Tom delivered unto the world and vocalization can be heard,
Sound echoes out across the ocean, gliding, on wings of a bird.

The mother's abdomen is swollen with a foetus so large,
One that has been gestating for 17 months, the pods first charge,
Stranger swims around displaying some discomfort,
Her restless commotion drawing a little concern for effort.

She rises for breath, expelling mist, to atmosphere she gave,
Remaining there, just below each softening wave,
She can feel the soft breeze upon her skin,
The warmth did shine upon her, scene enough to draw a grin.

Her first born is about to make its way into the world,
She swims about and then suddenly pauses, her mind twirled,
Her flukes and head are lifted up, in sunlight, the glare,
Her back arched; she gives birth right then and there.

All other killers surround her, hearts happily torn,
Protecting her and the newborn,
Watching now their bated breath to be rewarded,
Of this newest member to the pod, to be well guided.

Her thrashing about, which is necessary, visually learned,
Is natural and nothing in which to be concerned,
Somersaults and barrel rolls do aid, does not desist,
For good delivery one must be active, in pain, persist.

It is normal for the flukes to be seen first amidst ocean and sea,
Rarely the head, and the calf emerges to greet the glee,
And just a short period of delivery, for some a dramatic delight,
Delivery to reward the mother with greet reflection far from fright.

Tom is jettison delicately away from the mother of birth,
As Stranger gently accelerates forward and gives shallow girth,
The calf seen amidst red mist of blood from the torn umbilicus,
A sheen of gleam, shimmering, as though a form of mucus.

138

It dissipates as Tom now (if not clumsily) upwards does strive,
To surface just above, suck in his first lungful of air, to be alive,
Tom is born at last; the calf's triangle dorsal fin droops initially,
Fore flippers rigid, his flukes unfurl and thrashes deliberately.

Into the watery world in which he has been born,
Tom is free at last, to swim and splash about until worn,
To breathe the air above the surface of the ocean and to explore,
To have his heart filled with wondrous sights, more upon more.

He is lifted into the air on several occasions, seemingly ritualistic,
Much rubbing of skin on skin taking place, joyful, simplistic,
For all are overjoyed to see him born unto the world of serenity,
A little percussive activity takes place, never lacking in security.

He will maintain a very close connection with his mother of birth,
For the first year of his life, and beyond, for what it is worth,
Grow of maturity, become stable, a part of the pod ever growing,
To be taught, looked after, escorted, to always be in the knowing.

Always to have other members of the pod on which to rely,
To be there, one for the other, now and in the by-and-by,
But the first year will see him in his mother's shadow,
To her whims and ways, to always be ready, to always bow.

Sheltered by her very body and flippers, his family,
Protected by her and pod in way most simile,
Provided good motherly support and sanction,
Pod ready to make secure by action.

But for the moment, the here and now, Stranger is a little tired,
Exhaustion dependant on delivery, though often feeling retired,
But happiness keeps her so optimistic and content,
Feeling of love so strong you can see it, from pores it does vent.

Tom now joins his mother to learn of this new life,
Away from comfort of womb: grow, kill, possibly find a wife,
So much now though to learn on the swim, forever more,
To breath, to learn the dialect and of the pods law.

They have much to be thankful for at present,
But Stranger is a little concerned, on pods safety spent,
For there is great safety in number and theirs is but few,
To see more killers within their pod would provide good view.

A matriarch with great hunting ability and strategies to share,
She is worth her weight in gold: or should we say dietary fare,
Stranger recalled a place where blossoms could be looted,
A place where hunting whales could be recruited.

She had seen another pod in action,
One of similar interest and faction,
Had even shared with them the sport of the hunt,
Several orca she knew could be influenced, not to shunt.

She would recruit on Typee's aid for he was majestic and quick,
Good at hunting, good at killing, called to anger no short wick,
Grand at reading the thoughts of others, seemingly easy for him,
But he beheld one small factor which was requiring a slight trim.

He was too much of a commandeering sort in his nature,
Never to be made the leader of a sub-pod, to grow in stature,
But he did have abilities which she could milk, could bait,
Stranger reflected upon Typee's mate, Humpy, mind and state.

Humpy was a vicious type, by and large,
Not afraid to lead a head-on charge,
Not afraid to take a risk as may be the need,
Easy to manipulate and no need to plead.

Stranger would use her as a sub-pod contender for sure,
When the time was ripe Stranger would employ a lure,
But currently would allow Humpy to remain close by her side,
Yes, Stranger would have Humpy as an ally, along for the ride.

This would keep Typee close and others even closer,
For those intimidated by Typee would remain all the tighter,
All would henceforth be subjected to Stranger, her road to win,
For the pod to grow in number and strength, currently too thin.

But there was plenty of time to reflect on tactics,
For now she was simply content with life and the basics,
To see Tom now swimming near her right flipper, just behind,
Searching for the retractable abdominal nipples, forever on mind.

And so he soon begins to suckle for the very first time,
Touch is sensitive, sometimes commanding but feeling, sublime,
Where a calf requests feeding from mother, a nourishing source,
Nudges, nibbles, fore-flipper caresses, feeding strategy, its course.

After some time at feeding Tom has had his fill, a great morsel,
He now precariously takes up position behind a fin, the dorsal,
To swim effortlessly along in the slipstream,
Tom is 8.2 feet long, weighs 200kg, a part of the team.

THE BOATS OF GREEN

In the early Days and beyond a well-known fact did emerge,
Across the face of the whale-fishing industry, an interesting surge,
That seafaring vessels took in hand many different nationalities,
In particular South Sea Islanders, Aboriginals, for vast abilities.

As far as abilities go it must be spoken clearly, not to bork,
That for one reason or other some are called to particular work,
This is not racist or an attack on colour of skin but a wonder,
For some men are more apt at certain work, never to meander.

The Davidsons did learn this with the Yuin people,
A pillar of their enterprise at Twofold Bay, Eden, a steeple,
An industry set to harness that gift of the ocean to barrel,
Of New South Whales whaling, from small vessel most able.

Where can we find the town of Eden, one to come and love,
Near high cliffs that reach for the sky, so pretty at Snug Cove,
Close to the saddle and thereabouts, upon the plateau, the ground,
Quite picturesque and serine, of industry, the town can be found.

Eden does muse, to peer down at its harbour and over the bay,
Where a magnificent blue attracts, the eye upon to lay,
And sandy beaches of honeycomb break the line,
The line between ocean and forest surrounds, two to define.

The lookout [Boyd tower on South Head] was badly damaged,
Never repaired, lightning in the 60's, its cursed, cruel passage,
But still put to good use for it could be seen across miles of ocean,
Served whalers well on occasion whilst upon waves of motion.

It was May of 1863 that George Davidson, of Eden was born,
This was his world, great pride and privilege to be worn,
Into the lap of one unmistakable scene, of which many were keen,
True semblance of a bay whaling station to be found, to be seen.

Two weatherboard homes found situated upon the bank,
Broad and strong, not limp or lank,
And near the bay an open shelter procured from wood,
A shelter waiting for whale blubber to be delivered as it should.

Beneath the shelter is where the brickwork of the try-works toil,
Large iron vats and large tanks for the storing of oil,
A windlass would see a whale carcass heaved with joy and hope,
To be hauled and deblubbered by way of a large rope.

The whaling station also consisted of long ramp,
Those iron vats just spoke with vast array of oil lamp,
Changed little for the entire time in operation,
This great opportunity, this small whaling station.

It was here they would haul the quantities of blubber into position,
Blubber from which to extract the oil from vast lesion,
9-inch strips of fat are ripped from the carcass beneath,
All that remains: a shell of red and pools of blood from death.

Hope for good quantity,
Mandatory quality,
Hope for many hours of work,
Work hard, never to shirk.

Even when George was crawling on knees and hand,
He had become familiar with the boat house, where it did stand,
Where the shelter of 15 x 40 feet secured the boats,
To venture upon rolling waves, developing industrial moats.

The boats are shallow, carry a handful, are 29 feet long,
Sturdy and ready for rowing over waves so boisterous and strong,
Prepared for launch at a moment's notice, awaiting call to action,
Sitting, vacant the crew to power them over turbulence of ocean.

His grandfather, Set upon his way, Alexander Walker Davidson,
A Presbyterian treating everyone fairly, no matter the season,
Including the indigenous crews, hired and paid with a full wage,
Never to speak poorly of them, no pretence, no false stage.

He built a home from the wreck of the Lawrence Frost,
Along with a boatshed and workshop at little cost,
And for purpose at extracting information on the ship above,
We must extravagate a little for the added dimension we love.

The Lawrence Frost was a 1523 tonne ship made of timber,
Did not last long in life so clearly not sturdy but too limber,
Built in 1854 and sinking in 1856 would you believe,
Such a short life the owner could only grieve.

Having been severely damaged during voyage to Australia,
In August of 1856 it did run ashore, solid ground, a qualia,
Seemingly carrying more tonnage than for which it was built,
We must wonder if the owner or captain did feel any guilt.

But of this story we must, to history turn,
At least a little of this we must learn,
The ship was a mile from shore,
The stopper to anchor seemingly tore.

It was having sail shortened, men putting to work, to rope,
With strong northerly wind and flood tide, they lost all hope,
The anchor let out 45 fathom of cable, had given way,
Then the second anchor, no strength to remain, no safely to stay.

To stay on ocean, upon the wave, the vessel would not behave,
No hope at all, of all her strength, she already gave,
Gave all hope to the churning of wave, wind, and ocean,
Dragged along with both anchors, floating, free of notion.

Soon grounded hard ashore,
Harsh breeze increasing all the more,
Now a heavy ocean amidst strong gale,
Pumps not good enough, no big enough pail.

Ocean breaking clean over vessel,
Toiled in wind like curtain tassel,
The hold both fore and aft under siege,
The encumbering waves, the ocean but their liege.

All gone but still remembered, not truly lost in storm and rain,
Soon raised and repaired, to be up and running, set out again,
And now heading south after having taken trip to port in north,
She ran aground upon a spit, Twofold Bay, for what it is worth.

Set upon again by strong gale,
Bitter sweet its life, it did fail,
Driven to bay bed, not risen again to serve,
On second sinking, shattered completely, it had lost all nerve.

Washing aground near future whaling station to be,
Born of this wreckage, a family true, to work with glee,
The Lawrence Frost was condemned for all time,
But its body was recycled, to recall amidst berhyme.

Near the Kiah Inlet so small, positioned on the Towamba River,
1.6 miles across from town of Eden, employment to deliver,
On extreme side of the bay, away from mainstream bustle of life,
Many men came to work, not to drink heavily nor cause strife.

Varieties of crew stationed at Twofold Bay at one time or another,
Including the Barclay, Rixon, and the Walker [all brother],
The Whelan, Power and Newland,
Many names here as you can see, all come to make a stand.

But of all the men and boats that were cast into the ocean,
In an effort to kill a whale, the great devouring, a great action,
It was the Davidsons that had secured the majority of assistance,
From the killers directly, neither afraid to close their distance.

For Orcinus disliked the explosive harpoons, the great noise,
The devilish weapon of some crews, employed without poise,
When hunting baleen, no mercy for the behemoth of biology,
The Davidsons held little interest for this modern technology.

This favouritism seemed to infuriate the other crews ever more,
To such a degree that more artillery came into play from store,
Which saw to it that the killers assisted the Davidsons only,
Their green boats identified as worthy: not corrupt, not phony.

The green was based on the traditional Scottish Davidson tartan,
Each the same colour, worn with pride, like the shield of a spartan,
Not to mention the silhouettes, faces, and characteristics,
Coming to know so well, their mannerisms, their basics.

Davidson, his small band of five boats, of the whole, each a tiller,
Securing an ally for all time, winning the assistance of the killer,
All others being ignored by the black and white Wolves of the Sea,
A great, tremendous fortune falling upon Davidson with glee.

Great favour to shine upon the Davidsons, to be bestowed,
For right whales were declining in number, they rarely showed,
In tune with the culmination of the hunt for the sperm whale,
A decline stemming from Tasmania from 1841, supply to fail.

Learning was a two-way street, of society a steeple,
Not just with Orcinus but also with people,
Indigenous crews offered Alexander advice, he taking notice,
Understand the Law of the Tongue and putting it into practise.

In payment for the aid in catching the baleen each trip,
Killers were permitted to sup on the tongue and lip,
Greatest morsel of all that was caught,
Great delicacies which the killers always sought.

And not long into the strategies, forever aided, never coerced,
Familiarity did spring into thought, patterns to memory a nurse,
For dorsal fin and body markings were rather unique,
And as time passed by, each killer identified, names to speak.

Bay whalers found individual killers identity easy to diagnose,
Names derived from the Yuin deceased, now to disclose,
Tom, Hooky, Humpy, Jackson, Charlie, Typee,
Stranger, Montague, Old Ben, Young Ben, Sharkey.

Jimmy, Brierly, Walker, Kinscher, Youngster,
Skinner, Big Jack, and Little Jack, Cooper,
But incorrect identity did occasionally occur via the dorsal tail,
Some names are placed in error, both for female and male.

Many others remain unspoken for there are too many to quote,
Around 50 killers amongst three pods, often hard to keep note,
Each pod, in some cases, again split into smaller,
Sub-pods of varied size, no records to enlighten us further.

It was truly amazing how the killers would cooperate,
Not just with each other, but the Davidsons first rate,
In a concert of manipulation, and well-tuned, to orchestrate,
Tendered manoeuvres, a military juggernaut, precision spate.

Pods would attend their assigned choir, aligned and tasked,
Going through its paces, happily doing as was asked,
One pod positioning itself out to ocean to prevent escape,
To drive a baleen in towards the coast, of life to rape.

Another would cut off any escape to North,
Of the whales migratory route for what it is worth,
The third would hone in, attack, harass the prey,
In some cases this could take almost all day.

But a day of light,
Did not sourly bite,
Far worse could this be in getting food to table,
If no aid from whalers was made available.

So pleasurable it was to be working well together,
So seldom met was this deliverance, good standing, good tether,
As offered by the skilful throwing, most stoutly, of harpoon,
And lance from the bay whalers, driving it home, never too soon.

The poor baleen had no way of escape, no way out,
Even unable to dive, so painful it was, even unable to shout,
Running short on energy, unable to move or break loose,
May as well consider, already, flukes to capstan and noose.

For killers would surround their prey, approach from all side,
As well as from below, forever to torment, to ride and ride,
To throw themselves upon the baleen's back, so soul breaking,
An attempt to smother its blowhole, restrict its breathing.

Each year the killer whales moved from their Antarctic station,
To the coast of East Australia, tempering a weather negation,
Following the deadly breeze of winter as it maintained approach,
The streamlined move of baleen, swimming, ready to poach.

The winter months, a move into waters much warmer,
Not considered common amongst all pods, quite dissimilar,
For many remained stationed where food was more stable,
But the killers of Twofold Bay learnt to self-aid where able.

Here they lay, just off the coast, not that easily found,
In wait for prey as they made for their breeding/feeding ground,
Rarely far from shore,
An easy kill, an easy score.

For the migratory routes of the baleen brought the great whales,
Along the coastline, as fodder upon sheep fields, hay in bales,
Past Leather Jacket Bay and where it lay,
and then on towards Eden, Twofold Bay.

It was at Leather Jacket that the killers sprung their ambush,
In an attack of several phases, ready to push and push,
The prowling killer, on the loose, searching for his food,
There he was, always hungry, always in that mood.

The sperm whale fed mainly on diet of octopus,
The dolphin upon fish without fuss as did the grampus,
But the black and white of their close relation,
Fed upon them and grampus, great souls of this watery nation.

Whale was their tender choice, lip and tongue, a meal, a snack,
But mostly the killer whale was after the humpback,
But lacked much interest in the fin whale and blue for the present,
Both faster in the water, too much energy in the catch hence spent.

Certainly too fast for the rowing power of the men of Eden,
Unless aided by a pull on the ropes, attached, a boat so laden,
An easier kill was much preferred over hard,
No risk in over doing it, forced to retard.

This was the pods way, their chosen path, higher food estimate,
Some pods chose to remain in a much colder climate,
A minority preferred the warmer,
But all chose to occupy large areas to wander.

With purpose written upon face of one region compared to next,
Common sense factors associated with each in context,
If a particular fish is unavailable, cycle-of-life getting the better,
Then reason there is for diet or scenery change, no need to fetter.

For preference is always given to survival,
In particular to the young, being more temperamental,
So it was here that the killers had congregated,
Extremely fast to react and executed, their time well slated.

Watching as the identities of those beneath, their dorsal glide,
Effortlessly through the water, to unceasing pressures they abide,
Higher up, Tom with his mark and Hooky with his,
Distinguishing well, one from the other, hard to miss.

The pod makes its way to the grounds to feed,
Their home for the winter months ahead, to fill their need,
The matriarch has made her choice,
Given command, raised her voice.

Initially the pods are split, one a mile out from coast,
Another at two miles, and a third at three, at most,
Set upon an angle in order to channel their prey,
Towards the shore, a path of upheaval to lay.

And so a baleen is seen,
Not at all a smear or lean,
Not strange, a pregnant whale,
By herself, unaided, no male.

It is now, we see them dispatch two of their own,
Towards Twofold Bay where to them, unbeknown,
A lookout is positioned at Boyd tower on South Head,
Awaiting sign from the killer whale, awaiting sign to be read.

Here the crews of Davidson's boats will soon launch,
There so waiting with glee, mercilessly staunch,
When, soon to unveil, a cow and unborn calf to make appearance,
Heading northward and into the trap of pure nuisance.

On seeing in moonlight the spurts of a whale in due course,
The lookout at Boyd Tower would take to his horse,
Ride at a great pace the 2.5 miles to the Kiah Inlet,
Only to find that Tom's call had already been met.

Tom the killer, the best of the Orcinus, in more cases than not,
Swam to the mouth of the River, the best delivery spot,
Where the Davidsons were housed in two isolated buildings,
So constructed for life and leisure, their pleasure and feelings.

From within the bay Tom commenced upon his calling alert,
Calling the men ashore to act, with harpoon and lance, the expert,
Flop-tailing until the whalers made their way into the water,
Waters of the bay, aboard boats, to awaiting escort and slaughter.

Yes, flop-tailing, for the Davidsons alone, dropping hint, a clue,
Such visitation seen nowhere else upon the globe, this is true,
Tom and Hooky, seemingly acting as a sub-pod now detached,
Lead boats out to weary and tired baleen, for it to be dispatched.

The glowing bioluminescent trail they followed, this crew,
The stark morning light aided by moon, little light it threw,
It was to become fate, therefore, that Tom would become,
The most recognisable of all the killers, and sight most welcome.

Tom's regular contact with the men saw to it quite plainly,
That their trusting relationship did grow astoundingly,
Regardless of his sometimes annoying and playful nature,
Their working together was somewhat of a national feature.

The harpoon is thrown hard and it sticks fast,
HOORAH! bellows out for all to hear to the last,
For the whale has been stuck well, the bite does well adhere,
The unborn calf moving inside her now never to appear.

The mother fears for her young,
Holes within her, much blood sprung,
The baleen's presence of mind now clear to the killers,
And the killers like what they register, the stoutest millers.

And now the fear grows ever strong within the humpback,
It is her own undoing, courage she does now lack,
STERN ALL! then becomes clear and the boat is dragged,
All oars pulled in unison with great strength, cow almost bagged.

Oars are pulled back in order to help slow the leviathan,
It is part and parcel of the courage and plan,
The cow then tries to escape from the threat, an attempt to purge,
The whale turns abruptly and water begins to abruptly surge.

One of the boats is bobbing about upon the waves of the ocean,
And the turbulence of the fight is easy to see in its motion,
The boat is pointed at both ends, built for the stresses of the fight,
Built for momentum forward and aft, not in order to take flight.

Made of good cedar and built to last,
To ride out the ocean waves so vast,
But few can handle the thrashing of flukes now no longer mute,
The thrashing of a whale gone mad, it is in a wild dispute.

With the misfortune of a capsized boat, men will shout out,
The killers would assist, happily, freely, to give tout,
Tom now with the charged duty of ensuring their safety was keen,
Swimming around the boat's crew, protecting, it has to be seen.

Great assistance here in the commotion of the fight,
Battle against the whale, using fluke, no teeth to bite,
Men would struggle to stay afloat in rough ocean or seas,
Having pulled out of Twofold Bay, their desire to please.

Tom was truly a member of the family,
A friendship so strange but trusted heavily,
Such damage to boats was seen often,
But to the men's spirit it does never soften.

Tom lifted all of their spirit,
Had to be gifted with great merit,
And now the baleen continues with last effort to survive,
Now last, huge effort, for her and unborn to stay alive.

But the attackers concerted efforts won out,
Much pleasure in victory to shout,
Their maintenance of boats kept in-house,
Tended to like wife, like spouse.

Boats made to last, Alexander's son, John, helping with carpentry,
No easy skill, not to purchase from shop and place in pantry,
With their combined skill, and boats so sturdily built,
A great victory with Orcinus, towering high, not so easily tilt.

THE HUNT

George Davidson in 1877, 14 years of age, soon to take stage,
Upon his own whaling journey, ready to turn the page,
By picking up the struggle against the ocean, a fight to ever last,
And sperm whaling was considered by many as a thing of the past.

The whaling industry in general was brutal,
Had proved, for the sperm whale, to be fatal,
Slaughtered to near extinction,
An arbitrary stemming of life and eviction.

George wasn't tall in stature but was to become respected,
Amongst his peers and others far away seemingly celebrated,
For many, many reasons, to be toasted as a man, most remarkable,
To be placed within the annals of history, most able, most stable.

But for now we see a boy turning into a man of renown,
Mature and serious, and occasionally, as with all men, a clown,
His strengths were both hard and easy to see,
All he could do was dream of what was soon to be his reality.

He had a spring in his step, one to procure a smile and a stare,
Walked with arms swinging as though without a care,
Confident but certainly never cocky or juvenile,
Being more than he was; no, no, an utter denial.

He bore a distinctive arch upon his nose,
His eyes were a clear blue, tranquil, full of repose,
Most remarkable and seemingly hypnotising,
Though in a friendly way, to some were astonishing.

He wished to be a whaler,
Like his father, whale hauler,
And his wish was about to become true,
Right, humpback, and blue.

He watched from upon a hill, steadily firm and well perched,
As the men battled against a leviathan of the ocean as it lurched,
Gaining ground on whale, most remarkable, something to learn,
George, utterly astounded, to a great degree, never to spurn.

My God! how the killers felt the prolonged urge to feed,
This overwhelming encouragement and requirement, or need,
Not just food but to lay visit upon Twofold Bay,
Every year, one after the next, upon these quarters to lay.

Not missing a single season,
Not for any known reason,
They always came, to this place they returned,
Like a gathering of children, compulsion within them burned.

As though drawn to their place of birth,
A place keenly sought, this heaven on Earth,
But even with their exceptional hearing, within their surrounds,
It came to pass, occasional feed was missed within their grounds.

But were they missed or is that an incorrect view,
For man has little idea of their mannerisms, no real clue,
For more to the point the Orcinus is making a decision,
On which whale to attack, being more precise in their precision.

Scenarios had to be measured and food secured,
Always a preference on which prey should be lured,
From mans' perspective the situation was visibly shallow,
For it was they who failed in seeing source, advantage and tallow.

The Davidson's would hit the surface of the water to alert,
Orca to presence of humpback, though Orcinus was the expert,
Of their current position and need for support on the spot,
Killers turning in unison, either accept the ultimatum or not.

For it would save them much time in bringing down a whale,
Even if less worthy, much easier sport to wrap as in bale,
With the aid of men in boats, their harpoon and lance,
Regardless of their strategic position at a glance.

Tom could see, feel and hear,
The other killers around him, so near,
Those of the pod in which he did belong,
The pod commanded by Humpy, powerful and strong.

Humpy commanded over the pod with extreme precision,
Courtesy and steadfast will to procure good decision,
Leading by example and displaying a great understanding,
Of those within her pod and of the meal they were landing.

But before the formalities of the hunt could take place,
They were to be joined once more by Stranger as she made pace,
The two pods to join in the hunt as one,
Ceremony to prelude, from matriarch upon throne.

A ceremony that occurred from time to time, a must,
When a number of pods, of related killers, did readjust,
Joined back together after a degree of absence,
Having gone their separate ways in forage, now in their presence.

The two pods were lined abreast, opposite each other,
Facing off, preparing to be joined again as though lost lover,
Slowly but surely both groups do approach,
Drawing closer, closing the gap, no rehearsal, no coach.

They were now at 65 feet apart when they came to a halt,
Sounding delicately their calls, to habituate, secure by bolt,
Looking upon one another over the space between,
Seeing all, hearing all, temperate in pleasure, tapered clean.

After half a minute of ceremonial action,
Swimming together, again strong faction,
Submerged and surfaced shortly after, mingling again,
They were now ready for the hunt, unable to refrain.

Now the pods of strengthened unity make their move,
Towards Eden and Twofold Bay, in the groove,
For they can hear the movement of the whale,
Soon to find themselves in the fight, hard on tail.

The baleen, will however, put up a grand resistance,
Stubborn and worthy, the only victory, pure persistence,
From time to time the killers of the pod would vacate,
Vacate from watery surrounds to pressure and berate.

What do we mean by vacate and berate, what is this tale?
They leap from water, propel themselves upon back of whale,
To cover its blowhole, prevent it breathing, for it to drown,
Forcing the beast to suffocate, meal secured, life put down.

The whale would usually try to then dive, to avoid all grief,
But its efforts to do so would be thwarted by killers beneath,
Then another animal suddenly shoots itself out of the water,
In order to block the blowhole, its life now the shorter.

A gasp for air in the build-up of fear is denied,
For pregnant humpback, ample air supply is no longer supplied,
The humpback is heavily flanked,
Life expectancy not highly ranked.

Some orca head to the front, slow the escape, aid with the capture,
A concerted effort by all, a lengthy battle to butcher, their nature,
None will go without a meal, the youngest being fed first,
Hunger for blubber, for blood, that thirst for the win the worst.

The stress within the humpback mounts but doesn't peak,
It just keeps on growing, smell of fear to leak,
Thoughts falling upon the unborn calf that she carries within,
Carried for 11 months, two weeks, on verge of birth and grin.

She had departed, some time ago, the waters of the Antarctic,
Made for traditional breeding grounds, to find something tragic,
It is so obvious to this humpback, crying for condolement,
That there will be no solace from the predicament.

The humpback's concern now was for the safety of her unborn,
Nothing but cloak of terror to now, until death, be worn,
Her song-like choruses soon to be none, gone such purity,
And the birthing of calf never to be that joyous reality.

A killer made another strike upon her, being now so frail,
Her 39 foot length from head to fluke, the powerful tail,
Another chunk of blubber being taken from her side,
The pain searing, shooting through body, nowhere to hide.

What had she done to deserve such torment before death,
Was her unborn already dead, no longer to inhale that first breath?
She shook the thought from her mind, complete and utter denial,
To seek the only option open... complete and utter survival.

She wished to live, be free, to feed again, satisfaction to feel,
Her diet of capelin, herring, mackerel, and sand lance [sand eel],
To swim with mouth open, baleen plates delivering her meal,
To take as needed, plenty for all, no such thing as to steal.

Never to feel fish against 380 baleen plates as they stack,
The comb-like plates covered in a series of bristles, olive-black,
To feel the warmth of a full stomach; no, never more to know,
If she didn't fight now there would be no food, no tomorrow.

At the present all she could see was death as it teased,
Regardless of this a great surge of power within released,
Now fighting most heroically: her life, to self, now appealed,
Gone were all negative thought, her fate shall not be sealed.

And it is now that the bay whalers appear,
To aid in the killing of the humpback so near,
Providing assistance, and vice-versa, to the pods,
Orcinus in agreement, spy-hopping with nods.

Neither was disappointed with this alliance,
Quick in their decision and action, shared reliance,
Despite the killers being near exhausted,
Much more delivery of hatred must be sported.

The harpooner exchanges places with the headsman real fast,
As quickly as possible can be in small boat on ocean so vast,
The headsman positioned himself and readied himself with lance,
For the killing to continue, many hours of labour seen at a glance.

The cold of the night to be endured, the thirst: and the rapture,
The torn muscles and sore throat endured in effort to capture,
And with the concerted efforts of gigantic proportion,
The activity became hectic, of time they had no notion.

Tom would quite often be seen to jostle with the rope,
Already fastened to a harpoon, gifting men much hope,
Tom enjoying himself more than ever before,
A comical occurrence and sight to see for ever more.

Hanging onto the harpoon line for up to 30 minutes he did,
Being dragged by the force of the humpback, for survival it bid,
Swimming through surging ocean which grew and then subsided,
Tom being dragged along like a dead weight, effortlessly glided.

Tom was being pulled upon the surface of the ocean with glee,
He did this by biting upon the rope, in his mouth, all could see,
Or simply placing the rope beneath one of his flippers so strong,
Tom, a mature animal or not, in this action saw no wrong.

The battle continues well into the night,
Lances thrown with great effort, during the fight,
To be placed between the ribs of the whale not easily found,
To penetrate deep and cause that inflicting, deadly wound.

An incorrect placement of lance would see the effort wasted,
For little damage may be done, no victory to be tasted,
Or the lance might simply fall out and sink to the ocean floor,
Equipment lost forever, never retrieved, employed never more.

The moon then showed itself, and with sudden realisation,
A great commotion and vision, a great sensation,
Men stand, cheer, blood now rushing from blowhole most clear,
A sign that the kill, that victory, was so very near.

With this the whale suddenly commences with its death flurry,
Death now certain, vision blurring, no longer any need to worry,
The end is nigh, the humpback has no doubt,
With spraying of blood from blowhole, last of life gives sprout.

And the joy of the win is exuberating,
This to say the least, worthy of celebrating,
The men commence about the task of attaching buoy and anchor,
To secure the kill, an action adhered to, always a factor.

The Orcinus move in for their prize of the fight,
Forcing the humpback's mouth open, to tear and to bite,
Forcing their way into where the tongue sits ready,
Body of whale now unmoving, limp and most steady.

Calves are fed first and then those that remain most gratefully,
None taking more than they should; all is shared equally,
The tongue to soon be devoured completely, hunger gone, beaten,
Lips soon fed upon, appetising, very little left, almost all is eaten.

By the time the first of the killers has fed on this bulky shape,
Others further out to ocean, protecting flanks, preventing escape,
Move in and take what is for them and nothing more,
Having done their duty, keeping the whale close to shore.

The pods depart and leave all alone,
Now for the men to strip to the bone,
But not just yet, later the blubber can be dispatched,
At present they ensure the anchor is well attached.

The crew now returns home, to rest from work, not fun,
To claim the carcass later on, amidst light from sun,
When the gases of putrefaction goes to work upon this prize,
Around 24 hours after the sinking with anchor, it will rise.

And the killers below, both adult and nippers,
Finish feeding upon head, flukes and flippers,
The whale on ocean floor away from swelling and turbulence,
To be exhumed when gases provide that essential deliverance.

Yes; that's what George saw, without a mistake,
Looking over the bay, the scene unfold and end, in mind to bake,
Many more dreams by day of what he saw to his front,
One day, he, ready upon boat, hard work delivered with a grunt.

THE AGREEMENT

Two boats spearheaded towards the open water, easy to see,
Heading towards the entrance of the bay, wind to lee,
Competing for the prize that they had to have,
For oil from whale, for families sustenance, for poorer to stave.

The years did not favour too many partnerships competing,
Not for the same, right, humpback fin or blue, to be stripping,
Stripping blubber from carcass as turbulent times bided,
And the arduous competition at Eden slowly subsided.

The Davidson's vision to be the only whalers of the bay,
To grow and outlast, come of fruition, before them to lay,
But for present each boat surged forward, shoulders rolling,
Oars in hands, five oars apiece, amidst much friendly berating.

But the harpooner of Davidson's crew was already of mind,
To spring from position, desertion with pride,
To take his post with his thigh placed in the concave of his thwart,
To ready with a harpoon in hand, just as he was taught.

There was a great spout of water erupting from the surface,
A right whale had most temporarily shown a face of grimace,
Water foaming for an instant and the surface being disrupted,
By the gigantic lifting of flukes, ever dangerous, never disputed.

The tail then disappearing back into the ocean, dark as death,
Diving once more after having replenished its resourceful breath,
Seconds later the unmistakable dorsal of Tom was there,
Having erupted from the water, for his magnificence to be bear.

His entire body lifted out and seemed to freeze,
For just a second, in mid-air, amidst the strong breeze,
It was like a holy man witnessing a true vision afore,
A religious treat, a great specimen, there to adore.

Big Jack was alongside Tom and now headed to his port,
Endeavouring to cut off the right whale's dive, a last resort,
For no good it would do in the harbour of Twofold Bay,
For it was not that deep, the right had no chance this day.

But Big Jack was also aware of a possible retreat to be gained,
From beneath the waves where harpoon and lances now refrained,
Of those upon the boat, they could not see nor reach,
Not for love of money, seated here or from position on beach.

George could be seen, his silhouette upon a hill,
Overlooking the cliff where he stood, feeling the thrill,
Watching as the two crews thrashing at the ocean, sweated it out,
With all their strength, giving commands, many orders to shout.

They were trying with all their power to be the first,
Within distance of the whale, to quench their thirst,
To hurtle a harpoon against that great mass all knew,
The whale that had temporarily disappeared from view.

It was George's dad, John Davidson, his jet-black beard,
Much hair on face, his commands direct and calmly steered,
It was his boat against another, a boat manned by Bob Love,
Competition between each too fierce: two hands, one glove.

The screwed up looks upon their faces told the story,
And their every muscle tore at the oars for glory,
This was the fight of champions, the fight for 'fast fish',
The rule, securing rights to whale, each could only pray and wish.

The ocean was choppy and breeze strong, no real restriction,
The freshness doing little to upset the situation,
But the work was still hard enough,
You had to be extremely tough.

And as the oars continued to beat at the ocean,
From within the security of the row-locks of little friction,
Only time to stroke and stroke, to get ahead,
To pierce the body of whale with iron needle and rope for thread.

Davidson was making more ground than Love,
That extra asserted effort and seemingly praised from high above,
John looked behind him to realise the headway they had gained,
Seeing his men give no quarter, from hard work, never refrained.

He could see the sun as it set behind the bulk of Mount Imlay,
The sun quitting its quarters having given up its stay,
And a strong feeling of wholeness penetrated his soul,
His home, gentle surf plunging within the bay, this watery bowl.

It was home, upon the rocks at the foot of high cliff,
Where the swells of undulating ocean moved, constant riff,
The gentle waves caressing, music to ear so grand,
Long waves of white breaking upon the sand.

Long waves of white water broke along Whale Spit,
An elongated portion of beach, close to land was knit,
Debris of the Lawrence Frost still sticking up here and there,
Two white cottages glancing down as though to stare.

And the fight beneath the waves continued unabated,
To prevent the right from escaping to ocean, not related,
The right whale different in many ways and aspect,
Nothing here to truly decipher nor inspect.

The right whale was to endeavour,
To attempt the impossible, nothing in favour,
For even if he escaped to ocean and open water,
The other pods of killers were ready to slaughter.

Tom then abandoned his manoeuvre and raced to the surface,
The whale changing direction, tempers burning like furnace,
Both Big Jack and Humpy made the effort now to impede,
To act deliberately and with great speed.

Tom broke the surface and half turned,
Crashing down upon his flank, surface of ocean churned,
Turning to face the crew of the green boat,
He looked upon them momentarily as though to gloat.

He was trying to gain their attention, the headsman, John,
John saw then what was to play before his eyes, before gone,
He had seen Tom do this before but could not clarify,
What it was that was passing between them, but do not deny.

Tom seemed to look at him directly in the eyes,
Communicating his dire need, no hidden ties,
Tom then turned into the choppy waves and sped off, to tear,
Leading boat to whale's next surface, he requiring a breath of air.

Tom was showing them the way,
John saw all the cards fall into place, there to lay,
The connection between Tom's antics of the past,
The commotion now performed, every move, down to the last.

They were being escorted, pure and simple, from the front,
Shown the way as any usher would do, this was not a stunt,
Tom wished nothing more than to assist as best he could,
In the demise of the right whale, together, as they should.

Tom could easily see the dark flesh of Sam, he stood out,
He knew then that the harpoon would fly with encouraging shout,
For Sam placed his oar, opposite the thole-pins, into socket,
Harpoon then picked up, position sought, to throw like rocket.

He barely had time to place the weapon upon his right shoulder,
A grasp taken upon the shaft of iron, strong grasp of the holder,
The whale then surfaced briefly as Tom veered to the right,
Between the killer and the crew, and it was a beautiful sight.

Sam hurtled the harpoon forward and down, no mere morsel,
Into the fatty layer and penetrating deep beneath the dorsal,
The whale lunged forward with a suddenness expected,
Much water splashing over the crew but work never neglected.

They pulled back on the oars in tune, not too late, not too soon,
The manila rope holding tight, most secure to the harpoon,
The line was tight but able to run freely through the loggerhead,
Running smoothly, unrestricted, through eye of needle so thread.

All oars were now quickly peaked for good reason,
Pulled from the water in hurried unison,
Secured into position and out of harm's way,
Well clear of the surface of the ocean, there to stay.

The ocean could snap an oar instantly,
Like a toothpick and quite neatly,
To deliver against body a great wretchedness lacking negation,
Against flesh and bone, crippling crew beyond expectation.

The right whale thrashed mightily, dived, feeling stress,
The boat surging forward under great duress,
John manipulating the sweep in a manner of grasp and control,
Watching the right, the surge of the ocean, it beginning to take toll.

As carefully as one could he considered all possibility,
Watching for when the whale may turn quite unexpectedly,
For that dreaded moment when the whale might turn,
Capsize the boat with thundering power, he could never spurn.

Tom looked back again, seeing the harpoon stuck fast,
Considered for a brief moment the other crew, no prize for last,
Bob Love continued, hoping for harpoon to shudder and shake,
That the right whale might surface, for the hook's hold to break.

John stood, Sam and he to exchange position right now,
Sam taking up the sweep and John moving to the bow,
The commencement of the right whale's milling,
To ready the lances for the actual killing.

Tom reacted, dove beneath, to continue with his achievement,
Where Humpy and Big Jack commenced with their harassment,
No prolonged diving nor heading out to ocean permitted,
To be turned to the surface, movement to be restricted.

They surged out of the water and upon the whale's back,
Trying with all their might to cover the blowhole, their attack,
Breathing now harder to perform, no longer available,
To hurry the arrival of death, to draw good air, no longer able.

158

The first lance was then expertly thrown, a throw to last,
It penetrating deep, between the ribs, sticking fast,
exactly where it was aimed as good as any could throw,
The right whale moving in circles, absurdly nowhere to go.

Taking the boat and its crew with him, he swam wildly,
John throwing another lance which also hit its mark most tidily,
And within minutes a spout of red erupted from the blowhole,
A short dive and the whale was dead, Orcinus to take their toll.

John saw, as the others did, the orca move fast and without fail,
They in turn quick to set buoy and anchor to whale,
To set it adrift, to sink to the sandy floor,
Where killers could have their fill of lips and more.

Gases would see the whale afloat in a day or two,
To then be collected for deblubbering, a task they knew,
And so both Orcinus and men were pleased,
Each getting the gift they wished, their needs appeased.

The call was made to pod out to ocean, their cordon, their shield,
They came thundering in for their part of the yield,
Where each and every one of them would get their share,
None more than another, all equal, always fair.

There was more to come in the following days and many a week,
With or without the help of the Davidson's, a season yet to peak,
Though the help was a benefit to the killers, strategically rated,
For their energy reserves would then not be so depleted.

Stranger watched over the feeding, upon it she would glare,
Ensuring that none took more than their fair share,
But greed wasn't something in a killer to easily find,
Wasn't even a contemplation of mind.

These mammals were family, they were one and the same,
Of the same pod, of the same line, minds of similar frame,
They owed one another more than any man could realise,
For each one acted freely and willingly, each seemingly wise.

Sure, they were each an individual, one and all,
But never alone, part of a team, a pyramid so tall,
Their pod: their religion, true faith and miracle,
Everything to them, from base to pinnacle.

Humpy was looked upon as a strong and powerful pod leader,
Stranger knew her well, felt attached, by measure a pilaster,
She also looked effectively at both Tom and Hooky,
Of Hooky we have not spoken, hauntingly beautiful, not spooky.

Hooky was Stranger's second son,
Of his father, of information, I have none,
For there is little to say of this thing,
Of a mid-Antarctic ocean fling.

Animals may act as much for self, as they do for the group,
For pod: in this we should not deeply delve [archaic] stoop,
For to search for ever and a day, needle in stack of hay,
We may find it hard to understand customs as they lay.

But to employ a stranger for her need,
Not for selfishness or for greed,
Possibly still an animal instinct and the need to feed,
We shall not speak of whether from her own pod she did breed.

To uphold her splendidness,
To maintain her vision of boldness,
To assume her great effectiveness,
To always, in her, behold trustworthiness.

Hooky was male, as per Tom, and only a little younger,
Born of a father whom shall always remain a stranger,
And Stranger preferred it this way,
Fathers of whom would have no future sway.

Her faction is currently strong in number,
But split into pods and segregated by much water,
They saw little of one another when hunting,
They all knew they were of the same bunting.

Favourites: necessary to ensure longevity, and Stranger did have,
Kept them close, under sway, moving forward, a way to pave,
Typee, Humpy, Cooper, Big Ben, Tom, Hooky and Big Jack,
All loved, all grand and worthy, through seasons as they stack.

Each of them knew the men aboard the boats of green,
All capable of working with them, all very keen,
But for now they swam 1.9 miles south for Leather Jacket Bay,
Thirty members strong, for a short rest, for a short stay.

THE MINKE

George's task, at the beginning of his long and rewarding career,
Rewarded by its love, equation of money did not appear,
Was to assist his Uncle Jim upon the lookout,
One of square shape and footing, the ocean all about.

Of where do we speak? Well it is close,
Leased by his father, and good advantage rose,
All the land leased in fact, from South Head to Towamba River,
Great advantage over competitor, worth far more than a stiver.

Not only did he have the best post,
From which to look for whale-sign the most,
But the killers for farming that prized casket of oil from blubber,
Whale worth its weight in gold, if wood, a vast source of lumber.

It is Boyd Tower of which we speak, a very fitting building,
Damaged by storm many years before, to eye, pleasant, appealing,
It offered a scene, from south to north, of strategic importance,
Allowing the Davidsons to launch boats first, a great assurance.

And where whale-sign was missed, obscured, nothing to assist,
If some dark cloak, shrouding mist, or did unexplainably desist,
There was the comfort in knowing that Tom would appear,
Flop-tailing to his heart's content, to lead on, to cleverly steer.

When whale-sign of any description did speak out,
There was only one action to take amid shout,
Jim would find himself straddled upon his horse,
Racing home near Kiah, the beast beneath knowing the course.

Near approach of home he did raise the alarm,
Alerting all of the approaching whale, of which to harm,
To massacre and farm, to beach and snare, to harness and work,
This is how it played, not easy, not like taking baby from stork.

He sped on to raise the alarm of approaching foe,
The sound of the hooves most penetrating: hear it, you know,
The still of the night failing to masquerade,
Not mistaking the sound, this was no charade.

This was the still of the night,
A messenger to pass on great delight,
News which was to be acted upon, without a doubt,
Message received before Jim could dismount, men running about.

Three boats made the water and in good time,
To make their way across the smooth surface so sublime,
Water reflecting the star amidst clear skies high above,
Moving out towards the mouth of the bay they did all love.

And here we see that Jim may have misinterpreted a sign,
Nothing immediately seen, nothing on sight to align,
So an early morning patrol commenced from here,
To search for whale-sign, to all hope, hold it dear.

They could only hope their efforts would be rewarded,
By quick find, quick catch, time on water not retarded,
Continuing to work the oars they moved ever on, into the night,
Towards the shelter at South Head, on occasion a delightful sight.

A large rock, reasonably easy to see by day, red in colour,
A wharf [so to speak] close to cave of occasional favour,
A cave here of substantial size and cover, a tether,
Great place to temporarily reside during inclement weather.

The crews deposited a few stores here,
An opportunity now to replenish, seldom did opportunity peer,
A place of rough comfort in time of great need,
Not a place to willingly submit, but get away from with speed.

They continued to stroke the ocean and moved out of the head,
And here they could see spouts from orca most easily read,
Coming up from Leather Jacket Bay,
The sun commencing its reveal, light transcending upon the grey.

The orca seemed relaxed and complacent,
Neither thrashing about, flop-tailing, or making a statement,
And further behind those up front,
Another spout of water, ready for the hunt.

The waterspout jettison from within,
The force pushing with it much water to air, to thin,
Misty vapours spouting about the ocean now calm, not wild,
Greeting the morning, so brilliant and mild.

They were at work, listening intently,
Upon the sounds and movement of the ocean most discreetly,
Endeavouring to catch that ever elusive signal,
Of a whale within distance most reasonable.

The pods were positioned at varying intervals and in good fashion,
Three pods not far from coast, ears awaiting for that percussion,
Combined they acted as a barrier, a curtain,
Deciphering sounds and movement, soon to be, most certain.

And if a whale were to be moving too far out at ocean,
The killers would decide if whether or not to give compassion,
Or draw and force the whale towards the harpoon and lance,
For the men on green boats to have their chance.

It was a reality of the varied situations,
Of the killers' abilities and their reactions,
Whether or not the energy spent was worth the chase,
Each scenario must be measured from case to case.

Tom had seen the patrol of three boats and summed up the action,
Knew that the men were working with ocean, in conjunction,
Searching about and waiting for sign,
Hoping for a good sized baleen most fine.

Patrolling, waiting the opportunity to strike,
Hoping for chance not to sour, but situation to like,
Was it in fact a sign that Jim had seen,
From Boyd Tower, his eye so eager, so keen.

Was it a dream, false hope delivered to eye,
Was it an error, misfortune he could not deny,
Was there something to occur real soon,
Was there to be hope in reflection of moon.

For the moon was rising,
Giving its gift, not surprising,
Not good for the baleen but aiding the men and orca alike,
Orcinus to encompass, employ their very bodies, to strike.

Tom now turned towards the others nice and slow,
Movement deliberate, before commencement of the show,
It was then that a signal was received,
From several miles out to ocean, clearly perceived.

A small whale was bypassing the mouth of Twofold Bay,
A minke whale with unborn calf, alone, a stray,
Though not enough to feed three, let alone a single pod,
Sufficient enough to aid in hunger and so given the nod.

The teeth of the upper jaw fit snugly into the lower,
Cogs of a steel wheel, with just as much power,
Their mouths closed but ready to rip and tear,
They now shifted into higher gear.

The killers' jaws opened and closed in quick succession,
Clapping their jaws together in mounting aggression,
To press the fear of the impending doom,
Deep within the minke's mind, a clear, unfortunate gloom.

The signal was their call to duty,
A call to move forward, to gain on their booty,
Unbeknown to the men in the boats, orca beneath ocean face,
Mammals racing towards the ocean, with speed and much grace.

To the minke, to pester and provoke,
To embrace most diligently with restricting yoke,
By all means open to them, never to refrain,
No sympathy, just yield, a little sustenance to gain.

The minke would be fairly easy to catch,
No real competition, no equal match,
Hardly worth even this small effort,
Barely enough to provide any comfort.

But the facts of the case were mounted as normal,
No source of food shrugged off as dreary or abysmal,
And the mink would not tax them too harshly,
Quick and easy, over with briskly.

The normal procedure for the killers of Eden,
To undertake when hunting a minke, orca embolden,
See it stranded in the shallows, an easy win, never to fail,
And then consume it of all that was on offer, head to tail.

Although the same size as Orcinus, the leviathan of Eden town,
Was unable to outrun orca, being out of its class, to be run down,
In particular where a large pack of hungry mouths are concerned,
Looking for a quick fix, no time to waste, they cannot be spurned.

The minke swam through the ocean, through wave, to slaughter,
The beak, pointed shape of his head, gliding through the water,
Twenty-nine feet in length and powering along at great speed,
But not quick enough to escape, not as fast, the desired need.

Flukes broad and concave along the notched rear,
Fins pointed at the tips, body streamlined, symmetry to steer,
It dove, arching tail stock high, flukes beneath much wave,
The commencement of a deep dive, attack to stave.

The minke was forced to surface, dive cut short,
Two killers calling an end to her effort, an effort to abort,
Subdued to further torment, no more days in life to chalk,
To tear chunks from her flank, no longer content to simply stalk.

All were so eager to feed, to finish, to kill her,
Not caring for the terror within which they stir,
The rush of red billowing out and merging with the ocean,
Large clouds expanding out, growing larger, an interaction.

Several sharks in the vicinity could hear the calling,
The dinner bell ringing, the Orcinus mauling,
but fear prevented them from approaching too close,
For even the Great White feared this gluttonous pose.

The minke was utterly surrounded,
May as well be immobile, grounded,
Bulge in stomach an unborn, undeniable,
Easily seen, unborn whale, fresh stock, reliable.

The minke was not scrawny by any measure,
But not enough to satisfy three pods, no great treasure,
Preference, of course, was for a much larger baleen,
But there was none about, nothing heard, nothing seen.

Fresh dolphins, porpoises and fish,
Were always a welcomed dish,
But larger morsel was always their wish,
Small portion simply retarded... eish.

The minke was a krill feeder,
Harmless and often alone, easy fodder,
Life to end, to the wind seemingly thrown,
Unborn in womb, life to be never known.

The minke was eaten, of it all,
Nothing to hold the tide, nothing to stall,
Not an ounce of flesh or fat to remain,
Nothing but upon ocean a red stain.

And the men could only shrug off the situation,
Nothing for them to harvest, a purely sad position,
Normal patrol duty resumed, along with emotional stability,
Silence restored to the ocean, now strangled by tranquillity.

THE UNFETTERED

George burst through the door and exclaimed for all to hear,
With such exhilarated enthusiasm that heads quickly did appear,
A message for the crews to man their particular boat,
Great excitement reverberating through his throat.

A great anxiousness fell over them all, so sheer, almost pain,
Heart throbs, pushing the coarse excitement through vein,
Excitement for that word, the word to greet at culmination,
Culmination of wit, to call 'RUSHO', that single congratulation.

Tom could be seen, flop-tailing in front of Kiah Inlet,
Sandbar spit separating it from the bay, already met,
The bar where the Lawrence Frost does rest,
Ghostly remains, a tombstone at its best.

So rapidly men threw themselves upon the thwarts, lacking grins,
Grabbing oars, thrusting them into water via the thole pins,
Safety jackets pushed aside and boots forced on by the few,
So little time to respond to the words that they loved, they knew.

The boats practically flew through the air of this bright day,
The afternoon air fresh with several clouds racing across the bay,
And all indication lead to it being a long night affair,
The sun more than likely to fall before killers, of meat, could tear.

Quick kill is required, now more than ever, the need to be clever,
If whale was not secured by nightfall the air would cause fever,
Blasted cold, hindrance worse than a storm, a wind-chill factor,
A chill so devilishly severe: could shave a man of calm like razor.

Tom, having seen the rush of men to boats in good essence,
Was assured by their fast action, soon to be in his presence,
Turned tail, his flukes thrashing at the surface with grace,
Gaining a little depth below the surface in good pace.

Tom soon picked up on the signals of pods and right whale,
Signals through water clear as a bell, ripe and not stale,
And he was still some distance from the fight as it was heard,
Thrashing of flippers and flukes, amidst calm ocean, deciphered.

Echolocation engulfed the area, ocean a conductor, better than air,
Penetrating all, and in any direction you cared to stare,
The picture being painted in strong transcendent, bright colour,
Echolocation, a sensitive sensory system, chords of many flavour.

It was ten times more accurate than the best sonar in submarines,
Echoes, short pulses of sound, not indicative of machines,
Pulses; echoes emitted via staccato styles, high-frequency sound,
Each lasting a few milliseconds, but some longer can be found.

Produced in the nasal passage and deeper,
Below the blow hole, each the keeper,
Directed to the front, passing through fatty tissue of forehead,
Which in turn acted as a lens, musical vocabulary, easily read.

He endeavoured to focus his sound, for it to be well directed,
Hearing and advising, all taken for granted,
Segments of the emitted sound refracted, clearly understood,
Sound returning through bony walls of lower jaw, as it would.

There is so, so much here,
So much to clarify, to appear,
Such as sound being transmitted along the jaws length,
To acoustic conduits, magnificent evolution amidst such strength.

From conduits to sensory organs, their middle ear, sound to gain,
One on either side of the skull near the base of the brain,
This was an ultrasound in effect a clear picture, a distinct function,
Pictures painted clear, scene formed, acted upon, instant reaction.

The returning sound, travelling at four times greater speed,
Than that through the air, as fast as they require and need,
Providing detailed analyses, much information of varied texture,
Size, shape, distance, and composition, all as one, or as mixture.

Tom concentrated upon the object of his desire,
To bombard it further, information to acquire,
To be precise, to expose clear weakness,
For attack and closure to be one of neatness.

And the three boats of Davidson's men had much style,
Pulled in unison at first, slightly askew but all in file,
Each beckoned by their headsman to be the first in range,
For harpoon and lance to be thrown, a kill to arrange.

Colourful language was filling the air,
But these were hard men, hard but fair,
Voices carried haphazardly, far and wide across the bay,
Observers from the banks hearing each word as it stray.

But those watching paid little heed to each, foul, uttered word,
Men spurring each other on, words employed instead of sword,
For this was just a part of the play, it was all part and parcel,
Water off a duck's back, for this was a battle in which to marvel.

And the voiced encouragement continued, not seeming to abate,
Compared to the symphony of choruses below, how did it relate?
Were the killers speaking of same tone,
Of this it will never be known.

Then appeared one of their competitors, it was like a grievance,
Oars striking the water with as much unrestrained jubilance,
A competitor having launched two boats, how deplorable,
But all was fair in love and war, nevertheless, feelings ropable.

Spray lifted from the bows as muscles taut,
Pressing for a little extra speed, gain that naut,
surmounting efforts of gigantean proportion,
Stress reflected on all faces, a contortion.

Their teeth were exposed to the world,
Grimaces painted on faces, their minds twirled,
Deep lines of controlled aggression,
Upon their faces was bore great expression.

This was a race for survival, for the promise of wages,
For promise of purse, the writing of historical pages,
For a little coin, for the security of their families,
For the appeasement of all, and all part of the formalities.

Each and every one that manned an oar put in a great effort,
Dwarfed all else, the headsman's no less, great lack of comfort,
Each and every man full of character, measured by agility,
Performing each task, controlling sweeps, all with great ability.

Maintaining good direction,
To hone and deliver that perfection,
Enormous amounts of instilled confidence,
Encouragement pouring from all pores, the way of deliverance.

This was all for the sake of 'fast fish',
Nothing else mattered but this, their true wish,
But was this a fair fight, with the pods on Davidson's side,
Could this be condoned, as upon gentle waves they ride.

The total number of killers unknown, with three pods further out,
A second whale further still, bypassing: to strike, to clout,
Regardless, the tactics for the hunt did remain the same,
No variation from usual procedure: this was survival, not a game.

Tom turned then, instinctively, a sprint from starting gate,
Hearing the oars on water, time for whale to meet his fate,
Time to begin the wrestle, time for torment and achievement,
Time to dig that grave, a cup of victory, to brim with contentment.

The right whale was slow, turned towards the mouth of the bay,
Towards the boats that drew nearer, minds of men clear as day,
Each passing second bringing terror and death all the closer,
Boats continuing to surge forward, neither wishing to be the loser.

The gap between all parties now closed at a tremendous rate,
Each drawn as though a magnet to the whale, the beast, the bait,
And then the right sounded, diving beneath the ocean ceiling,
Sending all into turmoil, feelings reeling.

But this was just a temporary stay,
For the killers acted fast, not allowing it to stray,
The leviathan forced to surface and remain in sight,
For harpooner to try for that hard and fast, steel bite.

A harpooner's kiss,
If it did not miss,
The securing of whale to boat,
Fingers around a man's throat.

And the whale dove again but for only a short time,
Again to surface but so hazardous, a coin spinning on dime,
For Whelan, the contender, had a boat where it did surface,
Uplift of whale and water seeing a Whelan boat slow its pace.

168

No pace to attain, none to pursue, uplifted by strength and might,
For they were momentarily assailed, upon the back of the right,
Not just a look of surprise, but also shock and terror,
Fell upon the faces of Whelan's men together.

Now riding for brief moment upon the back of this hulk,
Held high aloft upon the crest of their passions bulk,
The seal between water and air broke,
Oars no longer in the ocean, unable to stroke.

Oars magically lifted from the water,
Still full of fight this great monster,
And the men aboard considered jumping from their boat,
Each no longer having wish, nor heart, to gloat.

Jump from this peril and into another,
Frying pan to fire, flames you cannot smother,
But suddenly and with great relief, sanity returning,
The boat slid harmlessly back to water, slightly turning.

Tom took an instinctive second to peruse the situation above,
To spy upon surface, attain position of those he seemed to love,
The green boats of Davidson seen close to Whelan's: too close,
This was reality, close call, a conflagration, too large in dose.

He could see, of Davidson's boat, the harpooner stand ready,
Weapon of trade upon his shoulder, surprisingly quite steady,
Thigh braced against the thwart and ready with strength to fling,
With great accuracy his iron, to kiss, to secure 'fast fish', to sting.

It left his hand then and fell towards the right whale,
Insufficient power behind the throw, and now for short tale,
For the harpooner was called Pigeon, employed for his skill,
But the wages from Davidson's could not meet the bill.

For over time evidence had been accumulated,
Pigeon's skill had been assessed and well rated,
The harpooner was cowardly being employed by Whelan,
Drawn by promise of payment and wage, good word and reason.

And so the throw was set to task with lack in power,
To provide assistance, upon Whelan, this fortune a shower,
A shower of blessings, to steal from Davidson and the Orca,
For Whelan to keep for himself, to be the deliverer of slaughter.

It was the last throw that Pigeon would, for Davidson, ever make,
There was simply too much here at stake,
The loss of the whale meant his immediate termination,
Paid off by Whelan, Pigeon's loyalty found at another station.

But the task at hand was still rather hazardous from all the boat,
Whale harried by the killers, restrained as though by moat,
And then suddenly the jaw of John Davidon did drop in disbelief,
From a man in Whelan's second boat, Bedford, a shout most brief.

Bedford had tossed his harpoon most expertly,
Secured victory most assuredly,
Energy, precision, a testament to his ability,
The 'fast fish' tied up, a situation of gravity.

Why gravity?
Lack of amity,
Read further,
An Orca tether.

Whelan began with his lancing,
Unable to stop his periodic glancing,
Looking upon the green boats with smirk on face,
For the Davidsons and orca alike, a sheer disgrace.

The harpoon, yes, did stick fast,
Did not fall, it was there to last,
For the whale there was no escaping the trap,
For it, there would be only that eternal nap.

Regardless, however, of the dire situation,
The right performed a gigantean persuasion,
It sprang to entrance of the bay, an attempt made for open water,
To embrace the wide-open space, be free of harpoon, of slaughter.

Pulling the boat, the men along for the short ride,
Upon the surface it did seemingly glide,
Endeavouring to escape the manila rope,
To try and achieve escape, to regain that lost hope.

John saw the dilemma and fell upon the only conclusion,
The battle had been lost due to an obscured conviction,
The unsteady hand, slow reaction time, of one of his own,
Pigeon, soon to be a figure on the unemployment line in town.

Davidson and crew could not believe what their eyes reflected,
The right whale giving up its fight for life, sooner than expected,
Pelted well by the two boats that were in good position,
One on either side, throwing lance after lance without question.

If not for the help provided by the killers, upon huge beast,
Then the kill would have been enduring, to say the least,
And now, in the cold victory that had been won, without stop,
Whelan was towing the carcass in towards his workshop.

Close enough to tow, no need to sink and await the bloat,
Just tow the dead whale in by power of oar, by power of boat,
And as they tugged on their oars the killers came for their reward,
To sup on lips and tongue, their just gift, the one men could afford.

Whelan's men would have none of this, no agreement bestowed,
Picked up tools-of-the-trade, tools on board having been stowed,
Their spades, square in shape and very sharp, very sharp indeed,
Those used in deblubbering, now served another desire and need.

They were striking at the killers, shear lack of remorse,
Keeping them at bay, provoking reaction, being coarse,
Holding back their attempts to take what was theirs,
Denying them food to survive amidst silent but snarly glares.

Tom surfaced and looked the men in the eyes,
Upon each and every one, for they, he did despise,
He took note of the boats, to remember them well,
Of this great rudeness, to the others he would tell.

Davidson's boats were green,
To help them the Orcinus were keen,
Combined effort to reward both in equal measure,
But Whelan: never again would he receive his treasure.

To always be remembered, never forgotten,
To the core they were very rotten,
Never again to be provided opportunity,
Endeavour to always obscure their ability.

No longer would they provide,
Unequivocal assistance, an easy ride,
Not as much as a wink,
No recognition, not even a blink.

THE FIGHT

The sun had not even commenced to light the day,
When two of the killers came flop-tailing upon the bay,
Throwing themselves out of ocean, to crash upon rolling wave,
The wind shallow but so cold, which hard work could stave.

Weather was an important factor within this industry learned,
In particular where the crews were concerned,
A hard south-west wind was cold,
The effect seeing the ocean become rather bold.

Choppy in the concave and here to stay,
Within reach and up to the mouth of Twofold bay,
For further out to ocean the waves did swell,
Though not enough to ring an alarm bell.

Rough by the layman's point of view,
The normalcy would not know what to do,
Hands of sweet work, not rough,
Would find it too arduous and extremely tough.

Swells could become worse,
Ever searching for that rancid curse,
Or settle,
To be gentle.

But for that present it was not that strange,
Within tolerances, within that range,
For the present, however, all was fair,
RUSHO so shouted, to boats from lair.

The chase to commence, blubber soon to be won,
George 14, full of vigour, extremely keen, finding it fun,
As all others, their jackets were thrown upon their bulk,
George was ready, well stoked, to work hard, never to skulk.

Scrambling out from the bunkhouse door,
Time of day and tiredness they were to ignore,
Running as fast as legs could carry them to their work,
Like greyhounds unleashed from pen, to whale which lurk.

The whale had entered the bay,
In search of fish, to do as he may,
To steal the solace, to enjoy his stay,
All alone and easy pickings, easy prey.

Suddenly it could be heard there in the night,
Some men slightly astounded: no, no, not feeling fright,
Excitement it was they felt within,
It was a whale, no false alarm, faces lighting up with broad grin.

Somewhere just inside the mouth of the bay, no longer at frolic,
Where many killers were present, organising tactics with logic,
To attempt to coral this beast with all their might,
To keep the whale from heading out to ocean this night.

It was a humpback, not in a good position,
Though plump and blubberous, in good condition,
Forced to remain within the confines of bay,
Between rock and hard place, how gloomy, how grey.

The killers could taste the tongue as they did move,
Reared and ready, in mood for killing, in the groove,
Adversely the headsman was considering his reward,
The tonnage of oil to be obtained, for he the steward.

The men wasted no time at all in closing the gap,
Between themselves and the fray, battling, no time for nap,
Muscles to be cleaved and hacked as they powered along,
Burning and working, men build hard, hard and strong.

Now fully awake and aware of their senses,
A straight and seemingly easy road to prize, no fences,
Knowing full well that the killers would be there,
You could not currently see them, but they were doing their share.

The lights from the bunkhouse and cottage now far behind,
Gradually growing smaller and smaller, comfort now out of mind,
No light of moon to aid them, the sky filled with cloud this night,
Only hard and strenuous work stifled the cold of its bite.

Somewhere upon this earth the sun was shining bright,
The crust of the earth feeling comfort so tight,
Elsewhere the sky was clear and stars sparkled above so high,
But here, right now, there was nothing, no slice of pie.

But something to appease, something here for layman to learn,
For all bay whalers know of one thing to which you could turn,
When stalking whale by night, there happened a small reaction,
The clear presence, phosphorescent trails, tracks upon the ocean.

George sat upon the front, the forward most thwart,
Providing direction, employing this natural aid as taught,
Trails left by the killers were seemingly easy to follow,
For whale, these pursuers, it was strange, hard to swallow.

But progress was still slow,
In this Tom did feel, did know,
So he moves back alongside the leading boat,
If human you would say he was there to gloat.

Tom felt that the men were not working to task,
Wished more from them now, but unable to ask,
Was something amiss? These men, so inadequate,
Time was of the essence, time most desperate.

Tom pushed against the lead boat, shoving it aside,
Endeavouring to point out, he could aid the boat, give it a ride,
If only they were to think on the situation,
Understood his clear thinking, his ideas, his passion.

If a harpoon had been thrown then there would be a rope,
A rope could be pulled by Tom to aid the boat, give it hope,
In gaining speed and much time, to close the gap,
To reel in the humpback, from abstract and grey, to sound in lap.

With the absence of the rope there was little Tom could do,
If only there was a way, if only the men knew,
But wrestling with the progress of the boat was doing little,
To invoke the imagination of those rowing was a battle.

Tom gave up, took off towards the humpback,
A few curses from the men beginning to stack,
Voices that momentarily bellowed out for miles and miles around,
Voices not mellow, picked up by the wind and carried to ground.

A wind was starting to pick up, to grow in its ferocity,
The cold night air now stinging at faces, a great sobriety,
Spray from ocean top,
Such weather you could not stop.

Coming up from the rolling waves, upon the bow so thrown,
Poor conditions commenced to make themselves known,
To the rowers of each boat doing duty, no spare oar to stow,
Each and every one feeling the chill commencing to grow.

As muscles tore,
At stroking of oar,
At battling each wave,
Great effort each man gave.

The headsman ordered for silence right then and there,
For the last thing he wished was to be forced to share,
If any competitor was to hear them chasing down a whale,
This very day's hunt and energy would be for nought and fail.

They had lost one the day before, another would not do justice,
Heading now past Snug Cover, Eden, no need to provide notice,
Where sleeping inhabitants of town were, just that, sound asleep,
So few lanterns ablaze from early risers, to work so few did leap.

Tom and two others, moving just below the surface, clearly seen,
Bulges of ocean moving with them, evoked and keen,
Tops of their backs and a little fluke worthy of glance,
It was clear they were ready, despite lack of readable stance.

An old friend then decided to pay them a visit,
The most temporary appearance of the moon a credit,
Provided them the opportunity to clearly see the humpback's tail,
They were beginning to pester: to pester the whale to great avail.

The night was dark and spy-hopping was no guarantee,
Of good visual with either the men's boats or whale to see,
A visual glance of blowing and sucking in more air for dive,
For humpback to attempt an escape, to live and thrive.

The killers then decided on another action to take,
To force the whale deeper, deprive it of breathing, life at stake,
To see it use its air once and for all, sustenance depleted,
To deplete it emphatically of its facility, to drown, death greeted.

These were the thoughts that ran through Tom's mind,
The tactic they should employ, depriving men of their find,
Gone the men's ability to anchor the carcass,
Not to be part of a play, as per Whelan's raucous.

But these were mammals of a society, of the oceans and seas,
Not men of selfish behaviours, of their steadfast pleas,
If the weather failed to improve and got any worse,
The carcass could drift out to ocean, most real, quite terse.

But Tom knew they needed man's power, to avoid a lengthy mess,
Needed the strength of harpoon and lance in order to relieve stress,
To siphon the humpback of will to live, increase the opportunity,
A kill by any means, no need to put men through great scrutiny.

And great achievement was received, the whale held tight,
Forced to enter further into the bay, lacking in thought, no flight,
Constantly parried by killers, remorseless strides of conviction,
Heighten the dilemma of humpback's predicament and restriction.

To savour the moment when they would gain the upper hand,
That mouthful of lip and tongue, the delicacy that was so grand,
But a sudden flex came, an ability to perform manoeuvres well,
The humpback shifted gear, gone the temperance, signs to tell.

It was now adamant to avoid the snapping of jaw,
Avoid the Orcinus as they lurched, reinforcing their law,
A great Chunk of blubber torn from his bulk,
These orca were not an animal used to shy action, to sulk.

The whale raced for the surface and broke it fast,
Great volumes of spray pelted here and there over area vast,
The rowers of a nearby boat smothered from head to foot in spray,
Shocking reality, a hellish dampening of feverish cold to stay.

The cold of the ocean penetrating fast to the bone,
Stinging at their flesh, stupor over them thrown,
Numbing all feeling in their hands, face and toe,
Feelings that were the most horrific one ever comes to know.

But quality of will is a bequest any bay whaler had instilled,
Men of heart, confident of mind, their very cores filled,
And so they put aside this drenching of life-sucking cold,
Remained steadfast in conviction, of sound mind, calm and bold.

George saw the opportunity provided him and lifted the harpoon,
High and steady above his head in both hands and not too soon,
He thrust down hard at just the right time, power and transition,
Phosphorus sign and movement pointed to whale's position.

The point of the harpoon penetrated deep, well secure,
Secure and strong within the beast most sure,
The 'fast fish' had been secured, no time in victory to bask,
And Alex Greig's boat was called to inaction, pulled from task.

The last thing they wanted was for two harpoons to be stuck fast,
Two harpoons in one fish would ensure safety was not to last,
In particular at night when the weather was not sound,
Where much difficulty there was, in controlling boats, to be found.

Fred Wilson moved to the rear and changed seating,
Placed immediately with the headsman, formality, no greeting,
John's own boat conducted the same manoeuvre,
George moving to the rear and changing places with his father.

The lancing of the whale was to commence immediately,
To secure good lance, not rash, but bold, not neatly,
The whale had reared its barnacled head at the initial stinging,
First harpoon and then lance, terror inwardly ringing.

The reality of the situation commenced to become clear,
A humpback of little threat to anyone or anything near,
Other than what was taken in his mouth and digested within,
Chased beneath and above the waves, having committed no sin.

He was meek and powerfully strong,
Meant no harm, did no wrong,
Wished only to move towards a breeding ground,
For mate to be secured, to be found.

To find himself a mate for the season of joy,
To secured and find, not to harass and destroy,
To pass on his genes at social gathering as per his peers,
To unknowingly secure the species for future years.

He sounded almost immediately on feeling the sting,
The harpoon entering his body, song for the thrower to sing,
And he dove as deep as he possibly could,
Manila rope dragging behind him as it would.

The rope looped around the loggerhead for control and ease,
Control which would not come easily upon worsening seas,
And whether Pacific Ocean or Tasman Sea,
Water was water, and to seamen no real discrepancy.

With the killers aid, a strong pillar,
The men had less concern for failure,
Though some things can be unexpected,
Occurrences which should never be repeated.

But today was a relief,
Nothing outlandish to issue grief,
A reasonable night upon the wave,
Reasonable work, to manhood pave.

Nevertheless,
The whale felt stress,
With such he became unsteady,
For a lance he was not ready.

The temperament of a harpooned whale was unpredictable,
Easily pressed into thrashing about in a manner unstable,
A harpooned whale is a dangerous animal, through and through,
As dangerous as they come, flukes capable of cutting boat in two.

The ploy of the killers had now changed,
They saw with clarity, and heard, the boats now ranged,
Lances could be thrown and landed with hopeful effect,
For the harpoon sat fast, firm and erect.

The call went around for the pod to change tactic,
No need to further press humpback deeper, keep it basic,
Avoid loss of energy, keep firm and strong,
Make all the correct decisions and none of the wrong.

Tom then leapt from the water,
His entire body lifting amidst the slow slaughter,
Coming down hard on back of humpback as though beckoned,
Sliding upon blowhole, restricting breathing, just for a second.

So impede that right, for the whale to breath, no reprieve,
To shorten his life, for it to vanish, to leave,
Remove his ability to think straight,
No longer able to act with precision first rate.

Tired to the core, from base,
Tired of the chase,
Tired of the restrictions imposed, a cloak of terror to wear,
Tired from the stress, strain, and overpowering fear

The whale was being forced to remain upon surface,
Killers either side and one below, their temperaments a furnace,
The boats closing in, drawing manila line through loggerhead,
Bringing the catch home, thread by thread.

George gave the order to turn towards the whale,
Picked up a lance before vision of monstrous tail,
He readied himself, thigh against thwart,
Steadying himself for whales fury, drowned in thought.

The gap was closed between them both,
He hurled the lance, his task to doth,
With great precision into the flank of the beast,
Between the ribs, soon upon the orca to feast.

It penetrated deep and the whale curled in pain,
His head lifting out of the water for air to gain,
Spray covering the crew once more,
What other effects were there in store.

Particles of moisture drifted quickly away,
Droplets upon clothing, to the wind, its prey,
The rough and churning, the rolling of wave,
White crests forming, breaking, not to behave.

The humpback endeavoured to sound one more time: or his last,
Flukes lifting out of the water, so near, so hugely vast,
Alex Greig's boat coming close to being badly hammered,
Crashing of tail unsettling those on board as they stammered.

A warning broke the air for all oars to be peaked,
To ready themselves for a fate, blood soaked and streaked,
Preparing themselves to be delivered into the waters around,
Amidst fury of whale and Orcinus, unsavoury death to be found.

For no one knew if the killers held a taste for human flesh,
Whether man-flesh, within their teeth, did ever mesh,
None found comfort in this thought by any distinct measure,
None wished to find out, if this was to be an orca pleasure.

The tremendous crash came quick and loud,
Failed to hit anything brittle, but much water displaced, a shroud,
A prayer said by many, to have escaped a watery tomb,
Boat not to capsize with men: nor oars of blade, handle and loom.

So the battle continued to be waged, a further two, sturdy lance,
Thrown at first chance, very next clear shot, clear glance,
Breaching the shell of the humpback and the 'red flag' flew,
A piercing, deafening noise erupted then, and everyone knew.

When finally the victory was achieved, most solidly won,
The carcass afloat, being mauled by the killers, mother and son,
Whale's mouth forced open, tongue and lips taken from beast,
The crews sat back exhausted, watched as the killers did feast.

It was now that George gave the order,
Certainly no time to saunter,
For a lantern to be lit, the beginning of their transition,
Each boat did comply, to aid them in their ambition.

A little light in order to acquire their desire and need,
For tomorrow, blubber! to appease their hunger, their greed,
The light was but to assist, attaching an anchor to whale, the toll,
And for positions in boats to be changed with ease and control.

The job was done, the fight lasting fifty minutes, no more,
And some to secure anchor, a task upon which for energy to pour,
No sooner had they finished and the sun made its appearance,
Right then and there it did show: goodbye to night, the hindrance.

All eyes then fell upon the biggest humpback seen in the bay,
Either dead or alive its size hard to fathom, not abstract or grey,
It was 52 feet long and quite literally dwarfed all before,
So hard it was to think of but a memory for all time and more.

Yes indeed, one to recall when drunk, to be stammered,
This day amongst many others would be remembered,
Another story to fill the ears of drinkers at public house,
But no real story here to share with lover or spouse.

This was a turning point that moulded George's life forever,
Sculpting his youth, to be part of him, a constant tether,
For he to follow in the footsteps of his father before,
From these his early years, to worship work, the orca, their law.

The glamorous side of things he would see to come and go,
Beginning with this short adventure: of all to come and know,
Men and orca working as one, to turn the tide of bay whaling,
Upon the head, to hammer, to fasten hope, to secure by nailing.

And this site of the slaying was visited once again,
Twenty-four hours after ending the humpbacks life in pain,
Orcinus having drawn their meal to watery depths to feed,
A temporary place of rest before rising, men to harvest their need.

The carcass had filled with gas,
Until it floated to the surface, a great mass,
Floating upon gentle wave, looking a real mess,
But now they must tow it, a relief, no stress.

Nigel B.J.Clayton

It was hard work but stress free and rewarding,
Unless shark did appear, a prize for gorging,
Floating upright, its back bare for the world to see,
Underbelly obscured beneath the waves, floating free.

The anchor retrieved, rower's arms bent to the labour, to deliver,
Deliver the whale, being turned in over near the Towamba River,
Bringing home the prize, to try-works for deblubbering,
Where capstan and boiling pots sat ready and waiting.

Boat spades were picked up by the men that had gathered,
Sharpened points, sharp as could possibly be, shapes not tapered,
The blubber cut into squares with great effort and much sweat,
Wiping salt of flesh from brow, shirt sleeves soaked, no regret.

Seagulls filled the air, brought together by that silent ringing,
Sound of dinner bell, to congregate amidst squawking, not singing,
Swooping in and pestering the work detail to no avail,
Making a right nuisance of themselves without fail.

The stench about was wretched, beyond belief,
From it there was little to no relief,
For the seagulls the perfume of any God,
To their approval they would give the nod.

The entire process was hard and extremely laborious,
Sheets of blubber cut from the whale in manner most serious,
Then turned up the ramp, further work undertaken on the blubber,
Each large portion being cut into strips: and not at leisure.

Strips that were 15 inches x 5 inches x 5 inches deep,
Deep as the blubber, as deep of that which they were to reap,
Strips then cast into a large vat to be minced smaller,
Portions placed within try-pots there on this spot, the boiler.

A man then has the duty to skim the surface,
Skim with a perforated utensil, for the smell a grimace,
Watching, attending, the boiling take place,
This was their source of wage, to render there was no race.

Some tasked with ensuring that all went well of their toil,
That all was rendered sufficiently, a pure, pure oil,
Pouring this into smaller pots, later into numerous casket,
Ready for shipping, for sale, ready for market.

THE POD

It was 1890, a sad time for all,
Three short years, time to fall,
Typee and Humpy to leave here today,
Mayhap to return, mayhap to stay away.

Never a crystal ball affair,
Nothing firm in which to stare,
The two orca spoken were birds of a feather,
Stuck hard and firm, always together.

To leave behind friends was always a sad time for all,
But there was never any hard fact, any hard rule,
If one felt a need to leave, to adventure elsewhere, to depart,
Then that should be permitted, to recommence, to restart.

A sad parting, in particular with Stranger, their living power,
More than matriarch, more than strength during times gone sour,
But the breeding season had come around,
Excitement to seek out, adventure to be found.

Breeding season: some would leave, some would show,
No way to be sure, no way to know,
But for the majority the pods remained the same,
But still, it was a terrible shame.

Perhaps Orcinus has different feelings than human mothers,
Different views and understandings unknown to others,
The love Stranger felt would be rekindled by the mean,
By the basic principles and balance of all that could be seen.

As averages go this could be considered a good turn,
Most had experienced similar, of it to learn,
But orca like Tom were here to stay,
Never to turn tail, never to stray.

For the whalers of the bay, the keen eye saw,
Changing each year the saddle patches thaw,
Then the new sprout to blossom and grow,
For each to be named, for each to befriend and to know.

Typee would be missed for his exuberance, his will to win,
Humpy for her ability to lead attacks, ripping blubber with grin,
Her dorsal, of all the other, a flag upon her back, forever,
Bent completely over, easily spotted from distance, fast learner.

The pod gathered around the couple at a place slightly north,
Not far from the icy coast of the South Pole for what it is worth,
Resting as they did between attacks on seals, oblivious they stray,
Taking opportunity for rest and before returning to Twofold Bay.

Typee and Humpy looked upon the members of their fraternity,
Their brothers and sisters like kin, their clan, their identity,
They stared a deep and longing stare, a submissive look,
Farewelling, feeling sad, sorrow, time together, pages from book.

But why leave now,
To seemingly throw in the towel,
It was to explore new environments, rear young, learn tactics,
To learn new routines, new feeding techniques, new 'basics'.

Typee was set upon starting afresh, strong in conviction,
Sling the reigns away and to live with no restriction,
And so with the goodbyes given the pair of killers turned tail,
Swam from those they knew well, to be relied upon without fail.

And time passed as it does, the older we are, the faster time falls,
Seconds, minutes, hours and years, never slows, never stalls,
It had been some time now that Typee and Humpy had departed,
When the appearance of another turned heads, hearts started.

Stranger was the first to approach the killer whale,
A strong resemblance to Typee, no significance to fail,
But despite similarities there was no relation,
Jackson was not a by-product of Typee and Humpy attraction.

At first glance,
Their very stance,
Their saddle patch,
All did seemingly match.

The pod gathered to introduce themselves, new member found,
A little vocalisation, skin rubbing and general nosing around,
Jackson, now member of the team, accepting his position,
Happy to fit in, happy to receive that 'new member' recognition.

It wasn't known from where he did feed,
Not overly thin, able to tend own need,
He was a stray from somewhere, of this all were sure,
Of no real importance, not yet, but one not prone to be immure.

Possibly discarded by another matriarch for disobedient behaviour,
Likely a transient looking for change, just another harbour,
A harbour that might offer him better opportunity in the future,
He, a new mind upon which to feed, did appear most mature.

He may even have lost a loved one and felt a strong urge to leave,
Depart the pod of which he was a member, start afresh, not grieve,
Regardless of circumstance, haply so fast, bonds to grow strong,
From outward appearance, all mused, he could not go wrong.

Jackson, a male of eleven years, average length from head to tail,
Saw immediate wonder and appeal in one of the younger female,
She was Sharkey and much time together they did share,
Each years from sexual maturity, friendship lacking in fanfare.

At first the attraction wasn't sexual or inappropriate,
Over no ruling did he stray, of bounds did not deviate,
Sharkey had appearance of one he previously knew,
A kindling of flame, of hard-felt love, a love which grew.

They were considered, through due cause, a pair,
To couple one day, all so pleasant and fair,
A time so great, to work together, always keen,
Vapours of mist upon dark horizon not yet seen.

THE PROTECTION

George lances his first humpback, a small animal by measure,
Providing confidence in these early years, and ample pleasure,
Not much pleasure for the whale so pierced, coming off worse,
The new headsman, seen as aspiring young man, seemingly terse.

Aspiration forming like the callous upon a working man's hand,
Great victory short lived, toast of company, man of the band,
But the kill was followed by many weeks of frustration,
No kill to be procured, no oil the render, nought to fashion.

George and his crew, along with John and his own,
Sheltered at South Head, wharf of rock, together, never alone,
Settled within the cave of substantial size,
Awaiting the call to action, that eluding prize.

The weather was fine and easier to put out boats from the cave,
Call for rapid response heard, for further misfortune to be stave,
Beneath the helm, South Head, at the ready, eagerness to grow,
Providing ability to move fast when whale decided to show.

The men had polished off lunch, now at rest with mugs of tea,
Tantalizing their senses when a sudden call came, a cry, a plea,
From atop the cliff and approaching fast, whale had been sighted,
Followed closely by six killers, the men were so delighted.

It was a right whale of large… no; massive proportions,
Filled with desire to mate and feed, of many notions,
And so far off it was hard to decipher, as killers did lure,
But two of the dorsal were those of Tom and Hooky for sure.

By the time the two boats were cast from the rocky wharf,
The whale, which killers and men in boats could never dwarf,
Had been pressured into the mouth of Twofold Bay,
In an attempt to harass, to kill, to feed upon as killers may.

Tom and Hooky separated from the mustering, with aching teeth,
Remainder of pod streamlining along on all sides and beneath,
The two keeping the front clear, paving the way, demise to cast,
Like the script of a movie, to fulfil each scene to the very last.

Tom and Hooky swam about the boats, instilling hope,
Just for short period, men preparing harpoon, lance and rope,
Each and all accessing the situation for what it was worth,
John's boat pulling away from George's, to go ever forth.

Kind and straight forward insults were pressed upon the crews,
Curse from headsman to headsman, encouragement, old news,
Verbal assaults of friendly gestures and coercion,
Aptitude, self confidence, in a word, inspiration.

Each man took control of his own ambition,
Here there was no hunger, no malnutrition,
Oars employed to their fullest, with great control they pull,
Potential of the crews, and individuals, never a lull.

And in time potential indeed did peak,
It comes to reason, no need of this to truly speak,
For great effort can only go so far with no rest,
To perform to the extreme, to one's absolute best.

The culmination of effort saw the boats approach their target,
All wishing within to win the day, get oil to market,
Tom and Hooky seeing the men making ground, faring well,
Departed the boats, to re-join their pod, amidst the growing swell.

The whale was heading for John's boat, John ready to stand,
Ready the harpooner, take position, get that iron firmly in hand,
The harpooner scrambled to position, bracing against the thwart,
Eyeing the whale with suspicion, preparing strike as self taught.

George acted upon the situation, moved to the starboard,
Shifting position and approach, to pursue that target and reward,
Wondering whether it may surface from beneath his father's boat,
Seeing it happen, right now, yoke temporarily fall from throat.

For Alex let loose with power, the muscle, of memory, it knew,
Harpoon racing through the air to target, slightly off skew,
The moving target too far, the shot did not penetrate,
Striking just below the dorsal, a poor throw, too poor to rate.

The fish was considered fast but that is too bold,
A whale this size could easily escape the hold,
Quite readily release himself of this embrace,
To continue on with this ultimate, survival race.

Sam Haddigaddi obeyed the order, prepared to sling another,
Another harpoon, but this like clap of thunder,
Peering momentarily at Alex, a friendly suggestion, competitive,
Harpoon steady in hand, gaining calculation, gaining perspective.

He savoured this moment, his take on the right whale,
To see if he could do better, where Alex did fail,
Commiserations for the one that did not achieve,
Achieve that fast fish, congratulations Alex would not receive.

Now, a throw which he had made many times in the past,
One which people would speak of, a victory to last,
One which would make him a legend of the bay,
An asset for the Davidson's, for ever and a day.

He hurled it then as the monster passed them by, not to be denied,
Hounded by the killers as they took chunks from each side,
Another orca beyond and one much further down,
The containment holding firm, the whale unable to leave town.

And as the harpoon was hurled towards the right whale,
The oars were dug into the ocean, ignoring any need to pail,
Quickly reverse, shift approach of the boat: go: halt,
Dig in deep to the ocean, see that whale trying to bolt.

Boat and whale just missed,
All fear now dismissed,
No collision, lucky in that, at least,
Avoiding ride upon back of beast.

The line was secure and the loggerhead attended,
Water now pailed out, poured over line, situation amended,
For the loggerhead was becoming too hot, smouldering,
Always vigilant, watchful eye the nurse, avoid floundering.

The headsman was changing places with the harpooner,
Commanded and completed, far better is to be all the sooner,
Two ropes now connected to the whale, beneath dorsal,
Two boats now in tow, oil in sight, for orca a great morsel.

John was closer to the whale than George, perchance,
George several boat lengths behind, further to throw each lance,
Both towed upon the waves, upon open ocean, quite unsheltered,
Killers trying to muster, the largest whale they had encountered.

The whale, having had enough,
Being large and very tough,
Tried heading out to ocean, open water,
Boats in tow, for killers no saunter.

Orcinus, their constant barrage, their preventing,
Not allowing the whale to dive, unrelenting,
At sides, beneath, snapping at heels, or so the speak,
Biting at flanks, covering blowhole, any favourable tweak.

But the whale kept on going, refused to say nay,
Heading further and further from neck of bay,
Out towards the east, the sun having deserted, to rest,
Last fragrant of light passing over range to the west.

To the west, where their home beckoned for the men to return,
Where warmth of fire and hot food sat ready for stomach to churn,
Alas, not much for it, but to sit back and wait for the whale to tire,
For boats in tow to finish with lance, for killers to eat and retire.

The work over time diminished, the miles behind them grew,
Their oars had been peaked, boats dragged behind, the wind blew,
Whale dragging, surf upon the bows, curling, sprouting outwards,
Surf to phosphorescent, day to night, stepping into the woods.

Approaching an unknown, coming fast, no star in the sky,
No moon to aid them, no pleasantness, all of this was to deny,
Though good it was that the weather was not out to destroy,
Wind fresh, slightly cold, but getting wet from water was no joy.

Jackets were placed on, more or less at the same time,
Some a little too small for the wearers, nothing to berhyme,
For when first they clambering aboard to give chase upon whale,
Each crew did go to incorrect boat, in decision they all did fail.

So long as oars were manned, a concern which did not atone,
For the cold now penetrated each and every one to the bone,
The wish for their own jackets on many of their mind,
To encase their bodies like a nut within shell, of orange in rind.

Discomfort did occur: men finding themselves seated at oar new,
New grip not used to: a seat change, though such cases were few,
No thrill to paw over an oar, but also no real call to complain,
Unaccustomed grip, not snug, not worn down by flesh on grain.

And many years of handling also saw the seat fit snug,
Like flea finding home upon dog, nice, lush, as though in a rug,
It was strange how the mind worked, how familiarity was firm,
Firm as in secure, peace of mind, mind never to toil or to squirm.

It was a little different for headsman and harpooners,
Here there was command and structure, they were not learners,
Each had a specific task needing attention, a required need,
Which included changing positions, iron into whale to feed.

A boat's worth was in its commander,
Or not, for he is worthless without good lancer,
Mmm, yes, all were one, part of the team, one and the same,
Also individuals, and mannerisms of mind do tire of the game.

The occasional sign of the whale's intermittent exchange,
Between water haven and surface, his open range,
Was made all the clearer by the phosphorus display afore,
The rope tearing through water, same again, a constant encore.

The whale was making no sign of giving up the fight,
Surrender far from its mind, to do as he pleased, it was his right,
The killers commenced to feel as though they had bitten too much,
More than they could chew, out of their reality, out of touch.

But was it not the whale whom had placed himself upon menu,
Even gone as far as to choose the venue,
Waltzing into the comfortable and serene appeal of Twofold bay,
To endeavour, to try, for a short and comfortable stay.

Now the whale insisted and had turned the power of the play,
The land far behind them, getting further and further away,
And before time they were 7.5 miles out to ocean as it beckoned,
Their momentum into the darkness didn't waver for a second.

George held his arms tight to chest when John's voice broke,
Slight terror to rise in mind, a vision beginning to smoke,
For the noise of the boats being dragged through the water,
Did advise, ropes crossed, George should cut his sooner, not later.

A sudden upheaval then delivered itself to the air,
A thunderous crash demanded a look, all to suddenly stare,
A sound which could be one thing and one thing only, right here,
John's boat, had been hit, smashed hard, hope gone, to disappear.

The smashing of boat reached their ears and Sam leapt too,
Leapt to action, tomahawk in hand, the line hit, cutting through,
Releasing the boat's connection with the prize that had showered,
Blossoms of spray amidst coercion of mind now empowered.

The members of the other crew had been cast into the ocean,
The whale turned back on the boat to create more commotion,
Smashing it hard with its flukes as it sounded briefly,
Then rose again beneath them, killing Peter Lia immediately.

Mass of fluke falling upon him with great strength,
A fluke so large and of great length,
No warning, the continuing momentum of the downward force,
Splitting boat into two, whereupon it sank: separation, divorce.

Mass of wood, lances, manila and thwarts, keg of water and more,
Rations and blond Norwegian, all drift helplessly to water's floor,
A man, always happy, his singing in the try-works, cheerful smile,
Where hard labour was always met, gone forever, now defile.

The work was now cut out for them and they had to act fast,
Water so cold that no one human life in it could last,
Cries for help appeared from out of nowhere,
The dark surrounds enveloping all, too much to bear.

A little phosphorus providing aid, someone was splashing about,
Some treading water, or swimming precariously without a shout,
All trying to get closer to the only boat afloat, their only scope,
The life saver to deliver eleven men to safety, to wish and hope.

A few of the killers then separated from the others, their pod,
To undertake a different task, immediately, without request or nod,
A task which went unnoticed by those in the water staying afloat,
Either plashing about or at safe harbour in their little green boat.

Under the sway of Big Ben, having now taken command,
Cooper, Tom, Hooky, Jackson, and Sharkey did understand,
Took positions around the scene to protect and to serve,
To aid the men they knew so well, as they all did deserve.

It was clear to the killers that they were far out to ocean,
That sharks might be about, not far from vicinity and action,
The last thing Stranger, or any of the others, did wish,
Was for their allies to be picked off by shark, a most tasty dish.

One by one the men were drawn out of the ice cold water,
Drenched, utterly and completely, but held from slaughter,
Chill of ocean devouring energy, this boat now their sumpter,
Depriving them of good spirit, their thoughts with friend Peter.

And the ring or orca surrounding the boat,
Was maintained during the ordeal to stay afloat,
From climbing aboard the vessel of desire,
Till onwards to bay, and killers did retire.

But the bay was a long way off, still no disclosure,
And the killing of whale had not been their pleasure,
Although Orcinus, one and all, did return to the excitement,
Back into the fray and the frenzy, for victories achievement.

The gunwale of the boat was barely above the surface,
So dangerously close to being sunk, in that, no solace,
And the saviour of the day, other than the orca in time of need,
That the ocean was still calm, the sun appearing, warmth to feed.

The sun on the horizon, began to shed light,
Gone was the torment, gone was some blight,
But weight of death was still on their shoulder,
Each and everyone felt it, the strong and the bolder.

And with the sun came the ability to see around,
The waters around them, the far off vision of ground,
Of the poor flesh and bone, those plucked from the ocean,
Having been, that night, guided by voice, a magic potion.

Positions in the boat were taken up, all,
Turn-taking at oars, still much work to fall,
Assurance and general comradeship providing a little relief,
Looking to sky, praying to God, no matter what their belief.

Instinct now took command and for the coast they rowed,
The whale they had forgotten, even as in the distance it bellowed,
They only thought now of the lights on shore, so far away,
Hoping for the water around them, below gunwale to stay.

After many hours of stroking the oars upon the watery grave,
And much time in thought and prayer, visions of church nave,
They came upon the sound of surf hitting the shore,
So close now, the entrance of bay, of Eden and home's door.

And Jim was on South Head, unlit lantern now in hand,
Waiting patiently for their return, there he did stand,
Saw from his vantage only one boat return,
Of the disaster he would soon learn.

As they drew into the bay,
Eleven men in a bad way,
Some worse off than others,
Wretched site, especially for mothers.

None would forget this day, enough to make drunk man sober,
The worst day that any of them could ever recall or remember,
Lost was Peter Lia and a sturdy boat, both now rest in grave,
Far below the surface of the waves rest Peter, Peter the brave.

In memory of Peter a stone was erected,
No less could this have been expected,
An inscription dated September 28th, 1881, for all to see,
To Peter Lia, who was killed by a whale: there to always be.

As for the whale, we shall never know,
Did he manage, of the killers, to throw,
Did he indeed make his escape, clear and far,
Harpoon still embedded, the point forever to jar.

THE MOTHER OF MARY

Far from Eden, far to the south,
Killers mingled freely, food to mouth,
Had stumbled upon a meagre minke whale of little delight,
Worth a play, but hardly worth the pleasure of fight.

And so Tom and the others broke off their quest,
Something caught their attention, thoughts on which to rest,
So, they were coming up from the rear of a steamer so grand,
SS Ly-ee-Moon, making its way towards Sydney land.

She was a steamer of great prestige and held in high esteem,
Built to be fast at 17 knots [20miles per hr], furnished to gleam,
Only the best that money could buy, looking so fine,
Initially built as a paddle steamer in 1859.

The ship measured 282 feet long and 27 wide,
Powered by a coal fed steam engine, over waters to glide,
Engines which turned the huge wheels, through water to power,
Within its pores, pride and prestige to seemingly shower.

She was originally rigged with three masts and fitted with sail,
Could make good speed where weather permitted, without fail,
Within 20 years [1878] was returned to service on modification,
By removal of mast, turned into schooner-rigged vessel of notion.

There were few lights on board and all appeared alright,
Ship plodding along at leisurely pace to everyone's delight,
All on board completely unaware as to what lay ahead,
No ill-fate from such calm weather could be read.

She had departed Melbourne on Saturday 29 May, 1886,
All 55 passengers and a crew of 41, relaxed and freely mix,
Captain Webber having left control of vessel in another's care,
In that of James Fotheringhame, the Third Officer, mind aglare.

James, having been handed much responsibility, rather discreetly,
So he, the captain, could retire to cabin, drink taken neatly,
Pro: the weather, not bad; Fotheringham mature and understood,
Con: a drunk captain of high responsibility was by no means good.

Later: they were approaching Green Cape, lighthouse of 3 years,
A blinking in far distance, a warning across many miles, appears,
A signal 95 feet high, 144 feet from level of ocean,
Sat upon crest, for eleven miles its warning to take action.

'Stay clear, there are rocks about,
This warning to you I do shout,
Do not approach, do not come closer,
Rocks abound, the ships' eraser'.

At this time, curiosity was ablaze, unbeknown to those on board,
The killers of Big Ben's pod escorted the ship, a playful reward,
Vessel of beauty, over gentle rollers pass, soon to ocean bequeath,
The sleek, beautiful creatures, masters of death, swam beneath.

White surf thrown up from the bow, music to the ear,
The sound of the ocean wasted upon night so young and clear,
And Green Cape was soon larger than life in the window,
James fighting concern for making hasty decision or fallow.

The captain had retired, orders made clear,
Do not wake him unless urgent, not to go near,
Green Cape was 16 miles shy of Twofold bay,
Leave me in cabin for a while, there to stay.

And the captain still sucked on the nipple,
Savouring his source and a snack to nibble,
Getting as drunk as a Lord,
This was the story, but not every word.

Tom could see as he spy-hopped a little, above water's lip,
A man stepping from bridge, towards stern of ship,
Throwing waste into the ocean as though to curse and spurn,
Unaware of the killers presence, still yet of little concern.

It was at this point that Fotheringhame made the hasty decision,
To call upon the services of the captain, to avoid any collision,
For him to be called to duty, James feeling inapt and fidge,
But the captain flatly refused to attend the matter on bridge.

After nine that night the captain returned quickly amidst dire call,
James seeing before him the drunkenness seemingly fall,
The sobering effect that plain rocks above ocean instills,
Is more empowering than one wishes or wills.

But he was too late and the ship hit rocks,
At the half hour chime of clocks,
Tom and the others could not foresee the danger to fall,
The hunger of rocks ready to mill, ready to maul.

Far unlike the captain with his years of mounted experience,
Years wasted within minutes due to shear arrogance,
Stern upon reef and bow floating precariously towards the shore,
There was too little one could do, before them death's open door.

The dangerous predicament was out of all proportion,
The rocks of Green Cape beyond wildest imagination,
The fight for survival commenced as though violently thrust,
The adrenalin taking place over clear thinking, survival a must.

Lighthouse workers heard the commotion, the grinding of ship,
The vessel tearing up, a battle against rocks, it beginning to rip,
Daniel Whelan and George Walters coming to the assistance,
Of those in dire need, they made a swift appearance.

Tom and the others of the pod moved in a little but most sure,
Steady at first, maintaining good distance, hearts most pure,
For even with their skill and experience of the ocean,
The rocks proved to be treacherous and unyielding in motion.

The foremast upon the bow fell and landed upon rock,
Where seamen and others started to crawl to safety in shock,
A fishing line thrown to the ship on which was attached a rope,
A line of safety, security blanket, something in which to hope.

With rope tied fast, Herbert Lumsdaine made for safety of land,
Rocks so savage, lighthouse aloft, ready and able to withstand,
Withstand the assault of all that nature had to offer him,
For life at that minute was like walk on edge of sword: grim.

Others followed beneath the line to safety, no easy lope,
Andrew Bergland, a passenger, Fotheringhame to follow on rope,
Making it to safety a further ten good people with boatswain,
Lastly the captain, only duty performed that night, it was plain.

One to die, Mrs Flora Hannah MacKillop, never again to saunter,
A legacy left behind in reminder of her most humble daughter,
Mother to Mary MacKillop, Mary: of figure and station,
Mother of Mother Superior of St Joseph's Provident Institution.

Needless of this, shall we speak of it more,
Of the killers and their trials, of their unspoken law,
Tom endeavouring to rescue some that clung to unsafe rock,
Whom fear for their lives, not knowing, he was not there to shock.

It was an effort, to attempt their very salvation,
Swimming as close as possible in this hopeless situation,
He being thrust helplessly against a formation of rock so large,
Some teeth knocked out, no shield against this, no [archaic] targe.

He retreated having secured, of this situation, no victory,
For it was too treacherous, a predicament of shear gravity,
And further screaming continued unabated for some of the night,
Twenty persons, upon stern, washed out to ocean, crying in fright.

Give in, the pod did not, as Tom gave direction,
His attempts to rally all and employ relative salvation,
Tom is not the matriarch, not female, but is a strong peer,
His persona had won law of the tongue, so could win here.

A rescue attempt must be staged,
This war with the ocean must be waged,
Do here as they do with the green boats, their contribution,
Treat those who appear with the same gravitation.

And Tom could quite clearly recall how Peter Lia had died,
Killed by the flukes of the whale crushing boat, life denied,
How the body sank lifelessly towards the bottom of ocean floor,
Visual picture clear in his mind as it then disappeared, ever more.

Again and again the killers attempted to move in with aid,
Trying with all their effort, but the people were too afraid,
To help them to safety where possible was not coming about,
Do justice where deserved amidst people, they scream and shout.

The Davidson's had served them well over the past year,
In return they should do the same, this was fundamentally clear,
This society, these humans, were part of their pod,
Whether in ocean they swam or on land they trod.

Like brothers and sisters, they were intelligent,
Proved to be emotional and rather diligent,
Showed semblance in many respects of their own,
As though ancestral in some way, cognition ingrained, well sown.

But still they feared the worst, that mental curse,
People preferred to remain upon sinking hearse,
To be dragged beneath the waves for that ever good night,
Fighting off the killers where one strayed too close: such spite.

And so many lives were lost unnecessarily, 71 to be exact,
Three of which were very young children, but does not detract,
Not detract from the overall numbers that died at Green Cape,
A loss that could have been avoided: of death, life to escape.

And so the killers swam off as the moon rose above the horizon,
To swim once more towards Leather Jacket Bay and good reason,
To head off a whale heard swimming near, large morsel indeed,
A large monster of a mammal on which to chase and to feed.

With distinct probability that others, would appear, other pods,
To aid them in their hunt with intelligence and teeth, not rods,
To then congregate prior to approaching Twofold Bay and glory,
To further furnish their memory with another hunting story.

And a surprise was found to be awaiting them as news fell,
Humpy had returned to the pod, one she had known so well,
Returned with her son, Walker, who was barely one year old,
Who would become just a number, never a legend nor bold.

It was strange she should return alone: had never been needy,
But it was not possible for Humpy to portray the tragedy,
A tragedy that unfolded during a clash with a humpback whale,
One with a calf that refused to die, to fight for calf in this vale.

Typee, her mate, had taken a fluke directly in the side,
Which was enough to split him open, too much to bide,
An uncommon and freak occurrence, sad to recall,
Typee died soon after, his life had come to its end, to stall.

Humpy had no real choice but to return to Eden and stability,
Leaving behind fond memories, but an estranged community,
Who treated her with defiance, no gratitude for hunting ability,
Treated poorly, no time for her majestic and athletic agility.

Humpy's time away from home was a reflection of her mind,
Cared not to recall, to search it corridors for importance to find,
She was here now, with calf, and Typee was gone to never return,
Walker to be looked after, accepted, one she could never spurn.

THE GREATEST AID

By the 1890s, G.Davidson, formerly known as Fearless George,
Had taken over the family business, mind built as of a forge,
Relying on ingenuity for survival during the off season,
Easy to see why he ran a small farm: good sense, good reason.

But where winter was waited upon, so the rewards were set,
A reward close to shore: fishing done with lance, not with net,
Tongue and lips for Orcinus, mammals, full of power and might,
Casks of oil for men of the land, not as cunning but very bright.

The relationship between the two species continued to evolve,
Problems and initiative, always a way, always something to solve,
When Orcinus became tangled in ropes, the men lent a hand,
When man was bound by water and shark, Orcinus would stand.

And so here we speak, of all things that evolved, of all to meet,
One was to be remembered forever, a memory to warmly greet,
The day killers had ventured into the bay, warning men ashore,
A humpback within distance, seemingly on leisurely tour.

Two other pods were shaken from nap,
Set into motion regards setting of trap,
Now patrolling the mouth of the bay,
In the hope that the whale would stay.

This great fish, required use of men's hands for impeding,
To aid in bringing her down, for pods to have their feeding,
Preferred the quick kill as opposed to the drawn out,
To hence set upon, green boats to launch with almighty shout.

Tom lead the way and all three commenced flop-tailing, their best,
Leaping from the water, hitting it hard, waking men from rest,
The unmistakable sound of calling traversing far and wide,
A beacon to secure the interests of man, calling him to tide.

Call the men to duty, to express without any doubt,
That there was a whale in their midst, waiting about,
One to be had, but it would not wait all night,
And from the dark depths of cabin, men stirred for the fight.

Men lying, in heavenly, blissful sleep, now a stirred commotion,
Dreams lost, alcoholic stupors torn, all clambered for position,
Shredding men of slumber and cloud-soft beds, no treason,
But happily stricken of the fear of a 'fruit and whale-less' season.

RUSHO! That unmistaken beating of drum, the sound and shrill,
Unmistaken command and call to duty, a hard to swallow pill,
There had been a heavy night of the spirits, drinks going around,
Commissary in misery, but now justice to be found.

Though only half the men managed to make it to the boats,
For they would not wait for the slow: George not taking votes,
Words strung to extricate more power, each to heave,
If unable to work under trying conditions then it was time to leave.

But men loved this work, enjoyed the hell,
Working the try-works, but not the beastly smell,
So give arms to the task they do, pull the oars under their charge,
To hit task hard, great efforts, not to gently tickle, or gently sparge.

George, as a student, looked towards the heavens above,
Studied his book before compiling a work he did love,
Looking to crystal ball, to the hours which lay ahead,
To foresee the weather of hours ahead, to be clearly read.

There was a half moon and sparse cloud spanning across the sky,
A westerly strong breeze, the ocean calm, on good weather to rely,
By all appearances they were in for an easy night,
But what of the whale? Would it be an easy fight?

Rising from the darkness the rowers then heard the familiar sound,
Of a humpback whale in the midst, of its demise inward bound,
A little further out upon the ocean, the pods and their hounding,
And the killers could hear the green boats, their oars pounding.

Tom remained at the stern having gained the men's attention,
Now leading the way, his phosphorus showing the direction,
The light from the moon hiding behind the occasional cloud,
A bond, friends of sea and land, something in which to be proud.

Tom came to the side of the boat, and time held much essence,
He needed the men, and men he, each other required that presence,
More so than not for there was only one boat here this night,
To do the work of two or three, and now with the lack of light.

He sideswiped the boat gently from beneath, oars pushed aside,
Drawing the attention of whalers as though asking for ride,
Eyes falling upon the mass, dorsal stretched out towards the sky,
A fin then struck them with fear, possessing such power, not shy.

Queries passed between breathes as they went for the prize,
Questions on his behaviour: would the boat capsize,
Would they all end up in the sea, thrashing to stay afloat,
To be hampered, lives taken, heads bitten off at the throat.

And the then one of the seated declared a solution as done before,
Tom Earl allowing a chuckle upon lips, inwards vision he saw,
Suggesting they throw him the painter [short rope] at the bow,
To see whether or not he was offering assistance, the boat to tow.

George looked inquisitively upon the suggestion and upon Tom,
Who was growing anxious, annoyed at slow progress, a bomb,
Tom feared the humpback would make its escape to deeper water,
That the youngest of the pod would not survive the winter.

They were all hungry but preferred to remain at Twofold Bay,
For the aid provided by the men and stick of iron, silvery grey,
There, dissension in their group, mothers concerned for the young,
But one good whale would provide enough, death hence sprung.

The killer hit the flank again, oars in danger, a possible loss,
George then gave the nod for harpooner, the painter to toss,
To see once and for all what Tom would do with the rope,
To see if the killer was in fact giving them hope.

The harpooner's face drew a collection of eyeballs, enthralled,
Looks falling upon the dark man, oar no longer pulled,
Oar lifted temporarily from water, for the painter he did reach,
Threw it into the water, to see if Tom was there to teach.

Jaws dropped then with the forward motion of the boat and Tom,
The killer opened his mouth, taking the rope as though to bosom,
A gentle grasp before pulling them over wave, the way so paved,
Clear access to humpback now granting them time, much saved.

This was a scene to remember, one for the books,
An incident never to be forgotten, but not escaping sour looks,
For many would not believe this, but the experience was grand,
One of the greatest feats of man and beast, not achieved on land.

The two killers that were with Tom looked upon his manner ,
Of action, mystic, the status of legend called to his banner,
But for Tom this was no time for fun,
He had a duty to perform, there was work to be done.

The boat was making good headway now, better than before,
Yet still the men rowed, true conviction, much sweat to pour,
But this killer whale, this Orcinus Orca, so brave, not naive,
Had done what no other could do, so much he did achieve.

Whistles, clicks and calls filled the ocean, it woken from slumber,
Echolocation, their repertoire of calls was quite large in number,
Sounds made when chasing a whale, commands to obey,
Signals, clear signs to adhere, the reaping of harvest, their prey.

The sonic signatures of the acoustic communication,
Consisted of pitch, harmonic structure, oscillation,
Tone, urgency, mood, loudness and action,
All an aid, enabled the killers to kill, the great tactician.

Sometimes employing click trains as opposed to singular clicks,
Dependent on the type of prey hunted, depended on their tricks,
Marine mammals could pick up on these, no dilapidating manner,
Where fish could not, as though into works was fed a spanner.

Passive listening was simply an extension of their abilities,
Sound commands and requests the strongest of strategies,
Straight conversation, calls indicating species and pod members,
That's all was needed, that's all there was, from their very fibres.

The very effort and commotion of the fight to keep,
The whale in the bay, of escape in waters deep,
And with this the boat nears its final approach, to close,
Upon this humpbacks daily life, a face-off, almost nose to nose.

The whale gave an almighty effort to escape the clutches of all,
Turning upon the teeth infected mouths, never to be in thrall,
An herculean effort surfacing, its raging scorn,
To be more than he could, to be the greatest thorn.

Great strength erupting like a volcano from its every sinew,
From every fibre burst an amassed energy, outwards it blew,
But escape? A humpback could only muster 7.5 miles an hour,
The killer could go 18: though at 100 a day and it began to sour.

Tom dropped the rope now, to join in the grind,
The importance of the game growing clear upon his mind,
A further escort of three killers joining in the final fray,
The humpback now coming towards boat, harpooner to pray.

The harpooner got ready in an instant for a frontal shot,
Another notch on his belt secured: if missed, then not,
Seeing the large mass of black coming full steam ahead,
The gap closing fast, harpooner hoping to put this to bed.

The headsman grasped the steering oar with both hands,
Pulled this into chest, further bracing as he kneels then stands,
Leaning back and stabilising himself as best he could,
Harpooner slightly askew, whale coming upon boat of wood.

The harpooner stood then, not too late, not too soon,
Cloud moving, most temporarily, in front of the moon,
Now sudden realization, the humpback, oneself did expose,
The harpooner struck hard, iron in head, straight for the nose.

Released a good throw that penetrated deep and stuck well,
The 'fast fish' was made, darkened moon no evil spell,
The harpooner had secured a good line for lancing to start,
Thinking himself proud, a great harpooner, possibly smart.

The whole issue of fight and slander had worked to a means,
Their purses to fill with colour of money, not magical beans,
Even before the try-pots could boil the blubber of carcass won,
He was counting his chickens, such victory, such hazardous fun.

But the humpback did not see this to his front,
And so reared its head, a tremendous brunt,
His head, broad and rounded, as from the top you saw,
A rounded protuberance beneath the tip of the lower jaw.

Fleshy knobs of barnacle covering most of its head,
Where blowhole sat a spouting, but not of red,
The vapours were of that reddish tinge so often sought,
Flew seven feet into the air and whale still far from caught.

Thrashing from side to side, back now arching, whale much alive,
The flukes coming up towards the surface in preparation to dive,
Seen here was a small dorsal fin, two-thirds down its back,
A nubbin of little consequence, of no importance should we stack.

Water fell upon them from beneath the crushing flukes, dissipated,
A convex shaped surge of surf that was disassociated,
Disassociated from the calm of the ocean, or of the sea,
A separate entity with one concern and one concern only there be.

To drench those within the boat, men who belong on shore,
To soak the wearers of jacket and shirt to the very core,
And gasps of shock erupted from their mouths, none alone,
As the cold of the water hit home, to the very bone.

The stabbing of the ocean's dousing driving home as it can,
That the waters around were dangerous, no playground for man,
Horrors now bland, stillness mused to come over the ocean wave,
The whale and the killers had disappeared, from sight they cave.

Several men surrendered their oars and quickly emptied the boat,
Bailing out water, all amazed that they were still afloat,
Working fast and furious to the best of their ability,
Before returning back to oars, their command, their duty.

The surface then erupted once more into a flurry,
The body masses of all involved surfaced again in a hurry,
The harpooner then changed positions with headsman real fast,
Lancing to commence immediately, hopefully not to last.

All of a sudden silence fell over them again,
And once more all appeared and seemed to be in vain,
Nothing but the cloud in the sky and the light of the moon,
The sea and its stabbing cold, but they had thought too soon.

By the time George took the stern the fighting was in full swing,
Two species of whale beneath, a ballet, a fight, to herald and sing,
Great chunks of blubber torn from the humpback, a near tonne,
But the fight below the surface was far from won.

The humpback was trying to head for deeper water,
To make for an escape, away from the slaughter,
And again they surfaced, surges of water, the oars pulled in,
Bursts of fury, a fight most furious, upon man not a single grin.

The killers were rallying together,
This their strength, their strongest tether,
Their ability to work as a team, providing support,
The orca swarmed from all sides, their frantic effort.

As the green boat continued to maintain its visual connection,
The strengthening of the humpbacks desire, a resurrection,
The harpoon still secure for the minute but lancing stalled,
Orca did all they could to hamper an escape, unabatedly mauled.

Killers threw themselves upon the blowhole of whale,
Others snatched on to lips without fail,
Ripping chunks from its bulk, Tom taking another bite,
With bites from fins and fluke, from any site.

In another effort to throw the assault into affray,
The humpback dived and turned, as though to stray,
The harpoon line falling slack, a bad omen, bad fate,
An order to counter the turn, for all to hear, came too late.

The movement of the rope and boat had caught George's leg,
Into the calm ocean he toppled, a tough man, who does not beg,
But the stabbing cold had knocked the wind from him most clean,
Like never before, the watery surrounds, its endeavour to demean.

Sam and Albert sprang to life and commenced to cut the line free,
Allow the humpback small victory: one they would likely not see,
The large mass of humpback heading away from them now,
Time of the essence, to aid George, somewhere near the bow.

For what seemed an eternity the headsman was being dragged,
Beneath the surface, no longer encumbered by rope, not snagged,
Of the cut rope George now fought his way clear,
Removed weight of shoes and jacket, for panic did smear.

Smear his judgement but not his cause,
To fight for survival, not to give in, not to pause,
He worked himself to he surface where the light from the moon,
Brought great slathers of relief and not too soon.

The boat was more than four football fields away,
He now alone, far from rescued, bobbing around, to gently sway,
The solace of ocean this minute forgotten, unlike unkind remarks,
As he tread water in order to stay afloat, he thought: sharks!

Cowards they were, one and all, these heinous carnivores,
Scared to death of Orcinus, no matter where one takes its tours,
But drawn to the actions of their fight for food, like a spell,
They come running, remain at distance, to this ringing of bell.

Nothing like supping on the remains of a humpback,
Whether a great meal or simply a snack,
Scroungers to devour and take what they need,
No opportunity passed on when, or where, to feed.

And where to find sharks of the ocean,
Forever on the move, forever in motion,
Everywhere, anywhere, an encumbrance of the deep,
Of water and shore, allowing them to take, to forever reap.

George could feel their presence,
He was sure of it, the very essence,
And then it came upon his ears, the disturbance of the surface,
Amidst the swirling of the sea, that dread, life to efface.

He was at more risk of death now, than ever before,
Alone in the water and so far from shore,
No boat by his side and no knife to ward off an intruder,
Dark annals of the waters about him, lurking was a marauder.

His eyes popped from his skull as a fin came into view,
Heading for him on a slight angle, closer it drew,
The unmistakable mast of a shark on the prowl,
No audible warning: no snarl from lion, or from bear a growl.

But what was this? Something thrown into the mix,
More fin rose; NO! A dorsal! Shear remedy to fix,
And the knob atop the fin... damn, it was hard to see,
Yes indeed, it was; it was Tom: Oh, glory be.

But was he to be relied upon,
Tom was like a formidable weapon,
He was a double-edged sword,
Either single or an orca horde.

Tom then filled George with slight dread,
A little terror upon face of George easily read,
He knew killers were more menacing than sharks ever were,
Shark feared killer, so killer was most feared, with wrath to incur.

No shark ever interfered with the joys of a killer whale,
As it fed upon its victims, this no myth or fairy tale,
Was Tom, who he knew, from the safety of his green boat,
Here to take him in jaws, crunch him like a peanut, then to gloat.

Many times had George seen a killer take on a shark or two,
Or seen one take on a whale so enormous and large, it was true,
By all comparison, that before him now was beyond all belief,
He imagined the worst, what it could do to him, and be so brief.

Tom looked upon this man, seeing George close up and personal,
Bobbing there, up and down, a salmon ready to take, to maul,
George grew more tense, the beast, closing the gap ever more,
It swam around him, George watched, to clarify what he saw.

He consoled himself, Tom would leave him be, not toy and eat,
Not tear him like rag, drawn into throat, eternal doom to meet,
And the minutes would tell, but safety then threw a lifeline,
For the cloud above gave sight to moon, a sight so fine.

Releasing itself from the clouds so high in the sky,
The green boat and its crew, he could not deny,
Out of the darkness, as a knight to the rescue,
The men at arms, the chivalrous, the ones he loved and knew.

And as spoken, George then saw friendship in Tom's eye,
Tom nodding his head, a gesture, no exaggeration, no lie,
And so with the shark having fled and George soon to be safe,
Tom returned to the fight against whale, to harass, to chafe.

The boat then drew alongside as he knew it would,
Plucked him, wrapped him in blanket as fast as they could,
The experience was unbelievable, this great monster of the sea,
Protector most friendly and warm, most humble and free.

He had surrendered himself until George was safe from harm,
Despite initial terror and within his head the ringing of alarm,
Had aided him until rescued by the others of his entourage,
So lucky he were for this experience, this stirring, by and large.

Tom was indeed a good friend,
There to aid, to help, to defend,
George almost a meal for a shark,
But light was drawn from the dark.

Tom then returned to his pod under Big Ben, most worthy,
Big Ben recalled how they protected men before, did agree,
How they protected them in their case of flesh, to assist,
But Tom had taken it to the next level, new contract to persist.

It seemed nothing more than stupidity to get so close to the men,
With danger looming, all so tense and fragile, but slightly uneven,
Tom could have been seen as the threat, men acting against him,
Skewered by harpoon and lance as he did protect, as he did swim.

Tom felt as though there was more than a common connection,
That there existed a greater understanding, just short of perfection,
Men served them, aiding the hunt, gifted them lip and tongue,
Ever since the Yuin of years past, worshipers and heroes unsung.

And so Tom had laid this question or immortal aid and law,
A foundation on which to continue the build, strong with no flaw,
They each seemed to have a better understanding of one another,
The bond between them strengthened, never to break or to suffer.

THE WHITE HEATHER

In 1901, 19 killer whales returned: Stranger, Youngster, Walker,
Big Ben, Tom, Hooky, Jimmy, Little Jack, Cooper,
Humpy, Jackson, Skinner, Charlie Adgery, Sharkey,
Big Jack, Young Ben, Albert, Kinscher, Brierly.

The humpback population would receive a reprieve this year,
Though still numerous in number, with this security does appear,
Easy pickings for the three pods working the numbers,
Pods under Stranger, Big Ben and Humpy, rope's core not fibres.

But bad news upon the horizon did show its ugly head,
Norwegian whalers in Australian waters putting resource to bed,
Shooting quite openly, Orcinus as they swam harmlessly about,
Clarified by Norwegians boasting, recklessly and with loud shout.

Norwegians concerned that the orca would eat their Godly ware,
Taking money from their pockets, more than their fare share,
A demoralising dilemma staining the traits of man, his ignorance,
Such so that the Yuin were moving from Eden and sustenance.

And so gone is a commodity of people, hard workers strong,
Annoyed by the whalers and all they did that was wrong,
Norwegian whalers, employing motors not oars,
A grievance and mistrust, insult to Orcinus and their laws.

For Tom it wasn't so much as a requirement to survive,
After so many years it was more about feeling alive,
With the aid of man they had learnt to thrive,
To collaborate with men on surface, or with pod in a dive.

They cooperated with the crews, the men of the green boats,
For the pleasure of the chase, of the hunt, a feeling that bloats,
For the thrill of the kill, part of human life, this magic potion,
People that walked on land, and also swam in the ocean.

During the final stages of Davidson's enterprise, do not deny,
With cost of oil falling, bay whaling was starting to die,
A friend named J.R.Logan aided the green by towing to ocean,
In reach of baleen by use of White Heather, poetry in motion.

203

White Heather, a yacht of lines and pleasure,
A joy to watch and to sail a great leisure,
To tow the row boats quite happily to where they need,
To the scene of the hunt, oil to harvest, orca to feed.

The use of silent and effective hand-thrown harpoon and lance,
Still great commodity employed, securing a kill, a good chance,
But the affection was the most formidable feeling, a golden gem,
Orcinus feeling more for the crews than the crews felt for them.

And this is the way it was all of those years ago,
Good memories to pour sour, mournful memories soon to sow,
Though for the present they apt to do as they could,
To hunt together as Tom knew they would.

THE FAILURE

The passing of George's father came in 1903,
Memories flooding back, scenes easy to see,
Dreams filled with the laughter and fighting spirit,
Whaling will continue, his life worthy of great merit.

The hunt must continue hence reflections held back,
Personal ruminations not permitted to stack,
For the mind was a fragile place, subtle, easy to cave,
No place for this on the ocean, thrashed by wind and wave.

George looked over the men in the boat as they rammed the bow,
Into the little surf that sprang up before them, high then low,
Each breaking upon the sleekness of their tool-of-the-trade,
Seemingly unbreakable, far from truth, though sturdily made.

He lapsed most temporarily upon his father,
Then saw the characters of those to the front in lather,
Another boat could be heard as it too entered surging wave,
The water encountered with a thud by the brave.

The men before him, stroking the sea with their oars,
As they knew how, harnessing strength from their very pores,
their backs were facing him as he came upon them from the stern,
Men of adventure, of ocean, men one-and-all, never to spurn.

Most were becoming old men with failing gears,
Not just in age but also through the tally of years,
Where hard-yakka piled on the age in double helpings,
Two serves for one, harsh upon the body, but a good innings.

Charlie, Archer [George's brother] and Boyd,
Boyd not to be confused with the opposition, no semblance toyed,
Each long in the tooth but on each George could rely,
Being satisfied with all men, the crews, where courage does lie.

And from the corner of his eye he caught glimpses of shadow,
Noises from afar reached his ear, shallow and narrow,
His senses heightened as he peruse the shore and bay around,
Looking for his opposition: Boyd and Glover to be found.

Both were as keen as he to see a 'fast fish' secured all the more,
Crews filled with ambition, to press their every muscle to the oar,
But there was more strength in character, persistence, ambition,
Than in the strength of muscles, sinew, tissue or perspiration.

Glover could be seen approaching from upon the flank,
Slightly behind George and his two boats: if only they sank,
But the competition wouldn't let up, not throw in the towel,
They might break an oar, but wouldn't quit, trying not to fail.

But George had the orca up his sleeve, his joker,
Of one thing he had learnt it was how to play poker,
For humpbacks and rights were all unpredictable,
Though with the killer's cooperation all was more stable.

The men continued to lean into the work, sweat-sodden shirts,
Their backs breaking as they asserted their Achilles efforts,
Muscle of character tearing up water, power, golden gilt,
Conviction of sustained power over every inch and yard spilt.

This was commandeering action, one learnt over many a year,
For it was an unknown, how many days or weeks would appear,
Before opportunity arose once more, to display how they felt,
Display this fortitude built of steel, dealing all that could be dealt.

With sudden realisation and the clarity of the chase racing back,
Falling upon their minds in flashes and splashes of black,
Ocean shrouding their boats, confetti upon glimmering wave,
The humpback bursting from ocean, no way to escape the grave.

The humpback majestically lifted itself from the watery tomb,
Only the flukes embalmed as though still connected to womb,
To crash back upon the ocean, to be greeted by Orcinus orca,
Killer throwing itself over the blowhole, a menace, a stalker.

The horror struck faces of the men in the green boat,
Was surreal, for such a scene was rare, so up close and afloat,
Time seemed to pause, or to simply slow down,
This action before their very eyes, whale of renown.

Orders to the rowers were issued amidst calmness and ease,
Loud bellows surely heard over theatre of war as it did tease,
But some men were haphazardly slow and oars bore the brunt,
Oars breaking, a whale gone crazy, thrash of body to their front.

Sam Haddigaddi paused for a second before thrusting a harpoon,
Thrust with much power, iron of death, not too late, not too soon,
Departing his calloused hand another oar snapped like toothpick,
Sam thinking he had broken his arm with throwing of iron stick.

The squelch of point entering the whale, unnoticed by all around,
All but the whale that bore the brunt of the throw, heard the sound,
For the noise went raking across and cascaded down his back,
Deafening at the least, this terrifying assault, this blatant attack.

Every throw was the same, no matter the whale, the species,
The heart-wrenching threat, Death calling for death, no mercies,
The agony of knowing was the worst but fight on he would,
Even if drowned, by hand of man or devils of ocean as it stood.

But fight he did and continued with a great spurting of energy,
Coalesced force so supernatural, a drawing from pores, a synergy,
Racing towards the face of the cliff which overhung ocean wide,
Turning abruptly, melee entered, killers and men, side by side.

How it stood: the channel to freedom not open to the humpback,
He turned again towards the cliff, powerful flukes it did not lack,
And the killers felt as though the time had come, once and for all,
To finish off this beast of beasts, a death he did strenuously stall.

With pure suddenness the humpback disappeared under the water,
The green boat turned as though upon a leisurely saunter,
And the whale began to surface with the boat upon its back,
The men jostling for hold of the fragile shell upon mass of black.

As the head of the whale began to surface and the boat to slide,
George leapt to feet without second thought, and leapt to side,
Landing upon the whale's back, as though meaning to ride,
Before pushing up again so hard, back to boat, on thwart astride.

The looks upon the men spoke more than words ever could,
And for briefest of moments the entire world sang as it should,
That the name Fearless George was humble, had true meaning,
And the chase then continued with smiles on men all gleaming.

Demise of their situation then bit hard,
The humpback refusing to give a yard,
Would not fall victim to the whims of either killers nor man,
A last ditch effort made once more, a cunning, malicious plan.

Instinct to survive, so strong within this creature beneath the skies,
Now seemingly up to the killers to bring about his final demise,
This mass of blubber trying to escape the snapping of jaw,
Orca only wishing to feed, to bring whale into a ravenous maw.

With one last ditch effort the killers forced, quite undeniably,
The humpback upon the rocks near South Head, most inevitably,
Where the last breaths of life fused in rapid action, then ceased,
Panic and torment having taken its toll, of life the whale released.

It was a sad state of affairs for both man and beast,
For the carcass was going nowhere, to be had no feast,
Out of reach of the killer's mouths and in difficult surrounds,
For the securing of blubber, no, for it was out of bounds.

There was no need to anchor and buoy the carcass as usual,
No need to wait for the gases to re-float that sunken from visual,
This predicament out of the ordinary, upon the rocks to stay,
No easy access to secure the blubber and hence nothing to pay.

What God gives with one hand he takes with the other,
And in respect to this dilemma, it did nothing but smother,
It did suffocate their morale, for the whale was going nowhere,
Not able to tow it into harbour, almost too much to bear.

The mass would have to be deblubbered where it lay,
Upon the rocks of the shore where it stubbornly did stay,
From beneath the cliff, no afternoon sunshine, out of luck,
Where blasts from a westerly wind lashed, relentlessly struck.

It was here, amongst the rocks, the surf, and heavy wave,
Making strong legs unstable, stability upon brittle stave,
Strength drained like sorrows of a drunkard on bar stall,
To suffer this burden, to do all they could, to answer the call.

And the men looked out across the ocean on occasion,
Where swells further out crest higher, poor weatherly fashion,
A storm brewing, turning sour, to fill all hope with scorn,
Forcing fingers to work harder still, to bone seemingly torn.

They all knew well that they had several hours of work ahead,
But did not know how long it would last, this could not be read,
The crashing of waves upon them and the rocky outcrop,
The angry ocean growing in ferocity and anger, it would not stop.

It was as though Poseidon by name and by justice,
Angered by the taking of creature, from the ocean did notice,
Not pleased the humpback should be cut into chunks and strips,
To have its body slashed, to be melted down, and for orca no lips.

Further out the killers congregated and swam in a circle,
Annoyed to hilt, a meal of sustenance denied them, an oracle,
Men weren't to blame; and neither was it the fault of the ocean,
The damn whale, beached upon the rocks, to deny: its ambition.

The killers gave to spy-hopping and watched the men work,
Men securing the catch as best they could, all frowning, no smirk,
Tools ferried from the try-works and the carving had begun,
Blubber caked the rocks, sheaves of white, dreary, lack of sun.

But Poseidon was to gift them something special, a reward,
For with the storm came another opportunity, one not to hoard,
A call received further out, a whale bypassing their position,
A sperm whale with calf further out to sea, a grand commission.

An uncommon occurrence which grew scarcer each year,
An offering so good, less and less did such appear,
Extinction caused by man and his incessant need,
Man's unwavering destruction, his almighty greed.

But a mother and calf,
That was a meal and half,
And for the joy of taste and chase,
They swam to stare it in the face.

The signal came again, the calf being of reasonable size,
The pack of killers would do well to swim and receive their prize,
The sperm and her calf were on a course away from the pack,
The killers sure to catch up and by morning's first light be back.

To the sperm whale there was no real concern,
For the killers were so far away, but she would soon learn,
Yet she would maintain an open ear, pursue her purpose, her need,
Her quest for warmer waters, to feed, maintain her good speed.

The Hawaii Islands were a long way, she knew the waters well,
Knew of great abundances of food, delight on which to dwell,
And with her attention turned fully once more to the path ahead,
She moved amidst the noise of ocean and creatures of ocean bed.

Orca, on the hunt, dangerous and hungry, to deliver their skill,
To sink teeth into the best blubber of all, for them more than a kill,
To rip at the calf, a manipulative action, before resighting,
Then setting sights upon the mother, to continue their fighting.

It wouldn't be easy, for the female would hinder their every move,
Give her all to secure survival of her young, with much to prove,
But try as she might the killers would win their prize,
They would receive their fill, a mother of substantial size.

By this time the men upon the rocks had completed their task,
With no time to waste, no time to scratch: or for unpleasant bask,
And soon with their oars in the water they were going along,
The weather growing in its ferocity, sapping all feeling of song.

Mounting waves of surging white crashing with great intent,
Upon the place where the humpback's remains were spent,
Now washed into the ocean as though a gaping mouth so great,
A small meal for the smallest of fish to have a measly treat.

And crab would take their share, seagulls would make their move,
All creatures and critters of ocean and coast now in the groove,
Move now for a delay would see the storm wash all so far away,
So all who were to sup, joined in the feeding, a scandalous fray.

THE RIDE

The proprieties of bay whaling in 1904 were tasteless and stale,
The dashed ambitions of men, the infrequent appearance of whale,
The costs: good money required to run a bunkhouse full of men,
To run several boats and household, a luxury now and then.

It is true that idleness breeds dissatisfaction and discontent,
That sitting back with nought to do did not pay the rent,
Unable to afford the luxury of butter on bread,
With inappropriate behaviour so coloured and always dread.

Drink was permitted but not something one could easily atone,
Gambling an inbred vacuum sucking pockets as dry as a bone,
Most often winnings lost the following week, so weak the hold,
And pay was seldom offered until an harvest was sold.

So when the time comes for the call to be made,
Rousing itself from the roll of the tongue and easily laid,
Men jump into boats wrapped in layers of warmth, in comfort,
Scampering for thwarts and oars of their beloved with effort.

They do so with such urgency, as though the entire town is on fire,
And they the only firemen for miles around, their speed most dire,
For not only were they in competition with others of similar mind,
But in a timely chase against the hands of clock: don't fall behind.

For every breath was a milestone,
Every humpback, oil and bone,
Quite often escaping, easily lost,
Amidst winds laden with heavy frost.

Nigel B. J. Clayton

These men did not serve by way of a written contract,
Meagre wages not secured if there was no resource to extract,
But were paid with what the headsman could suckle from buyers,
Always quoting low prices, the best of the best, true liars.

In some cases this was substantial: no rich path to pave,
Even though prices rose and fell like the ocean wave,
But most rewarding of all was the work conducted,
A group of men toiling: a team well orchestrated.

Even so the men would not abandon their captain,
Knew there would be no riches flowing from fountain,
And wages paid islanders, whites, half-castes and aborigines,
Was the same all round: no racist boundaries, drawing of lines.

And so men sit at table, playing cards, hunched over a cup of tea,
When all of a sudden the call comes from aloft a horse at spree,
The beast breathing heavily and being ridden so hard,
Towards men awaiting call of RUSHO, word sung from bard.

A poetic call to action, for nothing else mattered this minute,
Crowd of men crossing cobbles in a sprint, each filled with spirit,
The ground around shook, the bustling steps, thundering of sound,
Call to boats, fresh morning air doused in mist, action to astound.

Individuals clambered aboard their boat with quickened ease,
Oars picked up and thrust into position, anxieties to increase,
Surface of the bay quickly stroked to propel them ever forward,
Towards prize yet unclear, beyond visual, fathom, inch and yard.

And then the spouting caught the eye of George so assuredly,
Two humpbacks, beasts hounded by dogs of the sea most forcedly,
The wolves of the water, encumbrance of the baleen,
Devils of the murky surrounds, black and white, out to demean.

They were the evil at the backs of angels,
The shackles of torment, abusive bangles,
Of the earth and sky great eagles,
Above all, the dorsal of death that mangles.

The two humpbacks, forced towards the boats amidst whale song,
Driven towards the battle of wills, and the will of man is strong,
A man is stronger than Orcinus for he is willing to die,
Would readily give up his life in order for his children to fly.

Where a killer whale would only stress itself to its limits,
Lacking that understanding, or inability, or lacking spirit,
A man will fight to the death, with all his strength and might,
A killer would fall back, conserve its energy, give up the fight.

210

And so Harpoons and lances were struck and stuck,
The two whales secured within an hour of fighting, such luck,
Two boats and sidekicks fight, two species against humpback,
Each of medium size, but still a great victory, a great attack.

They were both good kills, secured within good time,
And relief fell from the men's eyes as though doused in lime,
For their purses now had something, no longer a vacant berth,
Even if for only a short time, that magic paper of great worth.

The drought had been watered, the show was now on the road,
A great and heavy burden lifted from their shoulders, a sour load,
Everyone thought how lucky they were with this good fortune,
Of two such quick kills, one after the other, the lifting of evil rune.

And without thought the humpbacks were anchored and buoyed,
Killers taking their reward as usual, to east they deployed,
The men to return on the morrow to bring home the bacon,
But something was brewing, further out, something well shaken.

That night the winds blew as the men slumbered well,
The heavens being shaken by the very cores of hell,
As strong wind wakes deeply embedded roots of a gigantic tree,
For three days the weather grew against the men in ferocity.

The gases within the whales would have had their way,
Having increased within the carcasses, buoyant within the day,
Each floating to the surface, ready for harvest, waiting for tether,
But no move could be made upon them in this weather.

The water around Whale Spit Beach was like a kettle on the boil,
Far too dangerous for little boats, men so fragile, too large a toil,
The fortitude of men, so easily swayed by power of ocean or sea,
But that's the way it was, that is life, the way it will always be.

By the fourth day it was accepted no more, and so with loud shout,
The boats forced themselves into the ferocity, heart's so stout,
The coast scoured both up and down for any sign of the whales,
But they had broken from the anchors, were lost amidst the gales.

And the torn looks upon the faces of the men told the story,
Gone were their wages, destroyed beyond regain, here no glory,
Drought scoured not only farmlands but ocean as well,
With it the optimism, panic striking hearts like ringing of bell.

Now was the time to face the reality of the situation,
George walked in on the men as they sat at their station,
The gloom around the table, cups of tea nestled in hand,
Sourly toasted the few choices they had, of where they did stand.

But the men refused to hear of it, banged at the top of table,
Refused to admit defeat, rallied to their captain's side most able,
To remain loyal, to be strong, to be steadfast in their conviction,
They would stay and continue, like men, to face their perdition.

Each was sure in mind that their fate was not written,
That there was plenty more on which to feed, that could be bitten,
They were sure as sure can be that the tide would turn to better,
That more whales were just around the corner awaiting fetter.

And as miraculous as it was, their words were correct,
Their harpoons and lances would not rust with neglect,
For they caught themselves two whales just two days later,
Nine in total over the next three weeks, each greeted by laughter.

The conditioning, of both species, had sprung to life,
More than simple feelings, or gestures, came from this strife,
There was camaraderie amongst them, for each served the other,
Both men and Orcinus being... courteous, careful not to smother.

From the killers point of view the humans were nothing to adore,
Men were to be used to the best of their ability and nothing more,
And men understood that killers fell well to their duties,
Performed as desired and willed, an amalgamation of abilities.

Orcinus, competing for food: by such, escalating their abilities,
But also relying upon the energy and prowess of the other species,
But there was always room for improvement,
And plenty to learn and see, and great amazement.

To the men in boats it was part of the day, each working their roll,
Arduous work endured, but after time, like taking leisurely stroll,
For orca it was harvesting sustenance by means of collaboration,
The tethering of secular importance, and a great manipulation.

People and animals do all they can to secure a living, to survive,
Whether one receives money as reward, or a meal, each will strive,
It is of utmost importance, in life, to seek an opportunity,
To reap the rewards of harvest, of one's strenuous activity.

This was something that Tom knew well and put into practice,
He was no stranger, he was not simple, he was not novice,
He was more than adamant to learn and to influence,
To gain advancement and never be an inconvenience.

The night was reasonably calm and flop-tailing called out,
A call to boats, for men to attend their duty, a loud shout,
One boat, faster than other, did disappoint Tom within the bay,
More boats the merrier: a faster kill, no time to delay.

George's crew flashed ahead of Alex Grieg's boat,
Separated by a football field of misery, but they did not gloat,
Such brought on a suffering misery for Alex that night,
One short lived for George, nothing there to cause great plight.

Suddenly a right whale showed itself by spouting high and wide,
Moon beams glistening off skin of monster, waves he did ride,
Followed by the disturbance of water, the bubbling of surface,
As killers bit with all their might, thrashing about at fast pace.

Arthur Ashby took his position with pride and hurled his harpoon,
Threw with all the power he could muster, not too late or soon,
It stuck, fast fish secure, and it then turned tail, of sturdy mind,
Commenced to head out to sea, trying to leave the boats behind.

The whale was secured, the rope let out, a good, tactical strike,
Although further away from the shore then they would like,
Not only this but Alex and his crew were falling further behind,
Spurring themselves on by power of oar, speed playing on mind.

Tom then saw the dilemma and acted immediately,
Pulled away from the fray, stripping the others of his ability,
Pod members looked upon him briefly and with anxiousness,
Opening their mouths, exposing their teeth, an aggressiveness.

Noisily clapping their jaw together, voicing their anger,
Frustrated by Tom vacating his post, his audacity, his demeanour,
They displayed their dissatisfaction, their displeasure,
Tom's unpredictable act could lose them their treasure.

With sudden amazement, Tom grabbed onto the whale line,
Allowed himself to be pulled along, the act so hard to define,
The green boat just a dozen feet behind him as the whale slowed,
The men flabbergasted to say the least, Tom now being towed.

The very implication that Tom was helping, was sheer ludicrous,
But there it was; so absurd, hard to believe, so ridiculous,
Tom was slowing the progress of the whale to such a degree,
That Alex and crew were gaining ground: Tom, a legend to be.

It was painted clear as a picture for all to see,
The other crew catching up along their side, upon the lee,
And here the harpooner of the other boat stood, good stance,
Secured against concave of the thwart, towards whale did glance.

Alex let loose with the second harpoon for the day,
To secure a link, to remain fastened, lance to strike as they may,
Tom then released his hold upon the line and re-joined his pod,
Having gained much approval from all of the men with a nod.

Suddenly the space between the ribs was pierced by lance,
The death-throes of whale illuminating the killer's exuberance,
Forcing their way into the mouth of the dying whale at a flood,
Tearing at his lips as from the blowhole came much blood.

The whale was putting up a hell of a fight,
At one stage leapt more than 16 feet into sight,
Seen with three killers still attached to his lip,
A vision to behold as he tried to flip.

The right whale was losing his energy for no reward,
Five more minutes and it's all over as boats surge forward,
The combined efforts of man and beast having won the day,
Life over for another mammal, so great was the fray.

With the whale was marked as usual, anchor and marker attached,
Dawned then upon George an opportunity, a new scheme hatched,
He looked over the men, gave orders, oars to ocean, to embrace,
As into the murky waters the killers, with meal, did race.

Orcinus would do as they pleased, in 24 hours George to return,
The humpback would re-float, ready to be towed, ready to churn,
George then announced of his moments thought and reflection,
To secure yesterday's kill early, drag her in, men called to action.

And fortune served the whalers, gases having completed their job,
Now ready to tow her back to try-works, 4.5 miles, no short lob,
But the night was pleasant: cold, the moon shone above,
The task most achievable, one to warm the core, not to love.

The markers were sought, pulled in and the anchor too,
Several ropes attached to the carcass, tied well as they knew,
And the men braced for the hard slog home, to work all night,
Heading for the coastal town, for their beacon, their light.

Their backs broke under the strain,
But as they say, no pain, no gain,
And 4.5 miles was a big ask, a large price to render,
The tide a little against them, the moon watching in wonder.

In time the moon would make its way across the sky to the west,
Bringing a little relief in the form of medium tide at its best,
But that was far away at present, not to be seen anytime soon,
Currently of thought was a warm bed, after soup with a spoon.

Although the weather seemed to be in their favour,
Their previous task and this long haul was too much labour,
With little energy they pushed on, not superheroes of action,
But of flesh and bone, disciplined by money, the true motivation.

They pulled upon the oars with all their strength and might,
Continued on as best they could against the tide this night,
The lights ahead of them showed where Twofold Bay lay,
But it was still very far off, so very far away.

After hours of pulling the monster behind,
So little progress having assaulted the mind,
With hardened hands starting to show signs of wear,
Men over-worked, a heavy strain, fabric of souls did tear.

Another thirty minutes and George waved the white flag,
Their bones worn, bodies shot, exhausted, strips of rag,
They now head on home without the cargo hence tied,
To return in the morning, after good rest, sleep no longer denied.

THE HEINOUS CRIME

In 1904 the number of killer whales was altered by one,
Unprecedented and unfortunate, to their cores it stung,
Before the eyes of most, including George, in boat, in bay,
With rudder in his palms, skies pleasant, open, and grey.

He was near where a whale had been buoyed and anchored,
Set upon entrance to bay where it had been stored,
Awaiting the gases to build, the bulge to move and re-float,
Any time now, dead whale to be seen, he cleared his throat.

And here it came, a gentle breaking, the surface disturbed,
No reasonable explanatory to employ, no decent word,
Ready for towing, to try-works to mend,
To deblubber in earnest, to cut and rend.

The try-works, men surrendering to work to be accursed,
Back-breaking at best and back-breaking at worst,
Suffering the intolerable smell and flies as they fly,
Seagulls on the light breeze, pestering beaks that defy.

One of the men in the boat was suddenly drawn to a chase,
Pointed it out to the others for cheer, not to abase,
For Jackson was alone, chasing a grampus over surf,
Gaining ground on the dolphin in violation of his turf.

The dolphin's all-inspiring effort to escape its devastating future,
A bleak and unconditional devouring which was to be a butcher,
Men smiled as they watched the chase and pulled upon their oars,
Ready to give momentary shout, ready to give open applause.

Suddenly they were all filled with fright,
Anxiousness that lasted mere seconds upon the fight,
Continuing to look upon the scene so far away,
So wide and expansive was the bay.

Jackson, so well through the shallows he propelled, he steers,
Breaking waves, crystal clear, upon beach and amidst leers,
But the chase was about to meet its end as grampus moved aside,
And Jackson fell upon the sandy beach; high and dry, end of ride.

Only his flukes felt the stimulus and comfort of water upon him,
He thrashed about in an effort to free himself of situation so grim,
As the grampus made its way safely back towards the open ocean,
And the men seeing the dilemma, Jackson and his lack of motion.

Too far from the water's edge to secure delivery into the surf,
Unable to move himself back into that place of his birth,
Without the assistance of the men of Eden and their green boat,
He was doomed to die there, on the beach, never again to float.

Without further ado they steered towards the killer as he thrash,
Trying to regain ground upon retreating waves, in them to dash,
The moon high in the sky, upon the other side of the globe,
Pulling tide from beneath Jackson, as though from man a robe.

The men felt that they had little time to procure a rescue,
Jackson would not function well upon the beach of hue,
And as they rowed, they saw, gulls make good of the opportunity,
Set on down and stand their ground, clear of harm's way in unity.

Gulls, looking upon the giant killer with eyes as large as saucers,
Squawking, stomachs to be filled, a gathering of scroungers,
Wishing with all their will to be able to peck out the drying eyes,
To take any advantage, to savour what they could with no ties.

And then a figure came into view as it walked Aslings Beach,
On towards Jackson, every step characteristic of body speech,
Harry Silks, homeless and obtuse, had seen the orca wash ashore,
With inward feelings so harshly felt, of orca he did deplore.

The men collaborated on Silks as he suddenly sprang into action,
He seeing George and men in their green boat, and their reaction,
Commenced to run fast towards Jackson, neither astute nor shy,
Seemingly wishing to be first upon the scene; but why?

The men continued upon their salvation of the killer whale,
Whom meant so much to them, of significance never to pale,
Silks acting suspiciously, without good cause or good reason,
Making ground fast upon orca, as though out to cause treason.

The whalers, wishing no more than to see Jackson safe from harm,
See him turned back into the surf, to aspire and calm that alarm,
The calming of inner terror, to impart their aid in this situation,
Unable to fathom the outcome to unfold: shaken from foundation.

And in full view of crew Silks withdraw a knife from a scabbard,
Stabbed the defenceless whale to death so very hard,
Followed quickly by his running away, so fast he bolt,
From the threats flung his way, of the verbal assault.

Several other orca had rallied to the scene of the splashing fluke ,
Poor Jackson unable to effect good move, of ocean to rebuke,
They too struck hard by the horrific scene, no laughable banter,
An astounding and heart-breaking offence, of needless slaughter.

And come what may, Tom and the others departed the bay,
Shocked and exasperated, for a few days, away to stay,
What would become of the contract between man and beast?
What was to become of Silks? Something at least.

Unknown to the killer whales of this town,
Silks was escorted away, never to be of good renown,
By the local law enforcers for his own protection,
Never to be seen of again, to help relieve the tension.

George undertook to repair the damage done, began legal action,
By first writing a letter to the Eden Progress Association,
To have the orca protected by law, to have them conserved,
To feel as though some form of justice had been served.

And within a few days another humpback was steered,
By fewer in number, fewer dorsal appeared,
The devastation of Jackson's slaughter, his killing,
Had seen the pods' number take a large milling.

THE DEATH

August 1907: Stranger was killed by a fisherman in Botany Bay,
Mother to Tom and Hooky, of her absence men pray,
These two siblings of ocean and sea, so fond of Eden and shore,
Felt the bite of separation more than anything, though little rancor.

And it wasn't just the matter of fact that their mother had died,
Nor that their matriarch long, aspiring life had been denied,
But of sadness, that human intervention had failed them again,
Upon their cooperation, their friendship, a great pain and stain.

217

Their mother had been killed by a fisherman for no good reason,
Death sentence to fall, for procuring fish from a net, not treason,
No orca had ever murdered a man, never heard in all of history,
But man had deliberately killed many Orcinus, some for glory.

What ensured that a killer whale 'did not' take the life of a man?
Was it the sense that a human was intelligent, a mammal, of clan?
Why should intelligence procure sanctity and life?
Why did Orcinus refrain from delivering man that great strife?

Not surprising should it be that Tom and Hooky were then absent,
Did not appear in the bay for a year, of their anger to vent,
To return the next, bringing new invigoration,
To start afresh with a greater determination.

But Cooper and Big Ben were more than just friends of Stranger,
Found the parting by death too much to bear, had too much anger,
And so they departed the bay almost immediately thereafter,
With their son Young Ben, though not Albert, their daughter.

Albert, their daughter, chose to remain behind, more to spore,
For she had mothered Charlie Adgery a few years before,
But others were in two minds as to whether to stay,
Or whether to follow the path of others and to stray.

Shortly after, further demise did strike the pod with bad news,
That Big Ben was dead, filling ocean with low-pitched mews,
Dying when stranded on the rocks at Leather Jacket Bay,
Young Ben returned alone, little solace secured, but not to stay.

It was a terrible year for the pod of killers of the bay,
Affecting them all in some small or large way,
First there was Jackson in 1904, and now Stranger,
Followed shortly after by Big Ben, always the eager.

Times were changing; vibrations and smells of ocean told the tale,
They were growing old, their minds seemingly weary and stale,
Vast reservoir of good memories evaporating, replaced by sad,
What was to become of them all? Were victories still to be had?

To the men, whaling was whaling, it mattered little,
Other than price they were to receive, of this resource so brittle,
Regardless of the amount of effort and time displaced,
Whether the whale was big or small it would still be embraced.

Equipment was important, boats best of all they did possess,
If a catch could be secured for little outlay as possible, little stress,
With no damage dealt upon the boats, then it was a good catch,
And one worth remembering on which memory could latch.

But one of the most recalled will be little reflected on by history,
Though a record of the grandest proportion exists, of this story,
Will never be excelled hereafter, for bay whaling is no longer,
And that was in 1910, its capture, a 98 foot blue, if not larger.

The sheer size made the catch a momentous occasion,
For those at the oars were in sheer awe and placation,
But it wasn't so much a case of capture, than one of surrender,
And so we shall extravagate a little of this monstrous stranger.

The blue had a calf that measured over half the mother's length,
A monster which totalled around 98 tonnes: muscle, fat, strength,
Enough oil and bone to tear the stitches of any money bag,
Regardless of form and manufacture, purse to wave the white flag.

The call of RUSHO! went out firm and loud as in the past,
The panting of horse from lookout and flop-tailing to last,
Boast manned, waters entered, ready to secure a humpback,
What they met was sheer disbelief, a blue, and size it did not lack.

By the time they were positioned, ready to deliver their prowess,
George sitting, shoulders back, to harpoon silently bless,
The killers had hounded the mother to such a desperate level,
She did breach upon the shore, great size on which to marvel.

Orcinus had performed so well that the blue was out of reach,
For them no lip and tongue, but the calf was far from beach,
It was the least exciting of all the catches they could remember,
Though so easy for the men, like draining water from manger.

The band of just six killers had done their job well,
A small group compared to before, each year their numbers fell,
Now further on, up the coast, close knit and in rank strung,
Not altogether displeased with the capture of the young.

It was a formidable task, that blue whale so large, no boast,
It could have taken much time to capture if further from coast,
Without the jagged shore the killers alone could not have won,
Not over this whale [she would be lost] weighing so many tonne.

There was still that exuberance from Humpy's pod, all pleased,
Pleasure that surged through them, pleasure which they released,
By show-boating and larking about, jumping from the ocean,
Breaching here and there upon surface, their home and station.

A trophy to be remembered amongst old saddle patches and new,
Remembered by Kinscher, Little Jack, and Big Jack as they grew,
And here they celebrated, showing off their skills and acrobatics,
Lessons taught to the young, handed down, their excessive antics.

But what of Tom; what made him so different?
What was it that drove his ambition, it so apparent?
What reinforced his strong, unequivocal tolerance?
Why did he display an allegiance to man at first glance?

Tom was a pioneer, a one and only in essence,
A creature bound by the fruits of intelligence,
Intelligence which left the others of his species far behind,
Of this situation... position... predicament: of different mind.

He understood, [a freak of nature], of mind most level,
like the lions, Ghost and the Darkness, but not evil,
Tom beheld unequalled knowledge, instincts of deliberation,
The lions devoured man through superior cunning and ambition.

Tom was a powerhouse of ability and procurement,
A wealth of interpretation within his head at the moment,
He was there to pave the way to the bright light of bonding,
Bonding even Darwin failed to see in the bloom of his bidding.

Tom was similar to man; he could feel hurt and embarrassment,
Feared death and displayed great courage, lived for the moment,
He, the ability to see beyond the makeup upon a man's exterior,
As an astronomer sees beyond the makeup of all that is superior.

THE LOSS

Jimmy fought well on this day [31 years since birth], so snappy,
He came to Twofold Bay several years after the return of Humpy,
A time of upheaval when some killers departed and others stray,
A time of prosperity, of minor issues, a structure in decay.

Little did it matter under the sway of Stranger in years past,
Who for her years and with the power bestowed was sure to last,
Who stood as a strong matriarch with a long list of signals,
Many attack manoeuvres accredited her name, unwritten annuals.

Being far less boisterous than Tom, Jimmy was a quiet mammal,
Was mated with Big Jack, a female of ambition, a strong animal,
Her mother and father being 'offshore' variants, living off fish,
Particularly salmon, than anything else, the perfect dish.

Tired of their life and position in large pod they decided to stray,
Had opted for habitual change, found their way to Twofold Bay,
Here they stayed for several years before moving on once more,
Jimmy, enjoying life with mate Big Jack, stayed on, close to shore.

Big Jack had mothered Kinscher and Little Jack,
A female and a male, neither courage nor beauty did they lack,
Over the year, Jimmy's persona had grown quite substantially,
Amidst this pod of 15, not large or small, maintaining good tally.

And this persona was not just from performance,
Not due to mistaken glance, or by pure chance,
Not because of any great feats noteworthy of praise or acclaim,
But since 1907 Big Jack had been matriarch, by name and fame.

Jimmy felt honoured, was of good position, suffered no neglect,
All brought on a blossom of change regards to effort and effect,
Such effort was accepted well by the other members of the pod,
Treated him well, always content to give him a friendly nod.

And there came a day when a humpback had been cornered,
Again their familiar assaults upon whale, all truly mastered,
Much effort sourced into tiring out this great beast so large,
To create that stress, horror, feeling of doom to hence discharge.

Again and again the blowhole was covered, humpback writhing,
Orca after orca thrown in order to impede its breathing,
Preventing the whale from sounding, to make for vast open water,
To escape through gate of Twofold Bay, to avoid the slaughter.

The men too, were present upon the surface of the ocean so wide,
Prodding away with their sticks of iron, over surface they glide,
Shifting positions, handling oars, yelling out above the noise,
Above the noise of war, to bring the whale to heel with poise.

Several harpoons had been thrown and one was not well secured,
The second had done its job well, lancing now assured,
Humpback putting up a good fight when Jimmy made his move,
To suffocate once and for all, then rip at its flank, nought to prove.

And then something went horribly wrong, a blunt conclusion,
With so many lines in the water and so much confusion,
Such a melee, much flourish about the scene so hastily stack,
Jimmy become entwined with line and sank with the humpback.

The other killers assisted the humpback to the bottom of the bay,
Unaware of Jimmy's predicament, of his position, his last day,
Even the men failed to see anything amiss,
And then Jimmy was heard to cry out, shattering the bliss.

Suddenly Kinscher and Little Jack were alerted to the situation,
Jimmy unable to break free of the mess, now drew much attention,
So little could they do: Jimmy died there, so lovingly prod,
Amidst Kinscher, Little Jack, Big Jack, and others of the pod.

And so several of the pod fell to the pressures of the loss,
Big Jack soon departed, it was too much, now no longer the boss,
Walker [son of Humpy] following in her wake,
And now Young Ben departed for good, to his core it did shake.

For Young Ben the loss of his friend weighed too much on mind,
There had been too much death in the past, nothing left to bind,
Last but not least the following turned their fluke and swam away,
Albert, Skinner and Little Jack, for deeper waters to stay.

The following day the carcass was retrieved by George and crew,
Utterly astounded by what they found as nearer they drew,
To the scene of the floating carcass with Jimmy attached,
Buoyed and anchored with humpback, upon their minds so etched.

A sorry sight, Jimmy strapped to its side, so secure and sound,
Like a baby strapped to its mother back, tightly bound,
A scene never seen before, a sheer jolt to the crew,
They cut the line away, allowing Jimmy to float from view.

Reminded they were, Humpy caught in lines of his making,
Though more fortunate for being noticed prior to whale sinking,
Humpy cut from the lines and set free before death,
Gifted chance at life, awarded another day, another breath.

The men remembered this day as the tragedy it was,
As too did the killer whales of the ocean, these grand orcas,
The whalers cut memory into the woodwork of Boyd Tower,
Along with Peter Lia, Jimmy to be remembered forever.

THE TIME TO FORGET, THE TIME TO RECALL

The Norwegians, in 1913, had mustered 9,500 barrels of oil,
From the east coast of Australia, from its waters, not soil,
Not to dally long, the last of their chasers, to tomb to lay,
In comparison to other companies; a small amount during stay.

But the damage was done and the killer whale was made vacant,
From the waters of Eden, for great stints of time, this instant,
Then a dorsal did appear, through gentle surf, a gift from grave,
Accompanied by smiling faces, of those who knew, giving wave.

Tom was back with Sharkey, Youngster, Humpy,
Kinscher, Brierly, Charlie Adgery and Hooky,
Now the cooperation, of beast and man, continued as per the past,
With reflection upon old times coming clear, but would it last?

Reflections of securing 'fast fish', that joining of destinies,
Reflections upon the unwritten laws between the two species,
Reflections upon the slaughter, feeding on lips and tongue,
Reflections of fun, men receiving their money and victories won.

Other killers came and went over the years,
Although few in number, when parted, always tears,
And migrating whales were killed as they had always been,
Amidst this effort, a legendary corroboration as never before seen.

By no surprise, Tom and George forgot the past: or did not know,
A time when laws sown [lips and tongue] took flower: to grow,
Each law opening a new beginning, the founding of friendship,
But the end was near, killers so few, in sight an end to kinship.

The most horrid of circumstance to hit, was the death of Sharkey,
Jackson's partner, a clash with the Norwegians most deadly,
Killed whilst feeding upon offerings of the ocean, now unclean,
Great Orcinus, the Norwegians so proud to sour and demean.

The Norwegians saw the killers as a pest and little more,
Little else mattered but filling the belly of ship with vast store,
And so Sharkey bought the brunt of their overzealous anger,
Brierly and Youngster then departed the bay of horrors for ever.

There was no bitterness towards those with whom they worked,
They were old and tired, less reliant, and mentally borked,
The whaling industry was faltering as orca numbers diminished,
Fewer each year returned to bloody grounds, they were finished.

WWII came, men disappeared, and once over, back to the ropes,
So many years away, hence their return saw many dashed hopes,
So few killers here now, new season, and a few new men to train,
Boats manned by casuals [not of iron] but unafraid of the rain.

Spring came and went and then summer, autumn and winter,
The same game played each year, mostly sweet, not bitter,
On some occasion there were three killers, at others five,
And the aggressive nature of orca: always heightened and alive.

Even though individuals slowed a little in their old age,
Tom always felt young: of history he alone did turn the page,
In 1923 Kinscher and Charlie Adgery departed, in clear view,
And as the pod decreased in size, George's own family grew.

George, as per Tom, in all comparison to his colleague of ocean,
Remained as fearless as always, as though by some compulsion,
They were peas in a pod, one and the same, dogs of different tail,
A strong bond struck between the two, never weak, never frail.

Never before in the history, save rumours of a man and jungle,
Had man and beast [wolves] performed so well, to truly mingle,
Such performance you would swear had been orchestrated well,
But no, familiarity and trust made them unique, not magical spell.

We recall how in the early twenties, the anchor rope, the painter,
How Tom would quite often grab it so men did not saunter,
It being thrown to him, how he did tow the boat towards whale,
To make good way, good speed upon humpback like strong gale.

Sometimes speedily overtaking George's opposition,
Those that prey on same target, upon them a deflation,
Holding dearly onto the 60 fathoms of 2 inch coir rope, so keen,
Hence preventing others gaining ground, before those of green.

Tom did this in order to secure the kill, to stay alive,
He, and pod, needed the sustenance in order to survive,
Without the aid of George, Tom would meet his end all the sooner,
Without the aid of Tom, the green boats would have been the loser.

Jackie Warren did witnessed the phenomena known as Tom,
In 1926 saw him grab the line of boat, to take it from,
And towed along the surface of ocean so longing and pure,
For the purpose of enjoyment, not for whale to catch or lure.

Or Margaret Brooks having her breath taken by such antics,
Tom pulling against the 'White Heather', of his heroics,
Tugging hard on tow rope, to prevent him taking the prize,
Seemingly depriving the orca, beast of ocean and sea so wise.

Yes indeed, they were times to remember, never to forget,
Times that saw little evaluation by historians which we'll regret,
Soon, however, there was only Tom and two others that remain,
Most having taken to different waters, for their meals to gain.

Neither joining super pods nor really deviating from them,
But remaining unto themselves, too old to grow new stem,
Yet some young members did bud new matrilineal linkage,
And some died, either peaceably or in fights most savage.

It seemed to Tom that his entire life had been spent with men,
His home at Twofold Bay, a history of its own to pen,
Two species having come together in times of hardship and need,
Whether bonding for years, or decades, they finally agreed.

As for Tom's family; well, he had little to show for his merits,
For his offspring had separated from him as nature permits,
Their mother, Tom's mate, refusing to leave her pod of transients,
Tom, never truly feeling alone, discouraging was life's variants.

And year after year saw fewer whales secured for savoury meal,
Orcinus forced to pursue other means of nourishment most real,
To other hunting grounds that did prove fruitful for their needs,
To the great disappointment of old friends and their creeds.

THE MIRACULOUS FIND AND SAD FALL

So many years behind him and so many deaths to date,
George, so ever thankful, that most experiences were first rate,
Each vastly good and few instances of horror and devastation,
But old memories die and new fill the void, no deliberation.

George, married, had a son by the name of Jack, one of three,
And this a recollection of how Tom gave him a dose of dignity,
Handing back to him, his friend so close, in need and desire,
In the year of our Lord, 1926, a miraculous saving, one to admire.

There came a day where the small family of five plus relatives,
Met tragedy, their dinghy submerged, weather endangering lives,
The three children gone missing not more than a dozen feet away,
Freak storm, no warning, a search well needed, on much to pray.

It was a sad fact of fate that saw three deaths in one day,
In a storm which lashed out its evil in more than one way,
The fact of the case is as basic as one, two, three,
A most depressing engagement worth cancelling with glee.

But now married to the fate so devilish flung,
George and family did all they could, no herald sung,
And if Tom were there at the time of the heinous storm,
He would have aided them all, with truth shall hearts warm.

This he proved over the days by entering Bay and approaching,
Closing upon the scene, many boats searching for the missing,
Searching frantically for the bodies of the three that were torn,
Taken from mother most cherished, age now hauntingly worn.

The first two children were found soon enough:
The girl pulled deceased from shallow waters once rough,
And a boy's body from the sandy bottom, his legs most visible,
As for Jack, nothing was found, and all remained most miserable.

Tom could see something amiss, but didn't understand what,
The men were searching for something, upon the area they squat,
Combing over the sea floor, time and time again in their boats,
Grappling hooks out, looking for sign, wrapped in warm coats.

Tom then bombarded the area with his skills taken for granted,
The signals received forming clear picture, he was so astounded,
He could see the body of Jack beneath the surface without fail,
Just beneath the sand where the boats had searched to no avail.

Over the next few days, after the weather beautiful and serine,
Tom continued up and down Whale Spit, hoping to be seen,
Trying with all his presence to show the world what he knew,
He had found the remains of the one the weather cast and threw.

George looked upon his friend of the sea with great admiration,
Tom's presence in his time of need, a mark of respect, a lavation,
For it suddenly dawned that Tom might have something to say,
Was here as a friend most dear to lift the lid on the days so grey.

Tom could see the expression upon George's face,
The sparkle of wonder in his eyes, a reflection of grace,
The methodical ticking away of the brain within his head,
The mind of a man whom is not that easily read.

Tom could see that George had realised the antics of energy spent,
Called for the boat to do another sweep where Tom lay persistent,
And soon found Jack beneath the sand, drew him upon the shore,
Tom followed the boat, paying his respects and very much more.

The other two were buried just two days before sibling Jack,
Now he, bestowed unto hallowed ground, of compassion no lack,
Forty cars, more; vast number having respects to lay, much to say,
Following the hearse as it drew into the cemetery opposite the bay.

Such a large congregation of people: great assembly, great lot,
All in complete silence, many in black, there on the spot,
Only the soft tones of the priest lifting themselves to the breeze,
Floating down towards the bay, no clear understanding to seize.

Tom had completed his duty well, a right hand man, a deputy,
Had offered assistance to his friend, beyond the call of duty,
The bond so strong between, one that could never be broken,
Above and beyond the law of the tongue, so openly spoken.

Such bond between them both was what made Tom so strong,
Despite many situations that had turned out to be so wrong,
It was doubtful that Tom would have lived as long as his did,
If not for the law which saw this tether, so secure and splendid.

The men had served him well, as he served them, from so young,
Not just a one-way ticket of servitude for taste of lip and tongue,
And the very sustenance that it offered was beyond all compare,
What they did with a whale's body after death, what did he care.

But the service he had paid this man of men was not forgotten,
And so, after the burial service George did attend, so here written,
George did pay visit to the shore; not to pay respects to children,
But to say a heart-felt thankyou to his true friend of the ocean.

It was then that Tom turned into the bay and made his way,
With the remainder of his pod to head off a humpback stray,
One with calf, allowing themselves to be caught unawares,
A fight with the Orcinus and his most awesome of stares.

He turned and thrust his flukes, through the water so fast,
Slicing through the waters of the bay, to join the fray at last,
Joining in on the waiting struggle which simply had to be won,
For they had not fed for quite some time, hence not here for fun.

And as George had lost his children to the ever waking ocean,
Tom too, lost a friend this year, to the calling of waves in motion,
For Hooky, son of Stranger, fathered by a stray,
Recognised by dorsal so bent, left forever the bay.

It was time to face the facts as they were staged before them all,
The crew was made up mostly of new, broad, short and tall,
They seemed inexperienced, inept, when compared to years past,
At a time before the war, which took the men away, fodder so cast.

The single boat now manned by crew, faces ever changing,
The ocean gifting fewer opportunities, all less engaging,
Orcinus orca growing old and weary, call made for substitute,
A move to easier quarry, less palatable, less astute.

Killers whales on the move,
Manned crews losing the grove,
Bay whaling changing as an industry,
The drawing of curtain upon ancestry.

But the men who served here would recall Humpy and Tom,
Frolicking freely in the bay, not knowing where they were from,
Having been here since a very young age,
To become a memory in history, written upon page.

And the two killers were not as agile as they once were,
Breaching the waters with less... ambition, but still sincere,
A stranger passing may think how free-spirited they appeared,
Watching them play, awake to the world, but somehow feared.

For the orca, no care in the world: they were aptly... longevous,
To bystanders who knew no difference, young and mischievous,
But George... he knew the truth, could picture it all, understood,
They were old, short in tooth, age to betray them all, for good.

1927 and the pod of two seemed to be of little worse for wear,
Once a pod of fifty more, strong in virtue, but no longer there,
A vast repertoire of song to corral humpbacks with great ease,
Allowing them to coral and secure a meal, one to please.

Humpy: older than Tom and frailer by action and thought,
Partnered with Typee, mother to Walker, so lovingly sought,
Knew of Jackson's death, by the hand of Silks: a demented mind,
But orca do not convey ideas in patterned speech like mankind.

She had once led attack after attack upon whales of all size,
Had ripped chunks from their lips and flank to gain her prize,
Had once become entangled in line and freed by George,
A conviction of mind therefore cast in gold, friendship to forge.

Humpy lead a pod until 1880, prior to temporary departure,
In 1885 was next in line for position of matriarch, to nurture,
Yes indeed, a great history, a story to be told, many memories,
But Humpy's days were almost over, so too the many glories.

They heard a humpback some miles out, followed in her wake,
Contemplating their next strategic move, much at stake,
A move without the aid of man, one that they would regret,
Like any other attack, apart from their number, therefore a threat.

They took chunk after chunk, pressing home the stress and fear,
So overwhelming, bitter-sweet aggression, a double-ended spear,
And so it is here that Humpy received a wound to the face,
An eye lost in the fight, inflicted upon her abilities: no disgrace.

The whale made its escape as Tom came in close to his friend,
A friend no-closer could he have been, right to the very end,
They fed on the whale, but this would not last them long,
Soon upon them both would be herald the end of the song.

The line had now been drawn for Humpy to see,
Within the week she was dead, gone her hunting ability,
Tom left to hunt food on his own, though no longer willing,
Maybe a small calf if able, but life was over, no longer thrilling.

THE DEPARTED

And so now there was just Tom, all alone,
A good life, having nothing for which to atone,
Dying on 16th September, 1930, shy of midnight,
The end of a legend in his own right.

A week before his death he had put chase to a grampus dolphin,
Taking chunks from the mammal until it died: a victory, a win,
It was a fairly quick death, a short fight,
It took a lot out of Old Tom, his last meal, his last bite.

The grampus was a meal, a king's ransom, not to be forgotten,
A great treat for an old warhorse, the blubber sweet, not rotten,
Lips and tongue taken great advantage of, better than most,
The fight seen by small crowd onshore, a splendid scene to toast.

And it dawned upon all those of Twofold Bay,
That Old Tom was alone, to eat and to play,
Not another killer to be seen anywhere about,
All quiet and bare, as far as the wind could carry a shout.

A week later and he was found dead,
After a day of frolicking, good life lead,
Flop-tailing into the breeze, on a day so bright,
And with the setting of the sun he said his good night.

His teeth bared the brunt of his years, now the worst of his flaws,
More worn in areas where he had taken the painter in his jaws,
His efforts to assist the men in their green boats now proved,
To be a devastating blow to his life, a life now removed.

Yes indeed, Tom had remained loyal to the end,
To all of those he had come to know, a great friend,
More knew of him than he could possibly know of them,
And that is where the tale does end and legend does stem.

Yes indeed, he enjoyed those last hours in this place,
Showing himself temporarily upon the surface with grace,
Onlookers thinking that something was amiss,
The next day his body floated into Snug Cove, gone the bliss.

Tom, recognised without mistake, his distinctive dorsal, his mast,
A fin which had been photographed so many times in the past,
A dorsal caught on camera in 1910, to forever last,
He died, simply, from old age, lived a life so full, so vast.

It was now, as his body lay still upon the beach,
That his genitalia proved once and for all, a lesson to teach,
That he was in fact a male, a long history so grand,
How had he managed near 80 years, so hard to understand.

J.R.Logan funded suggestion that preservation was the key,
For Tom's story to remain alive and well, for eternity,
And a suggestion saw to it that his skeleton was provided a home,
A museum built, history shielded as though beneath a dome.

The Eden Killer Whale Museum still exists today,
Puts the mind into a spin of all that visit the bay,
Over the tales that can be told or simply uncovered,
Of Tom, all in one place, history on plate so offered.

No one can deny the truth, for the truth is documented so well,
Tom was a male orca, 22 feet long, of abilities much to tell,
With a dorsal fin of 5.6 feet high,
Nothing of this fine specimen can anyone deny.

Tom was gone and bay whaling had come to an end,
In 1932 George hung up his harpoon, end of era, end of trend,
The crew disbanded to secure work in other fields,
To discover new sources of income, to discover new yields.

A few orca came back from time to time, memories to deliver,
Laying visit to the bay, upon the mouth of the Towamba River,
But these visits saw little action being carried out,
No humpback tackled, no prey, no "RUSHO" to shout.

The tide was changing across the entire country, so quick, so fast,
Whaling across the country was dying, from culture it was blast,
And it is strange to understand from the human point of view,
How the orca could alter human tactics, tactics of the hunt renew.

The orca were adverse, could make miracles from nature,
Saw change and hence relocated to other grounds, more rapture,
Understanding that their easy feeding was over with in the bay,
And so sought new choice, meals from new place of stay.

But even now as the darkness continues to fall over George,
Contemplating the life of the pods during the years they forge,
Of their presence and their interaction with the Yuin years before,
That maybe the killer whale will return to Eden, ever more.

Humpback whales frequent the bay and splash around in play,
Their calves by their sides enjoy the warmth of water in bay,
To relax and feed with little concern or danger from attack,
George and other men watching, to older times taken back.

And today, from the darkness of time comes a reminder of past,
For even now Orcinus can be seen near Eden, water so vast,
Where the picturesque port town and with its ocean views,
Continue to provide delight to passers-by, not whaling crews.

Now science is on the killer's side, to confirm, quite adamantly,
That they are intelligent creatures, naturally and mentally,
With acoustic senses, social coordination, and self-awareness,
Learn rapidly, are innovative, a sheer delight, nothing less.

THE END IS NIGH, TIME TO SAY GOODBYE

To an Orca, in general, the human race is a hindrance,
His desire and greed for commercial blubber his romance,
As he continued, without breath, to exploit the oceans and seas,
To settle those whims for oil, to do unto the species as he please.

Upon all countries of the world, in particular if coast does exist,
To turn the seas and oceans into paddocks and treat with iron fist,
To the Antarctic and Arctic, no measure, no explicit limit,
Where there was whale, there was oil, his credit, his permit.

And unbeknown to the orca of Twofold Bay, these killers of Eden,
In 1945 the International Whaling Conference, a whales warden,
Prepared extensive regulations for the part-protection of species,
To serve all whales as never before, to them great mercies.

This followed in 1946 by the International Whaling Commission,
Drawing conclusion that laws be adhered, without omission,
For international regulations should be put into place,
For these measures, henceforth, be maintained with grace.

Not simple conservation of the whales themselves,
But the stock levels of species so drawn from shelves,
And in 1949 a solar gathering of members did come together,
To maintaining principle and projects for protection, not to dither.

In particular of the females,
The calves and young whales,
Sanctuaries and limitations on the number of kills,
To offer a sacred number, limit how much blood men spills.

The lowering of numbers has since slowed but not ceased,
A stranglehold on killings did seem to be released,
Possibly good reason why Orcinus changed routines,
Deviating from routes, upon places it so frequently leans.

But in the case of Twofold Bay was a special case, one alone,
Where men and killer aided the other, reaping blubber from bone,
And it was the men who aided the killer whale,
The killer exploited man, not such a far-fetched tale.

Twofold Bay offered much to Orcinus orca, its potential seen,
Not only was it a natural corral for which to entrap baleen,
But it was shallow enough to restrict a whale's escape,
Its position alone migration routes and its general shape.

Leather Jacket Bay was also a natural wonder,
Employed well by the killers, this place from down-under,
For the season of whaling suited their endeavours, much to reap,
The pleasant currents permitting a leisurely pace, awake or asleep.

It was all a matter of strategy to the killer whale,
They chose the ground upon which to feed, with little fail,
Where such was to take place and the method to be employed,
By which means death was to be inflicted, a whale best annoyed.

And by 1952 George Davidson is dead,
Such a splendid bay life he had lead,
He was not alone in death, loved ones aside, Tom in head,
As Tom had died, alone beneath the ocean wave, so laid to bed.

The relationship between the two will live on forever,
A slice of history, Australia should be proud with fever,
Not for the relationship between these two different species,
But the acts of love, the affection shared, for all of their mercies.

If we look deep enough we can see how the men under George,
Gave up much, to work effectively with the orca, magic to forge,
Their equipment and techniques were of the old school,
Their foresight, courage and wit, not from any old fool.

These were not greedy men and nor were they wicked or cruel,
They had a job to do and did it well, the ocean their sacred tool,
But the men did believe they manipulating the killer whale,
Against all incursion, to prevail [Maybe you're doing it now].

How is it that a killer whale can put behind it the nature of the sea,
The nature of his species; the torments of their world that be,
That they can befriend man for gain, and all significance fades,
Learnt to work with man, maintain relationship for many decades.

If all killer whales were the same then should we assume,
That there be more of this cooperation, for growth more room,
Or are we drawn to a reality whereby this is one killer alone,
Made good a situation to suit the needs of matriarch upon throne.

The name Tom should be celebrated, for he was a one and only,
And if there is never another then the world would be lonely,
For we, as human beings, need these experiences in our lives,
Instil a greater commodity than killing, an ambition that thrives.

Maybe the future will behold another just like him,
If not then it is possible that life will be grim,
For George, possibly, the last memories that drift from his mind,
Tom: a friend who could never be forgotten, one so hard to find.

THE HISTORY

1712

It was in 1712 that the first of the sperm whale was taken from the safe harbour of its home in the sea near Nantucket, far from the waters of the Australian coast, but where several ancestors of those in the Eden pod had once frequented. The oil was considered much more valuable than that harvested by the bay whalers [shore fishing which had been a development of the Red Indians in similarity, but not a union as that of the Yuin of Twofold Bay]. Deep sea whaling was now an investment anxiously pursued; the curtain had been raised and the slaughter begun; an infringement upon the Orca's right to feed on all that swam in any of the oceans or seas.

1788

The settlement of Australia takes hold at the same time that the South Pacific is exploited for what it holds within its parlour of delights, 1,800 souls shipped to Botany Bay and they too, commence fishing within its waters.

1790s

By the 1790s sperm whale fishing had spread to more favourable grounds, where they were seen to be in such large numbers that the opportunity could not be refused, hence the decimation of the South Pacific did commence, and although the killer whale tended to lay more towards the coastlines of many countries for their sustenance, routes across the great expanses of sea were patrolled.

1791

Many shoals were seen by members of the ship Britannia, from Van Diemen's Land to just out from the coast of Port Jackson, at approximately nine miles, and the numerous sightings were recorded for the prosperity of the captain but divulged, in the end, to the governor for the Australian people and its fishing industry. The endeavours and efforts, therefore, of the human race helped dictate, within reasonable terms, that the killers should direct their attentions more favourably to the coastline where migratory routes of humpback were known to exist.

Within a few short years of this sighting another was recorded to the west of the Galapagos Islands where sperm whales were seen in large quantities, copulation a common occurrence. It was now a basis of

233

knowledge, something known by the killers for centuries, that one particular migratory route led along the coast of East Australia and out towards the islands so famous of Darwin and his findings. Not only this but the waters of the Pacific, to the north-east of New Zealand, were bountiful with sperm whales and their off-spring, so much so that the vast area, too large to contemplate, was combed by ships of many nationalities including those from Australia.

1799

Matthew Flinders stood upon the deck and saw that Twofold Bay could easily make a grand harbour, the skeleton of a right whale visible on the beach. A thought then traversed his mind where he was reminded of the days of Captain Cook, where he very nearly entered the east coast of Australia at the point where Twofold Bay opened itself to the world, but due to bad weather was forced to the north where Botany Bay was chosen for the first settlement.

1804

It wasn't long before the commercial value of whaling hit the minds of those that continued to colonize Tasmania, where right whales [sometimes referred to as black whales] frequented the bays with their calves from June to October. This provided great opportunity to hunt sperm whale during the summer months and then the bay whales in winter, through the exuberance of those that lanced the whales till their heart's content, fell upon the realization that hunting from row boats was as good, if not better, than ramming home their harvest from large ships; bay whaling was now a true profession and taken up by a few bays along the coast of Australia where migratory whales tempted the greed and thirst of human desire for oil.

Sites were selected with great care as many considerations needed to take point, namely shelters for the men, cookhouse, cooperage [where casks and barrels of all description could be made and repaired, to be filled to the brim with that marvellous substance], storehouses and try-works where slabs of blubber could be easily drawn up a ramp and prepared for boiling, extracting the gold so laboriously sought.

1828

It soon became an interest, the Yuin and their exploits, and Twofold Bay made the headlines in a Sydney newspaper, bay whaling adopted soon after as more of an experiment than anything else. The spoils were so great that the opportunity could not be ignored. It was shortly after that 16 white men of a dispatch from Sydney were killed and another five years elapsed before Dr.A.Imlay secured over a thousand acres of land in the area.

The indigenous people of the region around Twofold Bay are called Yuin and had a name for the killers; they called them 'Beowas', meaning brothers or kin, they were 'transient, a social organization of killer whale which was set aside from the 'resident' and 'offshore', but with many 'resident' characteristics; they were, in essence, a 'matrilineal' organisation of killers that were, to a degree, inseparable.

As per the Romans and Greeks before them, the Aboriginals of Australia looked upon the killer whales with great respect and admiration, believing wholeheartedly that they were the reincarnation of ancestors past, where the dead took the form of a wolf of the sea. Why?

The Yuin believed that the killer whales were the returned spirits of the dead, ancestors that had come back to the world of the living and to help provide sustenance to the indigenous population. If a monster of the deep was to provide such great amounts of food for the tribe then it must be nothing less than the reincarnated spirit of a recently deceased member for their society. They were, every one, treasured as original members of the tribe and known, not only to help feed the Yuin, but also to protect them whilst in the water.

For long before the presence of any white man, the Yuin – not exploiting – made good advantage of the situation where it was quite common for baleen whales to be herded into the bay and become stranded upon the beach, whereby the strategies of the hunt become a symbolised benefit to all in the tribe and the 'Beowas' were adopted into their beliefs. It was a phenomenon that could only be explained by the belief of the 'Beowas', for why else would a killer whale home in on a humpback caught in the bay, pester and kill, to feed upon the lips and tongue, and then allow all that which remained to be shored upon the beach in order for the Yuin to feed?

Much else was also sought by the Yuin, not just food and comradeship with a whale, but the more in-depth spiritual healing of infliction. It is here that rituals came into existence and all that the killer gave in jester to the people was to be used to full effect. A remedy evolved, where an individual so inflicted with rheumatism and the like would climb into a rotting carcase, naked and up to the neck in blubber, to gain the such sought-after relief gained by spending hours encased within the flesh and absorbing the stench and oil of the baleen's blubber.

1828 – 1830s

Thomas Raine was the first whaler in Twofold Bay in 1828, followed soon after in the 30's by the Imlay Brothers who employed several of the Yuin due to their keen ability to work hard, be reliable, and were easily skilled with the abilities of boat-handling; they were soon recognised for their talent and had good eyesight.

1838

Having sent for his brothers, Dr.Imlay undertook further exploits whereby his interest in breeding cattle continued alongside bay whaling.

1840

At this time the sperm whale industry took precedence for the humpback whale had become increasingly unavailable, learning over time to avoid the slaughter that occupied the bays of Tasmania, and although migratory routes were seldom changed and little voiced, it was in the interest of man to hunt where the value of the spoils could be secured in purse, hence the move from one species to the next; although, in all fair response, the sperm whale was also worth more in regards to oil.

1840s

In the 1840s, Benjamin Boyd set upon the scene and commenced to build a town in his own name; Boyd Town. It was his hope to have it grow in all aspects to one day be as big as any other city within Australia. He built a lighthouse from Sydney sandstone on the south head [Boyd Tower] along with a little church of red brick [the spire of which could be seen from 20 miles out to sea], houses, storage rooms, wharves, stock-yards and the Seashore Inn which is situated on the beach and draws upon the very romance of the area, all surrounded by the lushness of eucalyptus trees.

The bush itself was thick and descended to right upon the beach itself. Bay whaling was, however, not something that Boyd took too with great enthusiasm as the competition was so great, so sought to make an ambition from offshore whaling where the sperm whale could still be quarried in large numbers out to sea – for the sperm whale did not frequent the bays or the coast.

His crews were not successful, apparently bribed by the Imlay Brothers to miss-judge the thrust of a harpoon, but the oil from the sperm whale measured Boyd greed and filled him to the brim, his ships much more capable of bringing home the oil.

Oswald Briefly, a good friend of Boyd, who had arrived with him upon his yacht, Wanderer, made many written entries within a diary along with paintings and sketches of the activities of men and killer whales alike. It is from these accounts that the first encounter with the killers of Twofold Bay can be found, actually competing against the bay whalers as opposed to helping them, for the crews of bay refused to allow the killers a share and frequently attacked them with the boat spades used in removing blubber from the much sought after baleen.

It is here that the first of many strange incidents commences to take shape for the killers begin to show a liking towards those crews less callous in their treatment towards them.

And the men of the crews that fought the whales from upon their long and sturdy craft took little pity on the killers for their help in the hunt. The men watch as the killer whales flung themselves upon the back of the whale, charging in and taking chunks from its flanks, pestering it at every turn in order to prevent it from careering home into the depths of the open sea.

Lances continue to puncture the flesh of the humpback, the first catch in many months, but the fight isn't over just yet, for the whale must be killed and then secured, secured from the lurches of the orca as they come in for the lips and tongue. The crews endeavour to impede the killers' efforts, try with all their might to drag the dead whale away, to be deblubbered at their convenience. This is but one of the many reasons that the killers soon decide to take their catch whilst near the mouth of the bay as opposed to within it, for the men of Twofold Bay seem to think that the whale is their just reward and should not be shared, and it was only due to the lack of a baleen plates, and little oil to quench the first of the market and merchants, that killers were not rendered into oil.

Twofold Bay was changing face, there was now Eden to the north of the bay and two other small villages, if that, upon the south, separated by the Kiah Inlet. There was Boyd Town to the west and East Boyd to the east.

1843

It had become more than clear, even to those that lived in denial over the growing absence of right whales, that bay whaling in Tasmania was coming to a close. But in lieu of the bay whalers of Twofold Bay the call to boats was made, quite often, with great regularity; not by time of day, but by the appearance of whales from June and on into the long winter months. The sighting of whales in and around Tasmanian bays might have taken a turn for the worst, but the slaughter in and around Twofold Bay had just commenced.

The tides were turning and the great phenomenon was taking shape. Boyd's empire collapsed completely, and the whaling gear no longer needed was sold to Alexander W. Davidson and his business partner Solomon Solomon, to sit idle for several years until the boats hit the water.

1849

Boyd departed Australia in 1849.

1895

By 1895 sperm whaling was all but dead and the last unsuccessful hunt on the east coast concluded in 1896.

1955

The decline of humpback numbers, not due to the killers themselves, nor even the Davidson's, for the combined number of kills were rather deplorable to say the least; but particular investments such as those of the Norwegians, where whales were taken from Australian waters, certainly aided in the rise of situations within the world such as Frenchman Bay of West Australia taking the turn it did by commencing with sperm whaling and adding infuriation upon a depleted stock.

BOOK THREE

HOLLANDIA NOVA, 1712 - Song of the Coast

A BRIEF NOTE ON HISTORY

The Dutch United East India Company (Vereenigde Oost-Indische Compagnie – VOC) was the most powerful company at the time of the Zuytdorp, and the Zuytdorp was one of their largest ships. A great monopoly stretched from Holland to Asia (namely Batavia [Jakarta] where the VOC headquarters was established) and other countries which were a source of great wealth and commodity. Within time the VOC boasted settlements in Java, Sumatra, Borneo, India, Ceylon, Arabia, Persia, Bengal, Malacca, Celebs, Timor, China and Japan. Trade between these centres was also of strategic importance: where trade and wealth was concerned. Copper, tin, spices, opium and dyes were the basic requisites of commerce.

Spices were something new to Europe, tantalizing fragments of a whole that inspired great satisfaction within all across the country, each and every one tired of the tasteless morsels dished out at dinner time, turning to spices like a tidal wave upon a beach.

It was usual for more than one ship to be in the company on another and eight months forecast for the voyage ahead, being provided the mandatory and rather necessary rest stop at the Cape of Good Hope, Table Bay, for a period of ten days, a period of time which had been cut drastically from an extravagant three to four weeks. There was a fort here, established in 1652 for the sole purpose of providing medical aid and stores. A hospital of 200 beds saw many stationed upon the seafaring ships take harbour within the facility to fight that dreaded scourge of the seas, scurvy, so it was common knowledge that many hands would exchange places, those that had commenced a journey from Holland not necessarily completing the trip with that posting; it was another sad fact that all had to face and that was the death rate for those on such a long voyage, for quite a large portion of the ship's company would come to grief and be launched into the sea covered in sacking; pickings for oceanic life.

To avoid the dangers of the coast, from Table Bay to Batavia, at a time when the Portuguese were an enemy to be avoided, an alternate route was discovered: which also alleviated the problems in regards to wind direction. The ships would travel due west for approximately 1,000 Dutch miles before turning north. It was unfortunate for the time, however, that there was no means by which to accurately determine longitude at sea, latitude on the other hand was quite reliable. Eventually land was encountered and this then became the accepted method of voyage: to seek the sight of land and then head north towards the coast of Sumatra. For almost a hundred years sailors were fortunate enough to cast their eyes upon the west coast of a great mass of land, thought to have been part of New Guinea. Many names were cast upon the landmass, eventually Hollandia Nova taking hold. Only one real warning of impending danger was forecast to the captains of these ships and that was to avoid the Triall Rocks [Tryal Rocks - off the north-west coast of Australia] as the submerged capacity of the hidden encumbrance was enough to see a ship easily bashed, sliced, and quartered.

The Zuytdorp was the largest ship within the VOC and only two others were of equal size. It was built between 23 Dec 1700 and 22 June 1701, being 160 feet long, 40 feet wide, and the depth of the hold was 17 feet (283 millimetres to the Amsterdam foot). She was capable of carrying 250 lasts (500 tons) which towards the latter portion of her life was increased on paper and task: the Zuytdorp in 1712 carried in the vicinity of 576 lasts.

The Zuytdorp, due to the situation with war and pirates, carried ten 12-pound guns, twenty-two 8-pound guns and eight 4-pound guns (swivel cannons). The swivel and two 8-pounders were made of bronze; all others were iron muzzle loaders.

The Zuytdorp and Belvliet had set sail for the Cape of Good Hope, to journey for most of the voyage within sight of one another, but there were instances where they were to become separated, for one reason or another. The voyage was treacherous to say the least; a longer than expected journey being suffered as the ships had to sail up and around Scotland in order to avoid English ships of the sea patrolling the Channel.

The Zuytdorp arrived at the Cape of Good Hope on 23rd March 1712, and of the original 286 crew had lost 112 men and had 22 sick on board; eight having deserted at São Tomé; most deaths were attributed to scurvy but others of tropical malaria from São Tomé itself. The Belvliet fared little better, percentage wise, and arrived on 27th March, and from a crew of 164 had lost 60 dead and 18 sick, with two desertions at São Tomé.

Much time was then spent at the Cape to replenish men and stores when finally, on 22 April 1712, the Zuytdorp departed the Cape with the ship Kockenge; the Belvliet departing several weeks later on the 9th May.

The Zuytdorp pulled ahead of the Kockenge due to her being a much larger and faster vessel, a vessel of the first class, 200 'eaters' (people) on board, 80-90 of them being new to the ship. And as many do, the skipper decided to sail until sighting land before turning north for Sunda Strait, to take good advantage of the winds which presented themselves.

GENERAL NOTE

There was no single, homogeneous Aboriginal society, but around 250 different tribes and well in excess of 100 different dialects spoken, the difference between the languages [in some cases] being as different as English compared to Portuguese. With such a vast network of tribal backgrounds and varying ceremonial beliefs, where interaction between groups was a common occurrence, it is not surprising to see that members of a tribe were multilingual and able to quite effectively speak 10 different dialects or more.

The differences between tribes were as different as chalk and cheese: their language was different; their customs, kinship systems, ceremonial music and dance... all had its place.

Where subtle interaction was sought between the different clans in order to pursue marriage, partners for boys coming of adulthood and of girls ready to enter into sacred ceremony, groups were bonded by belief and enactment. New myths could hence be strung, beliefs exchanged, strategies of the hunt and food gathering techniques discussed. A cycle of life and survival was maintained and the gene pool stirred well to prevent the curse-of-ancestors from rising from the dead.

There is also one other aspect of aboriginal life which must be made quite clear, and it certainly isn't considered normal, and that is in respect to the genes. There is evidence [in the 20th Century] to show that Aboriginals of the Shark Bay area suffer from Porphyria Variegate, a gene mutation that is traceable to the Dutch, as is the disease in South Africa where 1 in 300 persons suffer from it. It is uncommon and rare, and there is no reason, other than the coupling of an Aboriginal with a survivor of the Zuytdorp, that currently explains the disease being discovered in Australia.

But for the most part there was peace amongst the Aboriginals, right across the land.

In 1623, Jan Carstenz placed colourful descriptions to several armed encounters with the Aboriginals. He spoke of how arid the land was, of how inhospitable and barren the entire place was, where no such horrid place existed anywhere else on earth. He spoke of the inhabitants as the most wretched and poorest that he had ever seen. These comments were carried quite literally back to the Netherlands, and the Dutch government decided that the land was not suitable for colonisation and no benefit could be won from seeking such an endeavour.

It is not surprising therefore that all the men and women that saw the land from far out upon the ocean felt the fear build up within them, a fear suddenly drowned by the so deeply satisfying and secure feeling within, in both knowledge and thought, that they would never have to set foot upon such a miserable place.

And then one day a ship approached this horrid place, its crew unaware of what was about to become of them, for the Zuytdorp had ventured too close to land....

AUTHOR'S NOTE:

Off the coast of Western Australia lies the Indian Ocean. To aid in the writing of this poem I shall often refer to these waters as 'sea'.

PROLOGUE

In 1829 the Swan River Colony was founded, hundreds strong,
A community as many other, settlers endeavouring no wrong,
Founded within short years upon the east Australian coast,
A land so bountiful, gifts for the plucking, much to boast.

The name Swan River, derived from that which it was christened,
By the Dutch, many decades before, as it so happened,
When black swans upon the river evoked a stirring of affection,
A beauty which men saw, feeling that natural connection.

So beautiful these swans were, much beauty well stack,
That they were drawn from the river and taken back,
A visual feast to be well endowed, a gift, a pleasure,
Shown well to the government and the people in good measure.

Just five years later and two aboriginals could be seen,
Within this district, walking leisurely but seeming keen,
Steady walking pace to see them delivered with spear in hand,
No hateful thought within them, of great tolerance, of good brand.

They were Tonquin and Weenat, lean, tall and dark,
Their darkened flesh unmistakable, eyes alight with spark,
Rather beautiful when it comes to the point of features,
Worthy and of great characteristics, with the desert no fractures.

Their faces were alive, a calmness and spring to walk,
Walking silently, looking about them, no need to talk,
A living script to the aboriginals, whom with the land did live,
A semblance to nature itself, and their people that did give.

The very structure of the skin and bone, their faces so undulating,
Skin and large noses that appeared to sit flat, to face much doting,
A reasonable testimony to a life well lived, one so gifted,
Life shared with nature and the land itself, seemingly related.

They had come to terms with white man, having settled from afar,
The way in which they hence founded, whites, a roaming star,
This wonderment of difference permeating this land so free,
They seemed peaceful, but the aborigines would not give a knee.

And so Tonquin and Weenat had something to offer,
Some information that may be of interest to these men, not master,
To provide information on a shipwreck that had come their way,
To offer courtesy for wad of tobacco, a comfort to have this day.

Nigel B.J.Clayton

Such information must be worth a little to these people so new,
Considering it was a white man's ship, sunk amidst ocean mew,
One smashed badly upon rocks some forty miles north of Kalbarri,
But their information was stark, misconstrued, hazy and glary.

Passed down from tribe to tribe, from elder to young,
Carried to sacred meeting, their corroboree well sung,
From other meetings to meeting where wives are won,
From hunting ground to hunting ground where speers stung.

The police officer sat rigid behind his desk before relaxing a little,
The story quite tense, but he listened, before him set his vittle,
The sentences delivered his ears missing words here and there,
The jest of the story is noted for what it was before confused stare.

There is a shipwreck to the north, a thirty day walk,
In the land of the Malgana, and they continue to talk,
Where the tribe Wayle lives off the land in pleasant solitude,
Visiting this place of wreck amidst curious attitude.

There is much money, that has been washed upon hard rock,
The officer imitates them a little, to understand, not to mock,
Silver coins that are so thick in the water, sand so hard to see,
So thick that it is ankle deep in places, a place so wild but free.

The ship has broken up into three main parts, this its grave,
A three-mast ship that will never again roll upon the wave,
But it also resembles much more than a pile of rubble,
A story hard to fathom, hard to piece together, hard to cobble.

Tonquin and Weenat look the officer up and down,
He takes his notes, writing amidst occasional frown,
Storing notes on the main points of the story,
Points of greater interest, awaiting him much glory.

They continue with their story of how the tall white men fell,
From the wreck and then upon the land, a little more to tell,
They are taken by the aboriginals where courtesy is exchanged,
A lasting relationship scored, relationships hence arranged.

The officer displays another frown, missing interpretation,
Thinking the wreck is most recent, ready for his administration,
Not considering for a moment that this is old information,
No clear understanding that he is scribing 122 year old dictation.

And further still, both Tonquin and Weenat provide advice,
That the white men lived in little houses, strangely nice,
Lived around three fires, dwellings made of canvas and wood,
And not so very far from the face of the cliff, here they stood.

246

The police officer must act quickly, provide aid to those in need,
A rescue prepared, to save these people, despite his inner greed,
Not knowing that nought will be found of any survivor,
Unless remains are so dug from the site, a site of ill-favour.

THE BREAKING

The 5th of June, 1712, on board the Zuytdorp are 286 souls,
174 seamen including those of higher rank, of many roles,
100 soldiers, 4 tradesmen and 8 passengers and stores,
Almost all will perish, washed upon unsavoury shores.

It came upon the men, women and children without warning,
A voice upon the wind coming closer, an incessant whining,
A great calamity that fell upon them in the dead of night,
The sky above was as dark as one had ever known, of no delight.

Intermittent sparks of light throwing themselves upon the world,
The decking and masts of ship lighting up, strength so hurled,
The savage wind and rain catching them unaware,
Thunder and lightning, together, striking out, so unfair.

The sheer force of nature stole people's voices away,
No verbal sound herald to ear amidst the heinous fray,
Shouts and screams on deck broken up by the wind,
Gone even garbled sound from bodies of terrified mind.

Crew members on deck continued throwing themselves to duty,
The last thing most would do in this storm of ill-fate, no beauty,
And upon their minds was the pressure to be successful,
To gift upon their endeavours a victory, to be eternally grateful.

The eight passengers below deck huddled together,
Bound by the horror of this most beastly weather,
The culminating of fear, the worst ever experienced before,
This journey to Batavia now sour, what more was in store.

And several oil lamps, secured upon hooks, alight and frail,
Swung back and forth, as the ship rocked, swinging upon nail,
Frightful looks all around them without doubt,
As shadows moved here and there, all about.

Three were wives heading to Batavia, to meet with husband,
A child in each of their arms, upon voyage to place so grand,
Fathers to see their child for the first time ever,
Men of high station, most important, earning much stiver.

There was another here, a man of which a lot was known,
But nothing of his younger life or from beginnings what town,
Heading to Batavia to work, a decision made of mind so strong,
To another country so far away, a decision made, now wrong.

Yes indeed, such a grand position advertised at home,
Of bookkeeper profession, of intelligence, not a [archaic] mome,
One to tax his mind to the limits of his skill and knowledge,
For him to work hard and establish good rapport, his pledge.

There was one other, a child of fourteen, in hammock he rests,
Older than the others cradled safely close to mothers' breasts,
He was alone, but did have a minder, that was the bookkeeper,
Who maintained vigil upon this boy who looked like a pauper.

The boy's name was Willem Steyns and of poor situation,
Cast upon an ill wind to carry him amidst his frustration,
To take him far and wide, until the limits of the earth,
To this new country unheard of, different than place of birth.

He was set forth by a poorly mother, a drunken, wretched curse,
She worthy of nought but the little money carried within purse,
He being cast aside by her, for him to be attended to by his father,
Who was a merchant in Batavia, of spices he did gather.

He was a lean man and worked hard to make a wage,
Ensuring much was dispatched to his wife from his cage,
Hands tied in this, a forced vocation, his only learned ability,
Unaware of wife's true state, so few letters received of surety.

He wasn't aware that Willem was on his way to seek him,
For the letter dispatched by wife was carried by the boy so slim,
Months and months on end spent in dreary isolation,
This on top of the dreary company he kept at his station.

The man, as tall as he was fair, tried to give comfort,
A little solace, some spirit, and that was no easy effort,
For the noise and raucous above their heads, on deck,
Continued unabated, furious activity they could not check.

And as the poor boy thought on matters he knew little about,
Fifty per cent of the crew raced upon deck, under threat and shout,
All trying their hardest to put to right the wrong,
Amidst a growing storm of great ferocity, so strong.

But let's jump back a little, to the man here within belly,
Within the hold of the ship Zuytdorp, so rotten and smelly,
His name was Pieter Pelsaert, 34 years of age,
Soon to be looked upon, to be the centre of stage.

The passengers were the luckiest of all those on board,
Within the best part of the ship, despite lack of luxury and accord,
Each scared to the core and not fully understanding the truth,
Sailors praying for the light of day, no need to be a sleuth.

Pieter had come to know the three women and Willem rather well,
Had spent the voyage strapped to their every yarn, under a spell,
Every piece of gossip silently taken in and savoured,
An assortment of characters, strongly flavoured.

He was a listener,
Not a talker,
A mover,
Not a loiterer.

As though herald to hear what each had to say,
Sometimes from within the shadows he would stay,
As they talked on their lives and the captain of the ship,
Of the crew and their misdemeanours, and sailors' lip.

They were thrown together in an area away from the main body,
A body of sole function, to work the ship well, not be shoddy,
The seamen whose job it was to see ship's cargo endowed,
To have it ported to dock in Batavia, no lenience allowed.

Pieter saw one of the women fall aside,
Atop her baby of just 14 months, as though to hide,
The babies face blue and crimson, the ocean a menace,
Resembling a mix of darkened sky and heated furnace.

He reached out to give aid,
To help up this stricken maid,
To offer solace for just a moment,
Pieter quick to action but not stringent.

"My God," Pieter bellowed into the woman's ear,
As he pulled her up from floor, into eyes did peer,
"What manner of transgression forced you to attend this voyage,
With one so young, to force your life to ocean and its rage?"

As Pieter picked them up upon rocking wave, he realised his tact,
For the woman felt as though she had be scolded, despite the fact,
And then the woman sobbed, looking at the man so kind,
Then down into the dead eyes of the one she held, no life to find.

Pieter's mouth dropped, life was truly riding upon a fine thread,
Said Willemtgen, most heartbroken, "My boy; he's dead."
She peered down again upon the form of flesh,
Pulled into her, a tightened grip, that their bodies would mesh.

So tight the hold, the child would never be pried loose,
Amidst raging storm, tossing of ship, no choice to choose,
The tears streamed from her face and Pieter tried to comfort,
Put an arm around her, with true conviction and little effort.

The other ladies looked upon the scene,
And then to their own young, love so keen,
Ariaantje with her 18 month old girl, used to laughter,
And Willemyntje with her 4 year old daughter.

Suddenly the door burst open and a seaman appeared,
Ariaen Leyden by name, it never, ever to be smeared,
Out of the darkness and into the light,
Fluctuating oil lamps illuminating his fright.

Shadows moved round,
Eerie shadows to be found,
The Zuytdorp creaked and groaned,
It bellowed, it cried and moaned.

"Pieter, Pieter, quickly man, we need you! All hands to deck,
NOW PIETER! All hands needed or we are a wreck."
And with more suddenness than the man, never to surrender,
The entire ship shuddered that unthinkable, evil shudder.

A noise from beneath her hull did grind and tear,
The most heinous ever heard, to heart a spear,
The entire vessel shifted upon axis, the stern drifting,
As though trying to overtake the bow, sinking and lifting.

Swinging around to port,
Vessel unable to abort,
Rocky seabed to report,
Work to be made short.

Of the damage being caused there was no remorse,
A rocky shoreline platform, of man, soon a [archaic] corse,
And the platform did crunch and grind,
The most heinous place to wreck, to find.

It was a platform to sit between rock and hard place,
Dwarfing the cliff either side with much ill-grace,
Much distemper displayed upon its sullen face,
Almost gone, all traces of survival in this race.

A race for survival, one to hold dear,
Far north and south the cliff does steer,
As far as the eye can see by day,
Rock, upon rock, upon rock, to flay.

The fear within the eyes of the women is one of sheer grief,
Their distorted faces of horror painting a picture of no relief,
Each clutched ever more the little ones so close to them now,
Willemtgen too, embraced hers with great vigour, never to bow.

Death was a strange thing,
Bad gift, Death to bring,
Some accepted it most freely,
Others refuting, seemingly [archaic] seely.

"We're going!" yelled Ariaen as he fell heavily from the doorway,
Knocking his head heavily upon the mast of the ship as he sway,
A mast penetrating all decks of the Zuytdorp, firm and secure,
Most rigid, unflexing, unlike fishing rod bending with lure.

And with great ease and horrible wrenching the mast did snap,
Enough to wake even the devil, deep down, asleep or in nap,
From just above the deck it fell away with the rigging,
Unfurled sail falling with it, rope cores ripping.

The Zuytdorp' short sail amidst of an early winter storm,
Lost all integrity, lost all semblance, all form,
This big, square-rigged ship, men forgetting its nativity,
The pending disaster unavoidable, a situation of great gravity.

Soon to be junk,
A mass, a chunk,
Gone the days of varnish,
The ocean now to tarnish.

Men upon the deck were thrown overboard, starboard and lee,
Gifted slow and fast deaths, each to the mercy of the sea,
But little mercy was received this night,
For the vast, vast majority, no more first light.

Barrels and crates, once secured, now rolled around the decking,
Cargo in the hold shifted suddenly, from slumber, now waking,
All aiding the abrupt shifting of the Zuytdorp towards disaster,
Gone all taming, hello calamitous, abrupt end, now the master.

The rats below deck rushed to find safe quarter,
Looking to save themselves from slaughter,
For even the most vile of life did thirst for life,
Did all they could to avoid much strife.

The Zuytdorp carried within her a great quantity of merchandise,
Precious metals, great wealth in the form of silver: most wise,
Coins being its largest hoard,
But much else here on board.

Coins in their thousands; Dutch ducatons, guilders,
Schillings, rix dollars, double stuivers and stuivers,
Spanish pieces of eight, pieces of four and pieces of two,
Spanish-Netherlands ducatons and patagons, thrown from view.

There was also gold which came in the form of Dutch ducats,
And many, many ingots of silver, amidst rat-chasing cats,
Such great quantities of wealth and riches carried in chests,
Packed and secured, hiding from view the rodent nests.

Two locks saw to it that each chest was bolted secure,
Each nailed down with sail cloth, to escape desire and lure,
Stored within the captain's cabin, below the poop,
Much more room and comfort than forborne sloop.

More luxury here for the captain,
But now gone the luxury and fashion,
Soon to go the silver coins valued at 248,886 guilders,
Gone 100,000 of newly-minted schillings and double stuivers.

But she also carried other commodities,
Needles, muskets and blunderbusses,
Lead, linseed, bacon, nothing on which to sneer,
She was filled to the brim with barrels of wine and beer.

1,813 pounds of fresh meat, ten live sheep, salt, pitch, paper,
Vegetables, potherbs, 2 hundredweight of beans, rope, copper,
2 hundredweight of peas, 300 pounds of rice, plates, sulphur,
Oils, cloth, canvas, sail yarn, medical stores, butter and leather.

And what good was all of this? It was ambition,
It was enterprise, for wealth, its ammunition,
Sanctioned from the hull of this grand ship, beneath every hatch,
And then Zuytdorp's return to Europe with an even bigger catch.

To return with spices, salt, pepper, textiles, china, silks and cotton,
Tea, coffee, nutmeg, cloves, cinnamon, mace: nothing forgotten,
All from Batavia and around, from this town,
And with anything else that could be tied down.

Damn it; damn it all, all to be wasted; on a ship no one can steer,
It was all loose, being thrown helplessly around, there and here,
Impossible to avoid the doom, whether below deck or upon it,
Men broken, being killed, made of flesh and bone, not granite.

Broken arms, broken noses, broken souls and mind,
Then heard the sudden call, snatched by the wind,
"Every man for himself", a call most dire,
Save yourself if you can, before life does retire.

And no sooner than being called by the man aloft,
He was speared by flying debris in gut of flesh, so soft,
As another of the ship's masts snapped and fell upon the decking,
The ship pitched further off its axis, far from soul-saving bearing.

Forced further upon unforgiving rock,
Into mind you cannot take stock,
It is surreal, nothing you can imagine,
A reality of horror, many shivers up a spine.

The Zuytdorp gives way to further, sudden bouts of lurching,
Upon the starboard side of ship, huge waves of terror thrashing,
Water now flowing freely within the hull,
No hope in altering the course, from it to pull.

Everyone trying to save themselves from the torments of the sea,
A time of few minutes for one thought only: to be free, to be free,
No time now to reflect upon anything except all manner of escape,
Each endeavour to disallow the heinous rock its merciless rape.

Pieter makes answer to the call, takes it as a command to act,
A call to duty, one not wished but he needed to react,
A hidden desire not to leave anyone behind,
Not to leave anyone here, upon the rocks to grind.

He could not leave an helpless woman with child,
Be the child dead or alive, the woman was mild,
Or the child known as Willem, he could not spurn,
For him there was life, much of it to learn.

"Quickly, Willem; you have to help me," and Pieter stumbled,
The shifting of the ship, grinding on its bottom, it rumbled,
And then further groans, mayhem being voiced from every fibre,
Further groans of mayhem being voiced in resonance and timbre.

The ship's core commenced to bend, to split,
The sound of cracking wood, integrity to quit,
The penetration of sound deep into their ears,
So loud, hardly believed, as the devil jeers.

"What do I do!" said Willem, the fright upon his face does grate,
Written in bold, the bulging eyes giving rise to the frantic state,
His near shattered mind and nerve. "Tell me, Pieter; please."
All this whilst the breaking of ship does continue to tease,

Pieter could not deny that the boy's frame of mind scared him,
To his wits end his feelings endeavoured to betray and to trim,
As though whittling his very fabric, a threat to characteristic,
But Pieter did react as a true man, overcome all to be realistic.

But the boy must be forced to endure and provide assistance,
For only then would he forget the fear within him and commence,
To commence his crawl from the abyss in which they had fallen,
To be brave before all, to grow up, not to be overly sullen.

"Give aid to Willemtgen and her son, do it now, no time to waste,
I'll attend Ariaantje and Willemyntje," said Pieter in haste,
And as Willem's mouth began to open, a movement at his brow,
Pieter added further, quite abruptly, so urgent: "Quickly, now!"

"Please, Willemtgen," said Willem, attaching his tether,
"Take hold of my arm and we'll scale the steps together."
Willemtgen's face showed a glare of hope then and there,
Even with her dead son still in her arms, so much to bear.

Willemtgen then reached out to grab hold of the boy,
A man to grow from one so young, strength to deploy,
At the same instant the worst thing to happen did transpire,
A monstrously huge wave struck the ship, all of it, the entire.

It broke into three pieces, hit hard by tremendous force,
Hitting the starboard side of the Zuytdorp without remorse,
But a wave has no feelings, no action to check or feel,
But Poseidon and the devil would provide a different spiel.

The bow broke away, 22 feet of her, and shifted 60 feet,
Towards the shoreline platform, many boulders there to meet,
With their bone-breaking knobs and points awaiting its delivery,
To gnaw upon it as man gnaws upon steak, gifting great quivery.

The stern headed in a most forward motion,
Towards a part of the shoreline, the nearest portion,
Delivered just 28 feet away from the main bulk of the ship,
To the base of this cliff, upon its very lower lip.

It broke up a little, steadying herself upon the rocks, it slowed,
Some 53 feet of her in which all the treasure on board was stowed,
The centre most portion, all 85 feet of that which remained,
Rammed home against the platform, no further ground gained.

The fallen mast upon the deck,
Shifted slightly upon the wreck,
Crushing several men looking to survive,
Who applied herculean efforts to stay alive.

Those few men that remained upon, or within, drew last breaths,
Within the bow portion of the vessel, died quick and slow deaths,
Broken bones and concussion in situation so serious,
By drowning, flying debris, or simply knocked unconscious.

Trapped within the rigging and unable to move,
Such death traps in the making, the rigging did prove,
And those tumultuous few of the stern fared little better,
But that portion of the ship availed strong character.

Pieter and Willem were both here,
Alongside the females and children so dear,
Companions and other members of the crew,
Some of them, until this day, they never really knew.

The higher the station a sailor of the sea held,
And the more with the upper class he could meld,
Closer to passengers, their sons and daughters,
More closely situated to the door of the captain's quarters.

Other than the skipper himself were the following: master gunner,
Stockmaker, under steersman, bosun; clerk and senior carpenter,
His 2nd and 3rd; upper steersman, master surgeon, bricklayer,
Coppersmith, comforter of the sick, under surgeon, firelock maker.

All were dead, spread throughout the ship, cast out upon the sea,
Dashed upon the rocky coast, pulled beneath the waves so free,
The surmounting weight of wave upon wave crashing about,
Upon their victims amidst callous, noisy and boisterous shout.

Pieter broke free from the ferocity of the ocean as it swelled,
Caving in upon him, encasing him, as though jelled,
Spluttering and gasping for breath in waters and night so swart,
To gain some form of initiative, of his predicament to thwart.

And the shimmering of light cast from lightning,
Gave freely, great clarity, of that which was frightening,
He saw a baby floating close by and then the body of a woman,
And then another body; and fear struck a chord, he not a pagan.

And Willem clawed his way from the bottom of his well,
Breaching the surface of the sea, to be rid of this spell,
With an outstretched arm he reached for the sky,
To seek assurance, to seek aid, to use his eyes to spy.

He was surrounded on three sides by the interior of the ship,
Which he had called home, his abode this long, long trip,
The fourth side was now wide open to the dark night air,
And with cast astonishment he saw a vision, one to declare.

It was as though he could perceive the glory of God,
Caste down upon him as though with a nod,
The opportunity of a lifetime taken into hand,
Before his sight, across the sky arced a band.

With the accompaniment of the lightning strikes he saw more,
Silhouette of the cliffs above, like doom, something in store,
Yes, they looked most evil, there amidst lightning strike,
But a vision of beauty, of promise, something in future to like.

"Are you okay, Willem? Are you hurt!" came Pieter from behind,
Shouting at the top of his lungs, Willem not alone, clarity to mind,
The open side of the ship now an open invitation,
For more noise to envelope them both, a great penetration.

"Yes; YES! I'm okay," came the reply and Pieter moved closer,
Towards the boy, the one he had grown a little fond of, no poser,
What you see is what you receive, company so seldom sought,
On a few occasions had lifted his spirits when they were wrought.

Now it was Pieter's job to see to it that the favour was returned,
By saving the child's life [and so, see, he has openly learned],
Remaining by his side in this, their hour of need,
Pieter, bookkeeper, now filled with a duty of care: he agreed.

There was a small gap between the stern and the shoreline,
The platform of rock which was vacant of sand, the coast's spine,
There was no soft landing, no offering of support from nature,
A gap to be breached before thrust against talons of stature.

To speak more than what was required, was wasteful,
At a time when gasps for air were pulled in by the mouthful,
And energy reserves were required to climb to safety,
Here instinct took over sacked bodies of flesh in their entirety.

Pieter closed the small gap towards the boy and grabbed hold,
Grabbed his arm, each then reaching for buoyancy, to be bold,
Found in the form of a large piece of debris, no need to be told,
An upturned barrel quickly filling with water, as though to scold.

They then grabbed hold of a chest, a foot locker with trapped air,
Offering to provide sufficient support, in this, their great despair,
It enabled them to make their way towards the rocky platform,
Which was within view below the cracking brilliance of the storm.

Piercing light was delivered, another lightning strike from stem,
Different shades of darkness outlining the scene before them,
A sudden burst of energy within them peaked their ability,
Where did the effort come from, this splurge of activity.

Within as little as half a minute they found themselves so near,
So near the edge of the platform that encompassed their fear,
The platform was covered in crashing waves and ebbing surf,
A giant cauldron at the boil, which was to become their berth.

Without warning a tidal surge of water lifted them both,
Up and over a jagged lip, over the mass of water's froth,
A miraculous salvation from harm for which they were grateful,
Tossed like a cork in a barrel after being so careful.

"Quickly! Willem; to me; grab my hand!" yelled Pieter so loud,
His voice penetrating the cold of the night, the darkest, the shroud,
Where the wind and spray from the ocean stung at their faces,
So unprotected they were, here at the worst of places.

Willem reached for Pieter, stretching beyond his doubt,
Until fingertip touched fingertip, their hands gripping about,
Now clasped together like welded metal, a single cast of iron,
Courage hence instilled within each, each now with heart of lion.

Pieter pulled Willem to, amidst the fury of gut-wrenching surges,
At the platform, made visible now and again, the surf edges,
In and out, undulating and fierce, ocean and rock, the thunder,
They scrambled now to a temporary safe haven behind a boulder.

The ocean continued to smash up and around,
Tearing at all in its way, upon all of the ground,
Followed by a freak wave of enormous size,
Encasing them in terror, of mortality to prise.

The lone man and boy gasped for air as the water ebbed back,
Easing off a little from its most heinous attack,
But the fury of the ocean was preparing for another assault,
The beat and bash, man, ship and rock, never to halt.

Pieter looked up and saw his opportunity for salvation,
A rampart of sorts, a mass of crumbling rock, gifting levitation,
Detritus in all its glory made for a steep but passable way out,
A clear way to the summit of the cliff face before them so stout.

Rock, stone and boulders had fallen away from the cliff,
Its true height obscured by dark of night, the ocean and its riff,
No sound heard from above, no sight of anything familiar,
No tree, only sound and sea, that cliff: in life nothing similar.

The height of the cliff, in fact, did obscure,
Did take from mind what was natural and pure,
Inaccuracy of perception provided the mind,
The insufficient light, it all did bind.

"Willem; with me; come with me, NOW," ordered the tall man,
Together they scrambled up gradient of detritus, this their plan,
Losing two steps from every three in their rush,
To secure safe haven, ever on, to push and push.

Each slipped numerous times, too many to count,
Fingernails splintered, blood soaked, pain did mount,
Much pain and caked in mud, they climbed higher and higher,
Ignoring abrasions and torn muscles, they seek their desire.

Every part of the body was a machine set to automatic,
Their every tissue that binds them working so frantic,
Ligaments and mind: both physical and mental: sheer panic,
No thought but of survival, they were berserk, crazed... manic.

Salvation wasn't too far ahead, they could see and feel it,
Looking up momentarily to see what was ahead, so close to spit,
But the light of night caused false crest to fill their vision,
They pushed on, evermore, shaking from mind this visual treason.

How much further did they need to drive,
In order for life to be secured, to thrive,
How long until victory was won,
This sheer misery, opposite to fun.

But reach the top they did, just as a little cloud moved aside,
Then disappeared and came, cloud racing, to ride and ride,
But they caught glimpse from atop the cliff on which they stood,
Exhausted but forced to endure, to watch below the great flood.

The Zuytdorp was in three pieces, thrashed and torn,
A few bodies barely seen, to sight a thorn,
And together the boy and man collapsed, their minds in a knot,
Upon the edge of the cliff, 115 feet high, there on the spot.

But conscious they were as they gasped for air,
From where they lay they could only stare,
A wave of relief empowering both to sit up and look,
Opened mouthed and in disbelief, Poseidon an evil crook.

Shock had momentary hold on their conscience,
Before clearly, a surge of adrenalin, not a science,
The natural bodies defence to protect and to serve,
They embraced the return of sanity, and feeling to nerve.

For now, out of exhilaration,
No adrenalin from action,
Torment of mind had returned,
Pain of injury now quickly learned.

Little by little it was all taken in,
Information deciphered, so thick, not thin,
The entire scene of destruction,
Cargo cast far and wide.

Barrels crashing against rocky platform,
Everything that moved was a weapon amidst this storm,
If anyone was alive then they required good prayer,
That was all they could do, this odd looking pair.

They could do nought of this situation,
Hands bound tight: to complete inaction,
These two skeletons of humanity, drawn to face their reality,
Now starved upon course, their voyage of obscurity.

Tired from the escape of sinking ship,
Tired from the fight across the cliff's lip,
Tired from the climb to higher station,
Completely exhausted beyond all imagination.

Guilty for doing nothing for possible survivors below,
The breaking of human conditioning, to sea, to throw,
Guilty of being alive whilst many others were now dead,
The laying of souls, never to rest in this wet tomb, their bed.

A few bodies could be seen, dashed against rocks,
In teasing action, as though the devil happily mocks,
But a silhouette falls before the surging of wave,
Cast upon them both now a vision from the grave.

"HEY, up here; we're up here!" shouted Willem as he waved,
His arms an invitation, most frantic, for company they craved,
But the vision was apparition, not true at all, nothing real,
The light and storm playing upon him, to savagely deal.

The stinging of rain upon his face was numbing,
His eyes betraying, and below the waves thrashing,
Pieter made Willem lower his hand, grabbing gently his wrist,
Wishing him to hold the pointless aid, to refrain and desist.

"Save yourself, Willem," said Pieter, eyes sincere and mellow,
Looking upon the boy of fourteen: a boy, this young fellow,
The boy returned the gaze, eyes momentarily tied by knot,
"They can't see nor hear you," the statement truer than not.

"Are we to do nothing at all, just sit here amidst the slaughter?"
"Avert your eyes, Willem. That's all you can do," advised Pieter,
"But I must do something to help," Willem replied,
Pieter realizing this minute that 'man' tag should be applied.

"Then do as I do, Willem. Keep your eyes open this night,
Ignore the pain you see; ignore the horrors, ignore the fright,
Watch, Willem; watch with your entire might,
Maintain a vision of where people lay until first light."

"Keep a note on where they may be found on the break day,
For us to venture down, pull all ashore, to soil safely lay,
We may find survivors, Willem, but we must focus,
We must hold our nerve, be the bull, be the Taurus."

"Harvest the fruits of our labour,
Keep all in our favour,
Set ourselves to task,
This is all that I ask."

Willem nodded acceptance of the task set before him,
Both casting their eyes upon the horrors of the shipwreck so grim,
The developing scene, a betrayal cast down from heaven above,
Willem thought: how could God do this to those he did love.

Quite rapidly now the cold of the storm penetrated deep,
Willem began to shiver, there upon the cliff so steep,
For the panic which had overridden the effect of the cold,
Had now dissipated, no defence hence scored, none to hold.

"Here, Willem," said Pieter. "Sit in front of me and keep warm,
between my legs sit tight, we must try and ignore the storm."
Pieter looked round, into the dark and saw nothing behind,
Infrequent exposures, open land, no good cover brought to mind.

"I see nothing," continued Pieter. "Nothing but open ground."
Willem was now seated in front of the man, some comfort found,
"Remain strong; stay as warm as possible, remain untainted,
Stay as strong as can be until the storm has abated."

"From our experiences on ship I think I can safely surmise,
That this cold is not common, but an unfortunate surprise."
"I've heard many stories," said Willem as his teeth chattered,
His body convulsed a little with shudders of pain that mattered.

"That this land is as cold in winter months, to encase and smother,
As it is hot, when the sun is at its fiercest, during the summer."
"No one has been around long enough to tell the difference,"
Voiced Pieter above the storm that continued its deliverance.

"This job of ours will be a hard one," added Pieter, "I was wrong,
I don't think we should remain aloft the wreck for too long,
I feel the pain of this bitter cold within me,
As I know you feel it within you, for I can see."

Willem was a shivering wreck, tooth and nail,
Pieter looked again, far from mind the throwing of towel,
"Willem; I don't think we'll find good shelter, but we must try,
A hollow, something sturdy to protect, on something to rely."

Without a further word the two stood up and proceeded away,
Stooped low with backs to storm they searched for place to stay,
Away from the cliff, away from the dismay,
In search for a haven and from which to pray.

It wasn't long before they came across a small re-entrant,
A small stream with banks of little concern but not pleasant,
They followed this a short distance before coming upon scrub,
Thick and impenetrable, upon their arms to severely rub.

"Maybe we should turn back," said Willem with growing concern,
"Up here, Willem. I see several boulders. Follow me, to stern."
They stepped from the low ground, halting beside large boulders,
Settled behind these as the wind hampered their weary shoulders.

Away from the blast of the wind and the soaking of rain,
Sought shelter for the remainder of the night, away from the pain,
Curled up and holding each other close, their misery to bury,
But could not sleep whilst the storm continued with its fury.

In the least they gathered rest, better than nothing at all,
Some semblance of energy restored, not all to stall,
Wanting to live on and to provide aid in the morning,
Thoughts on possible survivors, something on which to cling.

In time the storm did blow itself clear of the coast,
The sun was almost upon them, a warm and welcome host,
But currently it was time for some sleep,
Which fell easily upon them, and they in one heap.

LEADERSHIP

Birdsong was filling the air, birds from some distance away,
A melody of choruses that seemed unperturbed by the night's fray,
The sound rather mellow and pleasant, so sweet,
As two fragile forms awoke to the morning, the light to greet.

There was a bite of cold of the air, not a cloud in the sky,
The sun having broken the horizon, now quite high,
But the cold had less effect upon them than the night before,
When they were drenched to the bone, much misery to score.

Their clothing was torn and a little shredded,
A layer of protection gone, sure to be dreaded,
A little wet from the ocean and rain,
Suffering from bruises and a little pain.

Willem was the first to sit up, followed by Pieter, sound heard,
Both shivering as they opened their eyelids, now stirred,
And the vibration hit them both, resonant echoing, unfamiliar,
A long way off, a penetrating sound, mystifying but clear.

"Did you hear that, Pieter?" asked Willem, sound eerie but sweet,
"I did, Willem," the man answered as he stood up upon his feet,
Each looking out towards the north-east, each to broach,
From where the sound made its unwavering approach.

"And I think I know what it is," on instinct he relies,
"What?" asked Willem as he looked up into Pieter's eyes,
Willem saw the reflection of humanity, alive in the sodden body,
Scratches and bruises covering his arms and face, looking shoddy.

Clothes torn and tattered, his trousers ripped down one entire side,
Baring the flesh of his leg to the world, nowhere to hide,
His shoes missing and socks soaked with blood,
Patches of varying colour, covered by wet and dry mud.

"I think it's the men of this world, the owners of soil, this turf."
"Wretched souls," replied Willem, casting his eyes upon the earth,
Pieter corrected: "There has been much talk; much hearsay."
"Do you think they'll eat us this day?"

A false smile caressed Pieter's face, "No. But let's forget that,
Forget it for the minute, we are nothing on which to grow fat,
We must get back to the cliff, view the damage,
Find survivors if we can, if survive any did manage."

Leading the way back to the cliff face, Pieter looked behind,
Ensured that Willem was close by and at hand, kept on mind,
And before they knew it they were stepping up towards the ledge,
From atop the cliff , looking down, making silent pledge.

Such a site could never be explained; their feelings of despair,
Their depression, the horror of seeing bodies lying everywhere,
There upon the now exposed platform of rock, the ocean so mild,
And yet the night before it was so untamed and severely wild.

There was debris everywhere, not a single foot of ground bare,
Every part of the Zuytdorp now a wreck, dolour on which to stare,
Crates, barrels, cannons, cloth and sacks: all of these things,
Every single item of commerce was free of its holdings.

Everything splashed upon the scene as though in reckless doubt,
All former glory gone, the ship torn into three, losing the bout,
Losing the bout!! There was no coming back: a sheer misery,
When suddenly a voice leapt up from behind them, a victory.

"Pieter, is that you?" asked a weary voice,
A man we know, Ariaen Leyden; oh, rejoice,
Pieter and Willem turned to this presence,
Half startled to death by the broken silence.

"My God," shouted an exuberant Pieter. "We thrive, we thrive,
Ariaen; thank God... oh my... you're alive, you're alive."
He stepped towards the man of 28 years, a man of the sea,
Such a sight for sore eyes, it filled him with such glee.

Ariaen, a common sailor who had made many voyages to Batavia,
Three occasions, perchance, much experience held, now a savour,
He'd travelled between the countries of Asia for some time now,
Under the keep of the VOC: he quit the sea, he would never allow.

"I'm well," was all he could muster, no formal trope,
And from behind the man came further hope,
A mass of people, twelve all told, each as weathered as the first,
Dressed as lepers, in rags, but still they quenched Pieter's thirst.

And a majority were without footwear upon their feet,
Feet that had been lacerated by rocks, so harshly beat,
Some of those present were in shock, were soaking wet,
Cold all the night, from the early winter's storm already met.

"How many are there of you?" asked Pieter, pessimism cured,
"We're seventeen, including me, but four of them are injured."
"What kind of injuries?" asked Pieter wishing to hear more,
As those behind Ariaen closed the gap, looking bleak and poor.

Sunken faces worn by them all, seemingly gone, life's desire,
Like the embers disappear from the remnants of a blazing fire,
Life gone from their eyes, stripped bear of strength and power,
Nothing on which to gift praise, no gift in which to shower.

But they were alive and that it something better than nought,
What more could one ask, what more could be truly sought,
"Broken bones, mostly; and most of the walking, are whipped,
Cuts and abrasions in large number, skin in places so stripped."

Pieter looked upon Ariaen and saw a gash on his forehead,
A deep wound that had clearly removed some bone, easily read,
All had some form of injury, large and small. "You too are hurt,
We need cleaning materials, good cloth, any raggedy old shirt."

"It appears so. It hurts like hell to tell you the truth, a bother,
But there is more suffering here today than I can ever suffer."
"We need to move down to the wreck," started Pieter by choice,
Before looking upon the others and raising his voice.

"To look for survivors; others that may be trapped,
Who may require our assistance, well and truly sapped."
"No, Pieter," said Ariaen. "We've been dover the wreck already,
Two other men and I, but it is hard down there, far too unsteady."

"We've searched everywhere and not another soul has survived."
"Are you sure...? Maybe you missed someone; someone alive,
We can give hope; hope remaining for some unfortunate soul,
Someone stranded below this cliff, in this heinous, concave bowl."

Ariaen grabbed his friend upon the upper arms amidst stare,
"No, Pieter. We've tried. There is no one to be found there."
"Then what's to be done; what can we do?
For I refuse to believe it is all through."

"Supplies... we also need a firm shelter... maybe some wood,
Bandages and medicine for the sick would be immensely good,
We need tools for the cutting splints, but we need water the most,
Some food... anything to survive this place, our new host."

"And a cannon," voiced Cornelis Lieffers from behind,
A seaman of 19 years, of vast experience, but of poor mind,
"To signal a passing ship,
To aid is securing a return trip."

"Shoes," voiced another further back, "we also need shoes."
Pieter looked down at the man's feet, poor condition, old news,
Yes, indeed, there was much to be sought, much to secure,
Anything for their sanity; anything to keep them morally pure.

For it would be easy to go insane here,
To ridicule and pass on poor sneer,
To spite another for no good reason,
Upon land to cause treason.

Pieter looked at them all, saw a similarity: they were each a lamb,
Like babies in crib being tended, infants being rocked in a pram,
Freely admitting, flocking around a single soul,
It seemed that Ariaen had adopted the leadership role.

But Pieter felt that he had more to offer these people so near,
Each a soul to be catered for, each owed a life quite dear,
"I'm Pieter, I aided the administration by tending the rations,
I have exercised my ambition and expertise upon many stations."

"Upon land and the sea, I have laid visit to many ports,
All before I was nine and twenty, accurate in all of my reports,
I soon decided upon the comfort of dry land, both honest and fair,
And grew to change once more and decided to work elsewhere."

264

"I have many degrees and sound knowledge on navigation,
I maintain sound mind and ambition, high regard for civilization,
It would honour me if you'd all allow me the opportunity,
To help in this predicament of ours, for short stay or perpetuity."

A man took a few steps forward, those around him stirred,
"I am Hendrik Blaauw. Ariaen knows me, so I am assured,
I am seven and forty, have spent my life upon the sea so blue,
Why should the task of command and rescue go to one as you?"

Pieter opened his mouth, to attend further rhetoric, "I have—",
"Yes, yes; you have degrees," Hendrik replied, in effort to save,
Save good position by applying sarcastically, instilled hate,
Hoping all those, here and now, would take the bait.

He turned to look at the others around,
Could see all eyes upon him, interest found,
"Does common paper hold more authority than experience?
I have worked skin to bone, I am tempered, have much patience."

"I am simply offering my hand," said Pieter in defence,
"It's for you to decide what to make of my good essence."
"Well I say that we make of it right now," Hendrik said to tote,
"Who shall be in command of this shipwrecked crew? Let's vote!"

"Aye!" shouted one; "here, here," came another; and one there,
"All of those in favour of me, place your hands up in the air,"
Commanded Hendrik, pushing his own hand up in desperation,
And eight hands showed themselves after a little hesitation.

"The tally has spoken," said Hendrik. "Seven votes, and mine,
That makes a grand total of eight,
The other six will be yours,
Which makes a tally of seven, if you put up your paws."

And Pieter was pleased to see that Willem had voted for him,
It filled him with much pleasure, full to the brim,
"Wait! What of the lame, those that are injured and not here?"
Asked Ariaen in defence of his trusted friend, the votes to steer.

"Don't they have a vote?" pushed Ariaen, forcing the play,
"I have many years at sea and know, gangrene will have its say,"
Said Hendrik. "It will visit them each, and of this take note,
That a dead man cannot be relied upon to make a vote."

"And what of me?" stated Ariaen, "I have changed my mind,
I wish to make a stand. I'm of higher station and kind."
"There's no rank here," came a voice from the back,
A straight forward assault, a plain attack.

"That's right," confirmed Hendrik. "We're no longer on the sea,
Our survival depends on us living off the land, with you I plea,
Think hard on this, don't throw your vote away, we are so few,
I shall serve you all until a ship comes to our rescue."

"Which won't be long now," said Ariaen to all those listening,
Listening to the argument unfold as the sun sat glistening,
"I know that the Kockenge will be off these shores soon....
within the week for sure, whether by day or by light of moon."

"When we were at Table Bay I heard of others whilst on deck,
We can expect such ships as the Oostersteyn, the Zuyderbeeck,
The Belvliet, Popkensburg; the Corsloot,
And even the good ship Oude Zyp to boot."

"All to come this way over the next month, as soon as next week,
Not all will be seen; not all will come within range as we shriek,
Calling them to us with waving arms will do no good,
We need to build a signal fire and ply it with dry wood."

"For immediate ignition will be required when the time is right,
And we need to get a cannon," added Ariaen with eyes so bright,
They then falling upon Cornelis Lieffers, it was his idea,
An idea to save them all with cannon fire, a true seer.

"We must bury the dead and collect rations where possible,
And much, much more to come, but we are strong and able."
"Here, here," yelled Dirck Fret from the rear. "Let's be fair,
All those that vote for Ariaen put your hand in the air."

And to the astonishment of Hendrik a show of nine hands appear,
Each held high, including Willem and Pieter, who stood near,
"Not counting the soon-to-be-dead," added Pieter to the insult,
Extremely excited and overcome by the massive result.

"So as it is spoken, let it be done," said Hendrik in defeat,
The evil in his eyes brewing something behind mask, a sheet,
For it all sounded like a conspiracy against him and out of form,
He tried ignoring the comment against those injured by the storm.

SALVAGE AND SALVES

The storm had done its job well,
The pounding surf and the swell,
All having smashed the hull of the ship,
Driven it into shallow water, to tear and rip.

In watery grave,
And now gentle wave,
Two to ten feet deep, surrounded by water on all sides, this wreck,
Beside the shoreline platform, inside out, an unrecognizable deck.

Easy to see how many reached safety, only wishing it were more,
Tangled rigging alongside a fallen mast connecting ship to shore,
Precariously unstable, not to remain long where it currently lay,
It was a devastating site, beyond belief, faces now soberly grey.

A cliff of limestone [around 90 feet high at the actual wreck site],
At the foot a mass of jagged edges and boulders to spite,
Sharp-edged rocks and little sand of which to speak,
Stretching 65 feet wide, and 6.5 above sea level at low peak.

To all of those now looking upon the scene, seeing far and wide,
From the cliff, along the entire coast [for 155 miles] to either side,
An unbroken stretch of cliff disappeared into the horizon,
So daunting to say the least, but also beautiful beyond reason.

A carpet of silver could be seen far below, shimmering bright,
Glimmering in patches, here and there, in the morning's light,
Every chest broken, treasure inside revealed from behind shield,
The biggest decision was where to start, of their lives to rebuild.

Ariaen said: "We need to be systematic about our salvage,"
Looking at the others: "I see the wonder in eyes so savage,
The glittering of the silver below lighting up your eyes,
Listen to me, money is worthless if you're dead, I tell no lies."

"It'll all still be there next week and the week after that,
Help yourself if you wish but remember one thing flat,
What you salvage belongs to the VOC and will be taken back,
You'll receive no special favour, so of scruples don't lack."

"Some of you need shoes; that is a priority most worthy,
We need wood for shelter, if possible a cannon most sturdy,
Just the one will serve our purpose, if we can manage its weight,
But basic needs must be sought, choose wisely of this freight."

"A working breech block will help the most for the cannon's need,
Food and fresh water, and above all something on which to feed,
Barrels for storage, and anything else you think appropriate,
Anything not tied down, think clearly of plan, don't deviate."

"This is the calm after the storm, you need to all be bold,
For none of us truly knows what the future may hold,
We may not get another opportunity to gather our supply,
So let us make the most of it, on one and all our lives rely."

Ariaen then waved his hand frantically about, his face a stage,
Trying with great effort to release himself of bondage and rage,
For a fly did ingratiate itself upon him, even in June, winter,
Thanks to low temperatures, there being but a single flesh eater.

There were nods of agreement and the men went to work,
Climbing down towards the wreck, their life-giving stork,
Slipping upon the steep bank as they made for what remained,
Of the good ship Zuytdorp, another name the ocean had claimed.

Little was said during the task, the feeling of dread,
Clothing sought and shoes being pulled from the dead,
Bodies collected and moved towards the cliff, there to lay,
To hopefully be pulled to drier land, for men on which to pray.

For the need of man was a funeral and last words,
To seek eternal life, spirits on the wind, like birds,
For the sanctity of heaven and the bliss of afterlife,
To forsaken the natural life and all its strife.

But more still, no need for the corpses to rot and cause disease,
For horrendous smell to waft up to survivors, to mercilessly tease,
And if the ship was to be visited in the near future,
To visit unrestricted by unpleasant scene would be there pleasure.

There was no doubt of mind that visits would need to be made,
But confidence needed to be instilled, no need to be afraid,
And reminders of death was a curse upon itself, this we know,
Besides, the dead deserved burial, to keep spirits high, not low.

Several men tried to get one of the smaller bronze swivel guns,
Drag it ashore with breech block, and visit cabin, the boson's,
Rope needed to haul the large and heavy mass up cliff,
Surely something of desire and need, even a skiff.

So much to consider, so much on which to think,
Act fast but methodically, for the ship may drift and sink,
A tide to drag the remains of wreck far out to sea,
What would they do then, what would their predicament be?

Swivels were mounted on the poop, the highest part of the ship,
Currently quite accessible, but watch your footing, don't slip,
Several breech blocks were taken ashore in the end,
But swivel guns far too heavy, no way, of this, to amend.

Breech blocks were 12-18 inches long, weighed 28 pounds each,
Easier to portage if only they'd wrecked upon a beach,
And a pair of callipers and brass dividers scored, for navigation,
If later they should decide to build a boat, to avoid deprivation.

But for the most they searched for water and food,
Even Willem was much in the mood,
Everyone able was seen there, scampering about,
Looking and searching for salvage, of congratulations to shout.

Willem then fell upon an areas abundant in wealth,
Not entirely sure as to what they were called, here upon a shelf,
An area encrusted with… were they oysters, abalone, periwinkles?
Whelks, mussels and other shellfish, possibly rock barnacles.

Could they survive solely upon shellfish and nothing more,
How long would such commodity last, this limited store,
Willem was too young to consider the facts of survival,
Wishing and praying for another ship, for its safe arrival.

How long would any ship supply last all of those alive,
In the face of the impending difficulty where disease could thrive,
For there was a few on the brink of gangrene and death,
Lives on the edge of a sword, ready to draw last breath.

One of the searchers found dry powder for musket, but no musket,
Another a possible banquet, but found instead an empty basket,
A great stash of tobacco tins, but contents and lids missing,
Some broken bottles of brandy, not worthy of assessing.

The dislodged figurehead of a pregnant women made of wood,
From the Zuytdorp, thrown against rocks, it once proudly stood,
Now carried into a cavern below the cliff face for safe keeping,
A memory of the past, for their humanity is their thinking.

Far too large to carry to the top at present,
Maybe later, when time could be spent,
A memento of past life, a flag to recall,
A memorial of some description, strong meaning to all.

The figure was from the stern of the ship, a figure of passion,
She had a small plump face and bore a placid expression,
She was the only woman amongst them, none other to speak,
Carved of wood, not flesh, a prize worth saving, one to keep.

One by one, in there two's and three's,
Men appeared briefly upon the cliff top, their on their knees,
Placing down their salvage most gently as though baby to bed,
Before returning to the work, bodies wearily, but onwards lead.

And the bodies of the dead were collected below,
Accumulated on the platform, there to stow,
Stacked precariously, shoes taken by those that wore them,
Brief prayer to accompany their removal, the item a gem.

The ship's sails were torn apart – what was left – but taken,
Would be employed well as a shelter, to life a token,
And sheets or blankets for the bandaging of broken limbs,
For future breaks, of fingers and feet, and other things.

All men were different, in some large or small way,
And some here wished to doctor, to help where they may,
To give that gift of giving, to help where best they could,
Not knowing in some cases whether or not they should.

The collection of dead was the worst, a most horrid sight,
Silent and frantic calls reaching for the sky now bright,
But fight on they did against every normal sense,
Do all they could for dignity, sparing no expense.

And then a trove found like no other,
Like the breast milk for baby from mother,
Green bottle of alcohol for some men so weak,
Square in shape, filled with gin, some solace to seek.

Some of the more fragile-of-mind did hide poor intention,
Sought to carry many bottles off to hide in hidden station,
Somewhere upon the cliff face overlooking the sea, their store,
For drunkenness to pitch and play, to alcohol a whore.

Here sat Gerrit Jongbloet, Jacob Albertsz, and friend,
Jacobus Nuyts and Cornelius Brouwer, their sanity to amend,
They had wondered from duty not long after it did commence,
Drawing their bottles close into their chests, ready to dispense.

Wrapping their arms around the neck of a bottle,
To pour and pour, to throttle and throttle,
Caressing them as though they were wives of advantage,
Sucking the bottles dry, their moral sanctity in a rage.

Weaning the glass bottles of every drop,
Not knowing when, or if ever, they would stop,
Becoming drunk and loud amidst the misfortune so fallen,
Fallen upon them all, appetites so horribly swollen.

The four men with broken limbs lay not so far to one side,
Clutching their ears to prevent the awful sound, this tide,
Such drunken slander, so horrid, of their scruples it did tear,
And screams were emitted by those with breaks, unable to bear.

Dirck Fret, 35; and 29 year old Wiebbe Leuftink, sailors,
Had turned to doctoring, upon the needy great favours,
The strain of their task being very real and unparalleled,
At their wits end, their patience and anger just swelled.

Never before had either of them provided medical assistance,
And with no one of sufficient knowledge, was this a penance,
But for what they achieved the victims were most grateful,
And the drunken swine so close were unhelpful and hateful.

No one deserved this mockery, this absence,
An absence of morals and good temperance,
This drunkenness was beyond belief,
Did nothing to alleviate suffering or give relief.

The two good men, Dirck and Wiebbe, could do little,
As the drunks suckled upon their bottles amidst spittle,
Their passion for the green bottle, their precious gin,
Only aiding the weak in committing an audacious sin.

But the gin was a small saviour as well,
Given to the sick in small amounts, in pores to gel,
Was a passion which would help take the pain away,
To help those poor souls where upon the ground they lay.

Francisco Roelofsz had a broken leg and a punctured gut wound,
Seemingly forever on the edge of consciousness he swooned,
Johannes Snitquer a broken arm and fractured skull,
Constantly, forever, silent and still, in staring but full lull.

Marinus Leynsen had a broken arm and several broken ribs,
Fought hard to breath, on life he held but small dibs,
And Hayman Jorisz, of unsound mind, had two broken legs,
A poor condition, unlikely to ever walk again, for savour he begs.

Dirck looked to Wiebbe as the noise from the drunks drifted down,
Falling upon the shelter for wounded, they displaying a frown,
Several planks of wood and sail cloth melded as one,
A shelter from possible rain and the glimmering sun.

It wasn't the grandest attempt anyone had made at pitching,
Not a great architectural feat of hitching and stitching,
But for the time they'd been allowed they fared reasonably well,
Providing a little comfort, if any, from conditions a spell.

Out of earshot, Dirck said to Wiebbe, "I fear for Hayman,
That he won't last the week, and I am no worthy layman."
"Hmmm," acknowledged Wiebbe. "I fear for Francisco, he sinks,
I'll go and see Ariaen, ask him what he thinks."

"Don't give him too much credit, Wiebbe. He's just a man like us,
Do not provide him too much fuss,
Refrain from giving too much satisfaction,
It will go to his head, this granting of position."

"If it proves too much for him, if he fails to jump through hoop,
Then will be the time to change the leadership of this group,"
Said Wiebbe as he moved off without further word from Dirck,
Both good and clear-thinking men, of work never to shirk.

Dirck pulled a piece of cloth from a damaged bucket ,
Wiped the perspiration from Johannes' forehead, to pet,
The bruising upon his skull being very evident,
A large swelling and mostly red and a concave dent.

There was much pressure beneath the skull,
Seemingly pale, this flesh of man, this hull,
And the worst was feared for his well-being,
His fever was very strong amidst light mewling.

REMARKABLE FAUNA

Wiebbe approached Ariaen who had just appeared at the lip,
Above the cliff carrying one end of a plank, from broken ship,
Willem coming up from the rear, proving himself to be worthy,
Together they placed the plank down, tired, slow, and both filthy.

Willem was excited within, wishing to prove himself a man,
So patiently he worked, fulfilling his duty, a boy with a plan,
Lifting now, one end of the plank, and pulled it with great effort,
Over to a pile that he had growing rather large, bulky and stout.

"The boy works well," noted Wiebbe, smiling at the boy,
And waving away a single fly as it came in to annoy,
"He's a man now," said Ariaen, seeing Willem's mouth erupt,
Erupt into a smile, such a comment could never corrupt.

Wiebbe reflected briefly on the boy before making announcement,
For his reason of errand, of his anxieties which did ferment,
"The wounded are in a bad way... the gin did work well,
But won't last the whole night, and so gone our protective shell."

"There'll be much suffering later tonight,
But pain to be suffered before first light."
It was easy to see how genuinely concerned he was for all,
How strong in morals he was, how he held himself, lofty and tall.

Pieter there too, behind with sack, from work both sore and stiff,
Asked he: "What about those drunken bums over near the cliff?
Can't we seize the bottles they have, give them to those in need,
Prevent this absorbent waste, this tireless greed?"

Wiebbe added: "Oh, they have more than you think, that's no lie,
They've taken a great quantity of bottles, have them close by,
They've hidden them mostly, but maintain a few by their side,
They're settled in for a long and drunken ride."

"Take them by force," said Pieter, "do not be kind, don't woo."
"They have knives..." commenced Wiebbe. "What can I do?
What is it to us that they choose to crawl inside a bottle; really?
If that is their wont, their love, then let them hold them dearly."

"Inflicted by the devil. It will be to their own demise," Pieter said,
"We need the gin: can we take them when they go to bed?"
Ariaen commented then: "But if they don't sleep or stray..."
Said Peter: "We think. What is it that we can do for you anyway?"

"The wounded, as I have said; they're all in a bad way,
But some more than others, for them all I sincerely pray,
Most of us have something to remember the storm by,
But those four... I think time is short. Death, for them, does vie."

"Francisco has a broken leg as well as a punctured gut,
We can't do anything for the wound, no scalpel to cut,
Nothing to do except bandage it and hope for the best,
Endeavour to do all we can and provide them with much rest."

"Nevertheless, the wound will infect, unless we clean and close,
It's going to turn gangrene, and before we know it, on the nose."
"Can we attain anything from the ship's doctor, from his cabin?"
Asked Pieter of Ariaen, "Somehow maintain an uplift of chin."

"His cabin isn't far from the skipper's. Pieter, you were in there,
What was it like? Did you see supplies, or was it laid bare?"
"Last night it was like hell; this morning I conducted a search,
Of company or personal belongings... nothing but unsteady lurch.

"Even now the ship is wavering a little: a small wave hit the side,
But I continued on, knowing we are short on time, I did abide,
Most of the quarters are below the surface, a sheer hazard,
I prepared myself for the worst, of myself I did gird."

"But the cabinet in which the medicine is kept has been spoilt,
As much by the storm itself and also the waters of salt,
Everything will be ruined, for the ocean and rocks give no favour,
Gone all the goodness, smell and flavour, nought there to savour."

Asked Wiebbe: "Isn't it worth another try?
Something may be found, this you cannot deny."
"I'll have another look," volunteered Pieter, not confident at all,
Feeling no confidence in this effort, as though on errand, a fool.

And he was correct, for in the end nothing could be salvaged,
Neither doctor's belongings or medicine, all had been ravaged,
Said Ariaen: "Meanwhile we must provide them comfort."
Concluded Wiebbe: "I'll return to my station, increase my effort."

Another did then appear at the cliff, a scenery of sea and sound,
A regular seaman as could ever be found,
Jan Wysvliet put down a bucket: [his coming end due to denial],
Willem came in from the side and moved it to his stockpile.

"Jan, can I ask something of you?" queried Ariaen quite calm,
"Certainly. What is it?" Jan, easily lead astray: to hold in palm,
"Take another man with you and find a campsite,
Not too far away from the cliff; somewhere... just right."

"...but far enough to be away from the drunks over by the cliff,
They are just over there: drunken state and gin, easy to whiff."
"Sure," acknowledged Jan, tired reflection showing, easy to see,
As well as in the way he held himself. "I'll take Harmen with me."

Harmen Akkerman and Jan pushed on into the unknown,
Ready for anything, in their direction, to be thrown,
To a site where the Indian Ocean could be seen both far and wide,
And having quickly established a site for a camp they set to stride.

They decided to continue with a reconnaissance, to be gratified,
For it wasn't enough for these two men to be easily satisfied,
Men of the sea looking for adventure, for something to be met,
Not content with such a small accomplishment as previously set.

They commenced upon their reconnaissance of the area with glee,
Towards where the sound did seemingly grow, wishing to see,
The sweet call falling upon the light breeze and flowing their way,
The same one heard by Pieter and themselves, earlier that day.

From the edge of the cliff inwards for about 1,300 feet was void,
Nothing except a little low heath vegetation, solitude enjoyed,
Beyond that there existed very dense scrub for two miles,
Tea-tree and eucalyptus, a place favourable to criminal exiles.

The trees themselves well spaced, able to provide opportunity,
Ample enough for the making of raft or shelter, to avoid ferity,
To lease life more opportunity and saviour, that grand prize,
All was here for the taking should the need arise.

As it was, however, there was plenty of salvage from the wreck,
Enough to currently serve all of their purposes, keep life in check,
Which included material for the making of wild and blazing fires,
That is, once planks had dried, hence suited for their desires.

The going was tough on the men for they were already exhausted,
Tired from the salvage operation and not sufficiently rested,
Not to mention that they had gone without food passing their lips,
Since that day when sunk: forgone memory of salted bacon strips.

The sky was a beautiful blue and there was not a cloud to be seen,
Both knew winter was approaching, of this they were not keen,
And the clear sky so high above would soon be gone,
Winter storms and sullies, so close this future, not long.

Several gullies were present amidst a little undulating ground,
Each several hundred feet apart, small ridges and mound,
Each stretching out from the land and towards the coast,
Some being quite deep, a savage land, an unpleasant host.

Like small streams during winter after heavy rain,
But dry for the remainder of the year, underfoot a pain,
Harmen and Jan knelt down to drew handfuls of fresh water,
A small trickling from the night's storm, of dryness to alter.

Small rock holes were also found to hold up to 12 gallons or more,
Although an unreliable source of water, of requirements no bore,
Collection was the key, storage to become desire and need,
And next on the agenda was a source on which to feed.

Further inland there was a great expanse of undulating sandplain,
Stunted with low scrub, sheer desert by appearance, carpet so lain,
Like an ocean dotted with acacias, eucalypts, banksias and other,
To these men of the open sea, this was enough to smother.

Vastly different than the sights and smells of home and glory,
A land bound by cities at their fullest, amidst talk and story,
The scene before them was devastating to say the least,
This carpet of mystery, this awakening of unseen beast.

The heat of afternoon built up, dwarfing the cold from night,
And so, as it does at sea on long voyages, it played its delight,
Their feet started swelling up with the effort of the walk,
High above a migration of birds, squawking as though to talk.

As they continued on into the clearing, Harmen came to a halt,
"Look, Jan. Over there," said Harmen, pointing, but ready to bolt,
With his head low he tried to aim his finger with great accuracy,
As though it were a weapon, though in palm a vacancy.

"What do you see?" asked Jan as he looked off into the distance,
"A head, I'm sure of it," and so he searched for its reappearance,
"It moved... look... there it is again," Harmen said hurriedly,
"And now it's not moving; it's like a statue," he said quite avidly.

"Ah; yes. I see it too," concurred Jan, withholding a shout,
"It's not moving now. It has great ears and a long snout,
What do you think, for my mind is glassy with fog?"
Concluded Harmen, a satisfaction on self analysis, "A dog."

"No," disagreed Jan, looking upon friend with lowered eyebrows,
Signifying his puzzlement, as such a suggestion allows,
"Look around you, Harmen. This grass is almost chest high,
If it's a dog it'll be the largest dog I've ever seen, I cannot deny."

"It could be standing upon a recent kill, or a dirt mound,
Maybe searching for prey," suggested Harmen. "A great hound."
And then it moved, dashing off as it did leap and bound,
Against the open plains of grass-filled expanse, all around.

A kangaroo as never seen by the eyes of a white man before,
Harmen and Jan cowered in the long grass, afraid evermore,
Now breathless,
Now restless.

Holding their palms to chest, being caught completely by surprise,
The animal moving with such rapid action, small panic did rise,
"Did you see that?" asked Harmen, and then many more,
Fifteen other animals picked up their head, heads galore.

Each leaping off as the other had done,
Following the previous, a move to stun,
"My God. I don't believe it. What a sight."
"We must get back, Jan. Bring this to light"

"No, not yet," said Jan, looking at Harmen, within an anxiousness,
"They're just animals, Harmen. We should delve, be witness,
Go beyond where they stood, learn of them, find a weakness,
Clear our heads, learn hard facts, deny our minds this fogginess.

"But not too far, Jan. We don't want to get lost, unsettle the rest."
"Lost," scoffed Jan. "If so then we just head west,
It's as simple as that, but for the minute we must explore,
Come; let's go that way; east; let's look some more."

Before they knew it the day had closed its door,
By which they felt exhausted and fell to the desert floor,
There was no time for a meal of any sort... it had been missed,
The sun disappearing over the horizon: they had hunger to resist.

Their eyes were then drawn to watching that stunning sight,
The appearance of a myriad of colours cast across the starry night,
A great mass of sparkles came out, those made invisible by day,
Providing sufficient light to provide small comfort as they lay.

They lay in the dim light offered by the heavens above,
Being able to see in all directions, a serenity to love,
The cool night comfortable enough to keep them from freezing,
And the sounds of the night reached their ears, it was so amazing.

Huddled together like man and wife helped keep them warm,
Not so hard, gifted by that lack of storm,
It wasn't until the early hours of the morning that they felt cold,
A vacuum of evaporated heat present when they move, to scold.

It was all new to them, completely strange, and sadly,
Too tired from the night before they did sleep soundly,
They slept through the main chorus, the birds and their song,
Music of the morning, of the bush: everything right, not wrong.

And then out of the distance, more serine than first thought,
Sounds of reverberation across the land, that which was sought,
A ceremony taking place upon this strange land: near or far?
A drumming; a sincere acoustic; a fear it did jar.

There could be cannibals,
Maybe wild animals,
Creatures of the unknown,
Something heinous at them thrown.

THE DEVIL IN GIN

The night before Jan and Harmen did sleep,
It was for the others to…. Celebrate, not weep,
But before them now the sun drifting to horizon,
Fine work here, work to remember, to emblazon.

The salvage operation, early morning till dusk, well wrought,
Little undone, they did all they could, or so they thought,
All that could be carried from harm's way conveyed,
That too heavy left till morning, where it lay it stayed.

And before the waves moved in from an abrupt sea,
A shadow fell upon the camp, worries dampening their glee,
For there was still much to do, much to sort, much to consider,
Many resources secured from the wreck, much work for the leader.

The prizes unmoved would be going nowhere soon,
With or without high tide, with or without the moon,
Most too heavy to be carried out by smallish waves,
Or taken beneath the surging surf to watery graves.

Some were still attached,
Such as material employed as shield or thatch,
Even if precariously so, most would be available come morning,
In particular the swivel gun, to the deck it had good mooring.

But the bulk of the cheer, their cherished reward for honour,
Was port to cliff under hard sway, under harsh and hard labour,
But so much lost: barrels of wine and beer, the butter, ten sheep,
Rice, bacon and oils; nothing of these to save, to keep.

They were fortunate enough to have rescued some cloth and rope,
Peas, a few plates, many pounds of salted meat, all gave hope,
And vast amounts of meat had been lost to the hungry sea,
So much waste, gone forever, of vast resources now free.

Yes indeed, free they were of all that was home,
To be stranded in this hell, so little known of this biome,
Form measly chunks of bread and anything more lavish,
But they did manage some canvas, this to savour and relish.

That thing needed the least was illness and disease,
But nature was not on their side, not there to appease,
And that required the most, other than medicine was food,
But the salted meat would not last long, their situation no good.

They would make the most of the food whilst it lasted,
And maintain high hope for favourable wind well blasted,
For some source or other to come their way,
For pain of hunger to be held at bay.

The bodies of the dead had been piled on shoreline platform,
Unable to be moved unless hit by very heavy storm,
There they lay, ready to be moved, possibly the next day,
A huge fire and last prayer to send them on their way.

Of way we speak, and of this we must be fair,
For not all people are good, of heaven not to share,
Some were destined for place hotter than most,
For man with horns, to forever be their host.

A fire was intended for the deceased all at the same time,
A few words spoken, as best could be offered, some in rhyme,
No honoured guest available but learned men at least,
Someone there, better than none, even if not a priest.

A fire which would not only act as a point from which to cremate ,
But a signal to any coast-passing ship, of their situation to relate,
With the calculations suggested of the ships in port at Table Bay,
It was a reliable guess as to when eyes would easterly lay.

To fall upon them on the horizon, their signal seen,
And the survivors held good reason to remain reasonably keen,
For the Kockenge was expected over the next six or seven days,
Much slower than the Zuytdorp: to come near, to see their blaze.

Meanwhile the four men, drunk and beyond comprehension,
Lay near the edge of the cliff, creating much tension,
Each drowning their sorrows, to where they became oblivious,
Unaware of events amidst their gin, all the fool and treasonous.

A temporary fire had been lit by way of several lamps full of oil,
And a tinderbox procured by Ariaen, held from any great spoil,
Along with a secret maintained by him, a small box of tobacco,
A worthy possession, this and his fire-starter, left to fallow.

But the seamen did uncover the truth of his withholding,
Mostly halfwits, clear lack of intelligence, yet up to deciphering,
They could sum up two and two, possibly not three and three,
Ariaen had little choice and came clean of his tiny whee.

The firestarter, his tinderbox, now known by almost all,
But of the little tobacco he held he remained tight lip, to stall,
Stall the sight and smell of his delectable morsel of power,
And now he desired a tree root similar to that of a brier.

Any old tree root would do, in fact,
Something to hollow out, to carry on the act,
The act of puffing and inhaling, nothing near like it,
Forever on his mind was this thing yet made, he did admit.

From time to time,
A scent so sublime,
He sniffed the weed,
A perfume agreed.

Water was then brought to the boil for a dry satchel of tea,
It and a single tumbler rescued from ship of the sea,
Too little for all the survivors, some would miss out,
And a large portion of meat cooked in a pot quite stout.

With plenty enough to fill everyone most contentedly,
The warmth of food in stomach greeted most heartedly,
A small portion of tea would not go wholly missed,
Much more was on the mind, never to be held in fist.

The fire was heaven to have and to behold,
Most warily of its dangers, its ability to scold,
But likely wouldn't last, for fuel was low,
Wood needed securing, on fire of which to throw.

They hadn't managed to gather much wood,
That of salvage was, for shelter, reasonably good,
It would be a sin to throw such on fire as it stood,
A roof more apt to appease them as it should.

Even so it was still rather wet from the ocean and storm,
Pieter then made ready to speak and to inform,
For he held a lamp, which he shook to his ear,
And heard nought from within, it was a smallish fear.

That was the last of the oil for all they knew,
The remainder in wreck, or out to ocean as the wind blew,
He stood then with lantern in hand and threw,
Temporarily jolted by anger, by misgivings as they stew.

The injured had been moved closer,
To provide assurance, though they were wiser,
This was their time of need, but not of desire,
For one at least he was ready to retire.

Johannes Snitquer, with the broken arm and fractured skull,
His brain had haemorrhage, and before death the great lull,
Lull of feeling and remorse,
Wishing to live, of course, of course.

And death was like a dream to some,
Clear and understood, no feeling glum,
Some experienced little sorrow, but a small joy,
After life was to pleasure, not there to annoy.

In the company of others he wallowed away,
Uplifted within, his mind fogging, going grey,
His last thoughts simmering,
His life disappearing.

He fell into a sleep of no return,
Not right away of this did others learn,
But once realised he was aside,
Sail cloth placed over him, peace to hide.

Seebaer Phillipse and Joannes Spandaun sat by the small fire,
Wishing to speak, wishing to pour out their desire,
As they talk between themselves they glanced at Ariaen again,
They had something of importance to say, did not wish to refrain.

"You have something to say," said Ariaen, kindly,
 "I see it by the way you are looking at me so coldly."
Dirck and Wiebbe continued to examine the injured,
As others looked to the two young friends now inspired.

They were young seamen, on their first voyage for good wage,
Never before had they been to sea, waters so savage with rage,
"The fire should be bigger," answered Seebaer for the two,
"No passing ship is going to see this... thing: you have no clue."

"Have you been this way before, in front of this coast,
Ever passed this strange land, its endless tracks of little boast?"
Ariaen said this as he rubbed his head wound beneath bandage,
A white band covering his forehead, he, withholding his rage.

"We are both new to the sea," answered Seebaer as he shifted,
Pivoting upon the spot, embarrassed by inexperience so gifted,
Said Ariaen: "I've been this way many times, many times have I,
I have seen the shore from far out to sea, before my very eye."

"At this point, just off the coast, a ship will turn to the north,
And then head towards its destination for what it is worth,
Only during certain months of the year will one travel so far east,
Far enough that they will have much on which the eye can feast."

"In all my times, traversing coast from here to the Sunda Strait,
I have seen many fires, always there, early night to late,
This land is inhabited by black men of which we know little,
But they must be tough to live here, not weak nor brittle."

"They wear nothing upon their bodies, carry spears and shields,
From knowledge they are very ready for war, plough no fields,
No towns or villages seen upon the coast, nowhere seen,
Of their religion we know not, but we assume them to be unclean."

"They surely skirmish with others from this land most regularly,
And they do this after reconnaissance most discreetly,
For we have not seen them anywhere near,
But they know of our presence and have no fear."

"A small fire will not do anything to encourage great assistance,
But to do nothing will not satisfy all here, I see by appearance,
So should I insist and a larger flame, evoke more smoke,
To openly want and invite that dreaded, black bloke?"

"So I shall do as I think is best and leave it at that for now,
When the dead are ready for burial, the fire we can grow,
Time will then be right to build it high, built it strong,
We shall cast a flame upon it, cremate the dead, I am not wrong."

"We cannot bury the dead, it is too much work, we have no tools,
When the time is right, the fire will be lit as though we are fools,
I hope the Kockenge will be near at that time to see signal sent,
I hope to draw them near, wish not our toils to be so easily spent."

Ariaen looked around the campfire to all those that had survived,
All except the drunks: and Harmen and Jan: wishing them alive,
"If no ship comes within the next five weeks then we rethink,
Think of something new, to rejoin civilization, regain that link."

A Solid coughing spell then concluded his views on the subject,
"What shall we do?" asked Seebaer, as though trying to object,
"A ship arriving at Batavia will learn of our situation,
They may link our fire with those missing, fill us with elation."

"I say five weeks of signalling, conserving as best we can our fuel,
Linking efforts to the time table I offered: we must all be mutual,
Ships will pass, but their precise day of passing: I cannot say,
I simply offer a guess derived from what I heard at Table Bay."

"After the fifth week we will wait until the approach of summer,
Then make an attempt at launching our own boat, not to saunter,
I have no idea at this stage whether we shall be successful or fail,
But we shall require a good launching pad from which to set sail."

"I shall set out tomorrow," volunteered Seebaer. "I shall go south,
For one whole day and return," and to friend, opened his mouth,
"I'll take Joannes with me, we shall both go forth."
"Good," said Ariaen cheerfully. "Who will go north?"

Silence dominated the scene,
There were few who were keen,
"Seebaer and I," volunteered Joannes, "once we've returned,
Returned from the south, having found little or having learned."

"Even if finding something worthy you should still take a look,"
Advised Pieter as he then continued: "Water we need: a brook,
You might find something better in the north, learn from the south,
Be sure to take some cooked meat, to help sustain your youth."

"Something edible may also come your way,
But nearer the coast you must stay,
And ready access to the Ocean is needed,
And for God's sake, be careful, safety heeded."

Joannes nodded, "Very well. We shall go south, look yonder,
On return I shall venture north, to explore and to wonder,
For there will be much to consider and to formulate,
Of dangers and safe havens, much to extravagate."

Pieter added: "There are some blankets over there,
They will aid you by night when the sky, of cloud, is bare,
Courtesy of Willem and his collection, and so grows our store,
Take some with you, for weather dictates you need them more."

Joannes nodding acceptance with a smile,
His soul and mind ready to trudge mile and mile,
"Is there anything else that concerns anyone?" asked Ariaen of all,
"Not wishing to give voice of command, my desire is only to call."

"Yes, yes, that's it indeed, a call to organise our saving of soul,
We, seamen, even if young, deserted upon land to pay a toll,
And for what do we pay this price... possibly a test of our wits,
A test of conviction, to see whether or not we have merits."

"For the first time in our lives we must treat each as a brother,
So it shall be made clear: no one here is any better than another,
With different experiences and knowledge we must survive,
We need to collaborate more than ever, in order to stay alive."

The faces around the fireplace were easily read,
Each filled with agreement for what was said,
Willem stood up and sat down again beside his friend,
Ariaen, his father-figure, to aid where possible, to the very end.

"Shall I take meat to the drunks, the others?" Willem did ask,
"You're a good lad, Willem... in God's light to bask,
Considering others when they have done no work this day,
To aid those drunkards where they lay."

"We shouldn't turn our back on them," said Willem. "Should we?
I overheard one of the other men saying he wished it was he,
Then the other wishing he too were drunk,
Wishing to be oblivious, their miseries sunk."

"Wishing to be drunk, and getting drunk, is not the same,
It is two completely, different things," said Ariaen, feeling shame,
For he should be as good as Willem, not so quick to blame,
But it was hard to do when so many were lame.

And then Ariaen added: "But you give me an idea."
He stood up. "We shall both deliver them meat, try and steer,
Steer them from their drunken ways,
And if not successful... maybe just rid them of their stays."

"And whilst we are amongst them, if they appear incapable,
We shall throw what they have of their stash from table,
Refuse them access so easily granted,
Upon ground or over the cliff it can be decanted."

"I'll come with you," said Hendrik, feeling wise,
"I hope we can easily, of their possession, prise,
Casting evil drink into the ocean will be my honour,
Be rid, too, of their foul, drunken stench, that evil odour."

Both forgetting it could be used to aid the sick,
Their heads filled with this desire and trick,
To end once and for all the drunken behaviour,
To be judge and jury, to be their saviour.

As expected the four drunk men were flat on their backs,
Sleeping heavily, a chink in their armour, their cracks,
Drowned of all reality until morning's first light,
They would be unable to do anything, and too few to fight.

It took quite a while to find the spare bottles of gin,
Bottles hidden, now found with a grin,
Willem too, enjoyed throwing the bottles as far as he could,
Into the night air, to smash or wallow and sink as they should.

The noise of breaking waves upon the platform below,
Were now a sweet pleasantness, on them to grow,
And on return to their fireplace they all drift off into sleep,
The gin forever gone, of its medicinal purpose they did not reap.

CANNIBALS AND SNAKES

6th June, 1712, the survivors rose with the dawning of the sun,
The fire almost out, being hard to start, but warmth finally won,
The day was a little cloudy, but quite cold despite this,
Their second morning in a strange land, the ship they did miss.

It was at this same time that Harmen and Jan woke to motion,
Greeted by a *thwack* in the bush not very far from their position,
Jan shook his friend and got up upon his knees,
Head lifted to see across the expanse of grass amidst light breeze.

A greasy plain for as far as the eye could see,
Dotted with shrubs, and here and there a tree,
And where the grass died away, nothing but a scorched turf,
A prairie of softly undulating ground, a bare and stubborn earth.

Dotted with eucalyptus to break up the monotony of the view,
There was not much else, compared to yesterday, nothing new,
"What is it?" asked Harmen as a rumble came from within,
"What do you see?" rubbing his eyes, a lack of smile, no grin.

"Nothing, I see... Harmen, quick," insisted Jan with emotion,
Rapidly upon his feet and running in the opposite direction,
Running as fast as he could, body carried by fleeting feet,
The fright within Harmen was so high that his heart missed a beat.

Such an action stole his breath away for a brief second or two,
He shot up and looked around, stunned, not knowing what to do,
Saw then, Jan, running away, a hundred feet or more,
He thought, 'what a coward', such action he did deplore.

And then he, himself, turned to see what was the matter,
A near-naked man with spear and shield, his mind did shatter,
An aboriginal looking, as though mystified by his appearance,
Seemingly astonished but unafraid of this white and large nuance.

Harmen was quick on his friend's heels, so quick, so fast,
Running for another hundred feet or more, this land so vast,
To then turn and see once again the dark flesh, this ill-clad man,
The aboriginal seeking contemplation: a spirit of his clan?

"Who do you think it is?" asked Harmen, largely pathetic,
"I don't know and I don't care," answered Jan, rather rhetoric,
Some scepticism taking strong hold upon him, he unsure,
"He's a savage; possibly a man-eater," to peace of mind no cure.

"Shall we try and communicate with him?" Harmen did say,
Jan looked at the man standing there, three hundred feet away,
The black contrast, doing little but glancing in their direction,
Both considering the others mind-set as well as their complexion.

"We should leave him be, of stable disposition we cannot rely,
And there's no telling how many others may be nearby,"
With that said Jan looked around, feeling much fear,
Making sure none other was trying to move to his rear.

"I think he's alone," said Harmen, hopefully,
"Yes, probably," agreed Jan, within small depression, tiny gully,
Added Harmen: "He doesn't seem to be too concerned,
And he has a weapon—Hah! That's the first thing I learned."

"He's probably hunting food," concluded Jan who did recall,
"That creature we saw the other day, the one so tall,
Hopping across the ground in great stride,
The others won't believe any of this; they'll think we lied."

"Shall we return now? Pass on the news, get something to eat,
"Yes. Let's go tell the others, and wrap ourselves in a warm sheet."
And so they commenced the short journey back to their campsite,
As a little cloud gave way, the surrounding area turning bright.

And as they moved along they shot glances back upon their tracks,
Making sure they weren't followed by any blacks,
No other way to describe them, as they would the whites,
No better way of indication than where reality bites.

Several gullies were crossed, those same passed the day before,
Several rock holes presented themselves, far from cliff or shore,
Sources of water to supply the survivors over the coming future,
Source of food now the torment, thoughts on which to nurture.

The sandplains now behind them as the pair continued their walk,
Painstakingly back to the others, to share information, to talk,
Their stomachs feeling less hunger than the previous night,
Hunger dissipating slightly with their short journey, their plight.

They then fell upon an old camp, easily drawing their attention,
Seemingly of good vantage, slightly higher in elevation,
The ground surrounding it easy to view, not by chance,
The Indian Ocean able to be seen via studying glance.

Being of higher elevation made it a good choice,
Good vigil all round available, many pros to voice,
There were also several bare spots where people had slept,
An old lean-to laid flat upon the ground, looking rather inept.

A single large tree provided shading,
And a large rock employed for making,
Making of tools, or grinding of food, weapons to improve,
A smooth concave surface in rock, a rock too heavy to move.

Said Jan: "It looks like our friend employed this place,
But it hasn't been used for a while: of it they did not efface."
"A summer camp," suggested Harmen. "A temporary hide,
I will guess acutely: somewhere for hunters to reside."

"Do you think they'll return?" asked Jan, looking over shoulder,
"I don't know; but we'll have to keep an eye open, be the bolder."
Harmen then bent down, lifting a large portion of stripped bark,
"Maybe they left some tools behind... look, see this mark..."

"What is it...?" Jan said as he turned to the silence,
He then froze too, in terror-stricken semblance,
Hiding coiled and peaceful beneath was a snake,
Which was quick to lift its head, its tongue to rake.

Tasting the air,
A warning fair,
This his lair,
Be still, just stare.

Harmen had held himself well for the fright he had received,
Holding tight onto the bark in his left hand, hoping for reprieve,
He was in easy striking distance of the reptile and quite at a loss,
What should he do now, who in this situation was the boss.

The yellow scales of the six foot snake gave it a menacing look,
Not to mention the position it held: Harmen's legs shook,
Ready to lash out with a bite to Harmen's leg or arm,
Harmen's head rang in alarm, but he needed to remain calm.

Jan could see that Harmen wasn't going to move anytime soon,
He considered the situation, rather light headed, ready to swoon,
"I'm going to pick up a fallen branch, Harmen, to distract… it,
Don't move; for God's sake… keep still: it could leap, bite or spit."

Jan moved around towards the rear of the snake,
He took up a long branch, tested it with a single shake,
The snake turned its head to look upon Jan, just out of reach,
Harmen then moved his foot, a prayer he did preach.

Ah, a mistake, moving it a little further out of the way,
In an instant the snake turned to have its say,
And it struck out at the movement, as fast as can be,
Sinking fangs into the flesh of the calf, its venom now free.

Retracting his fangs it departed the scene, leaving the dread,
Jan's empty effort to beat down upon it hit the hard earth instead,
Harmen bent over in more shock than pain,
Grabbing hold of the wound with the palm of his hand in vain.

He then removed his hand and probed with shaking finger,
Over the site of the wound, some venom seen, digits linger,
"Damn; damn that thing!" cursed Harmen as he fell upon his arse,
"Of all the blasted luck, this worthless land: no benefit, no class."

"And now bitten by… what? Hiding in ambush, being sly."
"I never saw such a thing," a shocked Jan said in reply,
Jan gazed out, looking towards where the snake had slivered,
And then upon the frightful look of his friend, poison delivered.

"What am I to do?" shrieked Harmen, a cry, a shout,
"The poison… we have to suck it clean out."
"Quickly," prompted Harmen. "Get a knife."
"I don't have one, Harmen… how am I too save your life?"

"At the camp; get Dirck or Wiebbe," Harmen did yelp,
"Quickly, Jan, or I'll be dead. Run for your life, get help."
"Shouldn't you come with me? I can manage a carry."
"No; but you're right… I can walk. Quickly; let's not tarry."

Harmen got to his feet and started to move as fast as he could,
Close behind his friend Jan, not really knowing if he should,
Moving with speed, to be saved before the poison did react,
Before his body gave out: the poison they needed to extract.

They weaved in and out of the scrub, no given graces,
Pushing through the tea-tree, growing thick in places,
There was more than a mile to go over rough terrain,
In the general direction of the others, aid to gain.

The sweat commenced to pour from them both as they did move,
Jan, more than Harmen, believing he had more to prove,
To save his friend: something he had to do, this he knew,
And the distance behind them grew and grew.

Harmen suddenly halted and drew his hands to his heart,
He fell suddenly like a sack of potatoes, there to depart,
Straight to the ground in an instant, death overriding all will,
A grotesque contortion painted upon his face, he lay very still.

A MATTER OF COHABITATION

Seebaer and Joannes had commenced their exploration,
Going south on morning's first light, filled with inspiration,
Taking nothing more with them other than some small portion,
Burnt meat from the night before and full of good intention.

They had decided to try and return by last light,
In this way they could share in a campfire at night,
Again replenishing their energy before another long day,
Heading north for further exploration of coastline that lay.

The two had only travelled less than half a mile,
When they came across what afforded them a small smile,
It appeared to be a small beach fronted by gentle sloping ground,
Which extended out onto a rocky sea floor and lucky to be found.

They took note of the area for the importance that it offered,
Not so much for the ability to launch a boat, [if they bothered],
But for the landing of a boat from rescue ship, if one came near,
To see their signal fire, close enough to the coast, able to steer.

They spent little time here, wishing to be on their way,
More concerned in covering ground, not in causing delay,
And by midday their feet were rather tender,
Excessive reason to saunter, not to meander.

The effect of wet feet shoved either loose or tight,
Into the shoes of a previous owner, were not quite right,
Beggars can not be chooses in time of need or desire,
Offering little comfort but protection in times so dire.

The way south, as too, was presumed for the north,
Was full of many species of wildlife, many brought forth,
Mostly of feather: whistle, squawk; fluttering upon the breeze,
Of ground: ants, centipedes, lizards, beetles, and pests to tease.

"Our food won't last long, Seebaer," said Joannes out of the blue,
Trying to provoke conversation as they continued, speaking true,
"No. But time will be our reward, not all times will be bad."
"Maybe not, but there's plenty of time to be had."

"If no ship passes our way soon," Joannes did say,
"Ever more time than we can bear will come our way."
Said Seebaer as a few more steps were taken: "I was thinking...
These insects and beetles may be edible; and no, I am not joking."

Joannes screwed up his face as he considered the idea,
Of crunching into a beetle; of poison, of choking; the fear,
Pressing one between his teeth until its innards came rushing out ,
Faeces disturbed from its arse, onto his tongue and round-about.

"I mean to say," continued Seebaer, "the savages upon this land,
Well, they've learnt to survive, taken the surroundings into hand."
Joannes considered this for a moment, contemplating, being fair,
"Seebaer, you know what, you might have something there."

"Yes indeed; struck a chord you have," Joannes congratulated,
Nodding his head in an act approval, though not entirely elated,
Seebaer: "No better way to learn than from savages: so obvious."
Joannes stopped dead in his tracks "What? You can't be serious?"

"Why not?" said Seebaer as his shoulders shrugged up and down,
"They've lived here long before any ship saw this land so brown,
They survive day to day, and haven't yet attacked,
They have so much knowledge, so much experience well stacked."

Said Joannes: "But we haven't come into any contact as yet,"
Not knowing of Jan and Harmen, their encounter so met,
"What if they're hostile?
What if they live a life so vile?"

Seebaer: "If they're hostile then we are already dead,
The only way is to befriend them, to use our head,
Search them out, share in their secrets in order to survive,
Do all that we can to stay alive."

"Look, the sun is directly above us," Joannes said of time of day,
"We should return with the news we have; what do you say?"
Replied Seebaer: "I honestly believe it's our only way,"
He continued: "To seek out the savages, find out where they lay."

"And if a ship doesn't find us within the next few months or so,
Then we will have to trust the savages, in this I know,
Like the VOC trusts in those of Batavia and beyond,
But of eating beetles, insects and other, I'm not truly fond."

HARD CHOICES, SOFT MEN

It was just after midday, time for something to eat,
Time for the survivors upon the cliff to gather and meet,
Gathering at the place transformed into a temporary camp,
A small fire burning dull, unable to ward off cold nor cramp.

Kindling was quickly added and the flames stirred into motion,
A pot of water filled from a nearby source, to concoct a potion,
To boil what may be considered tea by some,
But others confess it's tasteless, bland and glum.

What meat remained was wrapped well, stored back in a barrel,
Sealed with a cover, placed in the shade, so not to spoil,
Gerrit Jongbloet, one of the drunks from nearer the cliff ,
Walked up to them, stood there, dishevelled, cold and stiff.

"I've come to see if I can get something for the others to eat,"
Said Gerrit, a shameful look of despair upon his face to meet,
All of the others looked upon him and then to one another,
Before shifting their view to Ariaen, as though their mother.

"You'll have to wait, Gerrit," said Ariaen. "The sick come first."
Hayman, the man with broken legs, voice cracking from thirst,
Quickly voiced his opinion, "Give them nothing, I say,
Give them nothing at all; for forgiveness they should pray."

"What is it to you, old man?" scolded Gerrit,
"You'll be dead soon," such tone carrying no merit,
Cursed Hayman: "Damn you to hell!
I wish, from the cliff, you all fell."

"Enough!" and Ariaen was upon his feet so fast. "You shall eat,
But be warned; you and your friends have choirs to meet,
You must make amends, help with the work, all day through,
And there will be no more drinks for any of you."

Said Gerrit. "Our supply is finished, only a few bottles we had,
For a rainy day… now gone. So ashamed I am, but also glad,
We all feel rotten to the core,
What can I say: what more."

"Every day would be raining in your eyes," scoffed Hayman,
Said Gerrit: "Okay, I was wrong, but I smell meat in your pan,
We are hungry, too, all of us are willing to conditions meet,
We are part of the crew, we deserve to get something to eat."

"Be warned, Gerrit, there are no other bottles left for you,
Every bottle was thrown into the sea, and nothing you can do,
You must all help or receive nothing. Be a man, not a whelp,
And, Gerrit; we are more than you, it would be wise to help."

"Is that a threat, Ariaen?" said Gerrit with a frown,
Responded Ariaen: "Make of it what you will, don't be a clown,
Discipline must remain if we are to be successful in our plight,
Stop squabbling amongst ourselves, ahead is a fiercer fight."

"Very well," said Gerrit, "I shall tell the others, but please,
Give me some food, go back with a full hand to appease,
The others are still drunk but will be ready to start work soon,
Will these terms be acceptable; to commence early afternoon?"

"It is, Gerrit. We're also going to rest, for the work is hard,
The salvage operation is almost complete, to every inch and yard,
A signal fire will be our next concern, the dead will be cremated,
This will prevent the spread of disease, and dull the work created."

"I understand," said Gerrit. "I'll go and tell the others and return,
To get some rations, give time for the others, of mistakes to learn."
Gerrit departed, leaving the main group to continue with cooking,
To allow them their rest, to avoid their stares, so sour looking.

A noise then came from beyond,
A familiar voice, of which some were fond,
"It's Jan," said Dirck. "I'd know his voice anywhere."
They all listened carefully and it came again upon the air.

Muffled by the background noise of the sea,
And some thick scrub of tea-tree,
Dirck yelled: "Jan, over here."
"Help me. I need help," came the voice of fear.

"Did he say 'help'?" asked Dirck: for he heard but could not see,
"Yes," replied Pieter as he, too, stood. "Quickly, follow me."
Dirck and Pieter raced off through the scrub as fast as they dared,
Calling out, closing the gap, their positions shared.

When finally upon him they saw Harmen upon shoulder,
Draped over Jan him like a rag doll, much there to ponder,
Though there was no time to be slow and easy,
For set in stone was that sense of urgency, the need to be busy.

There was Harmen, most of the colour drained from his face,
Jan let the body fall, and he fell to his knees, falling from grace,
Said Jan between deeply drawn breaths, tired right through,
"He was a good friend, but there was nothing I could do."

"What happened?" asked Dirck, seeing the man dead,
"A snake bite," said Jan, and with the word came much dread,
Unveiled now many looks of despair,
Poor Harmen had fallen upon a snake's lair.

Little thought had been given to such a danger,
Void of all contemplation, but then, none were eager,
But now more than ever they needed to tread warily,
To be always on the lookout, to walk most carefully.

"Come, Jan,' comforted Dirck, "you aren't to blame for anything,
There's so little that you could have done, absolutely nothing."
"If only I had a knife," said Jan, "I could have cut his wound,
Sucked the poison from within him, the bite was so easily found."

"It's finished now," said Dirck. "Come. We'll carry Harmen now,
Take him to the fireplace. Have a rest. Then you can tell us how."
"No," protested Jan. "I'll carry my friend, I feel the need."
"We'll all help," said Pieter, "together as one, we're all agreed."

GOD'S DAMNATION

"Help, come quickly," came the voice,
"What now?" said Wiebbe, wishing he had a choice,
"No, Wiebbe," said Willem, pointing towards the cliff, the west,
"Over there; it's Gerrit," Willem remained calm, doing his best.

"Quickly, help," gasped Gerrit as he raced towards the fireplace,
"What's wrong, Gerrit?" asked Wiebbe, for the worst he did brace,
He was feeling as though an injustice had been served,
Harshly dealt by Gerrit and the other three, not what he deserved.

"Cornelius Brouwer has fallen, off the cliff and down the slope,
I think he hit his head. He isn't moving. I need help, need rope."
Wiebbe looked down to the three men in his care,
"I can't leave these men, I don't dare."

"Look.... take someone with you... someone capable,
Not your friends; and see if he's hurt, if his condition is stable."
"I'll help," said Willem, standing and preparing himself for duty,
"You stay there, Willem, and cook the food, be my deputy."

"We all need nourishment. Hendrik, you and Gerrit go,
And see what can be done, I'm confident you will know."
"Aye," obeyed Hendrik in as quick as a flash,
Grabbing Gerrit by the arm, to be off at a dash.

The three men were taken to the accident site, to the very spot,
Willem sat back down and stirred the meat and peas in the pot,
Wiebbe looked down upon the open-eyed threesome in his care,
But in all true admission, was he being fair.

"This is a fine mess, Willem. Two calls for help, three wounded...
That's me and you, boy; that's it... just the two of us, surrounded."
Wiebbe to Willem: "I don't mind telling you that this very minute,
Right now is the loneliest I have felt in my entire life; I do admit."

Pieter, Dirck and Jan could be heard moving through the scrub,
The harsh land always there to remind, to lash out and rub,
And no sooner at the fireplace, and Wiebbe was at their side,
Ready to assist where he could, ready to give aid, ready to abide.

They laid the body of Harmen upon the ground, unshrouded,
And in full site of all there, and the three wounded,
Who in their state could only contemplate their near future,
It being the same, no medicine or sacred potion to nurture.

Of the three that lay upon the ground with bandages and splint,
Only one was unfamiliar with Harmen, no friendship to mint,
But he had come to know him during that first morning,
After the Zuytdorp had wrecked, during its unfavourable mooring.

The body of Harmen was laid upon the ground,
Wiebbe knelt down beside him, there being no sound,
Dirck was opposite and looking rather solemn,
Knew that he was gone, and without requiem.

And then the silence was broken,
Some words were softly spoken,
Said Wiebbe: "It's times like this I wish I were a priest,
To give comfort, a comforter of the sick, to be worthy at least."

Wiebbe looked Dirck in the eyes and understood his frustration,
For neither was a doctor, each held another station,
But both had intelligence, smarts you could not burn with wick,
Enough to understand the rudiments of providing aid to the sick.

It comes naturally after many years at sea where men fall victim,
Victim to scurvy and diseases of the tropics so heinous and grim,
Where the shells of men fall victim of God's own vengeance,
Or so it would seem by all outward appearance.

The silence was then pushed aside as Jan commenced stirring,
Standing there with something to say, unsure how; a warning,
He gave the news which all were dreading to hear,
"I saw a savage, a naked man with a shield and a spear."

The others tending the injured,
Those lying upon the ground hence hindered,
Even the breeze, all stopped to listen to the greatest dread,
To learn what was new, of what was to be said.

"I saw one of them, and Harmen too,
He was dark and stood erect, as though with nothing to do,
Holding his ground and eyeing us with hunger in his eyes,
I could see and hear his mind in play, I tell you no lies."

"I could see his wish to boil my flesh for eating,
My soul to roast upon a fire, my flesh basting,
His thin shell showing him hungry, and on flesh he relies,
His eyebrows provide shelter to those deep, dark eyes."

"The eyes, the evil that they cast in our direction,
Their look of greed, on community no reflection,
If it wasn't for the fact that he was alone,
He would have been after us, with spear or stone."

"Was he all of that, Jan?" asked Pieter, still standing beside him,
"He was indeed, and much more," concluded Jan, no fat to trim,
"Then we must prepare for the worst," said Ariaen at last,
"Several knives have been salvaged, their quantity not vast."

Said Dirck: "They'll do little against the thrust of a spear,
And what other weapons does he have near?"
"They're savages," reminded Wiebbe. "What can they possess?"
"They've survived here," advised Pieter. "But let's not guess."

"They've lived upon this land, naked to the world, and survived,
Survived the elements, beast; the snakes; yet they're still alive."
"And the damnation of God," said Marinus from upon blanket,
Rubbing his good hand across his broken ribs, much pain met.

"They're God's creatures too," said Willem, voicing his opinion,
Said Jan: "Savages like them don't have religion,
I saw the evil in his eye, almost close enough to smell his breath,
I wouldn't wish to confront a group of them for fear of death."

Gerrit and Hendrik then returned with bad news,
Cornelius had died in the fall from the cliff of views,
Having hit his head upon a boulder,
As well as dislocating his shoulder.

Said Hendrik: "We dragged his body to where the others lay."
He looked upon the form of Harmen, not knowing what to say,
"Poor Harmen," feeling saddened,
Seeing no blood, now confused: "What happened?"

Said Jan: "He was bitten by a snake and died,
But right until the end it was life that he vied."
And as this was spoken all eyes fell to the ground,
Fear now embedded in all, firmly and sound.

DEATH

Before dusk had arrived upon them this day,
The survivors had gathered at the site where the injured did lay,
Seebaer and Joannes had returned to the smiles of friend,
Happy to be back, but of their journey no end.

It was a miracle in itself, this feeling within,
The safety they felt being amongst this group so thin,
All of whom were in the same predicament shared the same fears,
Suffered the same miseries, shed the same tears.

It wasn't as if they'd be absent for any great length of time,
Or returning into the arms of a loved one so prime,
It was the comradeship that they needed, the comfort of another,
Another fellow that shared their will to live, happiness to smother.

Both men listened intently to the story told,
Of how Cornelius had fallen to his death, body now cold,
How Harmen had come to grief,
Of their efforts to aid the injured and give relief.

Of the savage seen beyond the scrub where the land was bare,
Like a motionless sea, undulating plains, savage and unfair,
Land bare of life other than trees which sucked the land dry,
Of the sheer lack of moisture and how by summer they would fry.

But the survivors provided each other with stability,
A small and yet rigid, unyielding commodity,
This, the centrepiece of their communion,
Their togetherness, their union.

Only two drunks, Jacob Albertsz and Jacobus Nuyts, out cold,
Possibly a gin bottle hidden too well: they were crafty and bold,
Remnants of broken bottles laying around,
Beware the sharpness of broken glass to be found.

Surprising it was that they were still alive,
But their poor condition didn't allow for them to thrive,
Despite this they had been provided warm blankets,
For pity and handouts they were like magnets.

Blankets to keep them warm, cold rolling in from the sea,
Where cloudless nights sucked warmth from man, beast and tree,
How on earth did the savages survive such weather,
Walking around naked as they did in skimpy leather.

Cornelis Lieffers then appeared from his work,
His devotion to keeping busy, none to shirk,
Bringing another bucket with him filled with fresh water,
Water scooped by hand, by gallon and quarter.

"Cornelis, young friend," said Ariaen to the young man, not old,
"You work too hard and need to rest; consider yourself told."
"I fear the thoughts within me will surface and explode,"
Said Cornelis, not wishing his mind to erode.

Willingly letting his guard down, his emotions to betray,
His exhaustion taking hold, the foundation now lay,
"You need to rest, nevertheless," continued Ariaen. "Behave,
There have been too many deaths already, you I wish to save."

Ariaen looked at the man coming of age: "Will you sit and join us?
Seebaer and Joannes have returned with news; on them let's fuss."
"Is it good news?" asked Cornelis, giving approving, his vote,
"We've found somewhere that may accept a sturdy rescue boat."

"Can this be true?" asked Cornelis, "But not to sail a raft."
"We don't think so, Cornelis," said Seebaer, no good as such craft,
And with a downturned eye: "But we intend to go to the north,
To search for another place, one of great worth."

"And work you've achieved alone will provide us with wood,
Enough wood for a small boat; I'm sure of it; it will be good."
"Yes," said Cornelis, his heart lifted. "Enough to make two,
And drag it from platform to embankment is all we need to do."

"Yes, indeed," said Ariaen. "There is much to do tomorrow,
So go with Seebaer and Joannes, of you they wish to borrow."
"They'd be faster with two," said Cornelis. "Wouldn't they?
And what of the work here? I think I should stay."

"We are plenty," added Ariaen. "And in number we grow,
Gerrit, Jacob and Jacobus will be joining us tomorrow,
To be put to work... isn't that right, Gerrit, good fellow?
With us combined the work will flow."

"Yes," said Gerrit, looking at Cornelis, into his eyes,
"The other two will have sore heads, but work... this we prise,
But with a little food and water they will do just fine,
And as for myself; my labour is yours, not mine."

Cornelis smiled and nodded, "Okay, I'll go; adventure to meet."
"Great," said Ariaen. "Now sit down and have something to eat,
Rest those weary bones of yours, for tomorrow you journey far,
And when you all return, your stories will make you each a star."

"It's just a day trip, isn't it?" asked Cornelis, now unsure,
"You didn't hear?" prompted Pieter, now leveraging his lure,
"Hear?" repeated Cornelis, unsure of where this was leading,
"Of Jan and the savage?" said Gerrit, who continued his feeding.

"No," said Cornelis. "What savage?" and the story did not derail,
He was told of what had happened, to the very last detail,
Said Pieter of this plight: "So you see,
In order for victory we need at least three."

Cornelis nodded acceptance, not wishing to let the men down,
And Willem consider, a desire to follow this example now sown,
To be willing and strong enough to do all that it does take,
To survive and devote oneself, to harden conviction, to bake.

Said Joannes: "I think, too, we stop thinking of them as savages,
We are not amidst a war here that rages,
For if a ship fails to come our way,
We may be forced to remain here, to forever stay."

"Our only means of survival,
Would be of an allies arrival,
Of this sunburnt land they are native,
And for us this may prove to be relative."

"Only time will tell, Joannes," said Ariaen. "Only time,
But you're right, one day this land may rub off on us like rime,
We to be encased in all it has to offer,
With the land itself to become its brother."

"But for now we need to explore towards the north the most,
Where much coastline is known to exist, of this, our host,
Many ships have used this coast to mark their progress,
Three hundred miles of it, if correct, to softly caress."

"And I'll go too," said Jan, looking at the others. "I can't stay here,
Not with my friend having departed from this world so dear."
Said Ariaen: "We'll be saying our goodbyes soon enough,
I'll understand if you don't wish to stay, for it must be rough."

"I have said my farewell, carrying him upon my back,
For many hours in the heat of the day, courage he did not lack,
I wish that winter was here already," and he kicked at the dirt,
His shoes well-worn, trousers dirty and shabby, a torn shirt.

"It's upon us," said Ariaen, scratching at the bandage he wore,
That covered the gash in his head, itchy and sore,
And looking out over the ocean he said "It has just begun,
And of all the wishes you make, only a single you have won."

Jan: "If it wasn't for the heat, that snake might not even exist,
If colder than now it may be away in a hole, not out to persist,
I guess there is much we don't know about this land,
Everything needs to be learnt, and knowledge is grand."

"The ways of one snake isn't necessarily the same as another,
Take that creature, the one I saw jumping, over and over,
In great bounds across the ground... that in itself is unbelievable,
How can such a thing exist? And there it is, achievable."

"We believe you," confirmed Ariaen. "If you wish to go north,
Well, we'll not stop you, but encourage you, for what it is worth."
And to change the subject he looked to Willem. "How's the meat;
Your peas; your broth? My stomach is waiting for it to greet."

"Ready," said Willem, proud as could be,
Looking around at smiles, pleased to see,
Happiness so remote with death all round,
So hard to avoid, so easily found.

Some may draw on this situation as condemning and sad,
A shortened existence on earth, terrible ends, this was bad,
But others would grow and see the many opportunities to take,
Shake the defeat from within, pour courage, confidence to make.

Moulding a new life for themselves,
Upon this new land as though picked from shelves,
For now they would consider the idea as suggested,
Joannes and Seebaer's thinking in mind, it to be digested.

The bounds of survival were commencing to surface,
For those with the courage to take it, to enforce, not deface,
Grasp ideology into an open palm,
To remain clear-thinking, to remain calm.

Of the man that had fallen from the cliff, a man clearly rotten,
He had fallen to his death and now practically forgotten,
He'd been so simply dragged over to the pile of dead,
A pile that currently existed on the shoreline platform of dread.

The mass of flesh was beyond them all to fathom,
Life wasted, death to young and old, taken from earth's bosom,
No clemency, no difference between command and structure,
Whether seaman, woman, or child: nothing now to nurture.

Of the little children, only one was found and placed at the pile,
The others had been lost by way of the sea, the sea to defile,
The waves taking the fragile forms of human remains,
To a burial site which none could claim, and the unknown stains.

What one does not know, must be learnt,
And here, now, all learnt must be clearly burnt,
Burnt to memory, new tricks and sites grasped,
Refuse to allow their lives hit hard and rasped.

That evening there was much to reflect upon and reflect they did,
But mostly in silence, behind a screen of security well hid,
They were all too tired to do much about anything at all,
So they lay, asleep, half asleep, to gather their wits, not to fall.

Silently contemplating the future, but also needing much rest,
Regards of little slumber or a lot, they must do their best,
Gather their energy, be ready for the morrow,
To greet the day, to be enlightened, or be hit by sorrow.

GANGRENE

7th June: The drunken men were now completely sober,
No alcohol within their system, not part of any fibre,
They could see the error of their ways, or maybe not,
But suffering a little from the shakes, there on the spot.

Here the new dawning of a day,
With the sunlight a fresh wind, but not all day to stay,
Dragging along a mass of cloud, mostly clear, a few quite dark,
But currently no sign of rain nor lightning and its vicious bark.

With broken bottles left upon the ground to stain,
A visual memorial there to remain,
To that single one who fell to his death,
Upon platform so far beneath.

These men sat there beneath the rays of the sun,
Unmoving, unstirred, but under mantle of social gun,
To appease the desire and need of the others,
Not yet truly accepted as brothers.

One other thing did greet them with the rising of the day,
Another body was relinquished to God from the fray,
Francisco Roelofsz, with the broken leg and punctured gut,
His ghostly spirit, his soul, from his body now cut.

Hayman Jorisz pulled his fingers from his bandage,
Placed them beneath his nose, the smell, of mind, to ravage,
Then withdrawing them quickly for the smell was overpowering,
The most horrid thing he'd ever smelt, his fingers quite disgusting.

The wounds smelt of decayed meat, of death, pure and simple,
He was gangrenous, terror coursing through him, to ripple,
Seebaer, Joannes, Cornelis and Jan had gone to the north,
But the others were there, to hear his news brought forth.

With an upturned nose he was about to request aid,
To wash his fingers, though not the emotion of being afraid,
When he saw approach both Jacob and Jacobus, men of disgrace,
Hayman simply watched in silence, hatred written upon his face.

He knew deep down that his legs would have to be amputated,
Cut off from above the knee, from thigh separated,
What was there to relieve the pain, for the pain to stop,
There was no gin... it was gone, every last drop.

Wasted upon drunkards who were weak, not strong,
Whom could not handle the disaster, knew not right from wrong,
He would show them, that he could hold back the cries of pain,
Prove his true convictions, to put on a strong face and be vain.

And the two men walked past him, glancing down but briefly,
Willem, Pieter, Ariaen, they could see,
Hendrik, Dirck, Wiebbe and Gerrit, there too, upon one knee,
And they continued their approach as each did agree.

"Sit down," said Ariaen in invitation. "Have something to eat,
Take the weight off of your feet,
There isn't much but we are hoping to secure food later on today,
Some shellfish and maybe other supplies to come our way."

Jacob was handed a piece of bark, a plate on which sat food,
"Thank you," said Jacob as he sat, for nourishment, in the mood,
Pulling the slightly curved piece of bark into his chest,
To guzzle it down and give his grumbling stomach a rest.

"And for you, too, Jacobus, a small meal."
"Thank you," said he, for hunger he did feel,
Gerrit looked upon his so-called friends who had corrupted him,
Forced him to accept the gin, to feel as though he was the victim.

"How do you both feel?" Gerrit did ask, as they ate their food,
Jacob: "I'm fine." Jacobus: "Me too." As they did sit and brood,
"And why wouldn't you be, you scum!" cursed Hayman, thinking,
Thoughts on the pain to be endured, of his legs and the stinking.

"You take all the gin and scoff it down, and now you come here,
You've not done a single days work, and behind backs you sneer,
And now you partake of our sustenance as though nothing at all,
You each have a tremendous amount of gall."

"It's from all of us," said Ariaen, indicating the food they shared,
Understood the hate, not the inability to forgive, why anger flared,
"Let's hear no more of it, we are in this together, one and all."
"It's easy for you to say," said Hayman, his back against a wall.

Tears slowly filled his eyes before drying in the breeze,
As it blew in from beyond one of the seven seas,
"I'm to be amputated and there is no gin left; no wine; no beer,
No medicine or anything else other than sheer fear."

Gerrit stirred and spoke softly to the man in anguish,
"I have a bottle, saved for you; you can have it if you wish."
The two drunks shot a glance apiece at Gerrit, full of hate,
"Where is it," stabbed Jacob, extremely obsessed and irate.

"Enough! YOU SWINE!" a curse that fluidly ran,
"Sit still, Hayman," ordered Wiebbe as he raced over to the man,
Hayman tried in vain to claw his way to Jacob, to kill with hate,
"You have sinned," said Gerrit, wishing to seal the bastard's fate.

"And so have you," answered Jacobus, under the collar quite hot,
"Gerrit is one of us," spoke Ariaen. "You two men, as yet, are not,
You've been given food and water, now earn the right to speak,
You prove only one thing; your greed for gin: you're weak.

Jacob held out his hand for all to see, shaking out of control,
Unable to stop the tremors from within, it was taking its toll,
"I'm not a doctor," said Ariaen. "Only you can overcome desire,
You helped yourself to the gin, so you must help yourself aspire."

"I can't," said Jacob in all sincerity and regret,
A look of terror upon his face, one never to forget,
Juice from peas and meat dribbled from the corners of his mouth,
"I must have it; please. I have no spirit left, it's all gone south."

Said Wiebbe: "There are others in need of it more than you,"
He leant forward and smelt the wound: what he said was true,
Sorrow filled his face as he stroked with great compassion,
The forehead of Hayman, to he would go the gin, the ration.

"Pieter; Dirck... will you help me?"
"What is it, Wiebbe?" asked Dirck, standing to see,
"It's time," answered Wiebbe with face, undefined and solemn,
"It's time to take these legs off; that is the problem."

The sorrow within Hayman's eyes was the look of an innocent,
A child, a hideous crime about to be committed most indecent,
The look upon Jacobs was similar, but filled with deceit,
Capable of doing anything he could for gin and its receipt.

Silence... the men moved to the task in silence,
Forgetting their food and water; now filled with patience,
Thinking only of the poor man about to be operated upon,
Wishing and hoping that he could and would remain strong.

They moved Hayman, away from the others, half mile or third,
Towards the south where the screams would not be heard,
Ariaen went too, with embers for fire carried by Willem: his task,
For it was his job, handed to him, this, of him, they did ask.

A fire which was to be employed in preparing the cutting tool,
To prepare the knife, a job suited to any man, child or fool,
It was large enough to be handled as a cutting device,
Could be used on bone and flesh; to chop and slice.

Willem returned to get some cloth and some rope,
And a little extra kindling for the fire amidst fading hope,
Several small logs would not go astray,
And these he grabbed whilst he pray.

And as he returned he passed Gerrit who was off to retrieve,
To retrieve the hidden bottle of gin, for Hayman to receive,
Close enough to see, but far enough so not to be heard,
Followed Jacob on his own errand, an outright coward.

Willem focussed upon his task, ignored what he saw,
To ready the fire and bandages for that man so poor,
Gerrit stepped out amidst broken bottles, of location to take stock,
To find that hidden, last bottle, the gin beneath large rock.

He got down upon his knees and commenced to excavate,
When a noise caught his ear, but he turned too late,
He saw Jacob standing over him face screwed up tight,
As he brought a large rock down upon Gerrit from height.

The strike killed him instantly, Gerrit's fate sealed,
Jacob grabbing for the bottle which had been revealed,
The neck now sticking out, a sore thumb: one not to shun,
The best site Jacob had seen his entire life, second to none.

He wasted no time at all and soon had it open, ready to drain,
Swallowing in great gulps all that it held, unable to refrain,
Before long it was empty, he just could not stop,
As though a flagon of water, drained of every last drop.

Jacob suddenly turned and saw Jacobus standing there,
Having followed soon after, unwilling to simply sit and stare,
Seeing that Jacob was up to no good, not out on walk for fun,
"You bastard," scolded Jacobus. "What have you done?"

Jacob looked down at Gerrit's body, the empty bottle released,
But Jacobus was referring to the gin, not the deceased,
Jacobus: "It's gone, every damn drop. You drank it all, its gone,"
All spoken before the reality of the situation hit him hard as bone.

"You've killed Gerrit, that's a sin,
Killed him for little more than a bottle of gin."
"I had to... I..." stammered Jacob, on feet so unsteady,
For the drunken state to befall him he was very ready.

Back at the fireplace, Willem had returned to secure more,
Hendrik looked to the boy, confirmation to score,
From far out, in the distance: "Willem, did you hear that sound?"
Willem: "God! It's Jacob, and Jacobus; Gerrit! The gin, found!"

Hendrik looked down upon the sleeping form of Marinus, asleep,
Oblivious to what was going on, no longer able to weep,
Having been awake and in pain for most of the night,
He had finally falling to slumber, to Hendrik's delight.

"I'm going to see what's going on; stay here, near this bed."
"Here," urged Willem, thinking straight from the top of his head,
"Take this," and handed the knife to him before racing off too,
Towards Wiebbe and the others, where impatience grew.

Hendrik took the knife without second thought,
Raced towards the commotion, conflict now sought,
Falling upon the scene in what seemed to be a moment's notice,
To see Jacob and Jacobus fighting, neither the novice.

Each was rolling around upon the ground, Gerrit unmoving,
Gerrit steady there, of his condition there was no need to sing,
Blood running freely from the wound upon the top of his head,
Like a script, all about him, it was all so easily read.

"What have you done?" said Hendrik in disbelief as they struggle,
The fight: Jacobus near the ledge, Jacob trying to strangle,
Jacobus now clawing at the earth, he suddenly slipped and fell,
Hendrik was utterly astounded, this was sheer hell.

Jacob turned, his eyes glazed over by the gin, his mouth in a snarl,
Civilization gone from his face, the truth he could not gnarl,
He was no longer a man but the devil possessed,
From all manner of human sanctity he had regressed.

With the bloodied rock still in hand he circled Hendrik now,
Motioning him to fight, of surrender never to bow,
"I have a knife, Jacob," advised Hendrik. "You have no chance,
Put the rock down, forget this fight, this death dance."

"We're here to help, all of us; I am... here. Let me help you."
"I curse you... damned, bloody fool. It is all through,
Besides, I have more than you," and Jacob held up his hand,
"I have the rock, right here; my iron, soon to be your brand."

He looked into Hendrik's eyes and raced forward,
The rock in motion, he footing most awkward,
And the stumbled as Hendrik stepped aside,
Jacob falling to his death, no wind to ride.

Hendrik just stood there, disbelief within,
His mind unable to calculate all of the sin,
This was not how man was supposed to survive,
This was no way for man to live, to live and thrive.

What manner of evil could possess another to commit such an act,
Such a heinous crime against his fellow man, the point of fact,
It then suddenly dawned upon him that he too had plenty to repent,
For his vicious treatment of others before now was easily spent.

He had tried to become leader, to have the ability to sway,
Sway judgement over those under his command, to have a say,
But now... he didn't want it; that is the way it should be,
He was glad that Ariaen had received more votes than he.

He was glad to have lost to a better man, for Ariaen was strong,
Day in and day out he had proven not to be wrong,
He was a good man with a clear vision for the future,
This leader was one, not to oppose, but one to nurture.

It's what was needed, a strong man to lead a volatile group,
A bunch of men whom had much to recoup,
Ariaen was helping them all find their way in this new world,
So cast upon a land with misgivings that swirled and whirled.

Hendrik could only whimper to himself, of the needless slaughter,
Feelings of sorrow filling him like a carafe is filled with water,
He would have to come to grips with it all, that had come to pass,
All that undone at the seams, this lesson learnt from this class.

AMPUTATION

Hendrik returned to where Pieter, Dirck and Wiebbe were readied,
For the amputation, removal of leg, for it to be burnt or buried,
Willem was tending the fire and checked over the supplies,
So placed neatly beside Wiebbe, and on these, much relies.

Ariaen sat silently at Hayman's head,
Ready to assist where possible at this makeshift bed,
Ready to obey orders as they were given,
Of true conviction, to be hard driven.

"Willem," said Wiebbe, "Thank you, but it's time for you to go,
Back to the main fire, there is no more for you to know."
"But I can help—," began his protest,
"You've done enough," concurred Pieter. "Time for you to rest."

He smiled at the boy. "Go and get yourself something more to eat,
Or better still, prepare something for all of us, solace to greet,
For we'll be hungry after the job is done,
Even if unable to eat, a little is better than none."

Willem nodded acceptance of the task and turned to depart,
Bumping into Hendrik as he stepped away, to make a start,
Forgetting Hendrik's intervention upon the two drunk men,
The others asked Hendrik for information, there and then.

"They're dead," said Hendrik in a half daze,
Not quite believing the words as the others did gaze,
Gaze upon him with open mouths so large,
The words tripping their ears, scrambling, as though to barge.

"Dead?" repeated Dirck, unsure of what he heard,
"All three," nodded Hendrik. "I know it sounds absurd."
Pieter stood, "Maybe you're wrong, maybe we should look."
A hand lashed out: Hayman, grabbing Pieter's leg, and shook.

"The bastards deserved to die," said Hayman, being blunt,
"No one deserves to die in this place," said Pieter, to affront,
Pieter looked down upon the man to be operated on soon,
"No matter their faults," came his lecturing tune.

"They're dead," repeated Dirck. "I saw two fall to their death,
And Gerrit has a wound to his head, a deathblow, easily read."
"Where's his body?" said Pieter as he grilled,
"Trust me, why don't you.... at the cliff where he was killed."

Pieter got up to attend, to see for himself, to do his best,
"Pieter," said Dirck. "Don't go, let him lay in peace, at rest."
Dirck looked at Hendrik, "There's nothing that can be done.
Our task now is to help Hayman; for a victory to be won."

"You're right," said Pieter as he took up his position,
To prepare for the task of holding the man during the operation,
And they were the last words for a while,
As Hayman's legs were unbandage: there remained no denial.

The smell of the gangrenous leg hit them all hard,
The mass of swelling revealed, putting them off guard,
The discolouration taking full effect upon their hidden emotions,
The fractured bone having broken the skin, its many lesions.

Wiebbe was to do the cutting; Dirck and Pieter were to hold,
Hold tight Hayman's arms and upper body, no need to be told,
To restrict, for him to be as motionless as possible,
For what was about to happen was extremely horrible.

Dirck stayed beside Wiebbe so that he could take over the task,
Of hacking through the bone if the need arose, he only need ask,
Hendrik sat at the ready at Hayman's feet,
Feet soon to be separated, no ceremony to meet.

"No, Hendrik," said Dirck, cautioning the man to the requirement,
"Get beside Pieter and help with restricting, for ease of treatment,
Hold firm the the upper leg... the thigh; keep it still,
We must act swiftly: an hourglass in seconds to fill."

Wiebbe had already separated the task from his friend,
Mental application, to deny any affiliation, sanity to defend,
He would separate the two so that no semblance did exist,
To shut out all that Hayman may say, to do all he could to assist.

He applied this thinking to actual practise,
To deny the reality of his being less than a novice,
In his mind the body to his front was unfamiliar,
As peculiar as a small tree trunk, a column, a pillar.

But his mind found it hard to dissociate flesh from friend,
About to deliver much pain of which no one can defend,
Pain and suffering beyond all contemplation,
And no way of creating a substantial distraction.

But he had conviction of mind,
Though not easy to find,
And no amount of screaming would stop him from hacking,
No amount of struggling would prevent him from slashing.

Once started the operation could not be stopped,
To be done in the shortest time, as he saw and chopped,
And before the screaming was netted to ear,
Leather was placed between his teeth on which to grind and tear.

Willem was sitting beside the fire, cooking as he sat,
Thinking of what was to unfold: alone, with no one to chat,
His only wish was for Hayman to survive the surgery,
To pull through this serious operation and its savagery.

But his thinking was obscured by a cloud,
Once the screaming started so loud,
The thick leather between Hayman's jaws having served little,
Of purpose it failed; was insufficient; its effect broken and brittle.

Willem could only wish for silence to reign,
For solitude to appear once again,
It was shear torture, the sounds of pain and torment,
The screams arrived in an unbroken cycle, in sight, no relent.

Tears then welled up within Willem's eyes,
The noise too much to bear, and here he cries,
He rolled over on his side, into a tiny ball,
Clutching palms tightly upon his ears, the noise to stall.

And yet the screams came reverberating,
Like the devil to unguarded soul, penetrating,
There was nothing that could compare,
With those fifteen long minutes of despair.

The screams finally coming to an end,
Silence to his ear beginning to blend,
The reverberation to a standstill,
No longer that awful shrill.

Willem was thankful that it was over, no more lament,
Praising the Lord that he had stopped the torment,
Thanking God for answering his prays, of his reply,
For bringing him silence, and he wiped his eyes dry.

It was only minutes later that Pieter appeared,
At the fire, his forlorn face, of peace, so sheared,
He stepped next to the hearth,
A look of solemnity, one of death, not birth.

"What is it?" asked Willem, thinking he knew the answer,
But afraid to say it out loud, his inbuilt censor,
"Hayman is dead," answered Pieter. "The pain was too much,
Even for a man of our nationality, a man most assuredly Dutch."

And Willem began to cry once more for it was his fault,
He, praying for an end to the screaming, and here the result,
It was his prayers to God without poise,
For an end to the torturous noise.

Yes indeed, it was he, Willem, that had asked for Hayman's death,
For it to be delivered this day, Hayman drawing his last breath,
"What? What was that?" came a tired voice as Marinus awoke,
Waking from slumber, having missed all, and he spoke.

Still half asleep: "Who's dead?" he did prattle,
The wind commenced to pick up a little,
Blowing harder than it had twenty minutes before,
Pieter's answer muffled by the wind as it tore.

WILLEM

Seebaer, Joannes, Cornelis and Jan were making good progress,
As they continued towards the north voluntarily, not under duress,
When their apprehensions were finally alerted,
Of the tension, no longer diverted.

The basic lay of the land was similar as it was to the south,
As it was to the west: experienced, not by word of mouth,
Although in the west there was slightly more for the eye to see,
But still a barren wasteland, a semi-desert, they did agree.

It was most inhospitable, commencing from the limestone cliff,
And in towards undulating, featureless sandplains, an ongoing riff,
A virtual monotony, thickets of acacia and banksia easily found,
Mostly sparse with some thickets, strewn across the ground.

Alike to islands upon a vast and open sea,
But often little happiness, no ounce of glee,
Perches for the birds and shade for some critters,
Those small like ants, and larger still, those with stingers.

But there was a tranquillity,
Though absent of any familiarity,
A margin between cliffs and barren landscape of trivia,
Of chalky earth covered in salt-tolerant heath and acacia.

The limestone platform continued along the coast,
As it was near the shipwreck of the Zuytdorp, for the most,
There appeared to be no permanent water source in the area,
From what the men could see, as scarce as trees on a glacier.

But the aboriginals knew the whereabouts of rock holes and soaks,
Well endowed with knowledge, relatively nomadic these blokes,
Water, liquid gold, needed for life, for life on which to binge,
Such water hides were five miles away, not on the coastal fringe.

The approaching storm had been building for the past three hours,
Weather, the instrument of torture and bliss, it held many powers,
"We'll have to make shelter, soon," said Joannes to all,
"We may be hit by a sudden and fierce squall."

"I agree,' said Cornelis, shifting his blanket upon his shoulder,
It being tied with thin rope [a loop], he now feeling colder,
"Where to, that's the question," stated Seebaer most realistic,
"This cloth we have isn't much against this wind, far too rustic."

Seebaer: "We need to find shelter; be smart, not dumb,
Asked Jan: "How far do you think we've come?"
"Why?" Cornelis did joke: "Do you want to turn back already,
Afraid of a little wet and hard work, on your feet unsteady."

Jan took the comment the wrong way, of tongue and mishaps,
Interpreting it as an insult, "What? scared; me, lazy perhaps?"
He felt injured, assaulted in some way,
But the feelings were not there to stay.

"No," winced Cornelis. "I was simply commenting... look,
It doesn't matter. I too would prefer to accept a clear brook,
A nice shelter, a log cabin, an oil lamp,
But even these we lack back at camp."

"You're right," accepted Jan, "I'm, sorry; please."
Cornelis was hence more careful to tease,
"Well, we need somewhere," said Seebaer, "maybe a large tree,
"And the sooner, the better, if you ask me."

Cornelis: "We've come about ten miles is my guess,
But then again it could be more, or a lot less,
It's so hard to tell when there isn't any sun,
Until these clouds have up and run."

Seebaer: "My feet are as sore as hell,"
"Mine too," added Jan, wishing to tell,
"Courtesy of the shipwreck and these damn conditions,"
conclude Cornelis. "So kindly spent upon us, with no restrictions."

"Let's try heading inland," he looked to Seebaer, for agreement,
"There will be trees there, will there not?" this a statement,
"One of worth?" questioned Seebaer with little emotion,
Hunched over and shielding his face in open palm action.

Nigel B.J. Clayton

And the heavens opened up and the downpour commenced,
A storm which would rage for many hours, of great expense,
The suddenness of the downpour precipitated by a lightning strike,
That shook the earth they were standing upon, not one to like.

"Come, let's go; quickly," voiced Cornelis as he lead the way,
Stepping off into the unknown without further delay,
The rain fell in buckets, the gullies filling up temporarily,
Water flowing away from undulating ground, and not sparingly.

Across sandplains and into the sea, soaked to the bone,
Torrents of water falling over the cliff of limestone,
And miles away, back at the camp, the same did adhere,
A great misery which worsened, though nothing left of any cheer.

Willem was hunched over and seemed very pale, a grave matter,
The shelter they had struck providing sufficient shelter,
Good protection from the pouring rain,
But of the penetrating cold, little warmth to gain.

The boy was shaking like a leaf and looked like hell,
Sweat started to fall from him freely, a ringing of bell,
The men gathered together, refusing to be beat,
Endeavouring with all their ability to harness body heat.

Only Dirck and Marinus remained apart, but not to suffer,
Quite a few feet away, half asleep and laying beside each other,
A large rock pile at their head where red hot embers from the fire,
So placed in order to maintain, keep them from a fate most dire.

With no embers to play their part,
Fire would be costly to restart,
Willem's symptoms had come out of nowhere,
Older boy, or young man, it seemed so unfair.

Wiebbe held his palm against the boy's head and shook his own,
"He has a fever; from what I don't know," and Willem did groan,
Hendrik: "This damn land and the savages upon it,"
Seemingly concerned for his own future, upon the land he spit.

Hendrik pulled away, possibly not wishing to catch the fever,
The sail above his head leaking slightly, to slowly deliver,
Several drops of rain penetrating the fabric and falling,
Falling upon his head, folding fingers into armpits for warming.

"No," said Ariaen. "I don't believe that. No one has a fever."
"So he's the first," said Hendrik, "That's all; the first to suffer."
Willem was clutching at his stomach, a small telltale signal,
He was in much pain and seemingly a little delusional.

310

His eyes darted, looking here and there,
Not at anything in particular, not to stare and stare,
It was then that he vomited all he'd eaten that day,
The meat, the peas, nothing in his stomach would stay.

"Poisoned by his own hand," said Hendrik. "It's greed,
That's the answer; poisoned, on too much he does feed,
God knows when one is being greedy, selfish beyond call,
It stands to reason that to the devil he shall fall."

"It's nothing to do with poison," said Pieter, holding the boy's arm,
In an effort to offer some comfort, as though to protect from harm,
"The food, you fool," said Hendrik sarcastically,
He's always alone, feeding himself, so full of folly."

"I know not, Hendrik," spat Pieter out of character,
"The boy has had no more than any here, he's no gluttonous eater,
It's not greed; we have all had the same,
He's playing by the rules, playing the game."

"Did anyone notice anything strange?" asked Wiebbe of others,
All shook their heads. "Dirck; Marinus; look here brothers!
Did you notice anything wrong with the boy?
There must be good reason; calculated thinking we must employ."

"What?" came Dirck's reply, seeing with sudden surety,
That Willem was in difficulty,
He yawned a little, stretched his arms wide, on his side he lay,
"What's that? What's wrong with Willem, what did you say?"

"You tell me," answered Wiebbe. "Did you see anything wrong,
With the boy earlier on? Anything at all that does not belong."
"Not, not a thing," said Dirck. "What symptoms does he display?"
"He's vomiting, has a fever, and in much pain; not at all okay."

"Maybe it's something he ate," came the reply from Dirck,
Upon Hendrik fell a look; a haunting smirk,
He then looked Pieter and Ariaen in the eye,
"I told you, didn't I?"

Wiebbe tried to gain Willem's attention,
Lifting his head and checked his vision,
Staring directly into him, seeing nothing at all,
Nil response, and he did softly call.

Wiebbe: "Willem; do you hear me?"
"Of course he hears, and he can see—."
"Shut up, Hendrik," the death stare sealing Hendrik's mouth,
Hendrick's conviction soon to be drained south.

"There's nothing," said Pieter. "Let's put him down,
Make him comfortable, until something further is known."
Said Wiebbe: "There may not be a later,
Whatever he's suffering is rather sinister."

Later that night, when the stars came out to greet life on earth,
Clouds now past and rain from the storm drained through turf,
Drained via gully and swallowed up by the dry land,
Invisible creatures could be heard, each song a brand.

Songs which were free for all to listen,
Sweet pleasantness of sounds, so bright they glisten,
Stretching as though the night and over the folds in the ground,
Mating calls amongst them made, and mates found.

Dirck and Marinus were asleep on the far side of the hearth,
Ariaen and Pieter fast asleep, near Willem, for what is was worth,
Wiebbe, on the other hand, was wide awake and listening,
To the sounds all around him, a loan ear to christening.

Here he tried to decipher what he could of the beetles and grubs,
Insects and nocturnal animals, many species amongst the shrubs,
He'd never realized such music existed,
It truly could not be resisted.

It seemed to him that the boy, Willem, had recovered sufficiently,
For he to be left unattended, to be checked intermittently,
A little colour had returned to left and right cheek,
His pulse was normal, fever gone, no sweat of which to speak.

He was sleeping comfortably and with his arms across his body,
No longer was he crunched up in a ball nor looking shoddy,
No longer holding for dear life to his stomach real tight,
Whatever was wrong was now put to right.

Wiebbe wasn't an educated man, but neither was he stupid,
He'd learnt a little of medicine, but of love no cupid,
Could tell the time of night by looking to the heavens above,
And of men and their sarcasm he did not truly love.

It was in this way that he could see that the morning,
Would be upon them soon with a magnificent dawning,
The storm having passed them by in their shelter,
And no real issue did they encounter.

He stood up and stepped from the shelter,
Headed towards the higher ground, solace to enter,
Through some thick scrub and following his intuition,
Some scratching noises then heard, their cause now an ambition.

He'd gone several hundred feet when he came across the ground,
The proposed camp site suggested by Jan earlier on, now found,
For the ocean could be seen quite clearly, as advised, from there,
But he did not loiter, he continued on his way from that so bare.

And then within minutes he came upon another great site,
Good for a camp, more rewarding than the other, just right,
Many thoughts then swept his mind, of life and death, disease,
Of cures, medicine, food and water, of his feelings it did tease.

The scratching noise now forgotten, he continued to wander,
Walking around, back to camp, under arm a little tinder,
He set the wood aside and bedded down once more for sleep,
But could not, his mind full of theory, no solution to reap.

The early morning had brought Ariaen and Pieter to the fire,
Wiebbe poking it with a stick, for a breakfast he was dire,
A breakfast of peas and shellfish,
The blandish and plain, dull dish.

Pieter asked Wiebbe: "Have you been up long?"
"Not long," answered Wiebbe. "I was feeling a little… wrong,
I couldn't sleep and so went for a walk for awhile,
I was deep in thought, but not more than a mile."

"I thought I'd get the fire restarted after the raining,
We don't have much dry wood remaining."
"It'll be enough," remarked Adriane, "enough for several days,
At least until the sun can loan us some wood-drying rays."

"I was thinking," said Wiebbe, "to make another camp,
Further away from where we are, a bit of a revamp."
"What in God's name, for?" queried Ariaen. "Why not stay."
"I went to where Jan and Harmen ventured the other day."

"I came across a great spot which offered a little protection,
Protection from the wet, and a rise in elevation,
From there we'd have a good view of the ocean,
Better to watch for, and see, a passing ship in motion."

"And just beyond that is another position,
A place for any sick, like a hospital, a good location,
Said Ariaen: "You're concerned over Willem, aren't you?
But you shouldn't be. He's not plagued; there's nothing to do."

Wiebbe: "Not just him. Look at Marinus. He seems well enough,
But what if he turns gangrenous... on some it will be rough,
They shouldn't all have to suffer that heinous smell,
Some of them would prefer to confront the fires of hell."

"Look," began Pieter, "I have no objection,
It may even alleviate a little tension,
But if we're going to have more than one campsite,
Then I think I should be with the sick, to help make things right."

"I see no issue," said Wiebbe. "Dirck and I will take turns,
Help look after any sick and there fever as it burns,
Regardless, it's a duty which must be performed,
But there is one other thing on which I'm concerned."

"And that is?" asked Ariaen, of information to fetch,
"A lookout near where the sandplains begin, for miles to stretch,
Just one thousand feet from the sandplains there's a place,
An old camp: Jan told me of it... told us all directly to face."

Said Pieter: "Ah; where Harmen was bitten by that snake,"
"Yes, that's right. We can maintain a vigil, a vigil to take,
Upon the natives we watch, see what they do, how they act,
Consider it an early warning, time for us to react."

"It already has a large tree nearby for preparing food,
For the hanging of carcass, providing good mood,
And there's a large rock there, seemingly used for grinding corn,
Of the natives it was purposely born."

"There must be food nearby,
Something on which we can rely,
Of food a descent supply,
For our survival this does apply."

"We must explore all options and keep our eyes open,
Staying in one spot will summon bad omen,
We need to commence with the laying of traps,
And strands of fibre are required, for the making of straps."

Ariaen: "Wiebbe; there aren't enough of us for three,
Two camps possibly, just open your eyes and see,
Having any more will not, our situation, mend,
Do this and we will all be condemned."

Wiebbe protested aloud: "That's rather a strong word,"
Ariaen: "Nevertheless, you suggest placing the sick in a third,
Either yourself or Dirck, in a camp with Marinus: the sick,
You're burning our candle, with more than one wick."

"These numbers: that accounts for three, with me, together;
And then with Pieter; that leaves seven, no other,
Is this entirely necessary?
Will it be but temporary?"

"We would only need two men at a time at this place,
The site near the sandplains; where animals jump and race,
The others could maintain the camp nearest the sea,
Watching for a passing ship; give us hope, fill us with glee."

Pieter agreed with this: "I think he's right,
It's against my better judgement, but this I shall not fight,
To separate Willem from the remainder is awful,
But I see the logic in it, for I am no fool."

Ariaen was silent for a few seconds and then nodded acceptance,
"Very well. We'll tell the others, despite possible askance,
As soon as they wake, we'll tell them simply,
Get things on the move and commence immediately."

"There is one other thing," said Wiebbe. "We must burn the dead,
Burn them now, where they lay, in preparation, to heaven be lead,
I don't see the point in dropping them over the cliff top,
It's a waste of energy... besides, where does our humanity stop?"

They each nodded in silent agreement, feeling that it was right,
They could not afford an epidemic, a rampant disease to fight,
Their lives were important and so they would act fast, be brisk,
The dead would forgive their grievances, understanding such risk.

SHORT HUNT

Seebaer and his companions fared reasonably well,
In the conditions that had fallen upon them: bequest from hell,
Considering that all they had was a little sailing material,
And several blankets to summon warmth, to health an arterial.

The tinderbox they had carried with them was of no use at all,
No dry material for which to start a fire, one could only mull,
And fire at such time when they needed it most, sanity to repair,
Such measly food; their stomachs feeling heavy despair.

The storm had played havoc with them, so rough its wake,
Strong and fierce, the earth did seem to shake,
They were thankful that it hadn't lasted as long as they dread,
Of good spirits there were so few to be read.

The misery of the men wasn't so much contagious,
for all were suffering the same, though not quite outrageous,
For misery of large weight won't allow a man to continue,
On a journey of little reward, A body of retainers, this retinue.

In most places the cliff proved to be impassable,
Therefore the gathering of shellfish, they were not able,
And as no other means of support availed itself,
Left to dream on, with visions of fruit-bearing land to tilth.

There was no rockhole nearby, nothing passed,
The supplies they did have, had not last,
An empty water-carrying device they had, yes they did,
Constituting an old pot with a loose piece of cloth as a lid.

But in this they were fortunate, for its neck was wide,
For lack of water they no longer needed to [archaic] bide,
Huddled around the old pot, fully replenished as new,
For due to the night's rain its level... it grew.

With blankets draped around them, they considered their options,
"We have to return immediately," stated Seebaer, head in motion,
There being no argument against such a vote,
Only more nods of the head, of clear understanding all did note.

"We all agree to that," said Jan. "Against my better judgement,
But what choice do we have amidst this aggrievement."
None could see an ounce of argument with that,
As they huddled in blankets, there they sat.

Seebaer nodded, "I'll lead the way if you wish and will start..."
The sudden fall of silence attracted all eyes to dart,
Ears erect, intent on hearing sound that Seebaer did not mention,
To hear what it was that had drawn Seebaer's attention.

"What is it?" asked Joannes as he whispered,
Seebaer held his finger to his mouth, all voice had disappeared,
And then the noise came again, not so far away,
Something moving towards them, seemingly to stray.

Possibly something close to the ground,
Dragging something along, something it had found,
It was a rustling noise of slow approach, coming straight,
The crunching of debris beneath a heavy weight.

Seebaer stood up, half crouched, now straining to look,
In the direction, his stance, and to the core he was shook,
Most temporarily his eyes grew large,
Not knowing what to do, either sit or simply charge.

The others looked upon him in terror, afraid for what it might be,
A savage, or a group of them, something heinous he did see,
Who knew what this land help in secret ready to be unleashed,
Against them so unvarnished, so unceremoniously dished.

"Seebaer, what is it?" Joannes asked again,
Feeling the need and desire for news, even one of pain,
"A large creature with small legs; as big as Willem that's no lie."
Said Seebaer, placing his finger against his lip, for silence to try.

Seebaer: "Listen to me carefully and trust in what I say,
Do you trust me this day?"
Everyone nodded, yes,
What was to happen was anyone's guess.

"When I say go you must all stand and take up a stick or rock,
Kick with your foot if you must... its head to knock,
Throw a blanket upon it, do all that you can,
All of us together, to the very last man."

"He will be slow because his legs are so small,
It is quite short, not very tall,
Are you, each one ready...
NOW!" and not a soul was unsteady.

The four men rushed to their feet,
To confront a new creature, one to meet,
Before them a wombat, so large and plump: of which none knew,
A great mass of flesh ready to be made into stew.

Blankets were thrust upon the creature so brown,
Stones and rocks taken from the ground and thrown,
A large rock lifted by Cornelis delivered a shocking blow,
Upon the creature's neck as it moved, blood to flow.

It moved hurriedly away as other blankets were recast,
Picked up again, and the chase was on, action fast,
The commotion of the hunt was in full swing,
All in complete disbelief at the sight of this thing.

It was something that looked like... nothing they'd seen before,
This could be a great victory, a resource, one not to ignore,
Colourful language filled the air as orders flew,
And within all their anxieties grew.

The energy now exerted was depleting,
There thoughts mainly focussed on eating,
An adrenalin rush for fresh meat,
Overwhelming and not discreet.

The wombat was under great stress,
The attack a shambles, a great mess,
Blankets thrown upon him not budging,
With rocks and sticks, taking a beating.

The men closed in on the creature and lashed out,
Raised voices in the commotion giving a shout,
Several beats to the head connecting well,
And it was then that Seebaer fell.

He fell upon it with the only knife,
To him bonded, as though a wife,
It penetrated the animal, taking its life,
Gone now was the wombat's strife.

But Seebaer wished to make sure,
Stabbing again, and again, more blood to pour,
And they knew that the creature was dead,
In its motionless state this was easily read.

The creature was now skewered from mouth to anus,
An action necessary, but most grievous,
A pole procured from sturdy branch,
The animal still bleeding, but no wish to stanch.

The pole was carried between two of the group,
On their minds, collectively, that of chunky soup,
But with no fire, unable to bring water to the boil,
There was nothing to do but commence their toil.

And so they commenced their journey,
With wombat on stick, not a gurney,
The men changing position from time to time,
Taking more rest breaks as their exhaustion levels did climb.

It was very tempting to bring their return to a momentary halt,
For small portions of the beast to be eaten raw with no salt,
But there would be no luscious flavour from fat of meat,
Nothing from chin to wipe, no great satisfaction to greet.

The trek back was of the most tiring,
The men were exhausted, hard was their inspiring,
And without proper nourishment they tired all the more,
Not an ounce left, all feeling quite sore.

But they had caught food for the first time, a great gift,
And this alone did aid their spirits, to uplift,
Pondering the meal to come, they almost felt like singing,
Pushing the thought from head, of their feet and the stinging.

And as the morning grew into early afternoon,
Seebaer looked up, saw something to his front, and not too soon,
Something that gained his immediate attention, for he saw smoke,
Thoughts all good, of optimism it did provoke.

"Do you see that?" shouted Seebaer for the others to look,
His finger pointing in the direction, a feast to cook,
For the camp was not far away,
Spirits lifted from minds growing grey.

"A signal fire!" presumed Jan, breaking out into a run,
In order to see for himself the white sails of a ship, saviour won,
Coming to the cliff's edge - but there was none,
Now at tethers end, feeling completely done.

"Don't; Jan," yelled Seebaer. "No ship is expected so soon,
Not until at least the eleventh of June,
Today's the eighth,
Calm down and just keep your faith."

"Leave him, Seebaer," said Joannes. "Let him alone,
He'll find out soon enough, his feelings to dethrone."
"But maybe it is a ship," said Cornelis with a smile,
"No, Seebaer is right," said Joannes, not in denial.

Cornelis: "Then what is it?" peering round, a look of lead,
Said Seebaer: "It must be the dead."
Bodies burning away,
Being rid of the stench and decay.

Back at the camp, Pieter moved up to the cliff ,
The wind askew, of stench they could not whiff,
With an outstretched hand he offered Ariaen a gift,
In his hand he held a pipe, emotions to lift.

Said Pieter: "For the tobacco you carry in that small box,
You might like to clean it first. I found it wedged between rocks."
"Thank you, Pieter," Ariaen smiled as he turned the pipe over,
Of tobacco he was a great lover.

He turned it in his hand,
Studying it closely, it make, its brand,
Seeing whether or not it would hold up to being smoked,
"It looks sound. I'll clean it tonight," and he was stoked.

"You should consider yourself lucky, through and through,
That only a few other men amongst us smoke as you."
"I guess so," agreed Ariaen. "But share I must,"
And turned to glance upon the flames, their past was sheer dust.

As the flames licked up the cliff's face, its surface to rub,
Hendrik stepped up from beyond some scrub,
And nonchalantly said, "It might concern some that the fire,
Will attract the attention of the savages, a situation most dire."

"My God," answered Ariaen with a little panic, "You're right."
Hendrik: "But, alas, if we are to signal a ship, a fire we must light,
So I guess it's of little concern,
Of any repercussions we shall soon learn."

And he walked away, continuing on back to the campsite,
"That's the first, real thing I've heard him say that's truly right,"
Said Pieter, to Ariaen, "and he just walked away,
Before I could tell him; before congratulations I could lay."

Ariaen shrugged: "Savage this, native that; no matter,
I guess we will encounter each other sooner or later,
It won't make a great deal of difference... do you think?
Aren't we already beginning to sink?"

"No, not really," answered Pieter; wondering,
He looked over to where Wiebbe and Willem were standing,
"They don't seem to care too much,
I believe they have much love within, to give at a touch."

Ariaen: "Maybe they haven't given it much thought,
Or maybe they only share, one to the other, feelings sought,
After all, Willem currently has needs; Wiebbe does too,
Their lives will be expensive: they are far from through."

Ariaen looked into Pieter's eyes,
Looking deeply, to uncover secrets, as though spies,
"Maybe we should be looking to the natives of this land,
They've lived here for their entire lives, with it, hand in hand."

PORPHYRIA VARIEGATE

"It's a sorrowful sight... very depressing," said Pieter as he looked,
Upon the flames leaping into the air, the corpses as they cooked,
"You're right," answered Hendrik and turned away, heading back,
Back to the small camp, to find food on which to snack.

He wasn't gone long before screaming out a mass of obscenity,
In respect to what confronted him, a breach of security,
For just beyond the fire, where the meat was stored,
Came a vision which seared and scored.

Their supply should have been tightly bound with a cover,
Maintained in the shade, at all times, shade to smother,
He found it was bare to the air around,
And not in the cool shade of hole dug in the ground.

The others came running, within them a feeling of fear,
Willem following up, at a slower pace, from the rear,
Willem feeling weak and mentally drained,
Of all his usual outpouring energy, nothing remained.

"What is it; what's the matter?" asked Ariaen drawing alongside,
Now next to Hendrik, waiting for a response, for his to confide,
Marinus looked over from where he lay, drowsed from slumber,
Finding it hard to see what was the matter.

"The meat," pointed Hendrik. "It's spoilt; every last chunk,
Every strip, and bone. Damn it to hell, now we're sunk."
A mass of flies of the likes they had not seen before,
Had swarmed upon the meat, more and more.

The cover to the prize had been dislodged,
By the wind earlier on, malignancy not dodged,
There were ants in the thousands, line upon line,
Coming and going, a banquet ready, a meal so fine.

"Maybe we can wash it," said Marinus, wishing to give aid,
Hoping to contribute something to the group as there he laid,
Feeling lazy, drawing his rations in water and food,
But performing no task or responsibility, but in the mood.

"Wash it!" cringed Hendrik. "Are you mad?
It's contaminated, beyond salvage." so much worse than sad,
And someone had left it out of ground,
Not immediately picked up, whereby it should astound.

"I'm afraid he's right," said Wiebbe so surely,
"Of course I'm right," came Hendrik familiar tone so severely,
Wiebbe: "We can't take a chance on it, there's no more to eat,
Willem has been bad and it could well be because of this meat."

"Willem is young and fragile, unable to take the abuses of disease,
Not like a fully grown man, to his body, of immunity, to lease."
"Ah!" yelled Hendrik. "The boy, it's his fault; it is, it is,
The meat was stored by his action; the fault is his."

Willem then stepped upon the scene, the uncovered meat,
The others surrounding the fire, upon their feet,
The dislodged cover bearing all to the world,
Accusations to be dodged before hurled.

"It wasn't me," said Willem, a pleading look within his eye.
"I placed the cover upon it; I did, that's no lie."
"It's okay, Willem," consoled Pieter, "It's not your fault;
It was the storm; don't feel distraught."

Hendrik fell upon his haunches, it was taking its toll,
"Blast, it. The boy should have placed it into the Hole,
The boy should have checked it, thrice each morning,
And thrice each night; to double check it, of its proper storing."

"It's too late now," said Wiebbe. "What's done is done."
"Yes," agreed Dirck as he moved over to Marinus, laying prone,
"Throw it into the ocean and forget it, its final day has been spent,
The last thing we need is to be divided by discontent."

Their faces were rather solemn,
This was no small problem,
Hendrik stared at Willem, accursedly, now and again,
A snarl, an upturned lip, of this action he would not refrain.

His face was betraying his feelings,
No one else around to make clear rulings,
The large fire behind them still burning,
The flames simmering, long from smouldering.

And then the miracle,
Amidst the debacle,
Seebaer was the first to be heard,
By the noise, not a spoken word.

"Seebaer," said Wiebbe, standing on his feet,
Going up and slapping him on the shoulder, happy again to meet,
So happy to see all returned safely, smiles upon their faces,
All in good spirits, not lacking in good graces.

"By, damn," said Ariaen. "What manner of creature is that?"
"I wish I knew," answered Seebaer. "But not an overgrown rat,
We caught it this morning, and have been carrying it ever since,
I'm sure you'll be willing to eat it, no need for me to convince."

Jan then said: "We also saw the smoke from the fire,
But no sails upon the ocean on which to admire,
And we don't see you dancing a jig upon the edge of the coast,
So quite sure there's no rescue on which to boast."

"You're right," said Ariaen. "We burnt the dead; all in one place."
Jan: "With or without sermon; with no steadfast grace?"
"Without. Who here is a priest or other man of the cloth?
No one, that's who; no single person able to [archaic] doth."

"So be it. I've already said my goodbye, before Harmen was cast,
Cast into the flame, to be drawn into heaven, forever to last."
"Go and say another," said Ariaen, understanding the torment,
Of friendship torn apart, in life comradeship so cast in cement.

Jan looked around and stepped away, his errand to do,
Not another word passing his lips as he disappeared from view,
"So; what news do you have?" asked Pieter, changing the subject,
Bringing joy back into their world, of sadness to deflect.

"No real news," said Seebaer. "We found it hard to continue,
The conditions were too trying, into the fire we flew,
We decided to return and have brought back this... thing,
Meat for us all to eat as you can see, to eat like a king."

"We'll have to hang it," said Wiebbe. "Skin it for the fur."
Ariaen: "Not here, Seebaer; we've been rather busy and eager,
And decided on changes, to make survival better... more relative,
And to increase our chances of communication with the native."

"Waste of time," said Hendrik, "if you ask me."
"It's necessary," said Adriane, standing up for Wiebbe, to agree,
"We're going to maintain three campsites: three."
"Three," voiced Cornelis apprehensively.

Cornelis pondered: "We can't even manage to care for one,
How are we going to manage three; how's it to be done?"
"We have to try," said Wiebbe. "There's a good position,
A little further inland... not far, one allowing for good vision."

"We can see the ocean from there, it's well suited,
Any passing ship will be easily spotted,
A little past that and we'll have another,
For the sick. For this plan we are relatively eager."

"The sick?" prodded Seebaer for confirmation,
Wiebbe: "Willem was gravely ill last night, with no solution,
We don't know the cause, no way of knowing what was wrong,
It may have been the meat. He still feels weak, not fully strong."

Seebaer and the others looked to Willem who seemed well,
As though, lifted from his shoulders, was a cast spell,
Seebaer looked him up and down,
A smack of the lips and a frown.

Wiebbe: "He had a fever and stomach pain, was extremely weak,
Seemed to forget himself for a while; worsened as we did speak,
He's a lot better now, as you can see, a great reliever,
So we know he doesn't have a disease or tropical fever."

Seebaer looked at Willem, "You look pale, too," he added.
"Even paler last night," said Wiebbe, "for nought he was avid."
Seebaer took a pace forward, "Do you know what I think?
With those symptoms, for him to feel so low, to sink."

Wiebbe was utterly flabbergasted, hit in the head with rock,
He was beside himself and in a little shock,
That Seebaer should know the cause of Willem's discomfort,
And in a matter of seconds, and with such little effort.

"He has Porphyria Variegate," concluded Seebaer. "It's not good,
I've seen it before, strikes mostly after childhood."
He looked to Wiebbe and back to Willem, not abstractly,
"Exactly as you say: suited to these symptoms exactly."

"The more severe cases can suffer hallucinations; skin damage,
Diarrhoea, muscle weakness and seizures, all hard to manage,
Blistering of the skin and scarring, and sensitivity to sunlight,
It will not be good come summer, when the sky is so bright."

"Fever and sweating is also quite commonly found,
Possibly unsteady upon his feet, not secure and sound,
Willem; your family... does anyone suffer like this, do you know?"
Willem answered, a good reply to this gauntlet of words to throw.

"Yes," said Willem. "My mother suffers badly of hallucination,
And much pain, weakness and fever, her ruination,
She's a drunk and cares little for me: but that name,
The doctors said what you just said... the very same."

Seebaer repeated the words of before: "Porphyria Variegate,"
"Yes, that's right," confirmed Willem, of confusion, no hate,
"Well, I think that's your answer," said Seebaer, a little pleased,
"And what's the cure?" asked Wiebbe, for answer to be released.

"There isn't one," said Seebaer, "but relief can be given,"
Sounding of little confidence, to home none driven,
"How is that?" prodded Pieter, so that, for the boy, he could care,
Wishing to aid Willem, for his life to be fair.

"Plenty of food," and those words prompted much traction,
Ariaen: "We do as suggested by Wiebbe, let's get to action,
Wiebbe, show us all where the campsite is to be,
And then to the hospital, of which I am eager to see."

"Cornelis and Jan can carry Marinus, Dirck his things, please,
Seebaer and Joannes, bring the... animal, our suffering to ease,
We can set up the third site and prepare our next meal,
Immediately, for Willem's sake, a recovery to deal."

"Throw it on a fire as it is," Hendrik said of the beast,
Wishing to get on with the eating, wishing to feast,
"Why waste your energy cutting away the skin,
And draining the blood; of blood it's already thin?"

Said Ariaen: "There's no need for more blood than necessary,
And it's part of what we call 'farming', Hendrik, it's not scary,
The skin can make boots and a hat, of which we are dire,
I shall not throw good material to the flame of a good fire?"

Hendrik didn't answer, he saw the error of his way, it was clear,
That the others had put more thought into the camps and gear,
He was overlooking many requirements, not to mention,
Of the animal and its by-products, of the general preparation.

"Let's get to work immediately and get Willem something to eat,"
Ariaen then added: "We start trapping soon, requirements to meet,
Let's get moving, for we have camps to set up,
And our food to catch and water to secure, to fill our cup.

Nothing further was said and the men set to duty,
Doing as they should amidst this land of beauty,
For beauty there was if only they should look,
Eyes to see and read, as though lines from a book.

By nightfall all had been secured: each and every site,
A small victory, their demise to smite,
All of the survivors came together as darkness fell upon them,
Marinus carried to the main camp, a view worth a gem.

Here he could view the sea,
Easily seen, a feeling of being free,
The meat of the animal had been cut away from the remains,
The ground caked in blood, upon clothing many stains.

The innards thrown aside for the ants and flies to have their way,
For the annoyance to be held back, for them to be held at bay,
The skin was laid upon the ground, for the ants and their raping,
Pegged into place and stretched ready the morning's scraping.

The ants clambered over it and would remove all of the meat,
From the skin, of this leather, of the remains, not being discreet,
And now was the time for a little celebration,
To congratulate one another amidst a common elation.

Each person held a plate of some description, there in the dark,
Whether it be made from wood or a large piece of bark,
Filled with well cooked meat and fat,
Willem wasted no time at all in having his fill of that.

And all around knew that from this day forth,
They would provide special care to Willem, of it he was worth,
To ensure he remained full and spared the more arduous chores,
This was one of their laid down laws.

Wiebbe could only think that the work the boy did earlier,
Contributed to his falling sick, a sheer must to consider,
He knew deep down that he wasn't to blame,
Willem was simply unstoppable, when to work it came.

There was more eating than talking,
Nothing like this meat, none found in all their walking,
Their main staple was shellfish and not always available,
Even though in abundance it was rarely brought to table.

"Do you know something?" said Joannes. "I was thinking,
Thinking that we could build ourselves an oven for cooking,
For the smoking of fish and drying of meat strips,
Jerky to serve us well during our long trips.

"What about the natives?" prodded Dirck. "How do they survive?"
"Don't worry about them," said Jan. "They know how to thrive."
Ariaen: "Which is why we should consider making them friends,
To learn of their ways, and all of their trends."

"It's good to be thinking along the lines of long-term survival,"
Said Hendrik, "but it's not going to aid in a boat's arrival,
We should wait for a boat to appear,
Do all we can to ensure they come near."

Dirck: "And what if one doesn't break our interlude?"
Hendrik: "Don't give me your defeatist attitude,
If a boat doesn't come then we build our own,
Set sail for Batavia, never again to be alone."

Dirck added good reasoning to this thought,
"It will do no good unless a launch site is sought,
It's no good building a boat if this can't be secured,
My mind on this matter is bland and cannot be cured."

"But there is a site," said Hendrik. "I heard it mentioned,
Just a few hundred yards away, to the south, there stationed."
Clutching at straws, and why not,
No thought was worthy of rot.

"Take a look, Hendrik," said Seebaer. "It's no good for launching,
We're stuck here and that's all there is to it, on this I'm vouching,
Our only hope is that a ship will be... this way blown,
See our fire, launch a boat: other than that we are on our own."

Silence struck again and the meal was finished,
An appetizing meal, one well wished,
It was then that Ariaen pulled a pipe from within his tattered shirt,
A speech to follow, being rather short and condensed, not curt.

"Do you see what was found by Pieter, a gift from the sea."
"Not much use without tobacco," said Hendrik, on one knee,
"Which I have," said Ariaen as he pulled his tobacco box,
From within his blanket on which he sat, like a crafty fox.

"By God," said Hendrik, "Real tobacco,
Give me some of that and I'll surrender my tomorrow."
"How much is there?" asked Cornelis with a smile,
And this fashion of happy faces did pile and pile.

"Not much," said Ariaen, "I must admit, I have very little store,
But enough to satisfy us each night this week or much more,
If we ration it, I see it lasting a good four week stroke,
But it depends on one thing... who here would like to smoke?"

Voices were raised,
And Ariaen was praised,
A sheer pleasure,
And in reasonable measure.

"We shall have one pipe a night,"
Said Ariane with delight,
"Do you agree?
To feel relaxed and be free?"

All agreed,
Men of single breed,
A tobacco to taste,
Not a single inhale to waste.

And the joyous song of satisfaction went up again,
Now was the time for none to refrain,
The tobacco may not come their way in the future,
And none around to grow or nurture.

Asked Wiebbe: "Shall we consider our order of business?"
"Yes indeed, let's deliberate," said Ariaen, filled with gayness,
Wiebbe: "From our earlier conversations it is clear that a ship,
May very well pass by this way in three days, during its trip."

We should make haste tomorrow and ensure that we are ready,
Ready with a signal fire, of our shipwreck to remedy,
Every able-bodied man should assist,
Help each other, do not resist.

Two persons to remain at the third camp,
To prepare traps, make new, or old to vamp,
A spear would be nice to have,
Thin and flexible, a well struck stave.

We also need a plan of execution,
To attain contact with the native population,
Consider, if you will, a reasonable gift,
We do not wish to cause a rift.

Said Jan: "I don't think that will be a problem,
They will show themselves soon enough; we'll soon see them,
In that I'm quite confident,
Just be free and strident."

"I agree," said Pieter, "but it wouldn't do any harm,
To keep our eyes open, a man to call 'alarm',
Let us try and make the first approach,
A good step towards friendship, not to sit and crouch.

"We need a gift," said Joannes, "something to offer."
"What do you suggest?" asked Hendrik, "for I wouldn't bother."
"I don't know, but something of much worth, something good."
"Food," said Willem. "Everyone desires food."

Said Pieter with a smile: "This is right,
It's as clear as the light,
They have been seen to carry spears,
A current war? None; or so it appears."

"So if not at war,
They must be at tour,
Hunting for food and game,
They too are in need, we are the same."

"We need to dry some meat,
As soon as possible, tendered, well beat,
If we get this done,
Then friendship we have won."

Hendrik: "And how do we know they're friendly?"
"We don't," said Willem, "but we can smile, and act not badly
Make an offering to them, with true conviction,
If they wished to kill us, it would be done, without restriction."

"Maybe," said Hendrik, "maybe not. Only time will tell,
But I tell you all this, right now, in my head, the ringing of bell,
That I care not for these schemes of yours, none at all,
I would much prefer to build a boat, than be speared and fall."

"Hendrik," said Ariaen, "so long as you don't take the wood,
The wood we intend to use on the signal fire, understood?
You can take what you want from the Zuytdorp, all you require,
And don't tempt our combined thoughts, our true desire.

Said Hendrik: "And when my boat is ready for the sea,
I shall only take those that make apology,
And those that pay for their place,
With so little time, against time I race."

"Maybe we should make you pay for the tobacco,
How's that Hendrik, a good enough echo?
And the place you keep beside this fire,
The one that you so much admire."

Seeing the error of his way 'again', Hendrik went off, alone to be,
Towards where the cliff top looked out over the calm sea,
The clear of the night growing colder but the wind having died,
Died down to practically nothing, upon the horizon he spied.

The next two days passed fast,
Marinus appeared to be healing, life to last,
Traps made by those at the third campsite were rather petty,
And proved to be ineffective, it was such a pity.

Several large fish were caught from the shoreline platform,
Separated from the ocean where small rock pools did form,
But the ocean was too dangerous to remain next to for too long,
The occasional crashing wave proving to be too strong.

Willem had prevented further attacks by remaining well fed,
Better when compared to the others, guilt on his face easily read,
But he continued to do all he could of the light duties,
Gathering of fuel for fire: *'feed it so that it never dies'*.

Two signal fires were made,
Here men constantly stayed,
Fires some distance apart,
Just to be smart.

Tinder was maintained at the main camp, well dried,
A camp from which they could see far and wide,
The availability of water was also a concern,
Of its procurement they would have to test and learn.

It seemed that everything was in order until the next morning,
The day the Kockenge was expected to appear with little warning,
All were anxious, all were afraid,
All wandered about, near the fires they stayed.

329

SHIP AHOY

On 11th June, Hendrik was hard at work, a working spree,
Fighting against the thrashing of waves from sea,
Gathering his wood for the building of a boat,
To take him to Batavia, and then he would gloat.

It was simply a matter of time,
Or so he told himself, as over wreckage he did climb,
A matter of time before a ship passed this way,
For him to consider option two, to chase and get in its way.

He maintained a steady watch towards the west,
Doing all he could, his very best,
In the least he provided the other survivors with pieces of wood,
Pieces that didn't serve his purpose, not because he should.

He knew deep down that he was pushing the survivors to hate him,
More and more each passing day, hatred filling to its brim,
But he couldn't help it; it was his way,
So he cast his thoughts aside to work his boat, there to stay.

All felt that the calculations were correct,
That today was the day, one not to neglect,
That a sighting would be made, the Kockenge to be seen,
With sails unfurled to catch the wind, upon the ocean to lean.

But how close the Kockenge was to sail was not clear,
If it was day then it might stay far out to sea, away to steer,
If by night then they would have to rely on a good moon,
Or noise from the ship itself, it could never come too soon.

The bells, bells upon the deck, that's what they would listen for,
The lookout at night would hear any noise, before ship they saw,
Night, however, was a long time off, currently just after noon,
The wait so hard, their need to feel a gratuitous boon.

Dirck took time off from the parties at work,
To check on Marinus and is condition, not to shirk,
Even though Willem had made this one of his sole duties,
Dirck was compelled to assist, one so joyous, not of pities.

For Dirck there was no ulterior motive for his attending this man,
He'd been looking after Marinus since day one, his personal plan,
A promise unto himself, to attend Marinus until fit and well,
Until able to walk upon his own two feet, and for no short spell.

330

Dirck, a man of faith and great inspiration,
Drew a dirty sleeve across his lips, an action,
A little blood having come from his gum,
He ignored the signature of blood, would remain stum.

As for Wiebbe, he was a man of command, not thick,
Certainly not a healer or comforter of the sick,
To Wiebbe their survival depended on decisions being made,
Not from inaction or from being afraid.

There was himself and Ariaen and Pieter,
The decision makers, nothing sweeter,
Each with the brains to organise and see things through,
Always aiding others and with much to do.

This was a council of three, to whom most would listen,
To heed their suggestions, and always for good reason,
Full of good advice, seemingly wise,
Each an individual, each that always tries.

Pieter had come from a good background,
Where family issues were more important and easily found,
He had a passion for living that his mother had cast,
Put into his mind forever, of conviction to last.

Pieter never reflected upon it much,
Never deliberating, in mind to touch,
He had been rewarded by his parents actions and self-confidence,
To work a solution through and with much patience.

Only held back by Ariaen, it seemed,
Whose very presence was so overpowering, it gleamed,
Ariaen shining through as the decision maker of the group,
Through combined motion of the council, never to stoop.

Ariaen: a man of distinction, a man of healing,
A man of good standing, a man of much feeling,
It was his easy-going nature that made his character,
Drawing an open ear and friendly smile, no actor.

Hendrik knew how to scoff and refuse,
But seldom did this act ever amuse,
Plodding away, gathering wood,
Upon his feet, unsteady he stood.

Just after midday, appeared a freak wave,
Falling heavily upon him, ill-favour it gave,
Bashing him heinously against the rock,
Of vision and consciousness it did knock.

Now washed out to sea,
A sea burial it was to be,
Flesh to be eaten of creatures about,
One man they could all do without.

Seebaer was near the edge of the cliff when the incident occurred,
All he could do was stand there and watch, he hardly stirred,
Despite the fact that the wave was too loud, too large, and fast,
There was nothing one could do, and to the sea Hendrik was cast.

Joannes, Cornelis and Jan were the first to be at Seebaer's side,
Looking down upon Hendrik in that last minute, taken by the tide,
What could be said? Very little,
So far below he looked like a beetle.

How fast the wave took,
How fiercely it shook,
Hendrik drawn mercilessly away,
Rock and wave to flay and flay.

Cornelis then saw something on the horizon,
Gave an emotional leap of joyous salvation,
Springing the news upon all around that a ship could be seen,
Nothing more than a little scratch in the distance, of sea a queen.

"I don't see anything," said Jan with hope in his voice,
Almost falling over, waiting to shout, to rejoice,
"It was there," came the exasperation from Cornelis. "I swear,
I swear to God that I saw a ship: for real, not mirage or glare."

"It must be the Kockenge," voiced Ariaen as he came running,
Confused by the sad look of Joannes, when he should be singing,
Compare this to the overcrowded joy of the other three,
"What's wrong, Joannes? A ship... you should be filled with glee."

"Hendrik has gone,
To the hungry sea alone,"
Responded Cornelis: "Leave it, just look for the ship,
Let's not let it slip."

Cornelis: "There it is, there!"
Jan: "I see it, a sight to revere."
"Me too," came a frantic call from Pieter most ripe,
Between sea and sky, the horizon, that fine stripe.

And before long everyone could see the ship in the distance,
Disappearing and then coming to view as it did advance,
The waves obscuring their sight of the ship, now and again,
Here in the sun, no clouds, no rain.

It was sheer jubilation, of great relief it proved,
As though all of their burdens had been removed,
But Ariaen was more sober in thought and gave the command,
To set light to the signal fire, to draw the ship towards land.

His three closest companions set themselves to task,
The signal fire was soon ablaze, uplifting their mask,
Unveiling their position for the world to see,
For the world this minute was a ship to set them free.

Pieter had alerted the others to the rear of the approaching vessel,
Before returning to stand by Ariaen, his emotions in a wrestle,
Pieter saw the expression, no smile or grin so painted,
Just a simple, sober look, rather grey and slated.

"What is it, Ariaen," asked Pieter. "Have you seen a ghost?"
"If we can see the ship, then the ship can see the coast,"
He answered nonchalantly, "which means that they will turn,
Turn to the north at any minute: in hell we're to burn."

"I'm sure as sure can be, there will be many eyes cast this way,
But fire not seen, and in our direction, the ship will not stay,
Men will be resting below deck or busy upon it, and rather keen,
Keen to be on their way, For I'm an experienced sailor, not green."

"They have no navigational reference for this region,
That will confirm their position,
So the lookout will have his eyes cast to the north,
Not to the east, no favour for us brought forth."

"I know: they seek the bay, possibly fifty miles to the north,
The best and only real navigation point they have of any worth,
Aye, I see the look in your eye, but I've taken many notes,
Scribed upon my mind is the layout of the stars, dots and quotes."

"You know as much as I of our predicament,
Of the ship; with the fire this moment,
The way men work on the sea is one of question upon question,
Confirmation needed on their position, not of fire to mention."

"Our only hope lays in the reality that the smoke might ignite,
Ignite suspicion when they reach Batavia, consider our plight,
They will then learn of our disappearance,
Consider this signal, a signal of our cumbrance."

Ariaen looked at the others, some having stopped in their tracks,
"Light the second fire, immediately; let burn these stacks,
Our only hope: that they will see our fire, to later be in the know,
Once in Batavia on learning of our failure to show."

And the men worked as they had never worked before,
Setting fire to the second, running for more wood they tore,
"If the natives didn't know of us," said Joannes, "they do now."
And to the fate of the future they must bow.

And that was the first and last ship they saw,
15th: Oostersteyn, 24th: Zuyderbeeck, 25th: Belvliet, and more,
29th: Popkensburg, 5th July: Corsloot and Oude Zyp: no sight,
All had bypassed them unseen, either by day or by night.

Too far out to be seen or passing further to the north of land,
Salvation not to come their way, no shaking of hand,
And so the signal fires sat at the ready until employed elsewhere,
Wood needed for their campsite, to survive a life so unfair.

PREPARATIONS

12th July: They all sat around the campfire of the main site,
These days, the beginning of winter, rain scarce, water rites tight,
They learnt to set traps for the smaller animals of land,
And tested morsels of carcasses found, being far from grand.

Beetles and small grubs, occasionally mixed in with other sources,
But this was always accompanied by a sour look upon faces,
Willem had suffered from minor attacks of Porphyria Variegate,
But never serious enough to see his basic health deteriorate.

At any time that an attack arrived out of the blue,
The men would give up most of their stew,
In order for Willem to gain a few extra days of nourishment,
An act of brotherly love, a gift of care, not of payment.

Marinus was forever on the recovery, health so slow to gain,
His ribs had seemingly healed but there was still plenty of pain,
He often joked about his arm and restriction,
The trouble with wiping his backside, and then the ablution.

"And you, Jan?" asked Pieter, "What are you contemplating?"
"Oh; nothing, really. I was thinking of these shoes and their aging,
They're near the end of their life," and Jan looked down,
Looked upon the big toes of both feet, dreary and brown.

They were showing through breaks in the leather,
exposed to the torments of the cold, the bad weather,
"I nearly burnt my feet the other night,
Toes bare to the flames of our fire so bright."

"Wrap another blanket," suggested Seebaer, "around your feet,
You'll do even better if you keep them dry: even an old sheet."
A few of the men looked around; they didn't have a spare blanket,
No spare shoes, clothes, shirt or jacket.

"I was thinking of getting shoes made from one of those furs,
Like you and Marinus," said Jan to Seebaer, "or like Pieter's."
"You can have the next one," said Ariaen, most sincere,
The truth being that all were in need most dear.

"What other needs do we currently have?" asked Ariaen of all,
"Apart from food, water; clothing and shoes; for summer to fall?"
Said Wiebbe, thinking of Dirck: "We need something for scurvy,
And I think we need it in a hurry."

Dirck did avail himself to the aid of all other,
Having neglected the effects: "I saw the way he did suffer."
They all knew that Wiebbe was right,
They needed good nourishment, scurvy to fight.

Roots were needed, some form of edible fruit,
This was their goal, on top of their list, this constant pursuit,
But how to secure this need?
Anything would do, even a seed.

"Dirck was a good man," voiced Marinus as he rubbed his arm,
The pain showing upon his face, a constant alarm,
The joining of the two bones not being as perfect as it should,
"I feel a little responsible for his death," as any man would.

"Don't," said Wiebbe. "He wouldn't want you to think that."
"He served me well," added Marinus, "beside me he sat."
"He served us all well," said Ariaen. "It wasn't your fault he died,
He died of scurvy. He hid the truth of his condition: he lied."

Cornelis: "He was transferred to the Zuytdorp from another ship,
He'd only be ashore one or two days, full of friendship,
No time at all to fill up on fruit or cabbage,
Hardly touching any fruit during his entire passage.

"Ah, cabbage," said Wiebbe, wishing to forget Dirck's death,
The way he suffered, his drawing of last breath,
Scurvy had taken its toll on his body, killing him over time,
"That's what we need now, something green, something sublime."

"There's nothing here but scrub," said Seebaer. "Nothing to eat."
Pieter looked at the others, "We need natives to meet,
For our survival it's the only way,
For we deteriorate more every day."

Ariaen: "I think it's time we voted on the matter,
Who's in favour of making contact, sooner than later,
Raise your hand,
Make your stand."

Seebaer: "But one thing must be said,
We must wait until the end of August, and then put rescue to bed,
If no ship has returned by then, then we should proceed,
Upon this point of fact we must all be agreed."

"NO," said Cornelis. "That's too late. We need to act now,
Not purposely wait for a boat, a solid raft, or a flimsy scow,
We can still remain here, until the beginning of summer,
But not rely, or waste effort, on this former."

"A vessel of the VOC is not going to come,
I'm being realistic, not glum,
Scurvy is treacherous to us all and Willem is suffering,
We need help now, for our health requires buffering."

"Good," said Ariaen. "So let's consider it agreed,
We'll remain here until summer, but must fulfill our need,
Joannes said: "And what are we going to barter?
Why would the natives help us? You believe them not smarter?"

"Well... we have nothing, really," answered Pieter in truth,
"Maybe some coins from the wreck, but I am no sleuth,
I believe we are smarter than the natives: we can build a boat,
But they know this land, they have it by the throat.

Concluded Ariaen: "All we can do is show good intention,
and hope for the best, and show no aggression,
I doubt for a minute they're aggressive,
Or we'd be dead already, sitting here most passive."

"He's right," defended Marinus. "Jan saw one,
Just a few days ago, probably alone."
"Yes," admitting Jan, reminding all of the encounter,
"And all he could do was stand there, to loiter."

"Watching me, clad in a single fur. I don't like them,
That's the conclusion I've come to, that's my problem,
It was raining and he'd come quite close but soon walked off,
He wasn't afraid, either. Just disappeared, as though to scoff."

"They're not animals," said Ariaen, "I'm sure he meant no insult,
They must've lived on this land for many years, achieved result,
They know the way of the land, something you may have forgot,
They know what is good to eat and what is not."

"We'll die if we stay here and do nothing,
I'm growing tired of waiting: within I'm seething,
We need to act,
That is a fact."

Seebaer volunteered: "Let me take a small party into the east,
Let me do this for all of us, bring to heel this unknown beast,
Bring to our lips a grand feast,
This the least I can do, the least."

Ariaen was silent for a moment and then nodded his head,
"Very well. Take as much water as you can carry, blanket for bed,
And eat well before you depart,
And always be ready, always be smart."

Seebaer: "We'll be gone just a few days, no more than four,
It'll only be a very short tour,
And this time we'll want to be seen,
To meet them we'll remain steadfast and keen."

"Very well," agreed Ariaen as he reached for his tobacco and pipe,
"I have enough for one more smoke," his mouth he did wipe,
"A large portion to do us all, the last,
Let's finish this tobacco, a thing of our past."

Seebaer, Cornelis and Jan all smiled, filled with elation,
Marinus then turned to Seebaer with a question,
"Who do you want to take along?"
"Cornelis, Jan and Joannes; together we're strong."

Marinus took the fur shoes from his feet and handed them to Jan,
"Take these with you: of them I am no fan."
"Thank you, Marinus, you liar," came the sincere gratitude,
Accepted them most happily, for to refuse would be rude.

Marinus managed to get Jan's old shoes on his feet with trouble,
Felt immediately the discomfort, understood why Jan did stumble,
No man could walk properly in these,
Of fine workmanship you could no longer tease.

But smile they did,
True feelings hid,
Marinus did the right thing,
Jan now happy, his feet could sing.

Nigel B.J. Clayton

OF CANNIBAL OR NATIVE

The group departed after having eaten enough to sink a ship,
Eating more than their usual share before commencing their trip,
They carried a receptacle each, differing in purpose and shape,
To portage their water, all that they could scrape.

They each carried a blanket,
A little sail cloth: a sort of jacket,
Able to be wrapped around them,
Or as a shelter, weather to hem.

They also had several pieces of rope,
Such commodity always gave hope,
For something always needed to be tied,
On it they most heavily relied.

They hadn't travelled far when they saw a familiar sight,
A kangaroo hopping away, scurrying off in fright,
Followed shortly thereafter by two more, Jan did smile and laugh,
And within a few more minutes an emu crossed their path.

They had never spoken of trying to catch an emu for food,
Too large and fast to chase, unless a young brood,
Did they taste similar to chicken?
Were they disease stricken?

Three quarters of the day had fallen before their first encounter,
An old fireplace, with sign of there being a shelter,
A hearth which had been abandoned long ago,
A sparse stick, or spear, but not ready to throw.

There were several bones, white and dry,
No way of knowing if it was eaten or did it simply die,
Cleaned well by the ants and the weather,
Or stripped bear with teeth and temper.

But on they went,
Their energy spent,
Two more hours before the sun said good night,
Goodbye to the day's last light.

But they exert themselves upon the current task,
Carrying their gear, and water in varied cask,
To continue on and do, no need of questions to ask,
No desire to stop in the late of day's sun to bask.

And then Joannes did make complaint,
Feeling on the edge of a faint,
"I don't know if I can continue like this for much longer,
I have no energy, I am not young and stronger.

At 37 years of age he was not that old,
But he was reasonable intelligent and bold,
Showed the signs of being worse for ware,
Amidst friends as they did stare.

Seebaer stopped dead in his tracks,
Hearing Joannes, seeing the energy he lacks,
Just behind Cornelis, who, being the youngest of the group,
Had pressed a little ahead, to look and snoop.

"Cornelis; wait," stammered Seebaer, turning to the other two,
"Let's camp here for the night; I think today we're through,
We've done enough, we should try and find something to eat,
Erect a shelter, prepare for slumber, some rest to greet.

Cornelis said not a word, moved back to join his comrades,
They were tired and weary, not natives, not nomads,
Each fell upon the hard floor of the sandplains,
Each sighing with relief, feeling those numerous pains.

Asked Jan of the others: "Doesn't this place ever change?"
"You came this way," said Cornelis of Jan. "To me it's strange."
"What do you see?" questioned Jan of his friend. "It's the same,
No matter where you go, a land you could never tame."

Jan: "Sure, the scenery changes a little, but its not arable,
For the most part it is dry and uninhabitable."
Joannes: "Hence why it's important to make good with natives,"
"No good can come of the natives," said Jan, as he freely gives.

"Then why are you here?" asked Joannes most rightly,
"Here or there, what does it matter?" replied Jan most sprightly,
"The inevitable will happen sooner or later,
We'll all die on this damn land, on that you can wager."

"Don't say that, Jan," insisted Seebaer. "There is always hope."
"Hope didn't help Harmen," continued Jan, unable to cope,
"Where there is God, there is hope," said Seebaer of belief,
Hoping the comment would provide a little relief.

"Yes, well," said Jan, his eyes upturned just a bit,
"If ever there was a Garden of Eden, this is not it,
God has nothing good in store,
Even if we obey his every law."

"We're alive," said Seebaer, "Even if not strong."
Asked Jan: "But for how long?"
Cornelis: "I'll try and find something to eat, walk out my cramp,
I'll take a look around whilst you set up camp."

"Joannes can come with me."
"I don't have the energy, can't you see?"
But Cornelis scoffed, insisted he attend,
Just a relaxing walk, his spirits to mend.

And quite a while later, the dark sky commenced its move,
And a howling in the distance, of which not to approve,
An howl shaking both Seebaer and Jan awake, sleep unexpected,
They'd fallen asleep shortly after the shelter had been erected.

"That's close," said Jan, quite afraid,
"Too close," agreed Seebaer from where he laid,
"Where are Cornelis and Joannes, do you know?
They've been gone a long time: why don't they show?"

Jan looked around as fear took a grip,
He knew that no good would come of this trip,
"CORNELIS... JOANNES," yelled Jan with all his might,
Several dozen birds in a nearby tree taking flight.

The sky was beautiful, a band of orange spanning the horizon,
From north to south. "CORNELIS... JOANNES." Going, the sun,
They both listened, nothing, heard, no reply, no howling dog,
Nothing: no overture of birds, insects, no scurrying lizard or frog.

Just a few seconds,
Eerie, and fear beckons,
The unknown was scary,
Time to be weary.

Seebaer: "That damn beast isn't far. I saw one the other week,
A great reddish-brown animal looking at me: such a mean streak,
Watching whilst I cooked upon the campfire a meal,
I guess he wanted to come in, an attempt to steal."

"Are they big?" asked Jan, with his fear in touch,
"Big enough," answered Seebaer. "It doesn't take much,
Even a small wolf can bring down a man or two,
CORNELIS... JOANNES, WHERE ARE YOU."

Seebaer stood silently and listened with his entire might,
"They aren't answering: out of range; out of sight,
We'll have to get some rest, take turns maintaining watch,
A task we need to do well, not one to botch."

Seebaer looked into Jan's eyes. "We'll get some firewood,
And see if that tinderbox Ariaen gave us is any good."
"I only hope we live to be able to give it back."
"Don't talk like that, Jan. No dog is going to attack."

Further away: Asked Cornelis: "Did you hear that; so eerie."
"It's just a dog," said Joannes. "It's far away, don't worry,
I can hardly hear it, for the most,
I'm more concerned about being lost."

Insisted Cornelis: "We're not lost; I've told you before,
All we need to do is to turn west and head towards shore."
"That's over a day's walk," Joannes pointed out,
"And here we are, leisurely walking about."

Cornelis: "We'll have to stay here tonight,
Find our way back with the morning's first light."
"You know something strange?" said Joannes. "I feel tired,
And yet I don't think I can sleep. I feel alive: inspired."

"The exhaustion I feel right now is the worst I've felt,
But the thoughts in my head are being dealt and dealt,
It's as though I see a hundred images all at once,
Each having something to say, something to announce."

"Yes, well; We'll just sit and talk awhile, listen to the land,"
Said Cornelis, "see what it has to say, see where we stand."
"Yes, I think..." and Joannes' jaw dropped sharply as he looked,
Up and beyond where Cornelis was seated, his vision hooked.

Cornelis had a look of bewilderment and froze there on the spot,
His eyes darted from left to right, but to look back he dared not,
"Joannes; there's someone behind me, isn't there?"
"Yes," replied Joannes, as he continued to stare.

"Please don't move quickly,
Do nothing at all too abruptly,
For there are six natives standing so near,
And each is carrying a sharp-pointed spear."

"Looking for food," Cornelis said blankly and praying,
Unable to think of anything to say that was worth saying,
"Probably," answered Joannes, thinking of their immediate fate,
And I think we're it, unable to do much, and in a bad state."

LIVE OR DIE

For both Jan and Seebaer the night had been long,
Each having taken turns to stay awake, until mornings first song,
Concerned for the welfare of their comrades and their own,
The fire remained reasonably well lit, upon it wood thrown.

The two men tried effortlessly one more time to call upon friend,
To call them home: huh, home; was this to be their trend,
And after another two hours of sitting and waiting,
They decided to return to the cliff, no need for debating.

It was quite obvious to them both that the other two would show,
Would come of their senses, head for the coast they did know,
Jan quickly doused the fire, the last embers smothered,
Considering now the much ground that needed to be covered.

The sun was hotter today than any over the past week,
And of this neither man needed to speak,
The land around them seemed worthless beyond all contemplation,
The ground unable to offer a single ounce of good traction.

But what the eye failed to see was a land of great offering,
Many gifts going unnoticed by the Dutch amidst scoffing,
For much food and water was available, if only they looked,
The land they walked filled to the brim of much to be cooked.

Again the day grew long and commenced to draw to a close,
But not before the two men could hear a noise as it rose,
The familiar sound of ocean breaking its back against platform,
Of where the Zuytdorp was hit so harshly by storm.

They literally staggered in, Ariaen and Pieter the first upon feet,
To provide assistance as needed, there to readily greet,
A crackling fire, warm and inviting,
To be here was both sad and exciting.

Willem scrambled to help but was quickly asked for aid,
To quickly throw some food upon the fire, a meal to be made,
Marinus dragged out a water container for the men to drink,
And then came the questions, with no time left to think.

"Where's Cornelis and Joannes?" asked Ariaen most concerned,
"They're gone," replied Seebaer, the onlookers had now learned,
News gifted through cracked lips, barely audible but understood,
No hiding of the truth, no speaking of falsehood.

"Let them sit and drink," urged Pieter, "They're thirsty."
"You're right," agreed Ariaen, "Their throats must be dusty."
And then a little silence, no further question to ask,
Until they had eaten and drank, and were ready for such a task.

Several mouthfuls of water later and after a deep breath,
Seebaer broke the news all were eager to hear, but not of death,
"They're lost; they wandered off for just a few minutes."
Said Ariaen: "tell us all, I'm sure you have no secrets."

Said Seebaer: "Last night: we'd been walking almost all day,
Needed somewhere to bed down, somewhere to stay,
We'd gone much further than Jan and Harmen had gone,
Other than exhaustion, nothing seemed to be going wrong."

"With some time before nightfall, Cornelis took Joannes away,
To search the area for water and food, without further delay,
That night I took first watch, and when I woke,
All I saw was Jan and our fire, and a little smoke."

"We called to them forever, but to no avail,
That is about the length of our tale,
We had to return." He kicked out at the dirt. "This sodden place,
It's like hell on earth. There's none worse, a land with no face."

Pieter then broke the silence, "Do you think they're dead?"
"Time will tell," said Ariaen soberly. "Let's not fill our head,
With false notions or guesses: let's just consider them as living,
But as Seebaer has said, this place is unforgiving."

"Maybe it is, maybe it's not," said Pieter, "but it can be tamed."
"No," said Seebaer, "it will be taming us, of this I am ashamed."
"Seebaer is right," said Wiebbe, sucking his lips into his mouth,
"We have to try to live with the land, or we sink and go south."

"That's what we're doing," said Jan, "trying to live with the land."
"No," said Wiebbe, "We've been surviving, trying to stand,
But not melding with it. We have to become one, or its over,
Be truly a part of Hollandia Nova."

"To be whipped by land!" said Seebaer. "To become a savage?"
"Your so-called savages have lived on this land, they manage,
For longer than we've been sailing past it, here they've lived,
For hundreds of years, they've learnt, they've thrived."

"No," disagreed Marinus. "Where are their houses, achievements,
Where are the everyday signs of their accomplishments?"
"Maybe the land doesn't permit it," answered Pieter most sheer,
Wiebbe: "I agree…. Time for us to be the true pioneer."

Said Seebaer: "That's what we've been trying,
And all that's happened is we keep on dying,
We've been south, north and east, and nothing has been found,
Limited, yes, but we've made that asserted effort, one to astound."

"It's not enough," said Wiebbe. "We have to do more than swoon,
We have to make contact with the natives and soon,
When winter has gone and the last of storm has come to pass,
The days will become hot upon this land of little to no grass."

"It will be like walking across the face of an anvil,
Look around you; all of you; a sheer hell,
This land doesn't know anything but the harsh realities of life,
And we must learn to live with all of its strife."

I've seen other lands which have succumb to the torments of heat,
Heat upon heat, upon heat; so hot it burns through the sole of feet,
I have seen other lands which have been spared no remorse,
A sun so hot it melts the mind of man; and in minutes of course.

But I have never seen a land like this, beaten harsh by a hot rod,
The ground so savagely treated by the open hand of God,
Where no Dutch flower can blossom nor a bee gather nectar,
We must prepare for the worst, to stand, not lay upon stretcher."

"What makes you think," scoffed Seebaer. "We won't die,
Right on this spot, beneath a heinous sun and cursed land to fry?"
Said Wiebbe: "Because I'll always hold onto the hope within me,"
"If I lose that, I lose all; even the right to die right: don't you see."

DEPARTURE

18th July: The weather remained rather moderate,
And over the coming the days a little rain at slow rate,
Not enough to fill the gullies with running water,
But enough to cause some misery and moods to alter.

Willem and Pieter stood before the third camp laid,
And secured into place, upon a tree, an arrow they had made,
It consisted of a shaft with two shorter pieces of wood attached,
To resemble a pointer, a bread crumb, and so niched.

"Do you think it will work, Pieter?" asked Willem unsure,
"I don't know, Willem," he said in return. "But it's a good lure,
Any man could see this from reasonable distance, but honestly,
I don't think we'll ever see them again, and that sounds ghastly."

"But if Cornelis and Joannes do come back this way,
They're sure to check each of the camp sites without delay,
Searching each for materials they might be able to use,
When they see this marker, they'll know the direction to choose."

Pieter helped with the final knot and he stepped back,
Of distinctness the sigh did not lack,
They hence turned to join the others, a timely arrival,
All manner of items to go with them in their forage for survival.

Each carried his own blanket and anything else on which to think,
Every second man a container for the porting of water to drink,
A few others carried one of the three knives or makeshift spears,
These weapons themselves helped shave off their fears.

They stood around the burnt out fire, a slight glow emanating,
Hotter embers deep within the mound of charcoal venting,
"We should have made a note for them from the charcoal,"
Said Marinus allowed, their despicable situation taking its toll.

Said Pieter: "The arrow that Willem made is a good enough sign,
If they come then they will see, and then all will be fine."
Marinus said: "I just wish we could have done more for them,"
As he reflected upon the realities of predicament and problem.

"Maybe we should wait a little longer; just a few days more."
Said Ariaen. "Our decision is made, survival we cannot ignore,
We can't keep holding onto false hope."
"You're right," agreed Marinus. "Let's go; let's not mope."

They commenced their journey, having committed no crime,
Their eyes falling upon their home for the final time,
A little guilt within each saying they had done wrong,
To continue with their singing, to continue with the song.

A seemingly sad farewell to a place they had come to know,
And now they were leaving it behind, their feelings low,
Northward to search for something more rewarding,
Ariaen led the way, followed by Pieter and Willem, now walking.

"Come on, Marinus," urged Wiebbe, "time to go."
Marinus tagged on, following the others, off into tomorrow,
Seebaer and Jan carried several poles for erecting a shelter,
Should the need arise when they stopped much later.

A temporary solution to aid in protection should it rain,
Something good to ward off the cold and the pain,
It would do them until something more permanent could be found,
Something more sturdy, more solid, much more sound.

Wiebbe took up the rear of the file, holding to chest his worries,
Glancing one final time over the site which had many memories,
Most of which he looked forward to forgetting,
Now to the future, where he hoped to find plenty of growing.

He said his goodbye to the site,
As though a last rite,
A camp he saw mature,
For laziness a sure cure,

DELIBERATION

They'd not been gone long, when Marinus stopped in his tracks,
"What is it, Marinus?" asked Seebaer, trying to see any cracks,
The others now stopping to see what mattered,
What was the cause for their trek to be shattered.

Marinus announced to all so that there was no mistake,
About what he was about to do, of an errand to make,
"I have to go back. We left no water for the other two."
"There's water in the rock hole," said Pieter, "They'll do."

"No," said Marinus. "That's almost gone,
If we leave them nothing… that's just wrong."
He looked to the ground and made his final decision,
"I'm going back to leave my water, in a good position."

"Marinus;" said Ariaen, "the animals will get at it."
"I'll hang it from a tree," insisted Marinus, quick with wit,
"You're wasting your time," said Jan, "and ours: all the more."
Marinus was silent, shaking a few of them to the core.

"Don't wait for me. I'll catch up: there's plenty of daylight,
All I have to do is follow the cliff;" said he; "right?"
"That's right," said Wiebbe, "the cliff and the sound,
You can also follow our footprints on the ground."

"Good; then you all go and I'll catch up soon enough."
"Are you sure?" asked Pieter, "With your pain it may be rough."
"Yes; very sure. You all go on ahead: a short stretch of the leg."
"Take someone with you," suggested Pieter, not wishing to beg.

Willem volunteered: "I'll go,"
Said Pieter: "You don't have the energy; no."
"No," assured Marinus. "Please; I'll go alone,
I need to do this for our friends, it must be done."

A silent nod was all that was needed,
Marinus, back to camp, he headed,
To hang his water from the tree,
For his dear friends to openly see.

Marinus stepped out upon the worn track,
Which lead, to the second campsite, all the way back,
And happy he was, for finding his way was easy,
As too was he thankful that at last he was busy.

The slight pain he felt in his arm and chest were shrugged off,
Now so used to it he could only scoff,
It being nothing more than a small hindrance,
To him it made little difference.

He stepped out onto the nakedness of the site and was confronted,
By sheer surprise, four sets of gnarled teeth well noted,
A viciousness he'd never seen or encountered before,
A small pack of dogs to lay down the law.

A deep throaty growl then surfaced from the first,
Of all before him he appeared the largest: the worst,
They commenced to encircle him, preventing any escape,
Smelling his flesh, waiting to tear, bite, scratch and scrape.

Dingoes; massive and hungry for easy prey,
They could sense the inabilities of Marinus, could do as they may,
They could smell the water and above all his weakness, his fear,
Smaller than a fully-grown, male kangaroo, he did appear.

For the dingo it was an opportunity, a matter of survival,
Marinus was simply an easy target, frail, wounded, unable,
Unable to control his fear, or to ward off a savage beating,
The dingoes would go to work upon him and end their meeting.

The animals closed in upon their game,
And then the attack came,
From the rear,
Viciousness at full gear.

The cry that filled the air was heinous to say the least,
The worst death cry that the men had heard from man or beast,
All they could do was stop, turn and stare, everyone the same,
looking out in the direction from whence the cries came.

And it soon fell silent, the screaming having come to an end,
"We should go back," urged Willem, "and help our friend."
"NO!" said Jan. "It was his own foolish decision,
He should have been careful, had a clearer vision.

"You're wrong, Jan. It wasn't foolish to want to help a friend,
No more foolish than it is for Willem to go and attend,
Attend to Marinus..." said Ariaen. "But it's now too late,
Marinus has met his end, of him you need not berate."

"Those damn savages," spat Jan. "They are simply no good,
We should kill them before they kill us all; we should; I would."
"He's right," said Seebaer. "On the savages you cannot rely,
We can't befriend them. They're heinous, of this I can't deny."

"You see," said Jan. "They're cannibals, every last one."
"He's right," said Pieter. "Why kill Marinus, he, weak and alone?"
"Maybe it wasn't the natives," advised Wiebbe. "You don't know,
Maybe it was a snake or something. We should go back; let's go."

"One of those dogs," suggested Ariaen. "And Willem, you stay."
"No. No, no, no; that's no dog," insisted Seebaer. "Not today,
A scream like that? And no snake either,
The savages were waiting, have been watching forever."

"They see us, they know where we are; they see,
But we've seen them before, haven't we?"
"Yes," said Jan. "They've had plenty of time to approach,
So why haven't they? Because our lives they poach."

Said Ariaen: "Maybe they're scared."
"No; they're not scared; but of hatred they've bared,
No man would wait as long as this before coming forward,
If his intentions were honourable; unless a coward."

Asked Ariaen: "Then what do you suggest?"
"Kill them," said Jan. "Without rest,
"Don't be stupid," spat Wiebbe. "We're too few."
"Only one solution exists," insisted Ariaen. "A rescue."

"And if rescue doesn't come?" asked Seebaer upfront,
"We stay clear of the natives, avoid them, never to confront,
We find somewhere to sustain us, a place to survive,
Find some savages that won't kill us, somewhere to stay alive."

"I don't trust you," said Seebaer. "I want a new leader,
Someone more readily able to see to our needs, someone bolder."
Ariaen and Pieter remained calm, standing rigid,
A call for a change in leadership could not be forbid.

"Listen to me," said Ariaen, unforgiving,
Of his post he was not leaving,
"If you wish new leadership, of our structure to quit,
Then you go off by yourself and try to find it."

"Pieter, Willem and Wiebbe are coming with me, with me to stay,
And Jan, are you with me or Seebaer, what do you say?"
Jan could see the manipulation of the talk,
As easily as Seebaer and he could walk.

"Stop," said Seebaer holding up his palms in defeat, in disgrace,
A funny little smirk upon his face,
"I see where this is leading,
Do you think me of foolish breeding?"

"I'll stay with you, Ariaen. I'll not cause any further trouble,
But remember this: we are not pieces of discarded rubble,
We all have the right to voice our own opinion,
Whether or not there is any good reason."

Ariaen: "So long as it's an opinion,
And not a confrontation,
Nor mutiny or war,
I'll say no more."

"You are free to voice all you want,
You are free to… politically confront,
I suggest we continue on our way,
Remain on our bearing north and not stray."

ANCESTORS

20th July: The sun broke the horizon when an aboriginal fell,
Fell upon the scene of Marinus ripped to shreds, no more to tell,
All of the signs were there; it was a pack of dingoes for sure,
And they'd made short work of Marinus, a semblance of gore.

He gazed around with his spear in hand and looked upon the tree,
A pointer made from wood, a curious device, easy to see,
Its reason for being did initially elude him,
And then it hit him hard, firm and trim.

The white spirits had left a message, both primitive and simple,
Through the Malgana territory and towards the Yinggarda people,
That was the direction they intended to go, to greet and interact,
That's why the spirits - these people - had failed to make contact.

But what of the other two spirits that had been found so recently?
Barega was his name, and he thought this quite discreetly,
He was an aboriginal of the Malgana people, of the Wayle tribe,
He was a tall fellow of handsome features, full of good vibe.

He had deep creases within his face displaying great character,
He stood naked with a small shield, and a spear to shatter,
Shatter the lives of animals for food, to cook on fire, or smoulder,
And had a small cloak of fur which he carried round his shoulder.

The cloak was a gift from the Nanda to the south,
The people of that vicinity who offered proposal by mouth,
With an interest in a marital corroboree in the near future,
For the tribes to commit, to be friendly, to give aid, to nurture.

He would provide this news to his elders, make them understand,
His tribe had heard, that white spirits had fallen upon the land,
Making visit upon them from across the ocean so vast,
It was all new to him, these people, their ships and mast.

Many times were ships seen passing them by and at full sail,
And in all that time it remained mystifying, it never did fail,
Such a strange unknown site; but now they knew instead,
The ships floated upon the water carried the spirits of the dead.

But something more troubled him, and confusion then rose,
How could a spirit of the dead be killed by a pack of dingoes,
If these visitors were indeed ancestors of the living,
Then surely they'd not be able to perish, undergo such misgiving.

Barega saw the obvious, a corpse where spirit was released,
Blood was everywhere, this man was living, but now deceased,
Flesh and tendons bare to the world as though free,
This wasn't the spirit of the dead; how could it be?

WHITE MAN'S CORROBOREE

The group of survivors continued reluctantly on their way,
To the north, pressing on in their misery, searching for a bay,
Seebaer could not restrain himself any longer,
He now feeling weaker, but of spirit much stronger.

The episode of death two days before was playing on his mind,
"Stop; wait," said he from the rear, the march coming to a grind,
Said Wiebbe: "We need to keep walking,"
"Stop, I say," repeated Seebaer. "Listen to me, I'm talking."

"All of you. Don't you see," and the others gathered round,
"They're killing us off, of their morals none can be found,
They intend to eat us, right down to the bone,
To cook us on fires, hot rocks, and hot stone."

"That's ridiculous," urged Pieter. "Why would they do that?"
"Why walk naked in the heat or cold?" said Seebaer as he spat,
"I don't know their ways but the intention is quite clear."
He turned to Jan. "You heard Marinus scream; his sheer fear?"

"Aye," said Jan, "The most terrible scream I've ever heard."
"Seebaer, you're ridiculous," said Wiebbe, "quite weird,
But presume you're correct about them, through and through,
What would you suggest, what would you have us do?"

"We must fight," he said, "stand and deliver."
"Seebaer," said Pieter calmly. "We have rope, a shelter,
Blankets, a little water and three knives,
No comfort, no water or food, no wives."

Seebaer: "I don't know, but we must think of something."
Ariaen: "We're going to head north, of more... there's nothing,
Return to the camp if you like, and be lost forever,
Or come with us, where lies your true tether."

Seebaer was silent for a moment but again came to his senses,
Realising that his petty feud was useless against this herd of asses,
That Wiebbe, Pieter and Willem would not do anything to disrupt,
The friendship between them and Ariaen, being politically corrupt.

"Okay, I'll take my orders as you believe I should."
Said Seebaer sarcastically: if only he could,
"No one's pressing you to take orders, Seebaer, and none given,
Decision rests with the majority, and always with good reason.

So they continued on their way with little further said,
Until only a few short hours later, midday to be read,
For the position of the sun, warned all that it was noon,
Time for a rest, and not a time too soon.

There was a frame of sticks, long and fat,
Upon which a fur of wombat hide sat,
They moved this without question,
What was found was no cause for tension.

For here they found what appeared to be a deep well,
Dug into the ground, into darkness it fell,
A poorly constructed hole in which to catch water,
It's precious worth quick to register.

The group fell upon it with excitement, filled with hope,
Quick to tie an empty water container to length of rope,
Lowering it into the seemingly shallow well,
To replenish their core and to rest a spell.

They each and everyone had their fill,
To harness water in this way you needed skill,
Wiebbe: "How do you suppose this came to exist?"
"Maybe shipwrecked sailors; they're survival to assist."

Seebaer stood up then, "I have to go for a walk... to relieve myself,
I have pains. Jan; are you coming, for protection; my health."
And the two walked off towards where the cliff did stand,
To take time from the group, from the unfriendly band.

Ariaen waited for the two men to disappear from view and earshot,
"Let them be. Don't argue, please. I've had enough of his rot."
"I'm not like you," said Wiebbe. "I can't put up with the poison,
You take it well, amidst his pessimism, and without good reason."

"I wish I were more like you. But I must say this, I can be—."
"Look," interrupted Wiebbe, "don't be startled. There... see."
The group of four looked up and saw six aboriginal men,
Not more than eighty feet away, a view to possibly condemn.

Four of them wore what appeared to be a small cloak,
Each a waist belt and arm bands, doing nothing to provoke,
Three of the men carried several small lizards from their belt,
Kills secured by the weapons they carried, or so each felt.

Several of them carried a spear,
[Boomerangs] And bent sticks did appear,
A thick stick with a stone head attached with human hair,
A small hatchet, accompanied by no friendly or unfriendly stare.

One of the natives then looked to the others, this was clear,
Their eyes fixed upon the survivors, with no stance of fear,
Several nods of the head were then seen as one stepped forward,
A graceful movement, seemingly at ease, not awkward.

"Show no fear," said Adriane. "Smile, be friendly; move slow."
"Are these the spirits?" asked Kulan, *"the ones you know?"*
"They look..." began Narrah, *"like the others from the bush?"*
"What did they say?" whispered Pieter, Wiebbe issuing a 'hush'.

The six natives fell silent and looked again,
Kulan stepped forward, not wishing to refrain,
And made his approach in peace with an offering,
A small goanna now in his right hand, of friendship to bring.

"Take this food; it's good," said Kulan. *"We have ample,*
The yellow fat of the goanna is a delicacy amongst my people."
"He's offering you something," said Pieter of the obvious,
"Quickly, take it or he'll be offended; or become furious."

Wiebbe took the food and smiled, bowing slightly,
"Thank you," he said, most rightly,
Kulan stepped back and turned, happy in what he did do,
"You see; they're happy to receive it, just like the other two."

Said Nioka: *"They look at it in such a strange way,*
And I understand so little of their ancestry this day,
Show him you killed it, a gift for him and his people,"
But make it short, pure and simple."

It was unknown to the survivors that dance was a formality,
Of communication in many ways, a great stability,
This was a corroboree and involved much movement,
Imitating animals and actions, of past or present moment.

Some represented hunters, or bouts of conflict,
None meant to ridicule, some made up and could not be predict,
All movement told a story and many new ones were developed,
To be told and recorded for all time in minds embedded.

The history of the tribe passed from one generation to the next,
Most accompanied by music, none scored via symbol or text,
And so Kulan crouched low, knees bent,
Buttocks almost touching the ground, little energy spent.

His spear taken good grip of and poised in a throwing stance,
Kulan moved around, then stood silently, to glance and glance,
Before the survivors, a grimace of anger portrayed upon is face,
The spear leveraged in Wiebbe's direction, as though to disgrace.

A knife suddenly appeared out of the blue,
Through the air, with great precision, it flew,
Penetrating deep the stomach of Kulan, a great knock,
The look upon the native's face was one of great shock.

Bewildered he looked up and saw Seebaer standing there,
Behind the other four, opened mouth of death, he did stare,
Nioka, Daku and Pindara,
Woorin, and the native Nioka.

All promptly readied their spears and pressed the survivors,
Voicing their anger, this act of betrayal from these... tumours,
The rudeness of this unprovoked attack,
This slap in the face, this great drawback.

"No! Stop!" yelled Cornelis as he and Joannes came running,
Up from the rear so fast, hearts strumming,
Followed by Barwon and Kalti, another two aboriginals,
White hands flying about, gifting their halting signals.

The stirred emotions of the other five were abated,
But only slightly - no need to be stated,
Vengeance had filled their mind,
Solace would be hard to find.

Ariaen, Wiebbe and Pieter could not believe their eyes,
Nor could Willem, the murder of a native, on whom much relies,
Seebaer endangering their lives, as though each meant nothing,
Committing the most heinous sin, Willem's heart now writhing.

It was clear, all of it, that they were about to meet their end,
Unless reprisal was performed, and their lives they must defend,
The presence of Cornelis and Joannes was proof beyond doubt,
That the natives were friendly, with a relationship to sprout.

They had given food and shown courage,
And Kulan denied future suffrage,
To be struck down for the whims of a single man,
A senseless death, against everyone's good plan.

Ariaen pulled the knife that he carried from his waist belt,
And did the one and only thing that his heart truly felt,
Within the blink of an eye rushed to Seebaer to penetrate,
To dig his knife deep within his flesh, filled with much hate.

The facial grimace of Seebaer was different,
Compared to that of Kulan's, it was more apparent,
Seebaer's grimace was of horror and pain,
His 'no-good' name now forever forbidden, a great stain.

The noise from the cliff,
No raff but much riff,
The ocean crashing about,
Gave freely its spirit, its shout.

Hard to hear from distance,
This current grievance,
And hidden by appearance,
Was the meaning of the dance.

The commotion all around was full of emotion, slow to end,
The aboriginals had congregated round their fallen friend,
Then Jan came to view, having crouched behind some bush,
To escape the horrors of being eaten alive, he remained hush.

He had believed Seebaer to the fullest, he understood,
It was true what he said, and now he knew, as he should,
Understood what it meant to be a flesh-eating native,
But he was wrong, didn't know it, none of it was relative.

Cornelis and Joannes did well,
As the seconds fell,
Showing they cared for the dead,
But within, filled with dread.

Kulan was dead,
And Seebaer of life no thread,
It was this alone that settled the calamity of the situation,
To bring to a simmer the built up frustration.

Wiebbe had pulled the bloodied knife from Seebaer as he fell,
Holding the blade he moved slowly to Narrah, to silently tell,
He held the knife out and offered it to him,
The blade blood-soaked from the fallen victim.

"No!" yelled Jan from the rear. "What are you doing; this treason?
Are you mad? You're insane; stupid beyond all comprehension."
He turned and started to run, running towards the cliff of the coast,
And at its edge leaped into the air, fell to his death, never to roast.

He was so sure, so sure of mind,
That they were to be eaten, the natives to grind,
Grind their bones, mix this with their flesh,
For a meal to be made of them, to be well mesh.

His mind was corrupted,
His thinking severely disrupted,
He failed to see what the others had seen,
Had believed Seebaer not dirty, but clean.

The afternoon had finally arrived, the sun seeking the horizon,
A fire blazed in all its glory, the men seated, victory emblazon,
They sat, not in groups of white and black,
But on equal terms, mixed: of friendship, no lack.

Said Ariaen: "I still can't believe that you're alive,"
"Yes," Cornelis agreed, "and here we are, to live and thrive,
Hard to believe that we fell in with such good fortune,
Now members of this great commune."

"We've had plenty to eat since Barwon found us,
He and Kalti, more than happy to give aid and with little fuss,
"You know them by name," said Pieter, "That's impressive."
"We've learnt a lot already, and believe their clan to be extensive."

"We haven't seen their main camp as yet,
But I believe it won't be long now before others are met."
"How do you know?" asked Wiebbe. "Is it just heart's desire?"
Asked Cornelis: "Do you see any women sitting around the fire?"

"*What are they talking about?*" asked Barwon, unsure,
"*I don't know,*" said Kalti, looking into Cornelis' eyes, the allure,
"What are you talking about, Cornelis, do you know?"
Answered Cornelis. "He heard his name called just now."

"Ask him about the women," prodded Wiebbe with interest,
"Where are the women," asked Cornelis for the rest,
With hand shaping the cup of a woman's breast,
His hands held at his chest."

"*Ahhh,*" said Barwon, "*He wants a woman, this he admits.*"
"*Then that confirms it all,*" said Kalti. "*They're not spirits,*
Maybe we should get them a woman,
Each and every man."

Asked Barwon, talking of Willem: "*Including the small one?*"
"*Especially him,*" answered Kalti. "*He should not be alone,*
For us, the Malgana, the time for marriage is near,
We'll pass the word with none to fear."

"*The Yinggarda have an agreement with the Nanda already,*
Having been struck, we must now confirm it and stand steady."
Said Narrah: "*The Yinggarda won't have room for them,*
Though for the Nanda I think this is no problem."

"*They're different,*" insisted Barwon. "*Maybe we can learn,*
A man that can float on water in a craft is not one to spurn."
"*Well,*" said Nioka. "*They come from somewhere,*
A place that can't be seen, a place with people of skin so fair."

Barwon looked into Cornelis' eyes, "*Later we can talk,*
Talk of women, when the sun crosses the sky after a short walk."
He indicated direction with lips; arm, the movement of the sun,
"A long day's walk," said Cornelis, "I think; just one."

FOUNDATION

21st July: They slept soundly that night,
And awoke the following morning so bright,
To be provided more water and food,
The natives sitting around the fire and in a good mood.

They were talking of the day's journey,
Eating some honeycomb filled with honey,
And after an hour of relaxed feeding and contemplation,
They began their trek of unknown duration.

Wiebbe and Pieter moved over to where their poles were laid,
And the cloth used as a shelter, full of holes and frayed,
But the natives shook their heads and tried with great effort,
That they were no longer required, unable to provide any comfort.

"Leave it all here," said Joannes. "Bring the knives,
And the water containers, those things that will save lives,
Nothing more, take only what they say we need."
They nodded their heads, they all agreed.

Cornelis looked at Ariaen as he was pulling his hand away,
Saw in his eye that there was something, in pocket it lay,
He found it hard to part with an abstract of his old life, his desire,
The tinderbox. Ariaen simply smiled and threw it into the fire.

He looked upon it there, sitting in the coals, upon this new land,
To lay undisturbed for 270 years before again in the hand,
Before being found by white man, a relic of the past,
He looked up, all departing. He followed on, the very last.

The survivors had taken their first real step in cohabitation,
With the natives of this land, and with land now their relation,
And as time passed they commenced to learn, lessons to sing,
With all the clarity, the fine tuning of time, happiness to cling.

Aboriginals lived together in tribes, child, woman and man,
Made up exclusively of these family members who formed a clan,
Each clan was responsible for ensuring the well-being of the land,
They lived with it, they did not own it, always together they stand.

Men hunted with spears and fished,
Some may say, to do as they wished,
They hunted during all seasons, amidst all the yearly blossoms,
Echidnas, kangaroos, wallabies, reptiles, birds, and possums.

They used spears and boomerangs to hit, catch and kill,
Could scale trees in order to get their food, to get their fill,
Boys coming of age went with their father: to learn life's lessons,
To learn how to hunt, and make and use tools and weapons.

Women gathering the bulk of the food which was eaten daily,
They gathered medicine, seemingly happy, they did so gaily,
Girls went with their mothers to learn about the bush,
Of food and medicine; how to grind and crush.

Each tribe had an Elder who prevailed over disputes,
Decided when to move camp, of ritual they had deep roots,
They were wise in tribal knowledge, on them much relied,
Decided when boys would be initiated, and girls to be married.

It was all such an intricate network of standards and rules,
Their way of life was simple, unhurried, of people no fools,
They abided by the laws laid down, and these the whites applied,
To their everyday living, a new way of life on which they relied.

WILLEM TO WED

21st November, 1712: It had been four months since adopted,
Into the Wayle tribe, to be accepted and gifted,
The campsite was split into family groups, it was their way,
Where each maintained its own fire at the closing of day.

Ever since the episode with the metal knife,
Where Kulan was killed by Seebaer, causing much strife,
The instruments of death had been cast aside as something evil,
A valuable tool but stained and unsightly uncivil.

It was now mid-afternoon and Ariaen approached the other five,
Sitting down amongst them as Willem stoked the fire alive,
Pieter and Cornelis shaped their spear points,
And Joannes prepared for the cooking of several joints.

"Where's Wiebbe?" asked Ariaen, to the point; blunt,
"Pindara invited him out for a short hunt."
Ariaen: "Well, I have some news," looking in Willem's direction,
"What is it?" he asked. "Looking at me with such perception."

"Least of all: I've just be communicating with a man for days,
His name is Barega, and of old news he relays,
The tribe tried telling us this some time ago,
It appears that Marinus was killed by a *dingo*."

Pieter: "I knew there was a perfect explanation."
Asked Willem: "So why are you smiling in that fashion?"
"Barega was organising a marital corroboree to the east, or south,
With the Nanda: so hard to understand his words by mouth."

"It took me awhile to understand clearly his meaning,
But now I know - I think - and I am beaming,
It's a few days' walk and all of the Malgana will attend,
We are to found, new relationship, new friend."

"And..." said Willem, under the worded cypher, feeling buried,
Ariaen smiled: "You're to be wedded, Willem, to be married."
"Married? But I'm not ready... not well; I'm still sick," he pleaded,
"It's the best thing for you; really: happiness I've really needed."

"You have a long life to live and there's only one way to live,
To be loved and for love to give,
It cannot be put off any longer,
As the days go by, with good food, you'll grow ever stronger."

"But we might be rescued," said Willem with a little confidence,
"Do you know what I believe, Willem?" said Pieter in essence,
"Once you've spent several years here with these people,
You won't want to return home; to a life so bland and simply."

"Don't talk nonsense," said Joannes. "I wouldn't care,
Even married to ten wives, I would not turn down a free fare,
I'd be firmly one aboard if I saw a ship sail past,
Whether the first man on board or the very last."

"Joannes; you'd have to live on the coast in order to see a ship,
And the coast doesn't provide all the food needed to pass your lip,
Yes, you know it's true; but life with the Malgana is great,
And I believe this to be our true fate."

"But married," said Willem again. "Whose idea was this?"
"It must have been one of the elders, something Woorak did wish,
It's so hard to understand these people sometimes, but I try,
But of their testimony and sayings I cannot rely."

"Do you know, the other day I was asking Daku 'how far',
He said *'Not long; little, short'*, of anything more I could not jar,
And then he indicated to me that it would take twelve or fourteen,
Fourteen days, I thought, not in the least very keen."

Cornelis stood up: "No, you can't. Not to the Nanda, not married,
We all like the women here, and so this idea should be parried,
I really have no dislike for them at all, and... I feel like a father,
As you all do to Willem, and I'd much prefer to stay together."

"Willem will wed and his wife will come here, it's my intention,
And as for you, young friend, I need to now mention,
One of the young women right here has taken a fancy to you,
I think the single life for you is well and truly through."

"Not Kyeema, surely," said Cornelis "Can I say nay?"
Ariaen: "Afraid not. The women folk have seen you two at play,
You should be more careful and play in the dark, you scamp,
Your manhood has revealed much to the women of this camp."

Cornelis: "And who here isn't man enough to have a need?
I'm not the only one that's been corrupted by my own greed."
"I'm sure you're right, but this comes from the elders, their voice,
So I don't think you're going to have much choice."

"How many days did you say till—?"
"Twelve to fourteen," interrupted Pieter, "So be still."
"And we depart tomorrow," finished Ariaen, "At first light,
And Cornelis, remember your old injuries; refrain from flight."

WALGA ROCK

A first for the survivors, to move from a main camp left intact,
And it was interesting to note that this was always the fact,
Grinding stones were left upon the ground where they sat,
Shelters left as they were the night before, on ground now flat.

Sheets of bark propped up and fire smothered but left to stand,
With hot pieces of half-burnt wood carried in sand,
Ported in other wooden containers to aid in starting the next fire,
Easiness in setting up the next camp to transpire.

The days were long and hard for the survivors,
Still suffering from acclimatisation, but they were strivers,
The soles of feet bore the brunt of the heat and vegetation,
It would take time to get used to the land and its condition.

They were travelling in a direction away from the setting sun,
They continued far into the east, but also far from done,
It wasn't for the survivors to question the direction,
The path taken was weirdly peculiar but offered much fruition.

And after eleven day of walking they came upon a rock,
But its distance from them was still quite a shock,
Daku came up to Ariaen and pursed his lips, direction so set,
Pointed with his mouth towards the object of rock silhouette.

"Walga," said Daku, *"Walga, Walga,"* towards the sun now rising,
"What's that all about?" asked Wiebbe as they continued walking,
"I'm presuming that the rock formation up ahead,
It's called Walga," announced Ariaen of what he read.

"Walga," said Daku again, confirming Ariaen's suspicion,
"The ceremonial grounds," said Pieter. "The place of our union,
"Maybe," agreed Ariaen, and then, "maybe not,"
And they continued with the walk, to that very spot.

Cornelis felt they were near the end of their short adventure,
For Kyeema gave him a great smile, a message, a lecture,
And he too smiled back though deep down felt unsure,
Though he felt the need for her was sincere and pure.

He didn't feel as though he was committing sin,
Possibly having children of coloured skin,
It made little difference to him, deep down,
What did it matter: white skin, black, or brown.

When they finally came upon the foot of the rock formation,
The women put about setting up camp, displaying much elation,
The men then stepped off to a place which they knew,
Where an opening existed within the rock, where shadows grew.

Ariaen and the others watched with great attentiveness,
Woorin and Daku commenced to draw, of feelings to express,
On a portion of the wall not far from the entrance but obscure,
And what they drew shocked the survivors for sure.

These two men who had lead them here were painting a picture,
A piece of art, using charcoal and red ochre, a permanent fixture,
With a mixture of many colours derived from plants so gathered,
A mural of dedication was hence, meticulously inhered.

It was a mural dedication to these strange men from across the sea,
They were accepted by the Nanda, a part of history, forever to be,
For right before them a sailing ship was being painted,
Of elegance and beauty, Ariaen felt overly sated.

A tear welled in Ariaen's eyes and Willem asked him,
"What are you crying for? Why are you feeling so dim?"
"Because we have found our way, we are at peace now,
With the land and with the people. I feel happy, not low."

"We shall never return to Europe, we have a future here,
This is now our home, and to me that is very, very clear."
Ariaen smiled at Woorin and Daku, they in turn smiled back,
This, the happiest day of Ariaen's life, of happiness never to lack.

The survivors over time were all married via great ceremony,
One of such splendour, you could not buy with VOC money,
The aboriginals did offer much more than they could ever dream,
The remaining survivors lived fruitful lives, topped with cream.